Paths to Development in Asia
South Korea, Vietnam, China, and Indonesia

Why have some states in the developing world been more successful at facilitating industrialization than others? Challenging theories
that privilege industrial policy and colonial legacies, this book focuses
on state structure and the politics of state formation, arguing that a
cohesive state structure is as important to developmental success as
effective industrial policy. Through a comparison of six Asian cases,
including both capitalist and socialist states with varying structural
cohesion, Tuong Vu demonstrates that state formation politics rather
than colonial legacies have had decisive and lasting impacts on the
structures of emerging states. His cross-national comparison of South
Korea, Vietnam, Republican and Maoist China, and Sukarno's and
Suharto's Indonesia, which is augmented by in-depth analyses of state
formation processes in Vietnam and Indonesia, is an important contribution to understanding the dynamics of state formation and economic
development in Asia.

Tuong Vu is an Assistant Professor of Comparative Politics in the
Department of Political Science at the University of Oregon. He
coedited (with Erik Kuhonta and Dan Slater) *Southeast Asia in Politi-
cal Science: Theory, Region and Qualitative Analysis* (2008) and (with
Wasana Wongsurawat) *Dynamics of the Cold War in Asia: Ideology,
Identity, and Culture* (2009). His articles have appeared in numerous
scholarly journals, including *World Politics*, the *Journal of Southeast
Asian Studies*, *Studies in Comparative International Development*, and
Theory and Society, and he is a co-editor in chief of the *Journal of
Vietnamese Studies*.

D0878824

Paths to Development in Asia

South Korea, Vietnam, China, and Indonesia

TUONG VU
University of Oregon

CAMBRIDGE
UNIVERSITY PRESS

CAMBRIDGE UNIVERSITY PRESS
Cambridge, New York, Melbourne, Madrid, Cape Town,
Singapore, São Paulo, Delhi, Mexico City

Cambridge University Press
32 Avenue of the Americas, New York NY 10013-2473, USA

Published in the United States of America by Cambridge University Press, New York

www.cambridge.org
Information on this title: www.cambridge.org/9781107618107

First published 2010
First paperback edition 2013

A catalogue record for this publication is available from the British Library

Library of Congress Cataloguing in Publication Data
Vu, Tuong, 1965–
    Paths to development in Asia : South Korea, Vietnam, China, and
Indonesia / Tuong Vu.
        p.   cm.
    Includes bibliographical references and index.
    ISBN 978-0-521-76180-2 (hardback)
    1. Southeast Asia – Politics and government.   2. East Asia – Politics and
government.   I. Title.
    JQ750.A58V83   2010
    320.95 – dc22   2009033078

ISBN 978-0-521-76180-2 Hardback
ISBN 978-1-107-61810-7 Paperback

To Ba Má and Lan

Contents

Tables and Figure

Acknowledgments

This book grew out of my interest in the revolutions and civil wars that violently shaped the history of postcolonial East Asia. As a survivor of the Vietnamese revolution and civil war, I have realized that analyzing these events is no less challenging than living them. Without the generosity of numerous individuals and institutions, I would not have been able to complete this book. Special thanks are due to Raymond Duvall at the University of Minnesota, who patiently guided me through my first research projects on revolutions and civil wars. At Princeton University, Lynn T. White III taught me much about Chinese politics and continues to be a caring mentor. For the dissertation on which this book is drawn, I benefited especially from the knowledge and advice of my committee at the University of California, Berkeley: Kevin O'Brien, Kenneth Jowitt, Steven Vogel, and Peter Zinoman. This book should show the profound influence they had on my theoretical approach. At the same time, Kiren Chaudhry, David Collier, the late Ernie Haas, Andrew Janos, and David Leonard were inspiring teachers who made Berkeley a truly stimulating intellectual community.

Beyond Berkeley, my work has been supported by colleagues from many institutions. At Smith College, where I was a Mendenhall Fellow during 2003–4, Donald Baumer, Mlada Bukovansky, Howard Gold, Jacques Hymans, and especially Dennis Yasutomo offered exceptional mentorship. Steven Goldstein tutored me on Chinese revolutionary politics and foreign policy over many lunches. At the Naval Postgraduate School, Maria C. Morgan and Kent Eaton helped me revise several chapters and provided generous friendships. Anne Clunan, Dean Robert L. Ord, Jessica Piombo, Zachary Shore, and Chris Twomey were likewise wonderful colleagues. I am also grateful to the officers I taught who contributed many ideas to my thinking on states and state building. At the Asia Research Institute of the National University of Singapore, where I was a visiting Fellow in 2007–8, Anthony Reid and Geoff Wade offered valuable counsel and collaboration. All my colleagues in the Department of Political Science at the University of Oregon helped me through the final hurdles of publication with enthusiastic encouragement.

During my two years of fieldwork in Indonesia and Vietnam, I accumulated debts to many teachers, colleagues, and friends. Harold Crouch, Eric and Cathy Crystal, Greg Felker, Christopher Goscha, Yong Chul Ha, Russell Heng, Ben and Melinda Tria Kerkvliet, David Koh, Bill Liddle, and Michael Montesano offered keen insight and introduced me to valuable contacts. Bill Liddle was always generous with comments on drafts and contacts in the field. Ben Kerkvliet read the entire manuscript, and his constructive criticisms saved me from numerous errors. William Collins, Don Emmerson, Adam Fforde, Vu Minh Giang, Jeff Hadler, Nguyen Van Huy, Vu The Khoi, Nguyen Van Ku, David Marr, Sarah Maxim, Andrew McIntyre, John Roosa, Arbi Sanit, Amir Santoso, Bach Tan Sinh, Bui Dinh Thanh, and Peter Timmer helped in various ways. I am especially grateful to the late Bui Huy Dap, Vu Dinh Hoe, and the late Doan Trong Truyen, who shared with me their knowledge as participants in historical events. Achmad Tirtosudiro, Sapuan Gafar, M. Hussein Sawit, and Noer Sutrisno were also generous with their time and knowledge of the Indonesian bureaucracy. My Indonesian language teachers, Indriyo Sukmono, Ninik Lunde, Sylvia Tiwon, and Prapto Waluyo, and my tutors at Sam Ratulangi University in Manado, Sulawesi, will be remembered for their kindness and patience.

My research in Indonesia would have been difficult without the help of Do Kim Dung and Aswatini Raharto and their colleagues at the Institute of Population and Manpower Research (PPT-LIPI) in Jakarta. I can never repay my debts to Dung and her family for their kindness. In Hanoi, I am grateful to Vu Minh Giang and Do Kien of the Center for Vietnamese Studies and to Le Dang Doanh and Vu Xuan Nguyet Hong of the Central Institute for Economic Management. In Singapore, the Institute of Southeast Asian Studies provided research space and access to valuable materials at its library. Acknowledgments also are due to the Center for Southeast Asian Studies at the University of California, Berkeley; the Hewlett Foundation; the Boren Fellowship; the Fulbright Fellowship; the FLAS Fellowship; Smith College; the Naval Postgraduate School; the Asia Research Institute at the National University of Singapore; and the

University of Oregon for generous financial support at various stages of research and writing.

I am fortunate to have as friends and colleagues Bill Hurst, Erik Kuhonta, Gerard Sasges, Dan Slater, and Kevin Strompf. Thanks are due to other friends who helped with contacts and ideas: Regina Abrami, Martin Beversdorf, Mike Boduszynski, Calvin Chen, Brian Folk and Yumi Iwai, Ken Foster, Myung-koo Kang, Conor O'Dwyer, Victor Peskin, Daromir Rudnyckyj, Scott Strauss, and Hung C. Thai.

Kezia Paramita took excellent photographs of the Pancasila Sakti Monument for the cover of this book. Portions of Chapters 1, 2, 3, and 5 have been published in *Studies on Comparative International Development* and *Journal of Southeast Asian Studies*, and I thank these journals for their permission to reproduce them here. I am grateful to Mary Sharon Moore for her help with copyediting, to Mary Harper for creating the index, and to Kelley Littlepage and Travis Waterman for research assistance. Emily Spangler and Brian MacDonald of Cambridge University Press deserve thanks for guiding the manuscript through publication.

Finally, I thank my family for being with me through this entire project. I am blessed to have caring parents, who years ago borrowed money to buy me an English dictionary, and to have a loving spouse who has made many sacrifices for me. I dedicate this book to them with love and gratitude.

Abbreviations

AIP	Annam Independence Party
BBI	Barisan Buruh Indonesia (Indonesian Workers' Front)
BU	Budi Utomo (Pure Endeavor)
CCAKI	Central Council for the Acceleration of Korean Independence
CCP	Chinese Communist Party
CEC	(Guomindang's) Central Executive Committee
CPKI	Committee in Preparation for Korean Independence
DCSVN	Dang Cong San Viet Nam (Vietnamese Communist Party)
DI	Darul Islam
DP	(Vietnamese) Democratic Party
DPR	(Indonesian) Dewan Perwakilan Rakyat (People's Council of Representatives)
DRV	Democratic Republic of Vietnam
EVN	Empire of Vietnam
GLF	Great Leap Forward
GMD	Guomindang (Chinese Nationalist Party)
GNP	gross national product
ICP	Indochinese Communist Party (Dang Cong San Dong Duong)
IMF	International Monetary Fund
IP	Indische Partij (Indies Party)
ISDV	Indische Sociaal-Democratische Vereniging (Indies' Social Democratic Association)
KCP	Korean Communist Party
KDP	Korean Democratic Party

KNIP	(Indonesian) Komite Nasional Indonesia Pusat (Central National Committee)
KPG	Korean Provisional Government
KPR	Korean People's Republic
LRA	(Vietnamese) Land Reform Authority
Masjumi	Partai Majelis Syuro Muslimin Indonesia (Indonesian Muslim Council Party)
MG	(American) Military Government
MIAI	Majelis Islam A'la Indonesia (Great Islamic Council of Indonesia)
MPR	Majelis Perwakilan Rakyat (People's Consultative Assembly)
New PNI	Pendidikan Nasional Indonesia (Indonesian National Education)
NU	Nahdlatul Ulama (Council of Islamic Teachers)
Paras	Partai Rakyat Sosialis (People's Socialist Party)
Parsi	Partai Sosialis Indonesia (Indonesian Socialist Party)
PBI	Partai Buruh Indonesia (Indonesian Workers' Party)
PC	(Korean) People's Committee
Pesindo	Pemuda Sosialis Indonesia (Socialist Youth of Indonesia)
PI	Perhimpunan Indonesia (Indonesian League)
PII	Partai Islam Indonesia (Islamic Party of Indonesia)
PKI	Perserikatan Komunist di India (Communist Party of the Indies, an earlier name of the Indonesian Communist Party)
PKI	Partai Komunis Indonesia (Indonesian Communist Party)
PNI	Partai Nasional Indonesia (Indonesian Nationalist Party)
PRC	People's Republic of China
PS	Partai Sosialis (Socialist Party)
PSI	Partai Sosialis Indonesia (Socialist Party of Indonesia)
PSII	Partai Sarekat Islam Indonesia (Islamic League Party of Indonesia)
RI	Republic of Indonesia
RTA	(Netherlands-Indonesia) Round Table Agreements
SI	Sarekat Islam (Islamic League)
SOBSI	Sentral Organisasi Buruh Seluruh Indonesia (Indonesian Central Workers' Union)
UNESCO	United Nations Educational, Scientific and Cultural Organization
VCP	Vietnamese Communist Party (Dang Cong San Viet Nam)

VNDL	*Viet Nam Doc Lap* (Independent Vietnam)
VNP	Vietnamese Nationalist Party (Viet Nam Quoc Dan Dang)
VRL	Vietnamese Revolutionary League (Viet Nam Cach Mang Dong Minh Hoi)
VWP	Vietnamese Workers' Party (Dang Lao Dong Viet Nam)

State Formation Dynamics and Developmental Outcomes

As the new millennium unfolds, the state is rising again in public and scholarly imagination. Two decades ago, the dramatic end of the Cold War fueled speculations that the state was an anachronistic organization that soon would be swept away in the coming wave of liberalization and globalization.[1] Such speculations were not without basis. As once powerful states from Yugoslavia to the Soviet Union collapsed like dominoes, while liberal ideology, the consumer culture, and the Internet revolution expanded their reach across the globe, the days of state sovereignty seemed to be numbered. States appeared no longer able to hold out against the assaults from such global entities as the International Monetary Fund, Microsoft, Citibank, CNN, and McDonald's.

Nevertheless, a new global order superseding states has been elusive. Numerous studies in the past decade have found that global forces, rather than dismantling states, may have strengthened them (Weiss 1998; Migdal 2001, 137–42). In the industrialized world, states continue to regulate markets in ever more sophisticated ways (S. Vogel 1996). Far from being pushed aside, state bureaucrats in many newly industrialized nations are leading the information technology revolution in their countries (Evans 1995). Whereas some states have responded to the global challenge through adaptation, others have launched dramatic counterattacks. After the initial shock following the 1997 financial crisis, the Malaysian government reimposed capital controls, while a new prime minister in Thailand kicked out the IMF. These telling examples suggest

---

[1] Notable examples include Fukuyama (1992); Lyons and Mastanduno (1995); Shapiro and Alker (1996); Strange (1996); and van Creveld (1999).

that the doctrine of state interventionism is still alive, and global capital may need to learn how to live with it.

A renewed appreciation for the continuing salience of states also stems from the rise of civil conflicts where states are absent or have collapsed. Frustrated efforts by the United States and its allies to keep peace in stateless Somalia and establish functioning states in Afghanistan and Iraq sharply underscore what is at stake for a stateless global order and how difficult state building is. As Theda Skocpol warned twenty years ago, states cannot be taken for granted for their role in national and international life. Questions of state origins and state power are back in the spotlight, guided by the accumulation of comparative knowledge about state formation and the complex relationship between state and society in various contexts.[2]

Such changing perspectives about states in a globalizing context provide the stimuli for this book, which seeks to demonstrate how state formation politics was responsible for the emergence of developmental states in some Asian contexts. Defined in the literature as states with cohesive structures and strong commitments to growth-conducive policies,[3] developmental states in Japan, Korea, and Taiwan have attracted significant theoretical interest not only among Asianists but also among analysts of other regions.[4] These states appear to hold the answer to a fundamental question in political economy that has been around since Adam Smith: why are some nations rich and others poor?

The central question that motivates this book concerns a narrower issue: what gives, or gave, developmental states their cohesive structures? The voluminous literature on developmental states has rarely tackled this question systematically. Through a simple comparative framework built on case studies from Asia, this book argues that patterns of intraelite and elite–mass interactions – especially but not necessarily during state formation – determine whether emerging states possess cohesive structures required for implementing developmental policies effectively. In particular, certain patterns of interactions generate cohesive structures, whereas others do not. Among elite alignment patterns, elite polarization and unity are conducive to the creation of cohesive states, whereas elite

[2] See Vu (2010a) for a recent review of this literature.
[3] This definition follows Kohli (2004, 10). "Commitments to growth-conducive policies" refers to state elites' narrow focus on the goal of industrialization while disregarding the social welfare of working classes if this hampers that goal (state investment in human capital that benefits industry directly is another matter).
[4] For literature reviews, see Wade (1992); Kang (1995); and Woo-Cumings (1999).

compromise and fragmentation are not. For elite–mass engagement patterns, controlled mobilization and suppression have a positive impact on state cohesion, but mass incorporation does not. More generally, accommodation is not conducive to structural cohesion, yet confrontation is.

This chapter begins by critically examining the literature on developmental states, which, I contend, sheds much light on the roles of states in late industrialization but lacks historical depth, overlooks ideologies, and fails to include socialist states. Then I offer a theoretical framework, which provides a useful background for a detailed outline of my argument. Finally, I discuss the six case studies presented in the book.

ROLES, CAPACITIES, AND STRUCTURES FOR DEVELOPMENT

The literature on developmental states pivots on the notion that states can play critical roles in industrialization. For instance, Gerschenkron (1966) shows how states acted decisively as planners, credit mobilizers, and entrepreneurs in late-industrializing France, Germany, and Russia. This belief in states as agents for economic development has been vindicated by the success of many East Asian "tigers." These successful economies emerged in the 1980s as a few bright spots in a landscape inhabited mostly by developmental failures. Scholarly efforts to search for the secrets of these "miracles" have produced a set of hypotheses about state intervention that revolve around three central concepts: roles, capacities, and structures.

State *roles* in late development preoccupied earlier works on developmental states. These studies were primarily aimed at discrediting the prevailing notion at the time that industrialization in the Asian "tigers" originated from laissez faire policies. The goal was to show that states matter, and that they do so through aggressive intervention into two main policy areas. Industrial policies constitute one area, including subsidizing inputs, promoting exports, imposing performance standards on industries receiving state support, and creating industrial groups in dynamic sectors (Amsden 1989; Haggard 1990). The other area concerns limited social programs ranging from land reform to investment in basic education (Johnson 1987). In brief, growth results from policies that allow a state to play the developmental roles of custodian, demiurge, midwife, and shepherd in the economy (Evans 1995, 77–81).

The issue of state roles is closely related to that of state *capacities* to transform the economy. Most states intervene in the economy and often play similar roles, but only a few succeed. Even these successful states do not always achieve what they want. Sound policies are clearly insufficient. State capacities are crucial. Without sufficient developmental capacities, states cannot play developmental roles effectively. Analysts of industrial policy particularly highlight three core capacities: to formulate and implement goals and strategies independent of societal pressures, to alter the behavior of important domestic groups, and to restructure the domestic environment (e.g., property rights and industrial structure) (Krasner 1978, 60).[5] These core capacities determine the success or failure of states' attempted roles in the economy.

Yet, if capacities explain success or failure in intervention, why do some states have more capacities than others? This question leads us to the way a state is structured internally and externally (Weiss 1998, 34). Rapid industrialization involves trade-offs, and a state's ability to formulate goals and implement them depends on centralized political will, bureaucratic autonomy, and coercive power. These in turn imply a state *structure* that comprises a centralized and stable government, an autonomous and cohesive bureaucracy, and effective coercive institutions (Johnson 1987). But internal cohesion is not sufficient to make industrial policies successful. State capacities to alter group behavior and restructure the domestic environment depend on the state's ability not only to dominate and penetrate society but also to establish growth-conducive relationships with particular classes. A developmental state structure requires an alliance between state elites and producer classes and the exclusion of workers and peasants (Evans 1995; Kohli 2004). This class basis enables a state, if it so chooses, to effectively formulate and implement strategies for industrialization with maximal business collaboration and minimal concerns about redistribution.

As the literature evolves through the three core concepts of roles, capacities, and structures, the conditions for developmental success have become clear. This success requires a state to play *developmental roles* effectively, which in turn entails a set of *developmental capacities*. Capacities in turn imply certain structural features of the state. A *developmental structure* includes cohesive internal organizations and alliance with capital at the expense of workers and peasants. Because capacities are largely derived from structures, we can simplify the essential requirements of developmental success to roles and structures. These two features are

---

[5] Weiss (1998) offers a systematic analysis of issues concerning state capacities and industrial policies.

interdependent factors that *together* explain successful developmentalism. Without developmental structures, states cannot play developmental roles effectively. On the other hand, structures do not guarantee that state leaders at any particular time are sufficiently committed to industrialization or that policies actually generate growth. As Peter Evans (1995, 77) summarizes succinctly, "Structures create the potential for action; playing out roles translates the potential into real effects."

While scholarship regarding developmental states is insightful, it suffers from three major weaknesses. First, the literature lacks historical depth. Most studies focus on proximate causes of developmental success but fail to address deeper links in the causal chain. In particular, many works are preoccupied with explaining economic growth or with identifying capacity requirements of developmental states while overlooking their historical origins. Although state roles and capacity requirements are important factors, this knowledge only begs the question as to why developmental states emerged where they did but not elsewhere. What gives, or gave, these states their cohesive structures? These historical questions have obvious implications for the contemporary debate about whether the model is replicable and similar policies are feasible in other lands with different historical legacies.

The neglect of ideology is another shortcoming of the developmental state model in the literature. Ideologies have been demonstrated to be causally significant in cases ranging from state consolidation in early modern Europe to social policies in modern welfare states (Orloff 1999; Gorski 2003). The scholarship on developmental states focuses on the "administrative infrastructure" of the state, or the networks and organizations through which state elites penetrate into society and regulate behavior. Little attention is given to the "ideological infrastructure," or the "symbols and identities through which rulers can mobilize the energies and harness the loyalties of their staffs and subjects" (Gorski 1999, 156–7). Besides centralized governments and cohesive coercive institutions, effective official ideologies and legitimizing discourses must be part of a developmental state structure.

The third weakness of the literature concerns its neglect of socialist states.[6] Two obvious differences exist between capitalist and socialist economic systems: the former relies mainly on private ownership and market mechanisms, whereas the latter does not (Johnson 1982, 17–24;

---

[6] Exceptions are Gerschenkron (1966); G. White (1988); and to some extent, Weiss (1998).

G. White 1983, 1). Another difference involves the class basis of the two kinds of states. Whereas capitalist developmental states rely on an alliance with producer classes and exclude working classes, their socialist counterparts draw power from direct control of productive organizations (e.g., cooperatives and factories). Here producer classes are dispensable. Rhetoric aside, working classes are treated similarly under this system as under capitalism.

I believe that socialist states, despite important differences, should be treated as a type of developmental state for three reasons. First, if Gerschenkron is right, the historical context of late development requires these states to play aggressive roles in their economies. Both South Korea and North Korea, for example, faced the same challenge of closing the huge gap with the industrialized world, a challenge that could be met only by coordinated efforts along a "broad front" (Gerschenkron 1966, 10–11). But Gerschenkron's view belongs to a minority in the literature, which frequently exaggerates the developmental roles played by socialist states relative to their capitalist counterparts. For example, in the 1920s Nikolai Bukharin, a Soviet leader and theorist of socialist development, wrote, "Capitalism was not built; it built itself. Socialism, as an organized system, is built by the proletariat, as organized collective subject" (cited in G. White and Wade 1988, 13). But we now have sufficient evidence that capitalism in late-developing countries did not build itself. More recently, Linda Weiss (1998, 66–7) argues that the task facing socialist states is *revolutionary transformation*, which involves breaking with an antecedent economic system, especially overthrowing the power of the dominant classes. For capitalist developmental states, Weiss claims that the task is less radical, requiring only *structural transformation*, namely the transformation from an agricultural base to an industrial one.[7] Yet Weiss overlooks the *counterrevolutionary transformations* that took place before structural transformations in capitalist developmental states such as South Korea and Indonesia under Suharto. These states relied on the political exclusion, if not repression, of working classes. As Chapters 2 and 3 show, peasants and workers had been organized by communist parties in both cases before structural transformations. Without counterrevolutionary transformations to defeat communists, capitalist structural transformations would have had little chance of success. The gap between

---

[7] Weiss (1998, 66–7) also discusses a third type of transformation, namely *sectoral transformation* (e.g., within industry from low to higher value-added industries). This is the task facing both industrializing and advanced industrialized economies. In this book, I focus on revolutionary and structural rather than sectoral transformation.

socialist and capitalist developmental states in terms of the tasks facing them is not as large as often assumed.

The second reason to count socialist states as developmental states comes from their structural features. These states have stable and centralized governments, cohesive bureaucracies, and effective coercive institutions – internal structures quite similar to those possessed by capitalist developmental states. Third, and finally, it is true that the modes of economic intervention differ between socialist and capitalist states. Modes of intervention determine how efficient and dynamic the economy can be and whether development is sustainable in the long run. Socialist systems in the Soviet Union and North Korea achieved rapid industrialization, only to eventually fall behind their capitalist rivals. Nevertheless, if our central question is about the origins of developmental structures rather than about the long-term outcomes of success or failure, modes of intervention do not matter as much. Theories that leave out socialist states not only overlook important similarities between socialist and capitalist cases but also exaggerate the importance of policy factors such as flexible planning and export orientation. Historical and political factors that account for the emergence of similar state structures in both systems are underestimated.

In a major study that seeks to overcome many weaknesses in the literature (Kohli 2004), the cause of successful industrialization is attributed less to state capacity than to patterns of authority understood as relationships between states and social forces. Patterns of authority in turn are determined by the historical patterns of state construction under colonial, nationalist, or military rulers. For example, in the case of South Korea, Japanese colonial rulers modernized the traditional Korean state, established an alliance between the state and production-oriented dominant classes, and brutally oppressed lower classes. This framework for a high-growth economy was preserved from the end of colonial rule until the 1960s when military leaders fell back to it and led South Korea to successful industrialization. In Nigeria, another case in the study, the British set the long-term pattern of a neopatrimonial state whose power was entangled in and weakened by particularistic and personalistic networks. The nationalist movement was feeble and divided, while subsequent military rulers failed to alter what they inherited from the British. In Atul Kohli's conceptual framework, history – especially colonial history – played a decisive role in shaping developmental outcomes.

Although Kohli's study makes a major contribution to the scholarship, he neither includes socialist states in his cases nor discusses ideological factors. Moreover, his typological approach aims to build *ideal types* of states ("neopatrimonial," "cohesive-capitalist," and "fragmented-multiclass" states) and tends to pay insufficient attention to the *historical processes* that produced cohesive East Asian states but wobbly states elsewhere. The resulting historical determinism is especially apparent in the Korean case. Here, Kohli emphasizes the colonial era (1910–45) and treats the early postcolonial decade merely as an "interregnum." Yet, as I argue in Chapter 2, the critical events that gave birth to South Korea in the aftermath of World War II not only transformed the Japanese legacy but also built new foundations for a developmental state that would emerge a decade later.

The discussion thus far suggests that the puzzle about the origins of developmental states has not been fully resolved. The search is still open for a theoretical framework that takes history seriously. Because the literature has overemphasized issues of state roles and capacities, it is time to shift the focus to state structures, as Kohli does. Ideology must be taken into account even if firm causality cannot be ascertained. Socialist cases, if included in the sample, also help to correct the bias in favor of policy factors.

THE ARGUMENT

This study hopes to advance this search by picking up where past studies left off. Like Kohli, I search for the historical origins of developmental structures as opposed to the policy causes of developmental success. Rather than constructing ideal types of states as Kohli does, I employ the comparative historical method to appreciate a fuller range of historical possibilities.[8] While acknowledging that colonialism is important, I disagree that it is the most important causal factor. Instead, I propose that colonial legacies are highly contingent on the politics of state formation in most cases. In analyzing the dynamics of state formation and the relationship between state formation politics and postcolonial state structures, I argue that states are born with different structural endowments; that patterns of intraelite and elite–mass interaction during state formation determine the degree of cohesion in emerging states; and that accommodation among elites and between them and the masses generates fractured and incoherent state structures, whereas confrontation produces opposite outcomes.

---

[8] See Mahoney and Rueschemeyer (2003) and George and Bennett (2005) for recent discussions of this method.

State Formation as a Critical Juncture

In the literature on state origins, "state building" and "state formation" are often interchangeable concepts.[9] This unfortunate conflation masks an important difference between the first modern states that emerged in Western Europe and most of the rest. The first modern states emerged over centuries by a process in which rulers built states gradually out of feudal domains and city-states (Elias [1939] 1982; Tilly 1990; Spruyt 1994). State structures, including organizations, bureaucracies, and territorial controls, were built commensurate with the functions and forms of what would be labeled a "modern" state. Modern state formation and state building were a long and incremental process.

In contrast, most states outside of Western Europe primarily emerged from imperial collapses or breakups. The Spanish, the Ottoman, the Chinese, the Austro-Hungarian, the British, the French, the Dutch, the Portuguese, the Japanese, and, most recently, the Soviet empires are in fact the mothers of the majority of today's states. Once founded, emerging states have been quick to adopt constitutional governments and claim full sovereignty over national territories. Yet the structures of these young states rarely match their modern pretensions: constitutional principles are not practiced, and government sovereignty often does not extend far beyond capital cities. For instance, while England has never had a written constitution, few states founded in the past two centuries were born without one. The English Parliament had centuries to negotiate working relationships with absolute monarchs before modern institutions such as party systems and mass franchises were introduced. Most late-forming states had no such experience.

Because late-coming states have sought forms first and structures later, the process by which they emerged and evolved has been radically different from the Western European experience. Speed replaced the *longue durée* and was a distinctive aspect of state-*forming* experience in non–Western European contexts. State formation comprised a series of rapid events triggered by the sudden collapse, or sometimes simply by a momentary weakening, of an imperial or colonial state. From a single empire, new states could break away one by one (e.g., the Ottoman and British empires), but they also could emerge with a big bang (e.g., the Austro-Hungarian and Japanese empires). The big-bang mode has indeed been the prevalent mechanism of state formation in the twentieth century.

---

[9] Whereas the verb "build" can only be used transitively (as in "someone builds something"), the verb "form" can be used both transitively (as in "someone forms something") and intransitively (as in "something forms" – i.e., develops gradually).

The rapidity with which most modern states were born has led some to classify state formation as a kind of "political crisis," defined as an "abrupt and brutal challenge to the survival of the regime, . . . most often consist[ing] of a short chain of events that destroy or drastically weaken a regime's equilibrium and effectiveness within a period of days or weeks" (Dogan and Higley 1998b, 7). There is some value in not separating state formation from crises that generate only regime changes. State formation shares with regime transition an extraordinary degree of uncertainty that makes "normal science methodology" less useful in studying these events (O'Donnell and Schmitter 1986, 3–5). In addition, an inventory of crises that range from struggles for independent statehood to breakdowns of authoritarian regimes contains a larger sample of critical events for comparative purposes (Dogan and Higley 1998b, 8–14). Yet excessive conceptual generality and the pretensions of objectively defined crisis situations introduce intractable conceptual problems and appear to outweigh the benefits of the approach (Knight 1998, 31–9).

In this book, state formation is used as a convenient analytical device that provides a clear-cut and useful starting point for the comparative historical analysis of state development over time. As mentioned earlier, intraelite and elite–mass politics during state formation – not state formation itself – is what determines the structural cohesion of emerging states. State formation enhances the impact of such politics because the occasion facilitates a wholesale institutional change, but state formation is not a causal factor.[10] Nevertheless, I highlight two differences between state formation and other kinds of crises. First, the outcome of the event is potentially more substantial than just regime change. Territorial boundaries, popular loyalties, communal identities, and political structures may be entirely remade, redefined, or renegotiated. The second difference concerns the event itself. The sudden imperial collapses that often precede state formation offer political and social actors rare opportunities to assert their will and exercise their collective power, which is normally suppressed. Generally, state formation involves a broader range of actors than regime change.

To be sure, there is no hard-and-fast rule that separates a state formation situation a priori from less severe crises. Political crises that involve a colony and claims of independent statehood, that occur in faraway corners of an empire (or a modern state that is structured or organized

---

[10] A disease analogy is useful here: viruses may cause more human deaths in winter than summer, but winter cannot be considered a cause of deaths. Viruses are.

similarly to an empire), or that involve a sudden regime change in an existing multiethnic state with pent-up ethnic tensions are the best candidates for state formation in the making. Still, a potential state formation situation does not mean new states will be born eventually, because the old empire may successfully recover and reclaim what it has lost, perhaps by military means. Furthermore, in cases where power is transferred gradually and peacefully from mother empires to baby states – as occurred in many British colonies after World War II – the legacy of state formation politics may be more limited. Colonial designs may have a more lasting legacy.

Political Dynamics of State Formation

In her book on democratic transitions in Western Europe and South America, Ruth Collier (1998) criticizes the recent scholarship on democratization as too much political science and too little sociology. By this she means the *political* dynamics of transition such as elite pacts have been overstudied, whereas deeper *sociological* processes such as class conflicts have not received adequate attention. The literature on state formation, in contrast, has been predominantly sociological. While sociological factors are important, this book places primary emphasis on political and contingent factors, especially on the interaction among elites and between elites and the masses in forming a new state.

"Elites," defined in the political rather than sociological sense, are the few hundred men and women who exercise the greatest political power in imperial or colonial centers or who are politically influential in their communities above local levels. They may be imperial officials or antigovernment activists. In colonial societies, they may belong to the dominant races, to the subject races, or to hybrid races – although in the era of nationalism people of subject races are perhaps more inclined to stake out claims for self-rule. Elites may be appointed by imperial metropolitans or recruited locally to assist in administration or to act as intermediaries in economic activities. Some empires permit the election of provincial councils that, over time, generate elites of status and reputation beyond local circles. In contrast with elites, the "masses" are local leaders, locally organized groups, and ordinary people.[11] The patterns of elite

---

[11] The definitions of elites and the masses here follow Feith (1962, 108), who adopted the concepts from Harold Lasswell. A similarly defined concept of elites can be found in Dogan and Higley (1998b); Villalon and VonDoepp (2005); Higley and Burton (2006); and Case (2002).

alignment and elite–mass engagement during state formation are argued in this study to have critical consequences for the structural cohesion of emerging states.

Elite alignment patterns consist of four basic modes: unity, fragmentation, compromise, and polarization.[12] *Elite unity* occurs when one single group predominates. Historically, elite unity seems rare perhaps because political groups take time to build cohesive organizations, whereas state-forming opportunities are often abrupt.[13] The opposite of elite unity is *elite fragmentation*, in which elites break into many small factions without any dominant group.[14] Fragmentation seems to be the most common pattern historically and can be the result of many factors. There may be too many social cleavages and politically divisive issues facing the elites, with too little time to work out differences and build unified organizations. In the case of vast empires, geography may pose another set of challenges to elite communication and organization; so does an overbearing imperial state that suppresses prior organizing efforts among elites.

Between unity and fragmentation are the intermediate patterns of *elite compromise* and *elite polarization*. In these patterns, elites are neither united in one single group nor fragmented into many. Although issues divide them, these issues are few and do not lead to fragmentation. At the same time, elite disagreement tends to be deeper and often involves identity clashes. Compromise means significant concessions in matters of ideology, organization, and material interests. Compromise often entails more than one step or decision. Initial compromises may be followed by more significant ones as certain elites collaborate on the common project of state formation, while other groups are marginalized. Compromise therefore is a process of forming a central bloc and eliminating extremes. In the same vein, polarization involves more than one step and means not simply a rejection of compromise by elites but the process of forming two or more (but not too many) opposing extremes and the elimination of moderate political options.

[12] To be sure, elites may decide not to act for whatever reasons. A notable case of elite inaction involves Malayan communists in August 1945. After the Japanese Empire collapsed, Malayan communists emerged as the best-organized political group. Yet they did not seize the opportunity to declare independence as did native elites with less strategic advantage in other Japanese colonies (Andaya and Andaya 1982, 252–7; Harper 1999, 48–52).

[13] The best example of the elite unity pattern is perhaps the formation of the Indian state in 1947 under the Congress Party.

[14] Spanish America is a case where elites were fragmented during state formation (Centeno 2002, 50).

Yet elites do not exist in a vacuum. Often imperial crises allow mass actors to riot and seize local power independent from elites. While elite behavior is typically motivated by an anticolonial ideology and involves organization, spontaneous mass actions are spurred by resentment against imperial rule or simply by some combinations of hunger, greed, and opportunism. These mass groups may have limited political ambitions, but they confront new state elites with a dilemma. If these elites choose to *incorporate* local power usurpers into local governments, they risk future insubordination because these groups have come to power by themselves and likely will not respect central authority. Alternatively, elites can choose to *suppress* mass actors. Often this is not really a choice because the emerging state is yet to possess a coercive force (unless it is willing or able to rely on the imperial coercive apparatus).

Mass incorporation and *mass suppression* represent two polar options. Elites often try and are sometimes able to mobilize large-scale mass support, especially if the process of state formation is protracted. This third pattern, which I call *controlled mobilization*, indicates not only a large mass following but also elites' ability to harness mass energies for long-term goals rather than rash and ineffective actions commonly observed in many mass movements. Controlled mobilization requires elites to build sophisticated organizations that sustain long-term elite-led mass actions.

The broad range of elite alignment and elite–mass engagement dynamics suggests numerous possibilities during state formation. Two additional points are in order to clarify potential confusion. First, the different patterns of each dynamic are not mutually exclusive. The imperial state may not collapse uniformly, and neither elites nor masses act or react uniformly. Thus, different patterns, such as mass incorporation and mass suppression, may occur at the same time. Mass mobilization may take place among certain constituencies, while the rest of the country follows a different pattern of engagement. Elites may unite at first but later polarize over the course of state formation.

Second, elite alignment and elite–mass engagement patterns are not assumed to be phenomena exclusively associated with state formation. Elites and the masses can undertake political action at any time, whether formally or informally and whether legally or illegally. During periods of regime change, intraelite politics can be intense and consequential. At the same time, mass revolts commonly occur in revolutionary situations that may or may not produce new states. State formation, if it involves major elite realignments and mass participation, as is often the case, is arguably a special and rarer case than the situations described previously.

TABLE 1. *Four Components of a Developmental State Structure*

- Centralized structure
- Cohesive political organizations
- Growth-conducive state–class relations or foreign alliances
- Ideological congruence

Components of a Developmental Structure

As found in the literature on developmental states, a developmental structure consists of an internal component that includes a centralized and stable government, an autonomous and cohesive bureaucracy, and effective coercive institutions. The external component of this structure involves a growth-conducive alliance with producer classes at the expense of workers and peasants. In many cases, especially for socialist developmental states, the alliance with domestic producer classes is substituted by state monopolies of the means of production and by support from foreign capital. Ideological congruence is added in this study as an important but thus far neglected component of a developmental structure (Table 1).[15]

Because others (e.g., Kohli 2004) have developed propositions about the importance of centralization, organizational cohesion, and growth-conducive state–class relations for developmental states, I focus here only on explaining how ideological congruence contributes to a cohesive structure. Ideological congruence is a broad term that indicates several kinds of relationships through which ideological factors impact the structure of a state. One such relationship involves the top political elites and the state bureaucracy. Ideological congruence in this case means shared ideological orientations between the two. A newly formed state in which a socialist party rises to power and inherits an imperial bureaucracy and army is an example of ideological incongruence: the radical ideology embraced by state leaders contradicts the conservative character of their apparatus. In contrast, a state in which a conservative government inherits a colonial bureaucracy and army poses no threat to, and may even augment, its ideological congruence.

Another relationship concerns the transformative goals of elites and the general ideological orientations of a society. Incongruence may not be fatal to transformative projects, but active social opposition or passive

---

[15] Ideologies can be defined as sets of ideas and symbols that "express or dramatize something about the moral order" (Wuthnow 1987, 145).

resistance can lead to delays and loss of momentum. For example, if German elites' goal is to liberalize sexual norms in society, they are likely to enjoy a higher degree of ideological congruence than American elites embarking on the same project because the historical legacy of Puritanism in the United States would probably generate a higher degree of social resistance. Unlike the previous case, congruence in this case is more difficult to evaluate because the general ideological orientations of any society are difficult to measure.

Still another relationship exists between elites' legitimizing discourse at different points in time (not assumed to be unchanged), or among various components in the same legitimizing discourse at the same time (not assumed to be consistent). Ideological congruence in this case simply means the internal coherence of elites' legitimizing discourse and its consistency over time. The assumption is that discourses lose their legitimizing power or are likely to trigger resistance if they change too rapidly or too radically, or if they contain contradictory elements. For example, an elite group may rise to power by using certain slogans calling for national solidarity but, once in power, reverse themselves by launching a developmental project legitimized by a divisive ideology such as class struggle. Here ideological incongruence reflects a discursive inconsistency. Again, this incongruence may not kill the project, but it can generate higher levels of political and social resistance.

To be sure, in theory elites can pursue and achieve any vision of development, however radical. In the long term, ruling elites with developmental ideologies can recruit new loyal bureaucrats, manipulate social norms and national cultures, and build consistent legitimizing discourses. At any moment, however, they are constrained by preexisting institutional setups, social norms, and legitimizing discourses.

In sum, centralized structure, cohesive organizations, growth-conducive state–class relations or foreign alliance, and ideological congruence are assumed to be essential requirements for a cohesive developmental structure.

State Formation Dynamics and Their Impacts on Emerging State Structures

We can now turn to the question how the dynamics of state formation impact the structures of emerging states. These dynamics include four modes of elite alignment (unity, fragmentation, compromise, and polarization) and three patterns of elite–mass engagement (incorporation, suppression, and controlled mobilization). Each mode of elite alignment and elite–mass engagement can have different impacts on state structures.

Elite Unity

Elite unity alignment pattern implies the cooperation of most elites under a unified leadership with the authority to single-handedly formulate and implement transformative projects. Other things being equal, this condition not only maximizes institutional coordination but also allows projects formulated to be more comprehensive. Furthermore, unity is the favorable condition for the creation of cohesive organizations, for developing class relations to elites' liking, for formulating a clear and consistent legitimizing discourse, and for disseminating ideologies internally and externally.

Elite Fragmentation

Elite fragmentation suggests that power is divided among many factions. Formulation of a comprehensive transformative agenda is unlikely, or at least difficult, because no single group has the authority to propose such an agenda. Fragmentation obviously imposes significant constraints on building cohesive organizations, on fostering relations with appropriate classes or foreign allies, and on elites' ability to forge ideological congruence.

Elite Compromise

Elite compromise also creates divided authority and suggests the embodiment of certain compromising attitudes in state organizations and in state relationships with various social classes. Lax rules for membership in those organizations and a poorly defined social base of the state are concrete expressions of elite compromise. Elite compromise requires elites either to downplay any particular ideology or to search for one broad enough to appeal to compromising factions. Nationalism or populism meets this requirement in many cases of modern state formation. However, these ideologies lack specific socioeconomic contents and may be incongruent with developmental programs.

Elite Polarization

Polarization is likely to produce violent confrontations and civil wars that result in either state breakups or the physical elimination of losers by winners. The ultimate outcome in the new state (or states) is not just elite unity but unity forged and tested through struggle. In terms of impact on state organizations, polarization necessitates the careful selection of members and early efforts to consolidate organizational structure and discipline. The likely outcome is more cohesive, if less broad-based, political organizations. In fact, organizations developed under the competitive environment of polarization must be even more cohesive than those created simply by elite unity. Finally, polarization generates pressures on elites to focus more on nurturing social bases and to clarify their ideological positions constantly in order to distinguish themselves from their adversaries. This environment is conducive to the formulation and diffusion of radical transformative goals within organizations but hostile to ideological diversity. Because of this radicalizing process, ideological congruence must be stronger than what is produced by simple elite unity.

Mass Incorporation
Mass incorporation implies that the new state must accept significant local autonomy from the outset. The structure of this state is wobbly because the center lacks control over local governments. Incorporation does not promise much in terms of cohesive organizations, growth-conducive state–class relations, and ideological congruence. For example, the armed forces of the new state may simply be a poorly integrated assemblage of local militias. Similarly, local groups are accepted as they are without necessarily sharing the values of the national elites.

Mass Suppression
Successful suppression helps the new state to curb local autonomy and impose central rule over local communities. Confrontation with the masses allows state organizations to be tested in a hostile environment. It improves their overall internal cohesiveness. Suppression eliminates open challenges to the new state's ideological hegemony and helps state elites to develop growth-conducive class relations.

Controlled Mobilization
Controlled mobilization can create more cohesive organizations than suppression can because, during the process of mobilization, elites are able to select the most loyal members of the masses. In addition, controlled mobilization allows the indoctrination of members with new values before admission into political organizations, translating into a high degree of ideological congruence. While suppression helps to consolidate state ideological hegemony by negative means (repressing alternative values),

TABLE 2. *Impact of Elite Alignment Patterns on State Structures*

	Elite Unity	Elite Fragmentation	Elite Compromise	Elite Polarization
Centralized, stable government	+	− −	−	+ +
Cohesive political organizations	+	− −	−	+ +
Progrowth state–class relations	+	− −	−	+ +
Ideological congruence	+	− −	−	+ +

Note: The signs suggest the varying degrees of impact that include four levels, ranging from weakly negative (−) to strongly negative (− −), and from weakly positive (+) to strongly positive (+ +).

controlled mobilization does so by positive methods (indoctrinating with new ideas). Positive means are more difficult to employ but generate more legitimacy for state ideology than negative means do.

Tables 2 and 3 summarize the impact of various patterns of elite alignment and elite–mass engagement on government structure, political organizations, state–class relations, and ideological congruence. In terms of overall impact, as the tables show, elite action and mass action may cancel each other out (if they carry different signs) or may reinforce each other (if they have the same signs).

While there can be numerous combinations of the two dynamics, this study focuses on four particular combinations (see Table 4). One combination involves elite polarization and mass suppression (positively reinforcing); the second, elite polarization and controlled mobilization (also positively reinforcing); the third, elite compromise and mass incorporation (negatively reinforcing); and the fourth, elite compromise and polarization together with mass incorporation and suppression (mutually canceling out). For convenience, I group the first two combinations under the

TABLE 3. *Impact of Elite–Mass Engagement Patterns on State Structures*

	Mass Incorporation	Mass Suppression	Controlled Mobilization
Centralized, stable government	−	+	+ +
Cohesive political organizations	−	+	+ +
Progrowth state–class relations	−	+	+ +
Ideological congruence	−	+	+ +

Note: For signs, see Table 2.

TABLE 4. *Confrontation, Accommodation, and Mixed Paths of State Formation*

Paths of State Formation	Combinations Dynamics	Impact on State Structure	Cases
Confrontation	Elite polarization	++	South Korea and Suharto's Indonesia
	Mass suppression	+	
	Elite polarization	++	Maoist China
	Controlled mobilization	++	
Accommodation	Elite compromise	−	Sukarno's Indonesia and Vietnam (1945–60)
	Mass incorporation	−	
Mixed	Elite compromise and polarization	− +	Republican China (1930s)
	Mass suppression and incorporation	+ −	

Note: For signs, see Table 2.

general label of "confrontation." The third combination is called "accommodation." The fourth combination is a mixture of accommodation and confrontation.

CASE SELECTION AND RESEARCH DESIGN

The theoretical framework of this book builds on six cases from four Asian countries: South Korea, Vietnam, China (the Republican and Maoist states), and Indonesia (under Sukarno and under Suharto). By all measures, these four countries are among the most significant in East Asia. More important, the six cases displayed different patterns of state formation and varying degrees of cohesiveness in their structures. The South Korean and Chinese Maoist states were among the most cohesive in the world. Both states were formed under the confrontation pattern, namely under the conditions of sharp elite polarization and either brutal mass suppression or effective mass mobilization. The Indonesian state under Suharto emerged out of confrontation and also acquired a cohesive structure in the process. In contrast, the Vietnamese state and the Indonesian state under Sukarno were formed through an accommodation path characterized by elite compromise and mass incorporation. In comparative perspective, these states had fractured structures. Finally, China's Republican state during the 1930s was created by a mixture of confrontation and accommodation: it came to possess a few effective organizations but also carried crippling defects in its structure.

The six cases are also distinguishable as communist and capitalist systems. As argued earlier, communist states harbored developmental ambitions, although they chose to pursue a different model. They were generally very effective in carrying out their ambitions, even though their effectiveness varied and the most effective among them never achieved a dynamic economy as their best capitalist rivals did. This failure, however, is due to the limitations of their model, not to their lack of effectiveness. By matching communist against capitalist cases, I hope to show the powerful impact of state formation politics on state structure, regardless of the ideological orientations of state elites.

Another innovation of this study concerns the use of the comparative historical method. This method has been useful in the study of revolutions, democratization, and welfare states but has not been employed to study developmental states. On the basis of carefully matched cases in which causes and effects are traced over the long term, this approach directs attention to the historical trajectories of state formation that would produce diverse outcomes in specific contexts. In addition, the approach enables the full examination of historical possibilities and contingencies, thus avoiding the historical determinism pervasive in studies that emphasize factors such as class relations (e.g., Moore 1966) and colonial legacies (Kohli 2004).

To strengthen the causal argument, I employ a "nested design." Nested designs are common in comparative historical research. They allow a researcher to enhance the leverage of a causal argument by examining the question at different levels of analysis (cross-national and subnational) with different kinds of data (dataset observations and causal process observations) (Brady and Collier 2004; George and Bennett 2005). Two levels are nested in this study. In the first part, six case studies are contrasted at the broad macrostructural level to demonstrate that different dynamics of state formation had different bearings on postcolonial state structures in these cases. In the second part of the study, the focus narrows to the accommodation pattern in the Vietnamese and Indonesian cases during the 1940s. Here the goal is to identify how this pattern was specifically institutionalized at the level of organization and in the discourses of the nationalist movements that would form the Vietnamese and Indonesian postcolonial states. By examining two variants of accommodation within limited time frames, the analyses at the second level add not only nuances to the argument but also causal process observations that increase its explanatory leverage.

ORGANIZATION OF THE BOOK

Part I (Chapters 2, 3, 4, and 5) offers a cross-national comparison of six cases: South Korea, Indonesia (under Sukarno and under Suharto), China (the Republican state and the Maoist state), and Vietnam (1945–60). Chapters 2 and 3 examine state formation and the rise of capitalist developmental states in South Korea and Indonesia. These chapters show how state formation dynamics following the collapse of the Japanese Empire in 1945 profoundly shaped the structures of these states in the 1950s. In South Korea, mass suppression was carried out by American occupation forces in collaboration with new state elites and the retained imperial coercive apparatus. At the same time, a sharp polarization among elites emerged. Ultraconservative factions eventually prevailed over radical communists, who fled to the North or were persecuted. In contrast, in Indonesia, new state elites compromised among themselves and incorporated the masses to fight for independence. I argue that the divergent state formation patterns in the two countries gave rise to a developmental structure in South Korea but not in Indonesia. Chapter 3 also explains the rise of a developmental state in Indonesia in the late 1960s. The cohesive structure of this state was born out of sharp elite polarization and brutal mass suppression – that is, conditions similar to South Korea in the 1940s.

Whereas Chapters 2 and 3 address the two capitalist cases of South Korea and Indonesia, Chapters 4 and 5 study China's Republican state during the 1930s and the two socialist cases of Maoist China and (North) Vietnam. I show that the Republican state was formed through a mixture of accommodation and confrontation, with accommodation as the predominant pattern. This state was able to build many cohesive organizations, but its overall structure suffered from critical weaknesses. In contrast, the Maoist state resulted from decades-long polarization. In the process, Chinese communists developed sophisticated techniques of mass mobilization. When they won the civil war, they had accumulated significant assets for a developmental structure. While confrontation gave birth to a cohesive socialist developmental state in mainland China, accommodation denied Vietnam such a state. Similar to Indonesia in the 1940s, state formation in Vietnam was marked by elite compromise and mass

TABLE 5. *Three Paths of State Formation*

Patterns of State Formation	Territorial Outcome	Impact on State Structure
Accommodation: Elite compromise and mass incorporation (Sukarno's Indonesia, Vietnam)	New states coterminous with colonial states	Wobbly state structure, incoherent political organizations, and ideological incongruence
Mixed: Elite compromise and polarization; mass suppression and incorporation (Republican China)	New state coterminous with imperial state	A few effective organizations; overall incoherent structure
Confrontation: Elite polarization; mass suppression or controlled mobilization (Korea, Maoist China, Suharto's Indonesia)	Old states broken up (Korea, China); state preserved but a major elite group eliminated (Indonesia)	Centralized state structure, cohesive political organizations, and ideological congruence

incorporation into a nationalist movement to fight the returning French. As a result, the Vietnamese state upon achieving independence lacked cohesion. Its premature launching of a socioeconomic revolution was thwarted, whereas the Maoist state had little difficulty pushing through a far more radical agenda.

Table 5 summarizes the essence of the argument in Part I that state formation dynamics shaped state structure in the six cases through three distinct paths. In the accommodation path taken by Indonesia and Vietnam in the 1940s, elite compromise and mass incorporation produced moderate and inclusive states in unified nations.[16] The path became institutionalized in fractured state structures, fragile political organizations, and ideological incongruence. In contrast, China, Korea, and Suharto's Indonesia took the confrontation path. There, elite polarization

---

[16] This pattern in Vietnam was interrupted in the late 1940s, when the communist leadership adopted radical policies, while part of the national coalition for independence broke away to help found the State of Vietnam (later changed to the Republic of Vietnam and relocated to the South). Due to this particular truncated pattern, only North Vietnam "suffered" from the legacies of elite compromise and mass incorporation. South Vietnam (which is not discussed) was formed through a different process marked by elite polarization and mass repression similar to the Korean path. Unlike South Korea, South Vietnam did not survive a protracted civil war.

and mass suppression (controlled mobilization for Maoist China) played midwife to states with cohesive structures in divided nations (China and South Korea). The rise of the Suharto regime in the 1960s did not break up the Indonesian state, but hundreds of thousands of communists perished, giving way to a new regime with a cohesive state structure. Finally, the Republican state was born out of a mixture of accommodation and confrontation. This state preserved the territorial integrity of the imperial state, but its overall structure lacked cohesion.

Part II (Chapters 6, 7, 8, and 9) aims to complement Part I with an examination of the Vietnamese and Indonesian cases, where state formation based on accommodation produced wobbly state structures. Part II offers substantial empirical details on the larger processes in two different colonial contexts. At the microlevel, accommodation was embedded in each country's respective nationalist movement that would transform over time into the new Vietnamese and Indonesian states. Part II investigates in particular how the dynamics of accommodation played out in movement organizations and discourses.

In terms of *organizations*, I argue in Chapters 6 and 7 that accommodation through compromise and incorporation helped both the Vietnamese and Indonesian nationalist movements to grow rapidly. Yet accommodation also created for both postcolonial states divided or decentralized governments together with political organizations that were characterized by blurred boundaries and weak corporate identities. To build a cohesive state structure, the Vietnamese Communist Party carried out a massive purge while launching its radical socioeconomic agenda. The backlash generated by the purge caused it to halt its policies and lose momentum. Similarly, the Indonesian ruling factions pursued capitalist development prematurely and eventually lost power.

While Chapters 6 and 7 examine the organizations of the Vietnamese and Indonesian nationalist movements, Chapters 8 and 9 focus on their political *discourses*. The central question is: how was accommodation institutionalized in the discourses of these movements? The focus on discourse is especially useful to gauge the degree of ideological congruence in both cases. In Vietnam, accommodation led to an emphasis on "national unity" and a strong resistance to the notion of "class struggle." When the Vietnamese state sought to promote class struggle in the 1950s, a serious ideological inconsistency or incongruence emerged. In Indonesia, accommodation helped to promote anticapitalist and populist themes, which dominated the political discourse. State leaders created a new discourse to encourage social acceptance of capitalism, but this discourse had to be disguised under populist and Islamic garbs to be accepted as legitimate. The nested analyses of the Vietnamese and Indonesian cases thus suggest how different configurations of factors in two cases nevertheless generated the same outcome of organizational fracture and ideological incongruence.

PART ONE

DIVERGENT NATIONAL PATHS OF STATE DEVELOPMENT

2

South Korea

Confrontation and the Formation of a Cohesive State

TRAUMATIC EVENTS AND A THEORETICAL LACUNA

On August 19, 2004, the leader of South Korea's ruling party, Shin Ki-nam, tearfully announced his resignation after his father's work decades before as a member of the military police force serving the Japanese colonial government became known.[1] "I still find it shocking and difficult to believe the details of recent reports about my father," he said. Shin was the first victim of an inquiry launched by President Roh Moo-hyun into South Korea's modern history, including the Japanese occupation from 1910 to 1945 and authoritarian rule until 1987. Just two years before, when President Roh himself was running for election, the news came out that his father-in-law had been a left-wing activist, was arrested during the Korean War, and died in prison when Roh's wife was a child.[2] When a rival took issue with Roh's father-in-law's record during the heated presidential race, Roh shot back, "Should I leave my wife just because of her father, who I never even met?"[3]

When these two recent episodes in Korean politics are placed next to each other, a great irony emerges. The two men now belong to the same ruling party, but one's father and the other's father-in-law used to be enemies. And the man who was not mentioned in the newspaper stories but

[1] Andrew Ward, "South Korea's Probe of Its Modern History Opens Can of Worms," *Financial Times*, August 20, 2004.
[2] Kim Hyeh-won, "Wife of Roh Believes in Korean Dream," *Korea Herald*, November 12, 2002. I thank Kang Myungkoo for pointing out this story to me.
[3] Kim Ji-ho, "First Lady Vows to Help the Underprivileged," *Korea Herald*, February 26, 2003.

who loomed large behind both was President Rhee Syngman (1948–60). Under his rule, Mr. Shin's father was protected and promoted, while Mrs. Roh's father languished in jail and died a premature death.

The events clearly left a deep scar in the Korean public mind. More importantly, the continuing trauma alerts us to a theoretical lacuna in existing scholarship. In particular, all dominant hypotheses about the origins of the Korean developmental state do not take state formation politics and the Rhee regime seriously. I noted in Chapter 1 that a predominant approach in the literature considers Japanese colonialism as the primary cause of Korean success and treats the period from 1945 to 1960 as a temporary deviance from the path preset by the Japanese (Kohli 2004). Most other accounts look no further than the Park Chung Hee regime (1961–79), when rapid industrialization took place. In these accounts, the state's ability to discipline capital and promote export-oriented policies that opened up foreign markets is regarded as a major cause of developmental success under Park (Amsden 1989; Haggard 1990). To be sure, the violent birth of the Korean state and the corrupt and personalistic Rhee regime are recounted, but these events serve merely as "historical background" or as evidence that Park started from scratch.[4] If the events (such as land reform) before Park's rise to power contributed anything, they were attributed to the United States, on which South Korea was highly dependent. Even so, those contributions do not play the central role in explaining Korea's later success and are at best secondary factors. The main causes are to be found in other periods.

The lack of an effective framework to analyze the historical context of state formation in South Korea generates inadequate explanations. For example, consider the argument that the land reform of the 1950s was a successful elite effort to reduce social conflicts and to buy peasants' compliance.[5] This argument overlooks the contested nature of land reform. There are many approaches to implementing land reform. In communist countries, even if landlords were not criminalized, no compensation would be given for their land. Under Rhee's land reform scheme

---

[4] Bruce Cumings has written the seminal study of events in Korea during 1945–53, but in his 1987 essay he promotes product cycle and dependent development theories and gives the period only a marginal role. An exception is S. I. Jun (1991), who focuses on the 1945–8 period and suggests that this period contributed to the later formation of a developmental state in South Korea. However, he does not show how. The serious neglect of the pre-1960 period in Korean modern historiography has been criticized in Stephen Kim (2001, 11–12), who also offers the best analysis to date of Rhee Syngman's role in winning American protection for South Korea.

[5] This was part of the explanation offered in Doner et al. (2005).

carried out in South Korea from 1949 to 1954, peasants had to pay land-lords by installments for the land they received. The Korean Communist Party that attracted broad peasant support in South Korea in 1946 and 1947 had opposed any compensation, and if the party had not been sup-pressed, land reform would not have been carried out as it was because the party would have mobilized peasants against it. The land reform may have reduced some social conflict but it could do so only after the violent suppression of communists. In the same vein with land reform, the argu-ment that "elite unity" under Park gave rise to the developmental state is not incorrect but nevertheless unsatisfactory (Waldner 1999). Again, one wonders whether this unity would have been possible in the 1960s if the Korean Communist Party had not been crushed by U.S. troops and Rhee's police by 1953. The causal chain goes deeper than the Park regime.

The explanation offered in this chapter centers on the politics of state formation under American occupation (1945–8) and subsequent state consolidation under Rhee (1948–60). This chapter attempts to show that the legacies of these periods were critical to later developmental outcome. By giving primary emphasis to the immediate postcolonial era, I do not assume that colonial institutions in South Korea can be preserved with-out indigenous actors (both elites and the masses) playing the central role. Similarly, Park's contributions are acknowledged but not assumed as sufficient. The arguments can be summarized as follows. In the Korean peninsula, the Japanese surrender in 1945 offered a momentary but crit-ical power vacuum. While elites scrambled for power, spontaneous mass revolts swept away local governments. Elite polarization between radical communists and conservatives gradually escalated despite three attempts at promoting compromise and collaboration. At the same time, the Amer-ican military government assisted by conservative groups and the colonial police carried out massive repression of communist-led mass revolts. By 1948, when sovereignty was transferred to a new government led by Rhee in the South, most southern leftist leaders had fled to the North and the entire southern communist organization had been destroyed. Thanks to elite polarization and mass suppression, emerging states in both South and North Korea became more cohesive and centralized under extremist ideologues.

This early extremist and cohesive character of the South Korean state was institutionalized further with two subsequent sets of events. The first was a series of repressive measures carried out by Rhee from 1948 to 1950 to protect the Japanese-trained security and administrative apparatuses, to assassinate opponents, to impose draconian security laws, and to root out communist influence in the population. The Korean War (1950–3), the second set of events, helped Rhee consolidate his anticommunist state even more. Polarization became entrenched not only among the elites but also in the general population, which helps to explain social submission to conservative rule in South Korea from 1953 to 1980. From the time when Park Chung Hee, the general widely credited for South Korean economic success, came to power in 1961, until he was assassinated in 1979, he never faced any serious leftist or labor challenge to his economic policies. Arguably he would never have had such a free hand in economic matters without a developmental structure built under Rhee.

In brief, elite polarization and mass suppression during state formation account for the origins of the developmental structure of the South Korean state. These events neither explain Korean economic success per se nor made that success inevitable. Rather, they explain how the cohesive Japanese-made state structure was reassembled and consolidated so that the Park regime could play effective developmental roles later on.

In this chapter, I review the record of South Korea's industrialization and the debate on colonial legacies. This debate is important not only to the Korean story but also for comparative purposes. Then I examine state formation politics and postcolonial state building under Rhee and demonstrate how a new developmental structure was created. While the state under Rhee did not play a developmental role, it is a mistake to dismiss Rhee's major contributions to the construction of a developmental structure. Finally, I discuss the impact of state formation dynamics and Rhee's legacies – in particular, how these factors allowed the Park government to effectively implement its developmental agenda.

COLONIAL LEGACIES AND KOREAN POSTWAR INDUSTRIALIZATION

As many have argued, Korean industrialization began in the colonial period (Eckert et al. 1990; Kohli 2004). Japan annexed Korea in 1910 and oversaw significant development until 1945. For all of Korea's sufferings under a repressive colonial regime, it was the Japanese who built the first modern factories, schools, and transport systems in Korea. In agriculture, the colonial government reformed property rights, facilitated land concentration, and contributed to moderate growth in production. Unlike Western colonizers, the Japanese invested significantly in developing industries and infrastructure in their colonies, including Korea. One study estimates that Korea's total commodity product increased at an annual compound rate of about 3 percent during the period from 1912 to 1937 – a rate considered "respectable" for an economy in transition from the traditional subsistence stage (Ho 1984, 359). Industrial growth rates were substantially higher, being nearly 15 percent during the 1930s (Kohli 2004, 51).

From independence in 1948 until 1980, economic development in South Korea proceeded in four periods. The first decade (1948–58) saw some growth despite massive destruction following the Korean War. This war killed more than one million people and destroyed nearly half of South Korea's industrial capacity, a third of its housing, and much public infrastructure (Eckert et al. 1990, 345). After the war ended in 1953, the economy experienced moderate growth and recovered thanks partly to U.S. aid (Reeve 1963, 125; Cathie 1989, 121). From 1953 to 1958, average annual GNP growth was 5.2 percent. While lacking an over-all economic strategy, the government implemented a land reform that effectively ended landlordism, a legacy of traditional and Japanese eras.

In the second period (1959–61), the economy slowed significantly, and growth rate was negative in per capita terms for 1960 (Brown 1973, 308). Electoral fraud and police brutality led to massive popular protests and the collapse of the Rhee regime in 1960. A year later, a military coup brought General Park Chung Hee to power. During the third period (1961–6), which coincided with the Park regime's First Five-Year Plan, Park implemented a wide range of macroeconomic policies aimed at stabilizing prices, liberalizing trade, and promoting exports. After this period, the South Korean economy underwent fifteen years of high growth, eight years of which saw growth rates reaching double digits. Total GDP grew sixteen times between 1965 and 1980, from $3.7 billion to $60.3 billion (Steinberg 1989, 123). The Park government also devoted massive resources to heavy industries such as steel, chemical, and shipbuilding. By the time Park was assassinated in 1979, industrialization in South Korea was clearly self-sustaining.

Although economic performance under Park was spectacular, to what extent this success was owed to Japanese colonization remains controversial. Those who assign a major role to the Japanese in laying the ground for postwar industrialization have relied on three main arguments. First, significant economic development took place under the Japanese. For example, by 1945 Korea boasted more than three thousand kilometers of railroad tracks and fifty thousand kilometers of motor roads (Eckert et al. 1990, 270). The Korean railroad system was clearly the best in Asia after Japan. Korea also had one of the highest rates of literacy (at nearly 50 percent in 1945) and enrolled the most elementary students (5.5 percent of total population in 1939) among all colonies (Kohli 2004, 39; McGinn et al. 1980, 80–1). Even though the bulk of colonial heavy industries was located in North Korea, much of colonial infrastructure was destroyed during the Korean War, the colonial educational system discriminated against Koreans, and ownership of most capital was in Japanese hands, Kohli (1997, 884) contends that "the knowledge of industrial technology and management, as well as experience of urban living, the modern educational system and the skills of workers survived, leaving a positive legacy for postwar industrialization."

The second argument for Japan's major role focuses on the transformation of the state under Japanese colonialism. The Japanese are credited with removing the corrupt and ineffective traditional monarchy, which resisted modernization (J. Yang 2004). In the place of a decayed agrarian bureaucracy, the Japanese built a modern centralized state with vast capacity and deep penetration into society (Kohli 2004, 32–44). An indicator of this new capacity was the number of government officials, which increased from ten thousand in 1910 to nearly ninety thousand in 1937, with more than fifty thousand being Japanese. The police force also grew from six thousand in 1910 to sixty thousand in 1941, being engaged not only in security matters but also in the mobilization of forced labor, birth control, and agricultural production. Much of this colonial bureaucracy and police force would be retained in postcolonial South Korea.

Finally, Japanese contribution is noted in creating an alliance between the state and propertied classes that excluded peasants and workers (Kohli 2004, 48–61). To co-opt Korean nationalism, the colonial government offered subsidies, loans, and contracts to many wealthy Korean entrepreneurs. Significant collaboration between the colonial regime and Korean capitalists led to the emergence of a Korean entrepreneurial class. By 1937, for example, there were 2,300 Korean-run factories of which 160 employed more than fifty workers. At the same time, the colonial regime imposed strict controls over workers to keep them working for low wages. Land concentration led to a high tenancy rate of 70 percent but extensive police surveillance kept peasant unrest in check. As Kohli points out, this pattern of relationship between the state and social classes under the Japanese closely paralleled that observed under the Park regime.

Overall, the Japanese were said to provide South Korea with a model of effective political and economic organization, an industrial base, productive agriculture, an entrepreneurial stratum, and a good educational system. War, political turmoil, and the corrupt Rhee regime did not erase these conditions and in some areas, such as agriculture and education, augmented them (Kohli 2004, 123). In a sense, Park simply "re-created" the colonial system on the basis of these conditions, although he can be credited for realizing its full potential.

While some truth lies in the core arguments, the thesis that colonial legacies were a disguised blessing is open to debate. In particular, the argument fails to explain convincingly how colonial legacies were perpetuated. There were massive social upheavals since the end of the colonial period until the 1960s, when rapid growth started. Critics have pointed out clear discontinuities between colonial and immediate postcolonial systems, as Japanese bureaucrats were replaced by Korean ones, and as fierce political contests turned the bureaucracy into a political machine capable of destroying opponents and distributing patronage. In fact, most of the largest firms in the 1980s did not originate in the colonial period but appeared and prospered thereafter, thanks to lucrative contracts from the American occupation and Rhee governments. Rather than being passive recipients of the Japanese legacies, these critics contend, both Rhee and Park acted in response to the political pressures of their time and reshaped the economy, society, and politics in the process (Haggard et al. 1997, 873–4, 876, 878–9).

Although I disagree with these critics in their total rejection of Japanese legacies, I take their criticism one step further by suggesting an analytical framework that centers on postcolonial Korean actors while still acknowledging Japanese contributions. The rest of this chapter analyzes the politics and legacies of state formation in the Korean peninsula and postcolonial state building under Rhee. Out of these processes, I show that essential elements of a developmental structure were created on the basis of the disintegrating colonial system and amid severe postwar political turmoil. With Park's policies, South Korea would reap the fruits of this structure, but one should not exaggerate his role.

CONFRONTATION AND THE FORMATION OF KOREAN STATES, 1945–1948

The establishment of independent Koreas after World War II consists of a series of contingencies that fed a relentless pattern of polarization. The idea of a postwar international trusteeship for the Korean peninsula first appeared among U.S. government circles in 1943 (Cumings 1981, 104–5). On the eve of the Japanese defeat, Washington and Moscow agreed to divide the peninsula at the thirty-eighth parallel. American forces would disarm the Japanese and prepare for the trusteeship plan in the South, which included Seoul, while Soviet forces would handle the matter in the North.

On August 15, 1945, the day Japan announced its surrender, the Japanese governor general's adviser met an underground figure with leftist affiliations, Yo Unhyong, and asked him to create a temporary administrative body to maintain order and to protect the Japanese from possible reprisals by Koreans (Cumings 1981, 71–81; S. I. Jun 1991, 108). Yo had helped found the exiled Korean Provisional Government (KPG) in Shanghai in 1919, attended the Congress of the Toilers of the Far East in Moscow in 1921, was brought back to Korea and imprisoned for three years by the Japanese, and worked as a newspaper editor in Seoul after his release in 1932 (C. S. Lee 1965, 130; Cumings 1981, 474–5). Yo had always been willing to work with communists but never joined the Korean Communist Party.

With the permission of the Japanese governor general, whose appearance with him was reported on national newspapers the next day,[6] Yo and his group set up the Committee in Preparation for Korean Independence (CPKI), asked Koreans to respect Japanese lives and property, secured the release of sixteen thousand political prisoners throughout the country, and called for the founding of local CPKI branches. Within days, local People's Committees sprang up in probably all the provinces (Cumings 1981, 273–5). These committees not only organized security teams but also assumed many government functions abandoned by fleeing Japanese officials.

After creating the CPKI, Yo apparently requested the cooperation of conservative nationalist politicians in Seoul but was rejected. In rejecting Yo's invitation, conservative nationalists argued that the only legitimate government was the exiled KPG. This failure to achieve collaboration was in part Yo's own doing (S. I. Jun 1991, 111–12). He did not consult these conservatives when he wrote the declaration of independence, which included sharp denunciations of Japanese collaborators (Cumings 1981, 72). Because many conservatives had collaborated with the Japanese, they would have disapproved of such a declaration. This lack of compromise was confirmed in the published roster of CPKI leaders a few days later; in

---

[6] Right-wing groups later would stigmatize Yo as a Japanese collaborator for this act. The Japanese allowed Yo to use the press and radio and to drop propaganda leaflets throughout the country. On the other hand, the CPKI went much further than the Japanese would have allowed in declaring a radical political agenda to prepare for Korean independence (S. I. Jun 1991, 109).

this list communists were in the majority, and the rest, with one notable exception, were members of Yo's group.[7]

The news that American forces but not Soviet armies would occupy South Korea reached Seoul only in late August. This prompted the CPKI to engage in a frenzied effort to set up a new Korean government while making a fresh attempt at compromise. On September 6, just three days before U.S. forces arrived in Seoul, the CPKI declared the formation of the Korean People's Republic (KPR), complete with a revolutionary program and a roster of Central Committee's members. Three-quarters of the names on the list were associated with leftist groups; the remaining were prominent nationalists (Cumings 1981, 115–16).[8] The latter, most of whom were still out of the country, were not consulted, and it was not clear whether they would agree to join the KPR. Even if the list were an honest demonstration of "generosity" on the part of the Left toward the Right rather than a gesture to impress the Americans, it was only a unilateral act, not the result of compromise.[9]

Nine days after Japan surrendered, Soviet troops arrived in Pyongyang with a detachment of Korean guerrillas led by Kim Ilsung (Cumings 1981, 121). Kim had been fighting the Japanese since the 1930s as a leader of a small guerrilla band, first in China and then in the Soviet Far East (Suh 1967, 314–15). After entering North Korea, Kim began to build up his base in the North under Soviet aegis, ignoring the scramble for power in Seoul at the time. By 1947, Pyongyang would turn out to be the Mecca for frustrated leftist politicians and communist revolutionaries fleeing from the South.

Arriving in Seoul two weeks after the Soviets had entered Pyongyang, U.S. commander General Hodge set up a Military Government (MG) run by Americans but advised by former Japanese officials and their Korean collaborators (S. I. Jun 1991, 137–8). Much of the colonial administrative and coercive apparatus was also retained. By early 1946, most of the seventy-five thousand Koreans serving the MG had been former employees of the colonial government (S. I. Jun 1991, 186). Apparently

---

[7] Many of these communists had tried hastily a week earlier to resurrect the Korean Communist Party (KCP), originally founded in 1925.

[8] The "Left" in South Korea consisted of several groups, from radical communists to left-center moderates. The "right" was similarly diverse. Politicians were bonded together not only by ideology but also by family and other ties (Meade 1951, 56; Merrill 1980, 151; Cumings 1981, 85–6).

[9] Cumings provides conflicting evidence of Yo's intention but (with sympathy) considers the list an honest albeit unrequited attempt at compromise.

influenced by his Korean advisers, Hodge refused to accept the KPR as a legitimate Korean government, and this nominal symbol of compromise died quietly to make way for two opposing groups. On the left, the Korean Communist Party (KCP) was resurrected on September 11 under Pak Honyong, a veteran communist leader (S. I. Jun 1991, 143–4). Pak had helped found the KCP in 1925, spent many years in a Japanese prison and in exile in China and the Soviet Union in the 1930s (Cumings 1981, 479; S. I. Jun 1991, 65). He later returned to Korea and attempted, in vain, to reorganize the underground KCP before 1945. After resurrecting the KCP, Pak wasted no time in organizing peasants and workers. By 1947, KCP-affiliated labor unions would claim half a million members (Cumings 1981, 198). Between August 1945 and March 1947, there would be more than twenty-three hundred labor demonstrations involving 600,000 workers (Koo 2001, 26).

On the right, conservative groups that included leading figures in Korean industry, education, and the colonial bureaucracy also united in the Korean Democratic Party (KDP) (S. I. Jun 1991, 146–7).[10] Some of these conservatives had impeccable nationalist credentials, but most had collaborated with the Japanese. While formation of the KCP and KDP triggered the polarization of Seoul politics, in late 1945 such a pattern did not appear irreversible. In October, Rhee Syngman, the most prominent nationalist in exile, returned to Seoul from the United States and founded the Central Council for the Acceleration of Korean Independence (CCAKI) (S. I. Jun 1991, 160–1). As a young man, Rhee had participated in a movement to reform monarchical Korea in the 1890s and spent more than five years in prison for his activism. After Japan conquered Korea, he came to live in the United States from 1905 to 1910 and again from 1912 to 1945, earned a doctorate from Princeton, served as president of the Korean Provisional Government (KPG) in Shanghai during the period 1919 to 1924, and founded the Korean Congress to lobby Washington for Korean independence (C. S. Lee 1965, 131–5, 310).

On Rhee's return, the KCP approached him but failed to persuade the man to exclude "Japanese collaborators" from the CCAKI and drop his hostility toward the Soviet Union.[11] While Rhee rejected any alliance with communists, not all right-wing politicians did so. An example was Kim Ku, a prominent exile of the Shanghai group who headed the KPG in

---

[10] For an account of the period 1945–50 seen from the perspective of KDP leaders, see Pak (1980, 28–55).

[11] "The Claim of the KCP: Concerning the Formation of the United Front of the Korean People," and "Fundamental Differences Regarding the National United Front" (*Haebang Ilbo* editorials translated by Lee Chong Sik; C. S. Lee 1977, 49–51, 107–8).

Kim Ilsung   Pak Honyong   Yo Unhyong   Kim Kyusik   Kim Ku   Rhee Syngman

Extremism   **Extremism**

◄───►

Fate of the moderate alternatives between the extremes:

Pak Honyong: fled to North Korea in 1947 and was executed by Kim Ilsung in 1955

Yo Unhyong: assassinated in 1947

Kim Kyusik: believed killed by North Korean troops in Seoul in 1950

Kim Ku: assassinated in 1949, probably by Rhee's police

FIGURE 1. The Polarization of the Koreas.

Chongqing during World War II (C. S. Lee 1965, 183–5). After returning to Seoul from China, Kim voiced his opposition to the U.S. trusteeship plan for Korea and sought help from leftist groups to overthrow the U.S. occupation. When the MG quickly repressed the coup d'etat, this second attempt at compromise among Korean elites foundered (Cumings 1981, 221).

The MG itself did not oppose elite collaboration and in fact sought to fight polarization by shoring up the center. It organized a Left-Right Coalition Committee headed by moderates Yo Unhyong and Kim Kyusik (Cumings 1981, 227–30). Kim Kyusik had been educated in the West, belonged to the Shanghai exile group, and was minister of foreign affairs in the KPG in the 1920s (C. S. Lee 1965, 130–1). The Coalition Committee excluded, and was denounced by, both radical communists like Pak and conservatives like Rhee (K. S. Han 1971, 53). As tensions grew between the KCP and the MG, leftist labor unions launched a general strike, followed by a massive peasant uprising to oppose the MG's policy of forced rice collection (Cumings 1981, 237–43, 252–8). The MG met the strike and uprising with force, resulting in thousands of arrests. American suppression forced communist leaders to flee to the North or move underground. Another opportunity for sustainable compromise had been wasted. By mid-1947, when U.S.-Soviet relations worsened, the MG let the Coalition Committee die and turned to Rhee as the most prominent politician who supported separate elections for the South. Rhee's extreme and consistent anticommunism had paid off.[12] Figure 1 shows that all the

---

[12] Rhee even went to the United States in early 1947 to launch a personal campaign accusing General Hodge of fostering communism (Allen 1960, 89–90).

moderate alternatives had been eliminated or expelled from South Korea by 1950, leaving the right-wing extremist Rhee in command.

In sum, Yo's dubious and unreciprocated effort at compromise, Kim Ku's failed coup, and the short-lived Left-Right Coalition Committee were three brief diversions from the relentless course of elite polarization in the South. During the same period, Kim Ilsung in North Korea also succeeded in defeating several moderates who challenged his leadership (Cumings 1981, 382–427). By early 1948, Pyongyang and Seoul had become centers of ideological extremism, with Rhee facing Kim across the thirty-eighth parallel. When American and Soviet forces withdrew from the peninsula in mid-1948, two separate states had been established, formally institutionalizing the process of elite polarization.

The sequence of mass uprisings and state repression interacted with elite polarization (Cumings 1981, 267–381). In response to the appeal of Yo Unhyong in August 1945, People's Committees (PCs) were founded all over the peninsula – one week before the Soviets entered Pyongyang and three weeks before the Americans marched into Seoul. These PCs were launched by various kinds of people: underground communist cadres, released political prisoners, migrant workers returning from cities and from overseas, and local traditional elites. Leftist groups did not always control the PCs, although over time many were able to do so, thanks to their superior underground organizing experience (Meade 1951, 55). Even so, these PCs were not necessarily subject to any central command or order from the KPR or the KCP (Cumings 1981, 267–350).

Left to continue, the PCs would have posed formidable challenges to the postcolonial state, as occurred in Indonesia (see Chapter 3). It was the MG's move to dissolve them in late 1945 that took Korea on a different path. This move was not easy because many PCs refused to disappear without a fight. During 1947 and 1948, local leftist groups led mass organizations in several strikes and attacks on police posts throughout the South (Merrill 1980). On Cheju Island off the southern coast, local PCs, including communist guerrillas, overran half of the police posts. According to official figures, more than ten thousand of the adult population of the island took part in the revolt. A regiment of South Korea's constabulary force, trained by the MG but infiltrated by communists, rebelled in Yosu – only two months after sovereignty had been transferred to the Rhee government. The strikes and rebellions gave the MG and later the Rhee government excuses to carry out massive repression of the left. The Yosu rebellion alone led to more than nine thousand executions and twenty-three thousand arrests from October 1948 to April 1949 (Koh 1963, 149, 150).

How did elite polarization and mass suppression shape the emerging South Korean state structure? First, elite polarization banished the best-organized and most-radical elite group – the communists – permanently from national politics. Communist organizations in the South were either relocated north or disbanded by 1948. Moderate alternatives and their supporters were similarly eliminated or weakened, leaving the political arena to a smaller circle of conservative collaborators and anticommunist politicians. Political power was now concentrated within this narrow group, which shared an intense anticommunist ideology, setting the stage for postcolonial political stability. While individual rulers such as Rhee and Park rose and fell, state power was never seriously threatened. The demise of the left as a serious political force ensured that the narrow alliance between state and capital would not be challenged.

Second, the fact that key elements of the colonial state structure, including bureaucrats, police, landlords, and industrialists, were retained under a new government led by a fiercely *anticolonial* leader was neither a coincidence nor a natural development. Rather, this predicament was the result of polarization along Left-Right ideological lines that trumped the old cleavage between collaborators and nationalists. Finally, the successful suppression of local PCs and mass revolts allowed the new state not only to build a new centralized state structure out of chaos but also to revive disintegrating colonial bureaucratic and coercive institutions, reorganize them under Korean command, test them in battles, and reorient them toward repressing communism.

Despite making solid contributions to building a developmental structure, state formation politics still left behind a feeble central government, in which power was shared between the executive branch and a factious legislature; intense popular resentment against former collaborators, who were now reemployed in the government; and perhaps some latent popular sympathy for communists or their underground organizations. These weaknesses in the developmental structure would have to be dealt with by Rhee.

THE CONSOLIDATION OF A DEVELOPMENTAL STATE STRUCTURE, 1948–1960

In 1948 when he became president, Rhee's most formidable opponents, such as Kim Ilsung and Pak Honyong, were in the North, and the southern communist movement had been brutally suppressed. Still, he faced institutional constraints and some organized opposition. The National Assembly elected under the MG was the main institutional check on

Rhee's power. In 1948 this body had vast constitutional authority, including the right to elect a president and approve a prime minister (Seo 1996, 82; Reeve 1963, 41). Even though the Assembly was divided and weak, with the majority in 1948–50 being independents, the state structure was insufficiently centralized with president and prime minister subject to parliamentary approval. While the MG and the division of Korea saved Rhee from major opponents, they hardly guaranteed him a monopoly of power. Similarly, the events during the period 1945 to 1950 removed top communist leaders from South Korea but were not sufficient to make South Korea a land of perfect elite unity. Organized opposition to Rhee in the Assembly came from a small leftist group (the So-jang pa)[13] and supporters of Kim Ku and Kim Kyusik – two moderate nationalists who advocated peaceful unification with North Korea (Seo 1996, 83). The conservative KDP was a minority group that did not always support Rhee (H. B. Lee 1968, 71–3). With his brutal maneuvers to eliminate rivals and his extreme anticommunism, Rhee contributed significantly (albeit inadvertently) to perfecting a new structure for the Korean developmental state.

Politicians can consolidate their personal power base in various ways, some of which may enhance state power, while others may not. For example, if politicians seek to build a personal network of loyal clients in the bureaucracy, this network helps them but not the state they run. Conversely, if they consolidate their power base by building effective coercive state apparatuses, these may stay with the state long after they have left the scene. By the same logic, if politicians orchestrate the assassination of their opponents, this often benefits only them. If they eliminate an entire swathe of the political spectrum (e.g., all members of an ethnic-based or leftist coalition), their perfidious acts may irreversibly alter the character of the state and the elites.

Rhee implemented all these measures. As many have noted, he built a massive network of loyal clients with U.S. aid (Haggard and Moon 1993, 62–3). Often overlooked is Rhee's certain power-seeking behavior, which built a solid state structure for developmentalism. In particular, the most critical contribution by Rhee was the construction of an extremely repressive anticommunist political system that effectively guaranteed long-term

---

[13] Zeon (1973, 141–84) discusses the role of the So-jang pa group in opposing the land reform bill. Unlike popular arguments (e.g., J. W. Kim 1975) that Rhee used land reform politics to curb the influence of the landlord-based KDP, Zeon provides more persuasive evidence that the land reform pitted Rhee and the KDP against the leftist So-jang pa faction in the National Assembly.

state domination and a social environment favorable to capitalist development.

Right after the communist-instigated Yosu rebellion, Rhee and the KDP collaborated to have a National Security bill enacted in December 1948. This draconian law was aimed at "any association, groups or organizations that conspire against the state" (Seo 1996, 85–6). Under this law, Rhee curbed press freedom, banned political activities by religious organizations and labor unions, and imprisoned anti-American activists and effectively all leftists (Reeve 1963, 41). This law and the coercive apparatus that enforced it would cast a long shadow over South Korean society. Rhee further revamped the law in 1958, giving broader authority to police to "suppress communists." Faced by legislators from opposition parties who organized a sit-in strike to protest this law, Rhee's security guards hauled them off the National Assembly floor and locked them up while his supporters passed the law (Hong 2000, 126–8). General Park would add a few more items to make the law even harsher, but the basic law is still in force today.

A second act with long-term consequences was Rhee's protection of former Japanese collaborators, who filled his police force and bureaucracy.[14] In August 1948, in response to popular demands, the National Assembly passed a law aimed at purging Japanese collaborators from the government. This legislation was protested by policemen and bureaucrats who had begun their careers under the Japanese and had been retained by the MG (Seo 1996, 90–1). Unable to stop the legislation, Rhee forcefully intervened to protect senior police officials, mobilized his supporters to demonstrate against the National Assembly, and ordered the arrest of seven Assembly members, including the vice speaker, ostensibly for being communists (Seo 1996, 98–9).[15] Their trials were the first cases under the scope of the National Security Law. Rhee decimated parliamentary opposition in this move, but he also, consciously or not, preserved the coercive state apparatus upon which Park would conveniently build.

Rhee was well known for his fiery anticommunist rhetoric. Speaking before the Taiwanese Assembly in 1953, he declared, "We do not know what makes the Communist what he is. When he becomes indoctrinated, he is no longer your friend or brother. He is no longer your fellow

[14] As late as 1960, those who had served in the Japanese police constituted about 70 percent of the high-ranking officers, 40 percent of inspectors, and 15 percent of the lieutenants in the Korean national police force (S. Han 1972, 11).

[15] Many among the arrested Assembly members belonged to the leftist So-jang pa group (Zeon 1973, 165).

citizen.... The only way to check [communism] is to fight it as you would fight cholera, smallpox, or any other contagious disease" (cited in Koh 1963, 138). Lesser known is Rhee's systematic effort to root out communist support in the population through a massive program in late 1949 to register, "reeducate," and monitor those suspected of having ties to leftist organizations. This program, ironically called Podo Yonmaeng (Preserving the Alliance), led to the arrests of about 300,000 people who were interrogated and forced to make confessions, name others, and declare loyalty to the government (Koh 1963, 104–6). By isolating, terrorizing, and maintaining surveillance of leftists, Rhee effectively eliminated their influence and institutionalized long-term social submission to conservative rule.

The civil war of 1950 to 1953 augmented what Rhee had done. This conventional war was remarkable in its swift reversal of fortunes for the warring parties in its first year. The battlefront first moved all the way south; three months after the war started, Pyongyang conquered nearly all of South Korea. The table was turned when United Nations troops under American command entered and quickly drove North Korean forces all the way north to the Chinese border. When Chinese armies entered the conflict, the outcome was a stalemate. The war caused severe losses and stresses for South Korea, but it also generated massive structural growth and maturity of the South Korean state as it mobilized and coordinated society to fight the war, suppress communists, and restore postwar order (K.-D. Kim 1981, 259–60). The clearest example of this growth was the South Korean army, which grew six times in size to 600,000 men at the end of the war despite its loss of more than 100,000 soldiers (S. J. Kim 1971, 39–40).

We have seen that state formation in Korea was marked by elite polarization and mass repression. The war was an extension of this process, and Rhee's role in the war must be acknowledged. Although North Korea made the first attacks, Rhee's strident and repeated calls for unification by force may have contributed to rising tensions that led to the war. He and Kim Ilsung oversaw the massive arrests and killings during each regime's turn of good fortune. For example, thousands of indiscriminate executions of alleged communist collaborators were carried out when the southern government retook Seoul in December 1950 (Koh 1963, 143).[16] The violence intensified what had already been northern extreme

---

[16] Similar events certainly took place when North Korea had control of southern territory but were not as well documented.

antiimperialism and southern extreme anticommunism (S. C. Yang 1972, 29–30; S. Han 1972, 44–5; Choi 1993, 23). The masses were no passive spectators in the process: during the war, millions of North Koreans, especially landlords and Christians, fled south, while many leftist politicians and activists in the South went north. Kim Ilsung was saved from northern Christians' festering resentment,[17] while Rhee Syngman gained an important staunchly anticommunist constituency. The war in fact homogenized the two societies and reinforced their extremist elites.

A major accomplishment of Rhee during the war was his successful effort to amend the constitution in 1952 to have the president elected directly by the people rather than selected by the National Assembly. To overcome overwhelming opposition in the Assembly to this move, Rhee imposed martial law on the grounds of fighting communist guerrillas, used army trucks to tow buses full of Assembly members to military police stations for questioning, arrested dozens of his opponents, and coerced them to approve the amendment (J. K.-C. Oh 1968, 39–46). Taking advantage of wartime conditions, Rhee further centralized power in the executive branch, making another contribution to building a developmental state structure.

In sum, by his efforts to increase personal power, Rhee radically reorganized postcolonial politics, added substantially to the developmental structure of the Korean state, and inadvertently prepared it well for playing subsequent developmental roles. For all the bloodshed, without Rhee's draconian but effective policies, communist networks would have persisted, creating political instability and contesting *any* developmental policies (as occurred in the Indonesian case described in Chapter 3). In his work, Rhee was aided tremendously by the MG and subsequent U.S. support. He contributed to making the war happen, and with its quick turns of fortune for both sides, the war further polarized both political systems.

As already mentioned, structure is not sufficient unless the state undertakes developmental roles, and the Rhee regime did not. Nevertheless, the Park government could not have played such roles so soon after it assumed power without the developmental structure created by Rhee, as a review of the relationships between the postcolonial Korean state and peasants, workers, and students from 1953 to 1980 makes clear. Given the frequency and massive scale of labor strikes and peasant uprisings during

---

[17] Prewar Pyongyang, where one-sixth of all Korean Christians lived, had been the center of the Protestant Church in Korea (Steinberg 1989, 89).

1947 and 1948, the absence of opposition from workers and peasants until the late 1970s requires explanation.

THE STATE VERSUS POPULAR SECTORS, 1953–1980

Except for a brief period from 1960 to 1961, state–society relations in South Korea from 1953 to 1980 were largely devoid of major contention. Peasant unrest, for example, was unheard of after 1953. This lack of unrest is puzzling because state extraction was heavy and state penetration intrusive. The government was a major buyer of agricultural products, collecting between one- and two-thirds of the annual marketed surplus of rice and barley crops.[18] Food prices were kept low under tight government control until 1968.[19] In almost every year up to 1960, government purchase prices were estimated to be 20 to 50 percent lower than production costs, depending on the particular year (Ban et al. 1980, 240). Until 1972, peasants were paid less than market prices for their produce. When General Park seized power in 1961, he paid lip service to the need to improve peasants' living standards. Yet his first two Five-Year Plans emphasized industrial development and invested little in agriculture (Ban et al. 1980, 167–91, 275).[20] Despite this neglect, Park received more electoral support among rural than urban voters.

With the Third Five-Year Plan, however, the government began to raise food prices, offer fertilizer subsidies, and increase investment in agriculture (S. Ho 1979, 650–1). This policy change was partly motivated by the regime's concern about the decline of food production and the large amount of foreign exchange required for food imports. Politically, Park may have felt threatened after the 1971 presidential election indicated some erosion of rural support for his candidacy.[21] As part of his strategy to boost local control, Park launched Semaul Undong or the New Community Movement (S. H. Ban et al. 1980, 275–80; Keim 1979, 18–23; Kihl 1979, 150–9). The ostensible goal of this movement was to upgrade the physical quality of village life through the spirit of cooperation.

---

[18] Data calculated from S. Ho (1979, 649). Rice and barley accounted for two-thirds of Korea's crop area.

[19] Food prices were also depressed because of cheap American food aid under the PL 480 program (S. Ho 1979, 649).

[20] Investment in agriculture accounted for less than 9 percent of total investments in the 1960s (S. Ho 1979, 648).

[21] He still won 53 percent of total votes compared to 51 percent in the earlier election of 1967.

self-help, and frugality.[22] The government spent only a small amount on assistance to villages but orchestrated a massive campaign that involved intense propaganda and excessive coercion (Kihl 1979, 152). For example, if peasants did not replace their thatched roofs with composition or tile as instructed by the campaign, local officials would come and tear down their roofs. There were occasional protests and resistance in some places but the overwhelming picture was a malleable peasantry unable to resist the state onslaught.[23]

State–labor relations were similarly peaceful under Rhee and Park. The 1950s saw three strikes and about fifty disputes annually. In the popular movement that overthrew Rhee in April 1960, workers played a small role. This brief democratic opening before Park's coup in May 1961 saw the birth of hundreds of unions and a surge of labor disputes. Between April 1960 and May 1961, more than two hundred disputes involving seventy-five strikes occurred (Y. C. Lee 1999, 100–6). After the coup, Park easily squashed this popular movement. With a few preemptive changes in labor law in the late 1960s, his regime was able to prevent the rise of a strong labor movement until the 1970s (Y. C. Lee 1999, 292, 297–300, 373). According to a careful study on labor law changes during this period, these changes were not made because of any labor threat, which was insignificant at the time. Rather, the changes during the period from 1968 to 1972 were part of Park's effort to stay in power and to expand state power in the face of changing international conditions (Nixon's detente policy and the North Korean threat) and the popularity of an opposition party led by Kim Dae Jung.

Despite a nearly threefold increase in the number of workers from 1.3 million to 3.4 million during the 1960s, the overall level of disputes remained very low (Amsden 1989, 325; Koo 2001, 29). Although labor disputes increased and unions expanded in the 1970s, only during the 1980s did these disputes reach the scale of 1946 to 1947 and become a serious threat to the economic order (Koo 2001, 29). The absence of labor activism from the 1950s through the 1970s by no means indicated workers' contentment, as is sometimes believed (Doner et al. 2005). South

---

[22] For example, see the following Park speeches: "God Helps Those Who Help Themselves" on June 10, 1970 (C. H. Park 1979, 42–5); "*Saemaul* Generates Rural Modernization," January 11, 1972 (97–114); and "*Saemaul*: A Direct Link to Increasing Farmers' Income" on March 7, 1972 (124–44).

[23] Samuel Ho (1979, 653) visited some Korean villages at the time and reported "intense" peasant resistance in the early phase of the program, when road construction took land from some peasants without compensation.

Korean real wages were low by world standards and their growth rates lagged behind productivity increases (Deyo 1987, 196–9). Submissive behavior also was not a Korean labor tradition. Labor disputes in the 1920s and 1930s occurred more frequently than in the 1960s and 1970s (Koo 2001, 25). We have seen as well how communist-led labor unions expanded rapidly and acted militantly during 1946 to 1948 but were crushed by the end of that decade.

Rhee was not able to forestall *all* opposition to his government. A huge student movement emerged unexpectedly in 1960 and toppled his regime. Although Korean students had a tradition of protest against colonial rule,[24] this movement had little connection to that distant past. The brutal practices of Rhee's police during the 1960 presidential election triggered the movement, and the rapid expansion of the educational system in the 1950s provided the shock troops for it. The protest began as a low-key event in a provincial town (Q.-Y. Kim 1983; B. H. Oh 1975). A group of high school students staged a protest against school officials who tried to prevent them from attending the rally of an opposition candidate taking place during school hours. Spontaneous protests soon spread to schools and universities in other cities and exploded after the police killed one student. When the professors in Seoul joined their students to protest, and the military refused to intervene, Rhee had no choice but to resign and go into exile. Although Rhee's fall was a spectacular event, students' demands were not radical and were only marginally related to economic issues (S. Han 1980, 146). Corruption, election rigging, and police brutality – but not social inequality, capitalist exploitation, or even the authoritarian political system – drew students into the streets. This fact demonstrates that the once powerful communist challenge to the South Korean state in the late 1940s had been completely wiped out, leaving no trace whatsoever.

After Rhee's fall, student organizations continued to mobilize support for various political parties and oppose the Chang Myon government's security bills. The military coup in May 1961 and its implementation of martial law significantly weakened but failed to stop sporadic student protests. Student demonstrations took place in the capital almost every year throughout the 1960s. These demonstrations targeted specific, noneconomic issues, including the U.S.-Korea status-of-force agreement

---

[24] Students played the most conspicuous part after religious groups in the March 1 Movement in 1919. Out of 1,251 schools, 203 participated; out of 133,557 students, 11,113 joined the nationwide protests (C. S. Lee 1965, 120).

(1962), the normalization of relations with Japan (1963, 1965), and constitutional revisions (1969). Some of these protests were quite large and violent, involving tens of thousands of students. In June 1965, for example, the government had to close down thirteen universities and fifty-eight high schools for an early vacation to preempt protest against its upcoming signing of the normalization treaty with Japan (Nam 1989, 38).

By the late 1960s, a new generation of opponents to the military regime had emerged, as evidenced in the cases of Kim Young Sam, Kim Dae Jung, and many student and Christian activists. Despite intense government pressure against him, Kim Dae Jung, who was forty-five years old and relatively obscure at the time, won 45.3 percent of the total votes cast in the 1971 presidential election (Nam 1989, 52). While Kim advocated the redistribution of wealth between urban and rural sectors, the thrust of his campaign focused on Korean relations with foreign powers, unification, corruption, and democracy.

The new opposition reflected demographic changes and, ironically, the very success of Park's economic agenda, which fostered rapid industrialization, urbanization, and international exchange. While about 7 million people, or 28 percent of Koreans, lived in urban areas in 1960, the number increased to 16.8 million or 48 percent in 1975.[25] The number of college students more than doubled between 1960 and 1975, from 100,000 to 240,000 (Steinberg 1989, 81). The rise of an increasingly resistant civil society threatened Park's political survival, forcing him to deploy more repressive tactics to retain power. In October 1972 Park declared martial law, dissolved the National Assembly, banned political parties, and arrested many opponents such as Kim Dae Jung. Brutal repression and the manipulation of the North Korean threat helped Park to maintain his grip on power until he was assassinated in 1979 (Nam 1989, 95–151). Yet political issues such as unification and democracy continued to dominate opposition agendas, even though the opposition became more radicalized in the last years of his regime.

The review of state–society relations shows that Korean leaders up to the late 1970s faced little opposition to their *economic* policies. By then, a radical ideology had emerged that went beyond the familiar issues to attack the regime's poor record on economic justice. Until this radical ideology called *minjung* consolidated in the 1980s, developmentalism, or the promotion of economic growth and industrialization regardless

[25] Data for 1960 are from Steinberg (1989, 15) and for 1975 from Kim and Donaldson (1979, 660).

of social distributive consequences, was rarely, if ever, challenged (Koo 1993). The unchallenged hegemony of the capitalist developmental ideology testified to the high degree of ideological congruence that the Korean state enjoyed and starkly contrasted with the contentious politics of 1946 to 1948. Counterfactually, one wonders whether the Korean state could have undertaken capitalist developmental roles in the 1960s without elite polarization and mass suppression that early on had created a cohesive and hegemonic state.

Because state–society relations were generally peaceful from 1953 to 1979, observers have tended to take these conditions for granted and have overlooked their origins. The problem with this neglect will be especially illuminated in Chapter 3 when we turn to Indonesia, a country that shared with South Korea many similarities but took a different path of state formation characterized by elite compromise and mass incorporation. State formation did not generate a developmental structure for the Indonesian state; not until the 1970s was such a structure built and developmental roles performed effectively.

CONCLUSION

The focus on state formation politics is useful in explaining the origins of the South Korean developmental structure. The Korean state by the early 1950s had already acquired a solid developmental structure. It was highly centralized with cohesive state apparatuses inherited from the Japanese but reorganized and restructured during state formation. Former colonial elites, including landlords, industrialists, and bureaucrats, were brought into a new alliance with conservative nationalists and protected by the regime. Radical leaders of workers and peasants were purged or fled to the North. Politics was limited within a narrow elite group, and even within this group power became gradually centralized in the presidency after several violent confrontations. Coercive apparatuses, including the police, the military, and security laws, enjoyed massive growth and were battle-tested. Colonial legacies were important; however, their preservation and the formation of a new centralized and hegemonic state were not natural developments as often assumed but rather the results of a particular pattern of state formation characterized by elite polarization and mass suppression. Successful developmentalism depends as much on state structure as on the willingness and technical capacity of state leaders to perform developmental roles effectively. Rhee contributed decisively to building a developmental structure but failed to embrace developmental roles.

Yet without Rhee's prior work, Park would have lacked the structure to launch his developmental policies only a few years after assuming power.

One lesson from the analysis of state formation in Korea is the need to study South Korean together with North Korean state development. Most existing studies of South Korean industrialization have ignored North Korea; this chapter suggests why this exclusion may be an inadequate or inefficient approach. State formation in South Korea cannot be considered separately from that in North Korea. During state formation, decisive patterns of elite alignment and elite–mass engagement took place throughout the peninsula and eventually generated ideologically opposing states in separate territories. The same process helped both emerging states to build strong developmental structures. If elite polarization and mass repression contributed to South Korean developmental structure, then the North Korean state also benefited from the same process. In fact, up to the early 1980s North Korea was still considered a case of developmental success like South Korea (Cumings 1987, 44).

The Indonesian experience of state formation, considered in Chapter 3, illuminates the Korean lesson about the causal relationship between state formation politics and postcolonial state structure. Unlike Korea, Indonesia saw very different dynamics of state formation at work, with profound consequences for its postcolonial development.

3

Indonesia

From Accommodation to Confrontation

POLITICS OF ECONOMIC SWINGS

Indonesia experienced a more tortuous trajectory of development than did South Korea. During the first four decades after independence, the Indonesian economy underwent two major pendulum swings. In the first seven years following independence, the Indonesian economy experienced moderate growth, estimated between 3 and 5.5 percent per year (Higgins 1957, 48; Paauw 1963, 189, 200–1; Mackie 1971, 19; Booth 1998, 61). Growth was highest in the first two years of this period, thanks to the Korean War that led to booming demands and favorable prices for Indonesia's primary exports. Although Indonesia faced a growing budget and foreign exchange crisis in late 1952, the economy continued to grow moderately because of government retrenchment policies, including import restrictions, export promotion, fiscal austerity, and foreign exchange controls (Higgins 1957, 1–39).

In 1957 ultranationalist politicians under Sukarno's leadership rose to power and decided to nationalize most foreign enterprises. Under conditions of poor Indonesian management and insufficient credit, the performance of these enterprises, which made up the backbone of the modern sector, worsened. An unrealistic exchange rate, government hostility to foreign capital, inflationary government spending, and large military expenditures were additional factors that devastated the economy (Dick 2002, 182–90). By 1965 the country was practically bankrupt with inflation rates surpassing 500 percent and budget deficits equal to 300 percent of receipts (Hill 2000, 1). After General Suharto seized power in 1966, his government implemented a stabilization and development program that included debt renegotiations, fiscal austerity, exchange rate devaluations, foreign investment, and export promotion. The new policies pushed the economic pendulum back. From its position as "the number one failure among the major underdeveloped countries" in economist Benjamin Higgins's words,[1] Indonesia saw rapid growth in the late 1960s and early 1970s. In two particular years (1968 and 1974), growth rates reached double digits. Thanks in part to oil windfalls in the 1970s, the economy continued to expand rapidly except for a brief recession in the early 1980s.

The economic pendulum swings Indonesia experienced from 1949 to 1980 suggest the limits of policy explanations. There is little doubt about which policies generated growth and which did not. Policies in the early 1950s and those carried out after 1966 did not differ fundamentally, and both were effective in generating growth. By contrast, policies in the period in between were indisputably disastrous. Clearly, politics rather than policies better explained the large swings in Indonesia's economic performance following independence. Politics brought the ultranationalists to power in the late 1950s but caused their downfall in the 1960s. Two interrelated puzzles thus emerge. First, why did Indonesian leaders who implemented developmental policies in the early 1950s fail to stay in power? Second, what did Suharto do to keep ultranationalist forces under control?

To address the first puzzle, I show how the politics of state formation was responsible for the defects in Indonesia's state structure, which made the implementation of developmental policies in the 1950s premature. We have seen that the South Korean state was born of confrontation; in contrast, the Indonesian state was born as a result of accommodation. Whereas Korean elites were polarized and the masses were suppressed, elite compromise and mass incorporation were the predominant patterns in Indonesia. Owing to its particular formation pattern, the Indonesian state had a wobbly structure. At the top, power was distributed among numerous political factions grouped in unstable parties that represented the whole spectrum of ideological, religious, and ethnic interests. Central authority was not respected by local governments, and local rebellions were common years after independence. Without a cohesive state structure, attempts by an elite faction to play developmental roles in the 1950s resulted in the rise to power of the ultranationalists.

The answer to the second puzzle is that Suharto responded by creating a developmental state. The cohesive structure of this state in fact

[1] Cited in Hill (2000, 1).

emerged under conditions very similar to the Korean case, namely, elite polarization and mass suppression. These conditions originated from the rivalry in the early 1960s between the Indonesian Communist Party (Partai Komunis Indonesia, or PKI) and President Sukarno, on the one hand, and the Indonesian military, on the other. Their rivalry exploded into a bloody confrontation in which communists were brutally massacred; the political system was forcibly centralized; and the state, domestic producer classes, and foreign capital formed a close alliance. For all the brutalities, Suharto's success in constructing a developmental state structure enabled his regime to play developmental roles effectively up to the end of the 1990s.

Before addressing these two puzzles, however, we first examine Indonesia's colonial legacies. The evidence suggests that these legacies were even less relevant to Indonesia's postcolonial development than in the Korean case.

COLONIAL LEGACIES

A standard text of Korean history starts its discussion of the colonial period by noting that "the Japanese assumed control of Korea with purpose and decisiveness" (Eckert et al. 1990, 254). In contrast, the Dutch competed with the Portuguese over the Malukus in the early seventeenth century but did not establish full control over the Indonesian archipelago until the beginning of the twentieth century. Their colonial project before its last four decades can be characterized as anything but decisive. This is not to say that Dutch colonial rule was inchoate and ineffective, especially on Java, where it was consolidated early on. In terms of extraction and penetration, Dutch colonialism ranked somewhere between the Japanese and other European systems. Compared to the British in India, for example, Dutch presence in Indonesia was far more intense. Toward the end of the colonial period, Dutch presence in Indonesia was about eight times greater than the British presence in India relative to total population. During 1921 to 1938, the Netherlands' net drain of income from Indonesia as a proportion of Indonesia's domestic product was twice the size of British income from India. The number of Europeans in the Dutch civil administration relative to total population was nearly fifteen times the ratio in India (Maddison 1989, 646, 656).

Nevertheless, Dutch colonialism did not match Japanese rule in Korea by all indicators. In the 1930s more than 240,000 Dutch and Eurasians were living in Indonesia (0.4 percent of total population) compared to more than 570,000 Japanese in Korea (2.6 percent).[2] In 1930 the number of Europeans employed in the Dutch colonial government (both civil and military) was about 21,000, whereas the number of Japanese civil servants in Korea was about 52,000 (Maddison 1989, 659; Eckert et al. 1990, 257).

Compared to the Japanese in Korea, the Dutch left behind an institutional legacy that did not clearly favor postcolonial developmentalism. First, Dutch rulers united scattered islands, transformed numerous sultanates into districts and provinces under a central government, built a modern bureaucracy that reached deeply into native society, and established a limited modern educational system (Benda 1966; Dick et al. 2002). Most postcolonial leaders received either college education in Dutch schools or practical training in the colonial bureaucracy. At the same time, the Dutch avoided changing local cultures and customs whenever possible (Vandenbosch 1943, 498). The colonial bureaucracy also systematically incorporated members of the traditional aristocratic class and employed them in positions parallel to European ones. While Dutch officials had the upper hand, traditional aristocrats were able to preserve their status well into postcolonial time.

Second, the Dutch contributed significantly to postcolonial development by promoting exports and foreign investment. During 1900 to 1930, average growth rate per annum in Indonesia was about 3 percent, equal to that in Korea,[3] and foreign investment exceeded $1.3 billion in 1940. Nevertheless, the colonial economy relied heavily on the primary sector that processed agricultural products or raw materials for export, with much less industrialization than occurred in Korea.[4] The Dutch also left less human capital behind than Japan did in Korea. Less than 7 percent of Indonesians were literate in 1930, whereas the Korean rate was close to 50 percent in 1945 (Emerson 1946, 499; Eckert et al. 1990, 263). UNESCO

---

[2] Data are from Maddison (1989, 660). Vandenbosch (1944, 171) provides the number of 212,000 total employees (including 29,000 Europeans) in the colonial civil service in 1928. There were about 170,000 Europeans in British India (0.05 percent of total population). In Eckert et al. (1990, 256), the data for Korea were 708,000 Japanese or 3.2 percent of total population in 1940.

[3] This is the combined rate of 1.8 percent per capita annual growth and 1.4 percent population growth rate (Lindblad 2002, 113, 122). Relying on Maddison, Booth (1998, 6) supports much lower rates of 0.2 percent for 1820–1900 and 0.3 percent for 1900–50. Data for Korea are from Kohli (2004, 27).

[4] Manufacturing accounted for less than 15 percent of Indonesia's domestic product in the early 1940s; Korea's ratio was 40 percent, including mining and timber (Lindblad 2002, 143; Eckert et al. 1990, 210). See also Booth (1998, 38–9).

sources show total enrollment of population from five to twenty-four years old to be 35 percent for Korea and 17 percent for Indonesia in 1950 (McGinn et al. 1980, 150–1). Racial discrimination exacerbated the problem of an inadequate educational system. The colonial regime used Chinese immigrants as middlemen and gave ethnic Indonesians few opportunities to develop into an indigenous capitalist class. Although Chinese capital would play an important role under Suharto, the ethnic minority status of the Chinese immigrants limited their contributions and hurt the legitimacy of his regime.

The Dutch also left Indonesia with no coercive institutions. The Japanese organized a police force of sixty thousand or one for every four hundred Koreans (Eckert et al. 1990, 259). This police force would be retained almost intact in the service of the postcolonial state. In contrast, besides a small police force,[5] the Dutch colonial army had about thirty-eight thousand men in 1938, or one for every sixteen hundred Indonesians (Elson 2001, 8). Although many of Indonesia's first military commanders were trained under the Dutch, the Dutch army as an organization was disbanded after the Japanese took control of Indonesian in 1942. The lack of a Dutch legacy in this matter was compounded by the Japanese legacy. The Japanese organized many indigenous militias during the occupation but dissolved these groups and took away their weapons right before the Japanese emperor announced Japan's surrender. Although many members of these groups would help to form and lead the new Indonesian military, many others would go home to become guerrilla leaders and local strongmen who would challenge the authority of the central state in the postcolonial era.

It is true that "the contemporary Indonesian state bears striking resemblance to the institutions which took shape in the final century of colonial rule" (Anderson 1983; Robison 1986, 3–5; Cribb 1994, 1). However, the continuity between the colonial and contemporary state was not predetermined, and the interests and actions of Indonesians should not be overlooked. In any case, the Dutch must be credited for starting a modernizing process, but their legacies were less significant than in the Korean case.[6] While these limited legacies meant postcolonial Indonesia was disadvantaged vis-à-vis South Korea, the argument advanced here is that state

---

[5] The most important component of the colonial police force appeared to be the field police, which included mobile units of about three thousand deployed in troubled rural areas (Vandenbosch 1944, 341–2).

[6] In some aspects the impact of the brief Japanese occupation may have been more significant than the Dutch period (Lebra 1975; Vu T. 2003).

formation dynamics were crucial to the extent that the Dutch colonial experiences became even less relevant.

ACCOMMODATION AND THE BIRTH OF
A WOBBLY LEVIATHAN, 1942–1949

More than two centuries of Dutch colonial rule in Indonesia ended in 1942 after Japanese troops invaded and occupied the archipelago. Whereas the Japanese suppressed nationalism in Korea, in Indonesia they promoted it to rally indigenous support for their war against the Allies. After establishing a military government, the Japanese set up advisory agencies on Java to help them mobilize local resources and manpower. They brought back from exile and promoted many Indonesian nation-alists and Muslim leaders to staff these agencies. By bringing together indigenous elites to work for them, the Japanese contributed decisively to the pattern of compromise later. The cases of Sukarno and Mohammed Hatta best illustrate this point. At the age of twenty-six, Sukarno gained prominence as a nationalist leader by founding the Indonesian National-ist Party in 1927. Subsequently imprisoned and exiled by the Dutch from 1929 to 1931 and again from 1934 to 1942, Sukarno was brought back by the Japanese to head various Indonesian advisory bodies. Mohammad Hatta led the Indonesian League while he was a student in the Nether-lands in the 1920s. Hatta's organization rivaled Sukarno's party in the prewar nationalist movement. After returning to Indonesia in 1932, Hatta founded the Indonesian National Education and was exiled from 1934 to 1942 for his nationalist activities (Anderson 1972, 421–2, 446–7). While both Sukarno and Hatta rejected collaboration with the Dutch, they were different kinds of leaders and, in any case, had never worked together. Brought to work as a team under the Japanese, these two leaders would proclaim the birth of the Indonesian republic three years later and stay at the helm of the Indonesian government for more than a decade afterward.

Elite compromise went far beyond a few top leaders, however. The Japanese convened a Study Commission for the Preparation of Indepen-dence in March 1945 (G. Kahin 1952, 121–7). This Indonesian body was created very differently from its Korean equivalent, which was headed by Yo Unhyong. Its members, who were all collaborating with the Japanese, met several times over many months to draft the constitution of the future Indonesian republic. The Japanese were careful in appointing to the com-mittee only older, experienced, and discreet men (Anderson 1972, 62–5). Communists and radical Muslims were not invited. Still, the Study

Commission's membership was broad enough to include most prominent Indonesian political activists with genuine nationalist credentials. The committee was able to achieve important compromises on the constitution and on Pancasila, five principles of the future state proposed by Sukarno. A major compromise was forged between secular nationalists and modernist Muslim politicians who desired an Islamic state (Noer 1987, 34–43). Pancasila's fifth principle, "One Nation under One Supreme God," which intentionally left God undefined, epitomized this compromise.

Although Indonesian leaders working for the Japanese were not quite ready to take over in August 1945, they were better prepared than elites in most other Japanese colonies. Two days after Japan's surrender, Sukarno and Hatta declared independence and formed a cabinet composed mainly of Japanese collaborators like themselves. These leaders immediately convened a conference of central and local bureaucrats to secure their collaboration and to confer on them a new legitimacy, so that they would not be vulnerable to popular reprisals for their service to Dutch or Japanese masters (Anderson 1972, 113–16).

With the Study Commission members as the core, Sukarno nominated leaders from various groups to form a Central National Committee (KNIP). New participants included such men as Sutan Sjahrir and Amir Sjarifuddin, who had thus far been active only underground. Sjahrir had worked closely with Hatta in the Netherlands and in Indonesia in the 1920s and 1930s and was exiled with Hatta. Unlike Hatta, he chose not to cooperate with the Japanese (Anderson 1972, 439–40; Sjahrir 1949). Sjarifuddin was a Dutch-trained lawyer who had worked for the Dutch colonial government and been a leader of some nationalist groups in the 1940s. Sjarifuddin collaborated with the Dutch but sought to organize resistance to the Japanese. He was captured and sentenced to death but later was saved from execution thanks to Sukarno's intervention. The cases of Sjahrir and Sjarifuddin indicated the broad and representative nature of the KNIP. Although this KNIP was only an advisory body, with broad and active participation by major groups, it took the first step that would pave the way for a critical compromise in October 1945.

This October compromise gave the emerging Indonesian state a new structure that would last for more than a decade. What went on behind the scenes was never clear, but we do know that this compromise entailed two elements. The first element was the creation of a national parliament and local committees. As chair of the KNIP, Sjahrir persuaded Hatta and enough KNIP members to approve the change of the KNIP from an advisory agency to a parliament to which the cabinet was accountable (Sjahrir 1949, 170–7). Given the Allies' imminent landing to disarm the Japanese, the Sukarno-Hatta duo must have realized that Sjahrir's non-collaboration credentials were needed if the republic was to win international recognition.[7] As a compromise, Sukarno and Hatta were retained as figureheads, but their Japanese-tainted cabinet was dissolved. In its place was Sjahrir's new cabinet.

The second element of the compromise was the organization of elites into political parties to take part in governance through the parliamentary system. At the same time that the Sjahrir government called for local committees to be established, it also invited elites to form political parties to participate in the parliament and in those committees.[8] This move generated further collaboration as new parties were formed and defunct ones resurrected so that they could claim seats in those committees. Within a few months, several dozen parties, including the dormant PKI, emerged. These parties were so hastily established that most were little more than alliances of personal factions. This lack of cohesion would contribute to political instability later, but in late 1945 these parties simply reinforced the pattern of elite compromise.

This compromise was robust enough to survive two challenges from the left to the Sukarno-Hatta-Sjahrir leadership. The first challenge was launched by Tan Malaka, a former PKI leader with a considerable reputation but no organization in 1945. Malaka became PKI chairman in 1921 at the age of twenty-five. He was exiled to Europe a year later, then served as the Comintern representative for Southeast Asia in the mid-1920s but broke with exiled PKI leaders and secretly returned to Indonesia in 1942 (Anderson 1972, 270–6).[9] While disowned by his PKI comrades in 1945, Malaka still possessed a considerable aura of a veteran revolutionary. Seeking to oust the Sjahrir cabinet, Malaka demanded that the Indonesian government stop negotiation and wage a war against the returning Dutch. Sjahrir had become unpopular only a few months after

---

[7] The Dutch, who were determined to reclaim their colony, were already portraying the duo as war criminals who would be tried the first day Dutch rule returned to Indonesia.

[8] See "Pengumuman Badan Pekerja Komite Nasional no. 3" (Announcement no. 3 by KNIP Working Committee), dated October 30, 1945, and signed by Sjahrir, *Ra'jat* (The People), November 2, 1945.

[9] After the failed PKI rebellion in 1926–7, Malaka was blamed by other PKI leaders for the failure; he would later be labeled a "Trotskyite." See "Tan Malaka – Pengchianat [sic] Marxisme-Leninisme" (Tan Malaka: The traitor to Marxism and Leninism), *Bintang Merah* (Red Star), no. 7, November 15, 1950.

taking office because of his pursuit of diplomacy as the means to achieve independence from the Dutch. For some time, Malaka appeared to prevail, and Sjahrir was forced to resign in February 1946. With help from Sukarno and Hatta, Sjahrir was able to split Malaka's coalition, buy off his main allies with cabinet posts, and eventually return to the premiership. Sjahrir's dominant position was weakened in this struggle, but elite compromise was ironically strengthened: the government became more inclusive as Malaka's supporters were invited in.[10]

The second challenge came from Musso, another exiled PKI leader, who returned from the Soviet Union in August 1948 (G. Kahin 1952, 272–303). Musso had been a PKI leader in the 1920s before the failed PKI rebellion in 1926–7 sent him into exile in the Soviet Union (McVey 1965, 168–9). On coming back to Indonesia just as the Cold War began in Europe, Musso introduced a new Soviet doctrine that called for communist movements worldwide to reject alliance with bourgeois groups (Reid 1974, 136–47). He took command of the PKI and pushed through a radical program of social revolution (Swift 1989). Musso's program supported Indonesia's close relations with the Soviet Union and called for the mobilization of peasants and workers. He won significant support from labor and peasant groups and from those elites frustrated with the protracted negotiation between the republic and the Dutch. The grand compromise among Indonesian elites may have unraveled if Musso had had more time. However, when a unit of PKI-affiliated militia revolted, Musso was stampeded into launching a premature military coup against the Sukarno-Hatta government. He was killed and his forces were decimated in a few weeks. Many PKI leaders did not participate in the uprising, and the party was denounced but not banned after the event. Even though the pattern of elite compromise was shaken, Musso, like Malaka before him, failed to break it.

As in Korea, the Indonesian story would be seriously incomplete without the masses. In large cities on Java, local groups launched massive attacks at the Japanese and the British.[11] Surabaya's Front to Defend the Republic of Indonesia, a spontaneous mass group, led an uprising of

---

[10] The Sjahrir government later arrested Tan Malaka and some of his associates on charges of treason (Anderson 1972, 310–31; Mzarek 1994, 313–16; Malaka [1948] 1991, 109–46). PKI supported the government, not Malaka, throughout the episode.

[11] G. Kahin (1952) and Anderson (1972) provide detailed accounts of the situation on Java. For cities on Java, see Smail (1964) for Bandung; Cribb (1991) for Jakarta; and Frederick (1989) for Surabaya. Other studies include Reid (1979) for Aceh and A. Kahin (1985) for various places.

about 120,000 that encircled British forces and killed General Mallaby, the British commander, in late October 1945 (Anderson 1972, 152–66; Frederick 1989, 230–77). In Aceh, East Sumatra, and Surakarta, radical youth groups dethroned local royal rulers and seized local governments despite the republic's policy to the contrary (Reid 1974, 65–8, 92–3; A. Kahin 1985). Similar upheavals took place in West and Central Java where local religious leaders led mass groups to attack local officials, including those freshly appointed by the new republic (Anderson 1972, 335–42). In a typical district of Central Java, for example, eighty – or nearly half of village heads in the district – were overthrown within a few months (Reid 1974, 144).

Indonesia's mass movements did not share the same fate with their counterparts in South Korea, which in turn had different implications for the two states. While the story in South Korea by 1947 was one of rebellion and repression, the story in Indonesia was one of mass incorporation, for two reasons. First, repression was not a real option. The Sjahrir government sought international recognition as the uncontested sovereign of Indonesia and made clear its disapproval of poorly directed mass actions such as the attack on British forces in Surabaya. However, unlike the MG in South Korea that commanded thousands of U.S. troops and Korean policemen, the infant Indonesian government had no real army until 1947. Lacking coercive power, in most cases it had to settle for incorporation rather than repression.[12] Local militias and other mass organizations were accepted as parts of new local governments together with remnants of the colonial bureaucracy. Although Sjahrir called for the formation of local councils in early November 1945, this move was not an attempt to mobilize the masses but to incorporate emerging mass groups that had seized local governments.[13]

The second reason for mass incorporation had to do with efforts by national political parties to mobilize mass support. These parties sought to incorporate mass groups as a quick way to expand their support bases. Amir Sjarifuddin, minister of defense and a leader of the Socialist Party (PS) in 1946 and 1947, organized under the name of the central

---

[12] It helped negotiate a truce between the landing Allied forces and radical youth groups in Surabaya, tried to rein in the rebellion in Surakarta against the Sultan, and suppressed the Tiga-Daerah uprising (Anderson 1972, 162–5, 332–69).

[13] "Pengumuman Badan Pekerja Komite Nasional no. 2" (Announcement no. 2 by the KNIP Working Committee), *Ra'jat*, November 2, 1945. See also G. Kahin (1952, 154). The announcement called for the heads of these local councils to be appointed by the central government.

government a youth congress with hundreds of delegates from various youth groups on Java (Anderson 1972, 252–61). At this congress, twenty-eight groups joined to form the Socialist Youth of Indonesia (Pemuda Sosialis Indonesia, or Pesindo). Pesindo would later become the PKI's armed wing when Sjarifuddin merged PS with PKI. Masjumi, the largest Muslim party, and its local branches also incorporated several local militias during 1946 and 1947 besides Hizbullah, which had been created under the Japanese.[14] The Indonesian Nationalist Party (PNI) incorporated Barisan Banteng (Wild Buffaloes Corps) as its armed wing.

In all these cases, local militias became members of nationally recognized political parties despite having neither interest in these parties' specific programs nor desire to be subordinate to any central authorities. These militias not only fought among themselves but also would not hesitate to confront the national army if necessary. The national political parties were often unable to rein in their own militias: the 1948 Madiun rebellion is a clear example, in which fighting between local Pesindo units and other militias forced Musso to prematurely launch his revolution against the republic (Swift 1989, 73–6). This event clearly showed how mass incorporation could destabilize national politics, as it would in the postcolonial period.

Owing to elite compromise and mass incorporation during state formation, Indonesia largely avoided the violence and the ideological extremism that engulfed the Korean peninsula during the civil war. A unified Indonesian nation-state emerged in 1949 after the Dutch gave up. Yet compromise and incorporation left behind a state structure very different from that found in South Korea. We have seen that the entire left side of the political elites was wiped out or relocated to North Korea when South Korea was formed. In Indonesia, several leftist leaders such as Malaka and Musso were eliminated, but power was broadly shared among numerous groups occupying the full range of the ideological spectrum.

Unlike in South Korea, where repression brought centralization and increased the state's coercive power, in Indonesia mass incorporation left severe defects in the emerging state structure. This structure was fractured, with the central government and national political organizations having little control over local governments and local political groups.

---

[14] Examples of these groups were Sabillilah (The Way of God) and Laskar Muslim Indonesia (Muslim Fighters) on Java, Tentara Islam Republik Indonesia (the Muslim Army of the Republic) on Sumatra, and Barisan Mujahidin (Corps of Islamic Fighters) in Aceh (Noer 1960, 78–81).

Where repression took place, it did little to bolster the Indonesian state's coercive apparatus: Indonesian rebellions were small by Korean standards. If casualties can be used as a measure of repression, the Cheju rebellion lasted for a year and claimed about sixty thousand lives. The Madiun rebellion led by Musso was crushed in a few weeks and could not have caused more than a few thousand deaths (Merrill 1980, 182; Reid 1974, 142–6).

Mass incorporation created conditions for persistent local revolts after independence. The Darul Islam movement (DI) on West Java, which was led by a former guerrilla leader, demanded an Islamic state and fought the central government for more than a decade (G. Kahin 1952, 326–31; Jackson 1980; van Dijk 1981; Noer 1987, 176–83). The Acehnese secessionist movement that broke out only a few years after independence is another example (Reid 1979; Morris 1985). The regional revolts in 1957 also had origins in mass incorporation.

THE FAILURE OF PREMATURE DEVELOPMENTALISM, 1950–1957

Thanks to elite compromise, at the time of independence Indonesia had a parliament encompassing the entire political spectrum from left to right and from religiously based to secular nationalist parties (Feith 1962). There were two large Muslim parties, parties of other religions, several nationalist parties, several communist parties, and other groups representing workers, peasants, the armed forces, ethnic minorities, and regional interests. A similar rainbow of interests and ideologies existed in local councils and governments. Compromise had produced an inclusive but fragile government based on poorly organized parties. While some parties were able to consolidate, none was able to dominate, and most would disintegrate into small personal factions (Pauker 1958; Lev 1967). Political stability was elusive: in its first seven years, Indonesia saw seven cabinets.

Factions having pro-Western outlooks led three of the seven cabinets in the first years of independence.[15] These factions guided Indonesia to formal independence in December 1949 through diplomacy rather than armed struggle. Under the terms of this negotiated independence, the Dutch government and Dutch firms would retake control of most

---

[15] The following discussion is based largely on Feith (1962)'s seminal work covering politics in this period. Glassburner (1971) provides classic analyses of economic conditions and policy making in the 1950s and 1960s. For recent accounts, see Thee (1994) and Booth (1994; 1998, 53–72).

plantations, industrial assets, shipping lines, and public utilities, as well as a disputed territory, Papua New Guinea. In the first five years after 1949, Indonesia's economic policies were made by Dutch-trained technocrats with advanced economic or law degrees. Under these men, the government pursued progrowth policies with the long-term goal of building a capitalist but socially progressive national economy. Western investment and technology were courted, while foreign property rights were protected. These elites lacked neither technical competency nor commitment to growth. Their mistake was to take on developmental roles without a developmental structure in place.

We have seen that South Korean rulers faced little opposition to their economic policy. In contrast, Indonesian technocrats' economic agenda met resistance from the very start. Opposition emerged not only from leftist and ultranationalist parties that supported the nationalization of all foreign assets and demanded government protection for labor and peasants against foreign management (Feith 1962, 131–4; van der Kroef 1965, 219–22). Opposition also came from inside the ruling parties, either among their factions or from local branches. All Indonesian parties had been formed hastily in late 1945 or early 1946 through the incorporation of various factions and autonomous mass groups; now it became extremely difficult even for those in power to hold their organizations together.

How the legacy of elite compromise interacted with that of mass incorporation to frustrate developmentalism can be seen clearly in the cases of peasants' and workers' resistance to capitalism. Under Japanese occupation and during the struggle for independence, peasants had squatted on large chunks of estate land that were now to be returned to their foreign owners. Government attempts to evict these squatters led to direct conflicts, the killings of several peasants, and the fall in 1953 of the Wilopo cabinet led by pro-Western technocrats (Feith 1962, 293–6, 308). In their struggle, the squatters were supported by the local branches of not only leftist parties but also some parties included in Wilopo's coalitional government.

The same situation applied to labor groups that were nominally affiliated with major political parties but were often autonomous (Hawkins 1963, 200–1). These groups had been incorporated into national political parties during the independence struggle; in their postcolonial movement the enemy was no longer the colonial state but its successor. They resisted the return of foreign capital even though this policy was backed by most national parties. The number of labor disputes rose from less than two hundred in 1950 to nearly four thousand in 1956 (Hawkins 1963, 232–42). Disputes between estate workers and foreign management led to widespread strikes drawing tens of thousands of workers. Widespread labor unrest was a main reason why Indonesia attracted little foreign investment except in its oil sector.

In the context of popular unrest and serious elite bickering, by the mid-1950s power had been transferred to populist and ultranationalist factions opposed to foreign capital and capitalist development. These factions championed a nationalization campaign to seize Western properties in the late 1950s and launched an invasion of Papua New Guinea, which was still under Dutch control. These adventurous policies not only destroyed the limited economic progress made since independence but also triggered a long recession (Mackie 1967).

The end to accommodation politics finally arrived with the armed revolts that erupted simultaneously on Sumatra, Sulawesi, and the Malukus in 1957 (Harvey 1977). These rebellions were led by disgruntled local leaders and army officers with the support of many leaders of the pro-Western, procapitalist faction now out of power. The origins of all these rebellions lay in the struggle for independence when local governments and armed units organized themselves after spontaneous revolts, but these groups were later incorporated *in toto* into local governments as well as into the national army.[16] Even during the struggle against the Dutch, these groups never fully obeyed, and often resisted, central command. Not surprisingly, soon after independence they rose up to defend local autonomy or to declare their own republics. These self-made guerrilla leaders viewed the efforts to centralize administration and army command by the government in Jakarta to be serious threats to their political future. Ironically, these forces that emerged during state formation and that frustrated the early pro-Western leaders were now supported by these very leaders. Premature developmentalism was not only defeated but also disgraced for its participation in an antistate, antination enterprise.

CONFRONTATION AND THE CONSTRUCTION OF A DEVELOPMENTAL STRUCTURE, 1960–1975

The regional revolts of 1957 threatened the very survival of the Indonesian Republic, and responses by state elites, especially President Sukarno,

---

[16] For history of the Indonesian military, see Sundhaussen (1982) and Crouch (1988).

were instructive in a comparative perspective. Recall that Sukarno had been pushed aside since late 1945 because of his collaboration with the Japanese. For several years he was merely a figurehead in the parliamentary system. As this system became paralyzed under tremendous factional conflicts, he gradually regained his power. The regional rebellions in 1957 offered Sukarno an opportunity to return to the center of Indonesian politics. He responded not only by sending troops to battle the rebels. Dissolving what he called the "Western-style parliament," Sukarno declared martial law, resurrected the 1945 constitution that gave the president greater authority, established a cabinet accountable only to him, and clamped down harshly on critics.

Sukarno's maneuvers no doubt helped himself first, but through these particular moves he also contributed to giving the Indonesian state elements of a developmental structure. With the dissolution of the parliament, state power became concentrated in the presidency. State structure was more centralized with Jakarta's victory over regional rebellions. Martial law allowed the military to infiltrate a weak civil bureaucracy, subjecting it to centralized command. In ways similar to what happened after the Yosu rebellion and the civil war in Korea nearly a decade earlier, the Indonesian state and the military central command were strengthened when the rebellions were defeated (Lev 1966b; McVey 1971; 1972).

However, the suppression of those regional revolts left intact the legacy of mass incorporation on Java, where most Indonesians lived. Leftist parties with a proclivity to mass mobilization naturally benefited the most from the situation. Surviving the Musso debacle thanks to elite compromise, PKI and other left-wing parties took advantage of the fractured structure of the state to penetrate the factionalized military, the politicized bureaucracy, autonomous local councils, militant labor unions, and numerous urban and rural groups on Java that had never been demobilized since state formation. As the crusader against capitalism and imperialism and as the champion of mass demands for land redistribution, higher wages, workers' rights, food subsidies, and price controls, PKI expanded exponentially and became the largest political party by the early 1960s (Hindley 1964; van der Kroef 1965; Mortimer 1974).

President Sukarno also contributed significantly to perpetuating the legacy of mass incorporation. Unlike Rhee, Sukarno lacked a loyal police force but offset this deficit with great oratorical talents. His strategy to consolidate power relied less on repression than on broad-based mass mobilization campaigns with themes of national independence and socioeconomic justice (Legge 1972). While Rhee ruthlessly suppressed the masses, Sukarno lovingly incorporated them into his national front organizations.

Toward the mid-1960s, a polarizing pattern among Sukarno, PKI, and the military became increasingly clear (Elson 2001, 88–98; Sundhaussen 1982, 162–225). As president and commander in chief, Sukarno had immense international prestige and broad popular support, and he stood in charge of a massive patronage network in the government. Without his own political party, personal charisma was his greatest asset. PKI claimed 2.5 million members, a nationwide organization of branches and cells, and the backing of many political factions, certain military commanders, and sometimes Sukarno. The military, the third pole in the polarizing trend, had become more unified and greatly expanded after successfully quelling the regional rebellions. Its top leaders were staunchly anticommunist and sought to counter an anticipated PKI coup by expanding military commanding posts to subdistrict and village levels. During 1963 to 1965, politics became sharply polarized as Sukarno attempted to curb rising military power by aligning himself closely with PKI (Sundhaussen 1982, 170–80).

Under these circumstances, a failed coup carried out by PKI sympathizers in the army brought the military under Suharto to power in 1965 (Elson 2001, 120–45; Roosa 2006). One of Suharto's first acts after replacing Sukarno was to coordinate a massacre in which the military and local Muslim groups killed about a quarter million communists (Cribb 1990). PKI was banned while radical union, peasant, and student leaders were arrested en masse. A massive purge – literally a manhunt – of known and suspected communists and leftists was launched throughout the state bureaucracy, military, local governments, and society at large (Emmerson 1978, 91).

Over the next decade, Suharto would carry out other systematic measures that together erased all legacies of compromise and incorporation of earlier periods and built a new cohesive state structure (Elson 2001, 183–91). The unstable multiparty system, the very symbol of accommodation and a serious defect in the state structure, was first to go. Suharto banned many political parties and forced the rest to amalgamate into two. He also established a new political party, the Golkar – in effect a grouping of bureaucrats, military personnel, and his political supporters. Except for this government party, parties were no longer allowed to campaign in the villages or in urban neighborhoods. This new party system would ensure the reelection of Suharto to the presidency and deliver political stability for the next three decades. On the surface, this move by Suharto appeared similar to what Park Chung Hee did in 1972 to establish the Yushin dictatorship on the basis of martial law. However, while Park's Yushin system helped him to maintain his personal grip on power, it contributed little to the Korean state structure, which had long been centralized with a strong bureaucracy and cohesive coercive organizations. In contrast, Suharto's reform of the party system was crucial to the construction of a centralized bureaucracy and military.

Another critical step by Suharto to restructure politics was the militarization of the state, a process that had begun under Sukarno. By the early 1970s almost all provincial governors and most district chiefs were military officers (Emmerson 1978, 103). State structure was further centralized with a new (and ironically named) "Regional Autonomy Law" enacted in 1974. This law finally completed the unfinished centralization project under the Dutch by imposing a uniform vertical administrative system across the country. Local elections were now formally replaced by personnel appointments by the Ministry of Home Affairs and ultimately by Suharto himself, whose power now could match that of the Dutch governor general (Elson 2001, 209).

On the economic front, Suharto and his team of young advisers, armed with American doctorates in economics, launched an emergency recovery program and a long-term plan for national development. This program brought immediate recovery and rapid growth rates, reaching double digits in 1968 and 1974 (Hill 2000, 12). Impressive economic progress, staunchly anticommunist credentials, and liberal economic policies earned the regime significant admiration in the West. This helped Suharto to build a close relationship with foreign capital: by the early 1970s Indonesia attracted $6 billion of realized foreign direct investment and became the second-largest foreign aid recipient among all developing countries after India (Robison 1986, 142; Thee 2002, 205–6). After restrictions on domestic capital were removed, intimate links between military commanders and Chinese businesses soon developed into powerful monopolies and became another important base of the regime (Elson 2001, 191–4). Together with a centralized government and effective state control over popular classes, alliance with propertied classes and foreign capital was another essential component of the developmental state structure that Suharto built in the midst of his confrontation with Sukarno and the PKI.

Less than a decade after assuming power, Suharto had fundamentally reshaped Indonesian politics and built a cohesive state structure.

However, destabilizing elements traceable to the state formation period would once again almost thwart his developmental policies in 1974. Although Suharto achieved early success in removing Sukarno and the PKI by 1966, anticapitalist and anti-Western sentiments ran deep because of the intense leftist mobilization in the previous decade. In addition, Muslim and other nationalist organizations dating from the state formation period remained intact and expanded as they participated in the massacre of communists. These groups were angered by Suharto's maneuvers to monopolize power, his slavishly pro-Western policies, and his disregard for Muslim concerns. Muslim groups had helped to bring the military to power, but soon they were back in the streets. Large demonstrations and riots took place in 1968 and 1973, but their movement peaked with the huge riots in January 1974 to protest Japanese prime minister Tanaka's visit to Indonesia. These so-called Malari riots involved thousands of students and led to many deaths and mass detentions (van Dijk 1975, 1–4). In these protests, the regime was accused of selling out national wealth to foreign countries and ethnic Chinese. Not just foreign investment but capitalism itself was put on trial.[17]

Shaken by the crisis, Suharto carried out systematic repression while retreating from his liberal economic platform. He created the Council for Political Stabilization and National Security both to effectively coordinate repression and to better channel dissent through state venues, such as the government party (Elson 2001, 209). By the end of the 1970s, university campuses had been brought under tight state control with the abolition of independent student councils and with rectors held responsible for campus order (Emmerson 1978, 125).

To appease its critics, the government imposed a range of policies to restrict foreign capital, require indigenous shares in joint-venture projects, and increase credits to indigenous entrepreneurs (Robison 1986, 167). The regime's foreign capital–based, export-oriented strategy was replaced by one that relied on domestic capital and import substitution for industrialization. Some close advisers of Suharto had long advocated economic nationalism, but the riots helped them to prevail over supporters of liberalism in the government (Robison 1986, 159–72). This strategic shift hurt the state-capital alliance somewhat but, thanks to the massive inflows of oil windfall profits during 1974 to 1982, the shift did not seem to affect Indonesia's long-term development. Rapid growth and industrialization

---

[17] Aspinall (2005) provides a thorough account of the anti-Suharto student movement.

continued, although growth could have been more efficient had liberal policies not been disrupted.[18] Without the oil windfall profits, however, Indonesia might not have seen *any* growth with its import substitution strategy. The significance of the Malari riots was diminished by the oil boom, but the event still exposed a structural weakness of the state – its fragile domination over society in particular – nearly a decade after Suharto assumed power.

In sum, the legacy of state formation explains why Indonesian developmentalism failed in the 1950s and had difficulties even after nearly a decade under military rule. Indonesia's particular pattern of state formation offered few developmental assets. By 1955 President Rhee of South Korea had essentially completed the task of building a developmental structure. In contrast, in Indonesia of the 1960s state power at the apex was still divided among Sukarno, the PKI, and the army. While elites became increasingly polarized, the legacy of mass incorporation persisted. Among other measures, Suharto engineered a systematic massacre of communists in Indonesia, similar to what Rhee did with his Podo Yonmaeng program in South Korea. Note, however, that Rhee did it in the late 1940s, while Suharto acted twenty years later. The military regime under Suharto must be given credit for erecting a cohesive developmental structure, which allowed it to perform developmental roles effectively thereafter. Yet by the early 1970s it was still hampered by the residual legacy of state formation, whereas Park had a relatively free hand where economic policies were concerned.

As in the Korean case, elite polarization and mass suppression dynamics were instrumental in transforming the ineffective Indonesian state under Sukarno into a developmental state. This confrontation pattern catapulted Suharto into politics after the tragic events of 1965 and was the logic behind much of his policies to reorganize state power up to the 1970s. We have seen that Korea witnessed confrontation during state formation. Indonesia experienced accommodation during the same period, which explains to a great extent why Indonesia faltered in its early attempt at developmentalism in the 1950s. For good or bad, confrontation eventually erupted in Indonesia in the 1960s in the struggle for power between the military and the PKI backed by Sukarno. Indonesia thus not only displays a contrast with Korea in terms of the different impacts of

---

[18] Hill (2000, 158) views the new strategy of industrialization as inefficient. Compared to 1974–82, growth rates were in fact significantly higher during 1988–96 after liberal policies were adopted following the second oil bust (Hill 2000, 16–17; Thee 2002, 215).

accommodation versus confrontation; it also reaffirms what we have found in Korea about the positive association of confrontation and developmentalism.

CONCLUSION

This chapter has attempted to explain why premature developmentalism failed in Indonesia and why a developmental state emerged when it did. The analysis centered on state structure, not on developmental roles or progrowth policies. In contrast with existing scholarship that focuses on colonial legacies, I have argued that intraelite and elite–mass interactions, especially but not necessarily during state formation, explain why Indonesia fell behind South Korea in obtaining a developmental state but achieved one eventually by the 1970s. Indonesia offers many interesting similarities and contrasts with South Korea. The two countries both were colonized and became independent at approximately the same time. While the Dutch were less interested in industrializing Indonesia than the Japanese were in Korea, the Dutch colonial regime was much more active than other Western colonial governments, at least in the last four decades of colonial rule. Indonesia was also occupied by the Japanese for three years. Both Korean and Indonesian states were formed during a period of extreme chaos and confusion following the Japanese surrender. Yet they experienced different paths of state formation and had different structures by the time they achieved independence.

Even more than South Korea, Indonesia highlights the importance of state formation politics and the limited impact of colonial legacies. Because of elite compromise and mass incorporation during state formation, the state was born without a developmental structure. At the top, authority easily crumbled under shifting ruling coalitions of fragile political factions that reflected the broad multiclass foundation of the state. In contrast with Korea, this social base was inclusive but oriented toward redistribution, not growth. The state was highly decentralized: local militias and local political groups were well organized and practically autonomous. State bureaucracy and the military were thoroughly infiltrated by political factions. A progrowth coalition was in power initially and attempted to play developmental roles but was quickly defeated for lack of a developmental structure to carry out its policies. These legacies of state formation eventually ended with the massacre of communists and with other systematic measures to build a developmental structure by the military government under Suharto. Only after this structure was firmly established around the mid-1970s could the state take on developmental roles effectively. Viewed in the long term, there may be some continuity between the colonial state and the military state in Indonesia. Yet colonial legacies here were more limited than in the Korean case and created many problems for postcolonial developmentalism.

The next two chapters turn to cases that have been largely ignored in the literature on developmental states. These are China's Republican state and its Maoist archrival, and Vietnam's socialist state. Among these, the Maoist state was born out of confrontation like South Korea and Suharto's Indonesia, whereas its Vietnamese neighbor took the accommodation path as Indonesia did in the 1940s. The Republican state was the product of both confrontation and accommodation. All three cases will further corroborate the argument advanced thus far, that elite alignment and elite–mass engagement patterns during state formation determined the structural cohesion of emerging states.

4

Rival State Formations in China

The Republican and Maoist States

Until recently, Western scholarship on Chinese politics was thoroughly
mesmerized by the revolutions that swept through China throughout the
twentieth century (Young 2002, 1). China's modern state formation and
state-building experiences have been either neglected or analyzed under
the rubric of revolutions (e.g., Skocpol 1979). This tendency has com-
partmentalized modern Chinese history into "the abortive revolution"
led by the Chinese Nationalist Party (Guomindang, or GMD) and the
communist revolution under the leadership of the Chinese Communist
Party (CCP) (Esherick 1995). The history of modern China became the
history of (first nationalist, then communist) revolutionary movements:
their leaderships, organizations, and strategies preoccupied scholarship,
obscuring all other important topics.

Conceptually and empirically, another history of modern China, centered on states, has been largely overlooked.[1] Until recently, only limited
research had been done on the Republican state that ruled China from
1927 to 1937 (Edmonds 1997). Scholarship shows that it was a viable
state that engineered important socioeconomic changes before its collapse on the mainland in 1949 (e.g., Kirby 1990; 2000b; Strauss 1998;
Wakeman and Edmonds 2000). After relocating to Taiwan, the leaders
of this state went on to develop the island into an industrial powerhouse.

---

[1] Notable exceptions are Bedeski (1981); Shue (1988); and Wong (1997).

The Maoist state has suffered the same neglect as its rival, even though as a revolutionary movement the CCP has attracted greater attention from scholars than the GMD. Yet Mao Zedong and his comrades did not just lead a radical revolution; they built a powerful state to realize their ambitions. Moreover, this state has outlived those wild revolutionary dreams and is now a rising global power. Despite recent attempts to place the Maoist state in historical and comparative perspective (e.g., Shue 1988; Wong 1997), the processes by which this state was formed have not been systematically addressed in the literature.

This chapter analyzes the formation of the Republican state, its Maoist rival, and the legacies of state formation politics for the structures of both. First, I examine historians' claims that the origins of modern Chinese states can be found in premodern times. Although these claims contain a core of truth, I argue that they do not address the issue of how China's modern states were formed and how past legacies were adopted or rejected. Next, I show that the Republican developmental state was formed with a mixture of accommodation and confrontation: with elite compromise as well as elite polarization, and mass incorporation as well as mass suppression. This particular state formation pattern gave the Republican state some cohesion but also critical structural weaknesses. Although its demise on the mainland was by no means inevitable, the defects in its structure were crippling. One defect was the divided power at the apex: although Chiang Kai-shek dominated the state apparatus, a significant opposition existed in the ruling GMD. Owing in part to this defect, the Republican state was constrained in its efforts to suppress communists. The other defect was located in the weak power of the central government over local branches. At its zenith, Nanjing had only nominal sovereignty over many provinces that were under local warlords' de facto control.

Then, turning to the Maoist developmental state, I trace the rise of the CCP to power not through the lens of revolution making, as conventionally done, but through the lens of state forming. In contrast with the Republican state, the Maoist developmental state was created through the confrontation path characterized by relentless elite polarization and by elites' controlled mobilization of the masses. This state was thus born out of conditions conducive to structural cohesion similar to the Korean case. Yet the legacies of state formation politics were not all advantageous to state structure. The cult of Mao Zedong, a legacy of state formation politics, caused the partial disintegration of the Chinese socialist developmental state in the late 1960s. The Maoist state offers a useful contrast not only with its Republican rival but also with socialist Vietnam, examined in Chapter 5.

TRADITIONAL LEGACIES AND MODERN CHINESE STATES

In comparing colonial legacies in the Korean and Indonesian cases, I have argued that those legacies were less important than state-forming experiences. Because China was never really colonized, the question is not about colonial but traditional legacies. How much must one account for them? This question has not been asked directly in the literature, but it is instructive to review the claims by some historians such as R. Bin Wong (1997) and Philip Kuhn (2002) about the clear parallels between the communist state and its predecessors. Wong asserts that all Chinese states from ancient to modern times have faced similar conditions of rule and, indeed, have pursued similar ruling strategies. They have emerged in response to a parallel set of common historical and structural constraints and shared fundamental characteristics. While he acknowledges the differences between the communist state and its predecessors, Wong (1997, 179–98) argues that substantial continuities and similarities between them exist if one looks at the relationship between the state, on the one hand, and the economy, the bureaucracy, and state ideology, on the other.

Economically, although the Maoist state in principle adopted a Soviet model, it in fact drew on traditional as well as Republican and Japanese practices. These practices included strong state intervention in the economy, the drive to create comparable economic activities across China's vast territory, efforts to promote agricultural production and regulate the grain trade, and emphasis on industrialization for military purposes. In terms of governance, Wong argues that bureaucratic expansion achieved greater depth and breadth under the communist state, but the tension between central and local levels was an ever-present issue that transcends Chinese history. Communist and traditional states shared the large-scale and systematic efforts to govern rural society, the refusal to recognize the legitimacy of sectional interests, and the strict control of nongovernmental organizations. Regarding state ideology, Confucianism and communism have comparable goals for regulating people's livelihood and comparable expectations for the elites to serve the government. Both are "fractal ideologies" that espouse a similar vision of proper order on any spatial level.

Wong does not suggest that communist leaders consciously adopted China's political traditions. He acknowledges that the communist state clearly had greater capacities than its predecessors. Nevertheless, the availability of such traditions limited communist leaders' policy options. Those policies that "resonated" with such traditions stood a better chance of success because historical and cultural memory of traditional practices would increase social acceptance of such policies. As Wong (1997, 195) argues, foreign ideas and modern models augmented traditional ones, but their persuasiveness depends in part on the receiving institutions. Furthermore, because the structural challenges facing rulers did not change much over time, rulers, whether traditional or modern, would tend to formulate similar responses. Thus, Philip Kuhn (2002, 92, 113) claims that, "although China's revolution wrought many changes, its constitutional agenda reflected some basic concerns of the late imperial and Republican states. . . . Underneath the practical and ideological imperatives of his own age, Mao found himself dealing with a modern version of a very old agenda." Hence, the emergence of the Maoist state on Chinese soil, but not elsewhere, resulted from the amalgamation of Chinese traditional institutions and modern ones adopted by communists.

The notion that state-making traditions impose broad limits on modern practices is a valuable insight. We have seen that similar arguments have been advanced in the Korean and Indonesian cases with regard to colonial legacies. However, it is difficult to know *how* traditional institutions came to be embedded in Republican and communist practices. Historical parallels tell us little about the political processes in which a new state structure was erected from traditional and modern raw materials. In these processes, human agents and contingencies played significant roles that cannot be overlooked. In many circumstances, communist leaders re-created structural realities by redefining social classes (domestically) or by challenging Soviet and American dominance (externally). The point is, historical parallels need to be supplemented with detailed accounts of how they were adopted or sustained despite the tremendous social turmoil and political conflict that intervened.

THE REPUBLICAN STATE, 1911–1937

The Republican state on mainland China was formed in 1912 following the collapse of the Qing Empire. This was a fragile state born out of accommodation that would soon break up. Because this early Republican state had a short life, I focus mainly on the period after 1923 when it was reborn. The pattern of state formation this time was characterized by a mixture of accommodation and confrontation. Confrontation gave the GMD state some developmental elements in its structure, whereas accommodation generated many built-in weaknesses.

The Early Republican State, 1911–1916

The genesis of the Republican state must be traced back to the politics of reform and revolution that led to the collapse of the Chinese Empire in 1911. During the last decades of the Qing Dynasty, the power of the central state was eroded gradually by massive domestic revolts, military defeats, and efforts at reform. Two main trends led to its eventual collapse: the politicization of the military and the devolution of authority to the provinces.[2] To cope with domestic and foreign threats, the Qing court sought to build a new military based on Western models (McCord 1993, 17–45). For many reasons, the court relied on provincial governments to implement military reforms. The result was the so-called New Armies placed under provincial control rather than a unified national military. Another source of instability came from nationalist ideas to which many New Armies officers trained in Japan were exposed (McCord 1993, 48–59). Besides the military, reformist leaders of the court also launched a reform to establish elected provincial assemblies, which met for the first time in 1909.[3]

These trends would eventually enable Sun Yat-sen and his associates in the anti-Qing movement to achieve their goal. Rising from peasant origins in Canton, Sun spent many teenage years in Hawaii and graduated from medical college in Hong Kong (Bergère 1998, 23–41). Inspired by reformist ideas, Sun started his quest to overthrow the Qing by raising funds from overseas Chinese communities in the United States, Europe, Japan, and Southeast Asia. As he traveled, Sun founded or connected loose anti-Qing organizations abroad: the Revive China Society in Hawaii and Hong Kong and the Society for China's Revival and the Restoration Society in Tokyo were three main groups.[4] The first group included mainly Chinese immigrants, whereas the latter two were strong among Chinese students in Japan (and later in China after their return). The

[2] For social changes induced by reforms that facilitated revolution, see Esherick ([1971] 1998).
[3] For analyses of these reforms, see Young (1977, ch. 1); Fincher (1981); and Thompson (1995).
[4] On key leaders of the movement who were students in Japan, see Hsueh (1961) on Huang Xing; Liew (1971) on Song Jiaoren; and Shirley (1962) and Boorman (1964) on Wang Jingwei.

Revolutionary Alliance (Tongmenghui), established in 1905 in Tokyo, was based on these three groups; Sun helped to found it and was elected as its president.

From 1905 to 1911, the Revolutionary Alliance conspired with secret societies to launch several local revolts in southern China; all were unsuccessful until October 1911. In this month, a small troop mutiny by a New Armies unit in Wuchang sparked a nationwide wave of spontaneous local rebellions led by New Armies units, provincial assemblies, and underground groups belonging to the Revolutionary Alliance. By December, rebels were in control of many provinces and elected Sun as the provisional president of a new Republic based in Nanjing. Faced with threats of desertion by his own commanders and urged by Premier Yuan Shikai, the Qing emperor agreed to abdicate. Yuan, who enjoyed substantial reformist prestige and military backing, then offered to collaborate with the Revolutionary Alliance to share power. The compromise between Beijing and Nanjing led to the establishment of a new government in Beijing in February 1912. Under the arrangement, Yuan became provisional president presiding over a cabinet composed of many Alliance leaders. Yuan's power was to be shared with a parliament to be established (Spence 1990, 262–81; Hsueh 1961, 118–36).

The compromise saved China from a bloody confrontation, but it created a fragile state that would not last. The newborn Republican state was fragile not only because of the continuing rivalry between the Alliance and Yuan but also because rebellious military commanders who had successfully challenged Qing rule now became entrenched in provincial governments. They continued to mobilize people and assert their independence from the central government (Young 1977, 76–137). Less than a year after becoming president, Yuan sought to centralize power in his government and in the presidency. By that time, the Revolutionary Alliance had become a serious threat to his rule. After the Qing's fall, numerous political parties were set up. Seeking to capture a parliamentary majority, Alliance leaders negotiated the amalgamation of their organization with several parties. To accommodate those small and more conservative parties, they changed the Alliance's name to Guomindang, softened its foreign policy goal from "striving for international equality" to "maintaining international peace," toned down the Alliance's emphases on people's welfare and on socialism, and dispensed with many progressive programs in its platform such as sexual equality, compulsory education, and obligatory military service for citizens (Liew 1971, 172–82; G. Yu 1966, 92–103). These compromises diluted the old Alliance's mission but helped the new GMD to secure the majority of seats in the parliament. In response to the looming threat from the GMD, Yuan ordered the assassination of Song Jiaoren, a key GMD leader, in March 1913. Song had been critical of Yuan's policies and appeared to be campaigning for the election of a new president. Yuan also weakened the GMD by bribes and by intimidating its parliamentary members (G. Yu 1966, 110–12). The final showdown came when Yuan dismissed the GMD military governors of Guangdong, Jiangxi, and Anhui in July 1913. GMD leaders immediately rebelled against Beijing but were quickly defeated (Young 1977, 129–37). No cohesive party to begin with, the GMD simply disintegrated in the wake of Yuan's repression.[5]

Although Yuan successfully eliminated the GMD challenge, Beijing still had precarious control over the provinces. Yuan overestimated his power when he announced in 1915 his plan to reestablish the monarchy and proclaim himself emperor. Unable to quell massive popular opposition, including military revolts in several provinces, Yuan abandoned his plan in March 1916. With his sudden death from uremia a few months later, central authority collapsed and gave way to warlord politics. The early Republican state was dead four years after birth.

The GMD's struggle to resurrect the Republican state in the 1920s was to have a more lasting outcome. Yet there was much continuity between the early and later incarnations of the Republican state in the sense that accommodation continued to be a defining characteristic of the pattern by which this state was reborn. The discontinuities included a significant element of polarization in the process of rebirth and the fact that Chiang Kai-shek was a more effective state builder than Yuan Shikai.[6]

The Later Republican State, 1923–1937

In the early 1920s, rival warlord factions dominated China. By the end of the decade, most of them had submitted, de jure if not de facto, to a centralized GMD state ruled from Nanjing by Generalissimo Chiang Kai-shek. The process of state formation was characterized by risky compromises made by Sun Yat-sen in return for Soviet aid. Adding to long-standing factional divisions within the GMD, these compromises almost

[5] Most GMD leaders survived Yuan's repression, regrouped abroad, and continued to oppose Yuan from there (G. Yu 1966, ch. 5).

[6] Young (1977, 249–51) offers an insightful comparison of Yuan Shikai and Chiang Kai-shek.

tore the party apart. At the same time, Soviet military aid and successful military campaigns of mass suppression (especially the "Northern Expedition" to subdue local warlords) strengthened a particular faction in the GMD led by Chiang Kai-shek. The purge of communists from the GMD in 1927 failed to disrupt the pattern of elite compromise among GMD factions, with serious implications for the structural cohesion of the GMD state.

The compromises made by Sun in return for Soviet aid during 1923 to 1927 contained three elements. First, the GMD platform now placed anti-imperialism above its long-standing antiwarlord mission. Many progressive programs that had been removed when the Revolutionary Alliance was reorganized into the GMD in 1912 were now brought back with even greater emphasis. Even though Sun rejected land redistribution, the new GMD Party Constitution bore many similarities with that of the CCP (Wilbur and How 1989, 91–3, 97–9). Second, the GMD was reorganized to have a centralized structure and strict discipline similar to the Russian Bolshevik Party. Sun agreed to have CCP members join the GMD *as individuals* if they accepted GMD programs and submitted to its discipline. Third, the GMD now set the goal of bringing workers and peasants into its support base. Victory was now viewed as depending on the nationwide participation of these classes (Wilbur and How 1989, 99). These compromises as a whole pushed the GMD further to the left than many of its leaders and members wished.

While some communist leaders such as Chen Duxiu initially resisted collaboration with the GMD (Wilbur and How 1989, 51–4), the CCP benefited from the deal without having to make any compromise. This party was founded in 1921 with assistance and advice from Comintern agents (van de Ven 1991; Dirlik 1989). It consisted of small groups of urban intellectuals and activists.[7] The CCP's organization remained separate from the GMD, but its members were allowed to have membership in the GMD. With this deal, the CCP gained access to GMD extensive elite networks in southern and central China and was free to mobilize millions of peasants and workers in Guangdong, which would soon fall under GMD control (elsewhere mass mobilization would have been quickly suppressed by warlords).[8] The CCP could openly accept Soviet aid while CCP members planted in the GMD could collect intelligence about this

---

[7] One of the founders was Li Dazhao, who was trained in Japan and was the head librarian at Beijing University. Another was Chen Duxiu, the dean of Beijing University and editor of *New Youth*, the most influential journal of the day (Spence 1990, 306).

[8] CCP membership grew from less than one thousand in 1925 to fifty-eight thousand in 1927 (Saich 1994, 101).

party for a possible takeover if the communists won enough support from sympathetic GMD leaders.[9]

On balance, it is unclear whether the GMD as an organization benefited from the deal. On the one hand, Comintern advisers helped to reorganize the GMD along the Bolshevik model, making it a more centralized organization. The Soviet Union trained and armed a new GMD army that would later form a key pillar of the GMD state. On the other, the GMD also paid dearly for Sun's compromises with the Comintern. Its leadership was deeply divided on the merits of the compromises. Its support base thus far had primarily been urban commercial elites and rural gentry, who were naturally uncomfortable with the radical reorientation of the party. Tense internal conflicts erupted immediately. Conservative factions warned Sun about communist subversive intentions. The existence of a party within a party was to them a serious threat to internal solidarity and cohesion (Wilbur and How 1989, 92, 103–5). Even though the GMD had been plagued with factionalism since its birth, ideologically CCP members were to the far left of the GMD center and posed a greater threat to internal cohesion than before. Personally, many party veterans resented being scorned by Soviet advisers and being marginalized when the GMD was reorganized (Wang 1985, 13). Internal conflicts intensified after Sun Yat-sen's death from cancer in January 1925. Bitter disputes among key GMD leaders over the roles of Soviet advisers and their communist protégés now in the GMD contributed to the assassination of Liao Zhongkai, a top GMD leader, by conservative military officers in August 1925. In response to the communist threat of subversion, conservatives in the GMD formed the so-called Western Hill faction and convened their own Central Executive Committee (CEC) meetings in Shanghai, rivaling the CEC in Canton controlled by the so-called left-wing faction (Wilbur and How 1989, 167–71, 188–91).[10]

The CEC of the GMD would split publicly into opposing camps many more times. The most serious split occurred in 1927 and was a direct result of Sun's compromises. In this split, tension between the GMD and the

[9] CCP intention to capture the GMD from within was expressed in Li Dazhao's speech at the Fifth Congress of the Comintern in Moscow in June 1924 (Wilbur and How 1989, 102–3). Three CCP leaders were elected in 1924 to the GMD Central Executive Committee (CEC) which had twenty-four members. One communist (Tan Pingshan) headed the important Central Organizational Department and was member of a three-person standing CEC (Wilbur and How 1989, 100).

[10] The "left wing" was a term used primarily by CCP leaders at the time. This concept does not accurately capture the ideology of assumed members of this faction. Before 1926, this faction was thought to include Wang Jingwei, Liao Zhongkai, Chiang Kai-shek, and the communists. For a discussion of the concept of "the GMD Left," see So (1991, 1–9).

CCP reached such a point that Chiang reversed his earlier membership in the "left-wing" group and sided with conservatives to purge communists from the GMD.[11] The left-wing-dominated CEC that had earlier moved from Canton to Wuhan immediately dismissed him as commander of the GMD army (Wang 1985, 132–46). He responded by convening a CEC meeting of his supporters and formed a government in Nanjing. The two GMD governments, one in Wuhan and the other in Nanjing, came close to fighting each other. Threats from warlords and an arrogant directive from Stalin eventually brought Wuhan in line with Nanjing and saved the GMD from self-destruction (Wilbur 1983, 112–46; Saich 1994, 115–18).

Not only did internal conflicts persist at the top of the GMD after the merge, but they were also widespread at local levels between radical and conservative party supporters. An especially hot spot was rural Guangdong, where peasants mobilized by GMD communist members were opposed by Sun Yat-sen-ism Study Societies organized by local gentry (van de Ven 1991, 165–76; Galbiati 1985). Even before the central party expelled communists from the GMD, purges of CCP members had been carried out in many cities during the GMD's Northern Expedition (Wilbur 1983, 94–112). What would have happened if Sun Yat-sen had not made his compromises can only be guessed, but these compromises clearly created serious defects in the structure of the Republican state when it was formed out of a divided GMD.

Sun's compromises unraveled in part after the purge of communists from the GMD during 1927 to 1928. Internal conflicts within the GMD now became open polarization between the GMD and the CCP. After 1928, GMD suppression reduced the CCP to scattered armed groups hiding away in mountainous Jiangxi or operating underground in many cities. These armed groups did not pose an immediate threat to the Republican state and appeared to be viewed by Chiang as a military rather than a political problem (Wei 1985, 155). Under his leadership, Republican troops launched several military campaigns and eventually forced the CCP groups to flee to Shaanxi with heavy losses.

The polarization between the GMD and the CCP after 1927 imposed much less pressure on the former than on the latter, given the great power

---

[11] Chiang had graduated from a Japanese military academy and spent several months in the Soviet Union to study the Soviet system. If his unpublished diary is believable, the young Chiang was sympathetic to many leftist ideas (T. Yang 2002; M. Yu 2002). He was an admirer of the Soviet Union and supporter of close collaboration with communists in his early career. For a detailed account of the purge in Shanghai that involved the Shanghai "Green Gang," see Martin (1996, 99–112).

asymmetry between them until 1945. The predominant pattern of elite alignment undergirding the Republican state remained elite compromise. Even as Chiang monopolized power over GMD military and bureaucracy after 1927, the party's top leadership remained inclusive and divided. As Robert North (1952, 19) observes from the GMD's rosters of leadership from 1924 to 1945, members of its CEC (with the exception of die-hard communists) were reelected by one Congress after another, or, if dropped, they almost invariably reappeared. At the time of the Sixth National Congress of the GMD in 1945, nearly 90 percent of the previous committee members were still alive, and almost all, with the exception of the communists, held positions of leadership in the party. In the GMD's CEC of 1931, Chiang's supporters accounted for only about one-third of membership, although they were perhaps the most cohesive faction (North 1952, 13). To be sure, the GMD's CEC by then was less powerful than it had been before 1927, but it nonetheless remained influential in national politics. Throughout the 1930s, Chiang often had to play one faction (e.g., Wang Jingwei) of the CEC off another (e.g., Hu Hanmin) to stay in power (Wang 1985).

If elite compromise was the predominant pattern of elite alignment during the formation of the Republican state, a mixture of confrontation and accommodation characterized the elite–mass engagement dynamic. During 1923 to 1927, this dynamic followed the controlled mobilization and mass suppression patterns. Radical leaders of the GMD collaborated with CCP cadres to mobilize peasants and workers to fight local land-lords, gentry, and merchants (Wilbur and How 1989, 106–12, 146–8). When local capitalists and landlords protested, they were suppressed, as in the Merchants' Corps incident of 1924 (Bergère 1986, 274–84; van de Ven 1991, 147–98; Wilbur and How 1989, 115–19). At the same time, the new GMD army fought many bloody battles with local warlords in Guangdong, Guangxi, and Yunnan (Wilbur and How 1989, 143–6, 153–5).

After 1927, the predominant patterns were mass suppression and mass incorporation. The Northern Expedition that began in 1926 to subdue local warlords and unite China was mass suppression par excellence (Jordan 1976; Waldron 1995; van de Ven 2003, ch. 3). Huge bat-tles that caused tens of thousands of casualties were fought between Republican and warlord armies. In the middle of this military campaign, Chiang turned against communists and ordered the murder of thousands in Shanghai (Eastman 1974, 6–7). Ensuing communist revolts in cen-tral China were similarly suppressed. Chiang also outlawed all mass mobilizing groups, in particular peasants' and women's associations that had been associated with the CCP (Schoppa 2000, 243).

While Chiang suppressed some warlords, he incorporated many others. When the Northern Expedition began, GMD forces were weaker than the combined forces of warlords. Chiang unified China not only by force but also by bribes and by the deft manipulation of the delicate military balance (Eastman 1974, 138). When he incorporated warlords, he often left their local governments and militias intact if they agreed to submit nominally to the central government in Nanjing.

The legacies of accommodation and confrontation explain the strengths and weaknesses found in the structure of the Republican state. Elite polarization after 1927 helped the GMD reduce internal conflicts and improve the cohesion of the state structure. Mass suppression allowed military commanders, of whom Chiang was the most prominent, to rise to prominence at the expense of more senior revolutionaries, such as Wang Jingwei and Hu Hanmin. For all the brutalities committed, the militarization of the GMD state gave it a more cohesive structure. Chiang's wars to suppress warlords and communists helped the GMD build a relatively effective core of coercive institutions such as the military and the "Blue Shirts" (Wei 1985; Chung 2000).

While earlier scholarship dismissed the Republican state as a complete failure, according to current consensus it was a viable developmental state with ambitious visions, many of which were put into practice (Kirby 2000a). These visions included the creation of a centralized, militarized state in the mold of Nazi Germany (Kirby 1984); the acceleration of economic growth under state leadership (Kirby 1984; 2000b); and cultural reforms to make China a more unified nation (Fitzgerald 1996; Bodenhorn 2002). From building a modern merit-based bureaucracy to organizing elite agitprop groups for mass mobilization and surveillance purposes (Strauss 1998; Eastman 1974, 31–84; Wakeman 2000; Chung 2000), from developing a modern military with great fighting capacity to organizing police in large cities (van de Ven 2003; Wakeman 1995), from making long-term economic plans to nationalizing most domestic industries and financial institutions (Kirby 2000b; Richardson 1999, esp. 84–97), the Republican state was active and often effective in its efforts to transform society.

Nevertheless, this state suffered from major structural weaknesses because of the legacies of accommodation. The conflict between radical and conservative factions in the GMD was never fully resolved, despite occasional confrontations. Internal fighting at local levels would dog the

Republican state for years.[12] At the central level, Chiang failed to purge his rivals from the GMD's central leadership. Most remained in the GMD leadership (the so-called Reorganizationists headed by Wang Jingwei and Chen Gongbo) and continued to criticize Chiang's policies and challenge his authority (So 1991). Together with urban intellectuals and warlords who had been incorporated into the GMD, these leaders exerted significant influence on public opinion in large cities even while they enjoyed little power over the Republican state apparatus.

Anti-Chiang forces were particularly influential on foreign policy issues. Under the banners of nationalism and antiimperialism, they mobilized student strikes and mass demonstrations to denounce Chiang for his failure to repulse the Japanese from Manchuria and for his policy to accommodate Japan's increasing encroachments on Chinese sovereignty (Coble 1985; Fung 1985; 2000). In 1931 they formed a new government in Canton and forced Chiang to resign for a brief period of time. In 1937 intense public pressure following the Japanese invasion of northern China and Chiang's arrests of the leaders of the National Salvation Association triggered the Xian incident (Coble 1985, 306).[13] This incident forced Chiang to make peace with the CCP, which saved the communists from being eliminated as Chiang diverted his troops to fight the Japanese. As a result, the CCP survived and would reemerge in 1945 to defeat the GMD.

The legacies of accommodation during state formation can be similarly observed in the ambivalent attitude of the Republican state toward capital. Recall that alliance with capital is a key feature of a capitalist developmental state structure. While anticommunist, the GMD state's relationship with domestic capitalists was testy, if not hostile. Anticapitalist and antiimperialist sentiments in the GMD were strong, not only during the radical phase under Comintern guidance but also afterward (Coble 1979; Bergère 1986, 229–41; Kirby 1984, 79; Fitzgerald 1990). Mistrust of homegrown capitalists encouraged GMD leaders from

---

[12] Geisert (2001) shows that many local GMD cadres remained radical long after 1927, and it would take years for the conservative leadership under Chiang to purge them from the party.

[13] In this incident, Zhang Xueliang, a former warlord who had submitted his army under the GMD government and who was sent to suppress the Long March survivors, kidnapped Chiang Kai-shek and demanded that Chiang form a united front with the CCP against the Japanese. Both the CCP and the Soviet Union were involved in the subsequent negotiations that led to Chiang's release and his agreement to form a United Front with the CCP to fight Japan (van Slyke 1967, 75–91; B. Yang 1990, 220–8).

Sun to Chiang to look to foreign capital to underwrite their economic development plans (Kirby 1984, 79; Richardson 1999, 92). Among foreign powers, Britain remained the nemesis of Chinese nationalism, while American investment was far more substantial in Japan than in China (Garver 1992, 4–6). Fortunately, Chiang was able to obtain German technical assistance and capital, which were instrumental to the construction of the GMD state (Kirby 1984). When Nazi Germany abandoned Republican China for an alliance with Japan in 1941, its role was replaced by the United States (Kirby 1984, 251). Ambivalence to, and unstable alliance with, domestic and foreign capital was a weakness in the structure of the Republican state. Arguably a sharper polarization with the left could have forced the GMD to fully reverse its radical origins and establish close relations with capital. From this perspective, the loss in the civil war during 1945–9 benefited the Republican state by helping Chiang to rid the GMD of many left-wing leaders who stayed on the mainland.

Yet the worst legacy of accommodation for the Republican state structure was the incorporation of local warlords. According to historian Lloyd Eastman's (1974, 138) metaphorical description, "China, even seven years after the revolutionary conquest by the [GMD], was like an ill-fitting jig-saw puzzle: most of the pieces seemed almost to fit, but they did not really interlock." Provincial warlords who had been incorporated, such as Long Yun, Fang Yuxiang, Yen Xishan, and Bai Chongxi, were constantly testing Chiang's authority and ready to challenge Nanjing directly at its weak moments. During the Nanjing decade, Eastman (1974, 85–6) counts at least twenty-seven rebellions and scores of lesser uprisings that attested to this weakness.[14] The relocation to Taiwan in 1949 that cut the Republican state loose from this burden of earlier compromises can be viewed as a major reason for its later success.

In sum, the Republican state was born out of a mixture of confrontation and accommodation, but a close examination suggests that accommodation was more substantial. As a result, the Republican state structure contained a few cohesive components and lacked overall cohesion, as Eastman's apt metaphor suggests. The structural weaknesses of this state were significant even though they did not make its collapse in 1949 inevitable. Its nemesis, the Maoist state, did have a different state-forming experience, one characterized by confrontation, which was to create a cohesive structure for the communist state.

---

[14] For an analysis of one of the most significant rebellions, the Fujian rebellion in 1933–4, see Eastman (1974, 85–139).

THE FORMATION OF THE MAOIST STATE, 1927–1949

The relationship between the GMD and the CCP went through many phases from 1923, when they began to collaborate, to 1949, when the GMD was defeated in the civil war. The relationship experienced limited collaboration under Comintern direction from 1923 to 1927, brutal conflict from 1927 to 1937, and a temporary truce from 1937 to 1940, ostensibly under a "united front" against the Japanese. This truce effectively ended in 1940. From then until the end of World War II in 1945, the relationship between the two parties could be described as medium-intensity conflict. This conflict exploded into a massive civil war from 1946 to 1949. Out of this war emerged two separate states that confronted each other across the Taiwan Strait: the Maoist state on the mainland and the GMD state on Taiwan. Despite brief diversions, elite polarization was the predominant pattern that formed the Maoist state. This long and brutal process of elite polarization, augmented by the way the CCP engaged the masses through controlled mobilization, changed the party from a feeble urban group of intellectuals to a powerful organization with a cohesive structure.

We have seen how the CCP accepted GMD leadership under Comintern guidance in the early 1920s, and how this deal collapsed in 1927 when Chiang Kai-shek purged communists. This purge triggered the polarization between the GMD and the CCP. While polarization affected both the GMD and the CCP, given the lopsided balance of forces in favor of the GMD, the CCP bore the full impact of the pattern. We have seen that Chiang made compromises with other factions of the GMD after 1927. Yet he categorically rejected compromise with the communists. Republican troops launched repeated attacks on communist bases in mountainous Jiangxi in southeastern China, where CCP forces regrouped after 1928.

Despite some success in resisting several GMD military campaigns, Jiangxi bases eventually became indefensible in the face of Chiang's effective use of the blockhouse tactic to encircle and isolate communist forces (Wei 1985). The CCP had to abandon these bases in 1934 and retreated to northwestern China in the so-called Long March. During this deadly journey, their forces shrank by 90 percent. From about 300,000 troops in 1933, their number fell to 30,000 in early 1937 (B. Yang 1990, 255).

In October 1935, seventeen GMD divisions were amassed in northwestern China in what was planned to be the final campaign to annihilate Long March survivors (Ch'en 1991, 105). Nevertheless, as in Indonesia and Vietnam, the Japanese invasion of China changed the balance of forces among domestic contenders for power. Japanese occupation of Manchuria since 1931 presented Chiang Kai-shek with a dilemma. Chiang was preoccupied with fighting warlords and communists, declaring, "First [let's] unite within then resist the enemy without" (Eastman 1991, 246). We have seen that only after the Xian incident did Chiang reluctantly agree to a truce with the CCP to fight the Japanese.

For its part, the CCP had every reason to desire a truce with the GMD and in fact had called for the formation of a national front to fight the Japanese since 1931 (Ch'en 1991, 106–7). A war between the GMD and the Japanese would relieve the GMD pressure on the CCP. The CCP's emphasis on the Japanese threat would frame the GMD as unpatriotic, especially in urban centers where anti-Japanese sentiments were running high at the time. The Comintern instruction in the summer of 1935 that ordered communist parties worldwide to form antifascist united fronts gave further impetus. After the Xian incident and several negotiations, the CCP agreed to terminate its armed struggle and its land redistribution program and to deploy its troops according to the GMD government's strategic plans. In return, it was allowed to set up liaison offices in the cities, nominate representatives to advisory bodies, and receive a government subsidy (van Slyke 1991, 178).

Elite polarization was interrupted for only two years after the signing of the truce. Hostilities ceased but no sincere collaboration ensued and the deal quickly unraveled. The GMD government, now isolated in Chongqing in southwestern China, tried its best to restrict the growth of the CCP. Since 1939, hundreds of thousands of GMD troops enforced a military blockade on the main base area of the CCP. Three years into the united front, hostilities resumed with the New Fourth Army incident, in which a clash between GMD and CCP troops led to nearly ten thousand casualties on the CCP side alone. After this event, Chiang Kai-shek ordered all liaison offices in the cities closed and direct contacts between the CCP and GMD virtually ended (van Slyke 1991, 227–39). Until the end of World War II, GMD and CCP forces fought each other perhaps as much as they fought the Japanese.

Unlike other cases in this study, the Japanese surrender was not a significant event in China. No real power vacuum opened up for local elites to mobilize. Two competing governments, each with more than a million troops, had mobilized and waited for some years in rugged western China for the end of the war. While they negotiated, the GMD government and the CCP rushed their forces to seize the vast territories recently opened following the Japanese surrender. After a series of decisive victories in northeastern and northern China, communist forces swept across central and southern China in a conventional military conquest (Pepper 1978; Westad 2003). As in Korea, elite polarization in China ended with a civil war and the permanent separation of two states.

With regard to the CCP's elite–mass engagement dynamic, the predominant pattern was controlled mobilization. As an antigovernment revolutionary party, the CCP needed peasants' support, and ordinary villagers no doubt played an important role in the communist victory. Their compliance and support resulted from the CCP's combined use of military coercion, material incentives, and ideological exhortation. The CCP's successful strategy of mass mobilization went beyond offering rewards to collaborators while imposing sanctions on opponents. Different alliances with local groups were created with a high degree of flexibility and adaptability both to local conditions and to changes over time (Wou 1994; 1999). At times, communist activists would form alliances with and recruit from bandit groups; at other times they would attack those bandits with the help of local self-defense paramilitary groups (Perry 1980). The goal was to maximize mass support at any given time under the general rubric of revolution.

Conflicting views exist on the nature of the relationship between the CCP and the Chinese peasantry. Early studies emphasized the democratic character of Mao's mass line (Selden 1971). More recent research has attributed greater significance to coercive aspects of the communist mobilization strategy and the diversity of approaches to achieving effective mass control and guidance (Y. Chen 1986; Levine 1987; Wou 1994; Keating 1997; Esherick 1998). Levine (1987) has shown that Chinese peasants did not make revolution by themselves; in various local contexts their participation was conditional on whether there was a Red Army unit stationed nearby. Peasants did participate; yet this collective action was preceded by the communists' effective control of the local political situation and was followed by an even higher level of control. This strategy worked because, where peasants were successfully mobilized in small groups, the party was also able to penetrate local relations (Keating 1997, 3). The party's deeper penetration broke up age-old local ties and institutions and created new social status hierarchies tied to political support and sanctions from above. Where communist organizations were effective (they were not always so), the masses had become malleable in accordance with fluctuations in party policies.

How did elite polarization and controlled mobilization shape the structure of the Maoist state when it emerged in 1949? Polarization triggered three processes that transformed the CCP as an organization, including ruralization, militarization, and centralization. After the 1927 debacle, CCP leaders realized that their forces were no match for Chiang's in urban battles. They withdrew to Jiangxi, where they set up a Soviet Republic and carried out a radical land redistribution program (I. Kim 1969). In Jiangxi, the ruralization of the CCP began as the party sought a social base to help it withstand overwhelming GMD forces. In the next two decades with the exception of occasional influxes of urban youths fleeing the cities to join the movement, the only source of recruits for the party was peasants. Given the CCP's class-based land policy during much of this period,[15] poor peasants naturally were attracted to and were welcomed in the party. In 1934 68 percent of Red Army soldiers had a poor peasant background, while 77 percent of Red Army recruits came from the base areas. The CCP had even larger proportions of members with peasant background than its army (Harrison 1972, 201). As more poor peasants were drafted into the Red Army, military needs gave further impetus to a radical land policy: party leaders viewed land redistribution as a way to motivate Red Army soldiers and to give them a stake in the revolution. When the CCP emerged from the countryside to seize the cities in 1946, its members were predominantly of poor peasant origins.

Ruralization was accompanied by militarization. Having painstakingly organized peasants and workers only to see their organizations crushed by GMD troops in 1927, CCP leaders now understood that mass mobilization without military backup was folly (van de Ven 1991, 188). Heavy and constant GMD military pressure made the militarization of the CCP urgent, if it was to survive. In 1929, the party called for all members to undergo military training (van de Ven 2000, 110–11). All males between eighteen and forty-five who were not class enemies were conscripted. At the village level, peasants were organized into militias linked together by guerrilla detachments. Militarization had become formalized and institutionalized.

The formation of a cohesive, stable, and centralized CCP leadership was another outcome of relentless polarization. How did this happen? During 1923 to 1927, the CCP underwent a period of fast growth, with membership expanding from less than one thousand in 1925 to fifty-eight thousand in 1927 (Saich 1994, 101). As the party expanded its activities in many new areas, its organization became functionally more differentiated

---

[15] CCP's land policy was most radical during the Jiangxi period (1928–36). Policy was officially more moderate during the second united front (1937–45), but Pepper (1978) has shown that such a moderate policy was implemented only in a few base areas.

and complex. At the same time, many new leaders promoted to leadership positions in these growth years were untested. In the wake of the GMD purge in 1927, the CCP not only shrank in size but also experienced a rapid leadership turnover, less because of executions by the Chiang Kai-shek government than because of policy failures and ensuing power struggles. As the party shrank on the run from GMD forces after 1927, party institutions became less differentiated, while policy lines became more so with every change in its leadership. The lines between military commanders and political commissars blurred while the lines between Qu Qiubai, Li Lisan, Wang Ming, Bo Gu, Zhang Wentien, Zhang Guodao, Mao Zedong, and other leaders sharpened, as they had to promote and defend their positions in so many power struggles.[16]

Leadership struggles appeared to make the CCP a less cohesive organization, but in fact the opposite was the case. By the late 1930s, the leadership that survived the deadly Long March had crystallized into an extremely cohesive group: that group would hold together for the next twenty-five years almost intact. A fairly differentiated "correct line" had emerged with a leader, Mao, at the core.[17] The rise to the top of a radical leader in the character of Mao was not entirely determined by environmental and organization-developmental conditions. Yet Mao had been an ardent advocate of a rural-based revolutionary strategy since 1927[18] and movement of the CCP away from the cities, a result of elite polarization, clearly gave Mao an edge over his rivals in the CCP leadership.

The trend of ruralization, militarization, and centralization would continue during the Yan'an period (1937–45). Polarization, in the form of a military blockade and repeated attacks by GMD troops since 1939, imposed ruthless pressures on CCP bases and forced its leaders to develop economic, social, and political programs in order to survive.[19] A political program that contributed considerably to the structure of the emerging communist party-state was the "party rectification" campaign (Cheng Feng) from 1942 to 1944. In this campaign, all cadres were forced to

---

[16] For a concise analysis of these struggles, see Ch'en (1991, 53–104). On politics during the Long March, see B. Yang (1990).

[17] Mao's position was secure by 1938 after he had defeated his potential challenger Wang Ming (Teiwes 1994).

[18] See Mao's Report on an Investigation of the Peasant Movement in Hunan, dated March 27, 1927 (Saich 1994, 198–209).

[19] For an analysis of the organization of the government in the Shan-Gan-Ning base where CCP headquarters were located, see Schran (1976). Other studies of CCP bases include Selden (1971); Y. Chen (1986); Hartford (1989); Keating (1997); and Goodman (2000).

undergo intense study sessions, read and demonstrate their understanding of theoretical and policy issues, and criticize themselves and others for mistakes. The campaign used the threat of physical and psychological violence to make cadres submit fully to the party and to Mao in particular (Apter and Saich 1994). Many cadres were arrested, tortured, and even killed after they had confessed their mistakes. With Cheng Feng as "a baptism in fire," the CCP came close to being reborn as a religious sect and the Red Army close to being molded into a holy army (van de Ven 1995).

The Cheng Feng campaign enshrined Mao's version of history and his supremacy in the party.[20] The texts that cadres studied came mostly from Mao, who rewrote the history of previous power struggles in the party to project himself as the savior of the CCP in its tortuous history (Apter and Saich 1994). Mao already had assumed control of the CCP on the basis of his personal charisma; he now sought to institutionalize it by constructing an orthodox interpretation of party history with himself at the center. By 1945, Mao's thoughts were written in the party's constitution (Wylie 1980); his rule from 1949 to 1976 has often been compared to that of an emperor (Teiwes 1990). While the strengthening of discipline in the party as a result of Cheng Feng contributed to the cohesiveness of the CCP, the cult of Mao would have ambiguous legacies.

The fierce terror imposed on the communists by the Republican state after 1927 generated the complete transformation of their movement. This transformation was not inevitable: the CCP was near total destruction at several points in the process. Nevertheless, enemy pressure forced CCP leaders to work hard to transform their party. By 1945, elite polarization produced a CCP that was essentially a party of poor peasants with a Mao-dominated cohesive leadership and a million-strong military. Victory in the four-year civil war further centralized and militarized communist organizations (Westad 2003, 328).

The ruralization, militarization, and centralization of the CCP left critical legacies for the structure of the Chinese communist state established in 1949. Two legacies of ruralization can be identified. First, the development of a relatively uniform (peasant-based) class character of the party increased its cohesiveness. Second, during its long process of ruralization, the CCP developed techniques and trained cadres for mass

---

[20] Mao would continue to be challenged, but every time he would be able to rally the top leaders behind him and defeat his challengers (as in the case of Peng Dehuai in 1959 during the Great Leap Forward).

mobilization. These techniques and cadres' experiences would become handy after the party emerged victorious in the civil war. With respect to militarization and centralization, the implications for the future state structure are obvious. Because effective coercive apparatus is a central feature of a developmental structure, the militarization of the CCP made a decisive contribution.

Elite polarization thus contributed decisively to the cohesive structure of the Maoist state. So did the CCP's controlled mobilization of the masses. Before 1945, the areas under the party's control held about one-fifth of China's population (Johnson 1962, 1). Success in mobilizing the masses to serve elite goals allowed the CCP to defeat traditional elites and establish a centralized government that reached down to village levels in these areas by 1945 (Y. Chen 1984, 504–9; Keating 1997; Esherick 1998). Violent mass mobilizing campaigns helped the CCP to recruit new local cadres who were implicated in the violence and thus became dedicated to ensuring that class enemies would not be reinstituted (Esherick 1994, 1073). These loyal cadres would dominate local governments by 1950. Second, cadres skilled in controlled mobilization tactics would help the Maoist state to quickly consolidate its rule over the rest of China after 1949. The state could effectively subject Chinese peasants and workers to greater demands for their labor to build socialism. This effectiveness perhaps explains the absence of any large-scale rebellions despite the deaths of twenty million peasants during the Great Leap Forward.

ONGOING SOCIALIST REVOLUTION ON MAINLAND CHINA, 1949–1960

By the time Mao proclaimed the People's Republic in 1949, the CCP had accumulated substantial structural assets to build a strong Chinese state. At the core was a seasoned Communist Party with a cohesive centralized leadership, a sharply differentiated and mythologized "correct line" associated with Mao, and a four-million-strong military wing.[21] The party and military were well integrated and had relatively uniform class character. Most Red Army soldiers were members of the CCP, and most CCP members were poor peasants. With the Cheng Feng campaign from 1942 to 1944, in which the cult of Mao and the methods of internal discipline crystallized, the CCP began to resemble a religious sect as much as it

---

[21] During the civil war, CCP membership increased from 1.2 million in 1945 to 2.2 million in 1947 and 4.5 million in 1949 (Schurmann 1966, 129).

resembled a modern political party (van de Ven 1991). In areas under its control, the party had extended its administrative power down to the village level with loyal and experienced cadres in charge. The party also had decades of experience in mass mobilization in the countryside.

With the hard work dedicated to organizing governments in base areas and with the massive victory in the civil war, by 1949 the CCP could form a state in which it monopolized power. The party had sufficient cadres under its command to implement its agenda in all policy areas and throughout the government bureaucracy and did not have to rely on any other groups.[22] Comparison with Vietnam in this aspect is instructive. In 1949, for propaganda purposes, CCP leaders offered several anti-GMD bourgeois groups token representation in a consultative body (O'Brien 1990). A few "democratic personalities" were selected to be ministers. Yet this was a totally different situation from the Vietnamese case in Chapter 5 where noncommunists shared real power with communists in the Viet Minh government during 1945 to 1949.

The state-forming experience also contributed to the structure of the state by helping the CCP win the Soviet alliance. The CCP's victory in the civil war greatly impressed Stalin and helped China secure Soviet aid for its socialist developmental programs (Zhang 1999). The ideological extremism of the CCP must also have impressed Soviet leaders. As Mao unequivocally declared in July 1949 after seizing Beijing,

The experiences of 40 years (of Sun Yat-sen) and 28 years (of the Chinese Communist Party) show that, without exception, the Chinese people either lean to the side of imperialism or to the side of socialism. To sit on the fence is impossible; a third road doesn't exist. We oppose the Chiang Kai-shek reactionary clique who leans to the side of imperialism; we also oppose the illusion of a third road.[23]

It should be noted that, up to 1948, the Soviet Union still maintained good relations with the GMD regime. At the same time, the Soviet Union had only low-key contacts with the CCP (N. Jun 1999). Chinese communists' military prowess and ideological strength persuaded Stalin to reverse his policies by 1949. The outcome was a Sino-Soviet treaty of mutual defense

---

[22] While the shortage of manpower was a problem here and there, the CCP always had sufficient reserves of experienced cadres to control the process in most large urban centers. According to a study of Wuhan in the 1960s, for example, cadres who had joined the revolution before 1945 formed the majority of provincial leadership (Kau 1969, 230).

[23] Mao Zedong, July 1, 1949 (Brandt et al. 1973, 453).

and assistance signed in early 1950. Given the long-standing Soviet relationship with the GMD government, the young Maoist state could not have secured this treaty without the decades-long process of confrontation that enabled it to develop extraordinary military capabilities and ideological sophistication. The treaty in turn offered it a crucial alliance that formed an element of its cohesive structure. Despite recurrent tensions in the relationship, throughout the 1950s, Soviet and Eastern European aid funded hundreds of industrial projects. Alliance with the Soviet bloc was critical for China to fulfill many goals of its First Five-Year Plan (Lin et al. 1996, 36).

The CCP was by no means guaranteed immediate and total domination in 1949. After nearly four decades of civil strife and four years of civil war, order was not easily reinstituted. The party controlled significant areas before 1945, but these accounted for only one-fifth of the population. Its experience in mobilizing rural masses was not particularly useful for urban areas where cohesive social groups such as labor gangs and secret societies had long grown their roots. Still, compared to the Vietnamese case discussed in the next chapter, the CCP had a more solid foundation upon which to build.

Clear evidence of a cohesive state structure can be found in the domestic campaigns and in the Korean War. The security challenges facing the Chinese socialist state, after having taken over most GMD territories in a quick victory, were daunting. These domestic problems were further compounded by external threats. Less than a year after the birth of the People's Republic, the Korean War broke out, bringing China to face the most advanced armies on earth. As it mobilized for the war, the Chinese state launched a series of vicious campaigns that lasted for three years: the "anti-counterrevolutionary," "three-anti" (waste, bureaucratism, and commandism), "five-anti" (bribery, tax evasion, theft of state property, cheating on government contracts, and stealing state economic secrets), and thought reform campaigns.[24] These campaigns sought to suppress domestic opposition while transforming society according to the socialist blueprint. Rampant violence was directed against former GMD members, secret society leaders, and other potential class enemies (Perry 1985;

---

[24] The Three-Anti campaign targeted corrupt urban cadres, most of whom were new recruits or holdovers from the GMD government. The Five-Antis was ostensibly aimed only at lawbreaking capitalists but in fact targeted the national bourgeoisie as a class. Thought reform was intended to purge intellectuals whose sins included, inter alia, sympathy to "American cultural imperialism."

Strauss 2002).[25] At least half a million executions and millions of sentences of hard labor, not to mention thousands of suicides, may have resulted from these campaigns (Teiwes 1993, 37–8). Capitalists and intellectuals had to go through mass denunciation sessions and mass trials. These campaigns also organized residents into groups, recruited loyal local cadres, and established local organizations (Vogel 1969; Lieberthal 1980; Strauss 2002).

Concurrent with the massive violence directed against urban elites was the "land reform" that targeted rural elites in former GMD territories.[26] "Land reform" had been implemented during the civil war in areas under communist control, followed by a radical campaign for the rest of the country in late 1950 (Shue 1980, 41–96). By 1951, "land reform" was mostly completed and Chinese leaders quickly moved on to the next stage of collectivization (Bernstein 1967; D. Yang 1996). At first, mutual aid teams were established in 1949 and 1950 following the completion of "land reform." Some peasant resistance caused a retreat, but the CCP launched a second drive in late 1953. By the end of 1954, 60 percent of rural households had joined one of the many forms of cooperatives, up from 40 percent a year earlier. After a brief consolidation phase partly in response to widespread peasants' resistance and sabotage, another "socialist high tide" swept through the Chinese countryside during 1955 and 1956. Going with the tide, more than 96 percent of households joined cooperatives, with 87 percent in high-level ones, by the end of 1956. Not only did more high-level cooperatives spring up, but the size of all cooperatives grew: from an average of ten households in 1950, to twenty by 1954, and forty-five by 1957. In a mere six years, the Chinese collectivization campaign overcame significant resistance to reach an unprecedented large scale.

Given the scope of the domestic challenges and the radical goals of not only suppressing opposition but also transforming society, the swift success of these campaigns was astonishing and pointed to a cohesive structure for the young Chinese state. The vigorous and close-knit secret societies and labor gangs in the cities could not have been subdued without an effective coercive and administrative apparatus well versed in

---

[25] For the Five-Anti campaign in Shanghai, see Gardner (1969); for the Anti-Counterrevolutionary and Five-Anti campaigns in Canton (Guangzhou), see Vogel (1969. 134–8). For similar campaigns in Tianjin, see Lieberthal (1980).

[26] In contrast with land reforms in most contexts, which primarily involve land redistribution, "land reforms" as carried out in China (1947–51) and North Vietnam (1953–6) were essentially rural class struggles (Moise 1983). See also note 2 in Chapter 5.

tactics of mass mobilization (Lieberthal 1980). Similarly, the successful "land reform" and collectivization that allowed the state to destroy local elites and bring rural society under direct state supervision could not have happened without a cohesive state structure. This structure enabled top leaders to formulate and implement unprecedented radical programs throughout their vast country over the resistance of class enemies. The Chinese success contrasted starkly with the suspended class struggle campaign in rural Vietnam. In particular, the Vietnamese case, discussed in Chapter 5, demonstrates that cohesive leadership and party organization were critical factors in Chinese achievements.

In terms of external challenges, the Korean War is instructive for what it revealed about the role of war in the Chinese case compared with the Korean case, and about China's cohesive state structure in comparison with Vietnam. First, the Korean War (and the continuing tension with Taiwan) clearly moved the CCP's socialist programs to the top of its agenda and greatly radicalized them. The Korean War shattered any Chinese pretensions of inclusiveness and brought the process of state and socialist building to full speed (Weiss 1981).[27] As Ezra Vogel (1969, 61–2) argues, "It is doubtful if the campaign against former soldiers and their sympathizers [in Guangzhou] would have been so severe without the Korean War." To meet the great costs incurred by the war, the government launched massive campaigns to mobilize manpower and resources and accelerated its program of heavy industrial development. War with "imperialists" exacerbated the tension between the state and its perceived class enemies, especially suspected spies for the United States and capitalists who took advantage of wartime scarcity to get rich.

Second, the success of the Chinese state in waging a war with the most advanced militaries in the world *while carrying through a radical social agenda* is instructive for our study of Vietnam in Chapter 5. Vietnam specialists have often argued that Vietnam was hindered in its socialist ambitions because of its war with France (C. White 1981).[28] Yet the Chinese case suggests that those specialists lacking a comparative perspective

---

[27] Lawrence Weiss (1981) argues that CCP leaders did not intend to engage in socialist construction right after 1949 and a moderate, inclusive PRC was still a real possibility before the Korean War. Weiss believes that the Korean War profoundly radicalized Chinese policies; in contrast, most other observers acknowledge the influence of the war but contend that these radical policies had been in the making for a long time (see, e.g., Teiwes 1993).

[28] Kerkvliet et al. (1998, 7) also cite wars as the main reason why North Vietnam lagged behind China in leading rural transformation.

omit a critical variable, which is state structure. With a cohesive structure, the CCP could overcome far more challenges; without it, similarly radical Vietnamese communists were simply stalled in their tracks.

Thanks to its cohesive structure at birth, the CCP was able to establish effective rule over the entire country in a short time; obtain crucial Soviet aid; suppress resistance from intellectuals, capitalists, and GMD leftovers; and successfully carry out radical "land reform" and collectivization campaigns. All of this was accomplished while China's Red Army fought the American-led United Nations' forces to a standstill in Korea. Domestic and external challenges did not weaken but in fact strengthened the state and radicalized its social agenda.

THE CULT OF MAO AND THE DECLINE OF THE MAOIST STATE

The previous section has demonstrated the positive contributions of state-forming politics to the structure of the Maoist state. Yet, although the Long March and Yan'an periods were decisive in forming a centralized and cohesive CCP, these also were the times when Mao Zedong secured his godlike status in the party. Mao's near-divine authority, coupled with his belief in mass mobilization as a policy tool, generated a series of grave mistakes that nearly destroyed the developmental state he helped to build.

The first mistake was the rectification campaign in 1957 that called on intellectuals and the masses to denounce "subjectivism," "bureaucratism," and "sectarianism" in the party (Goldman 1967, 158–242; Teiwes 1993, 77–85). While bottom-up feedback may be helpful for policy evaluation purposes, developmental states are effective primarily thanks to their internal cohesion and external domination over society. In response to calls from Mao for "a hundred flowers to bloom," intellectuals and urban citizens bombarded party leaders and government bureaucrats with increasingly harsh criticisms. Few of these criticisms directly challenged party rule. At the same time, they were not the "gentle breeze and mild rains" that the CCP had expected. Faced with demoralization among party ranks and unprecedented expression of mass discontent, Mao and his comrades sought to correct their mistake with an "Anti-Rightist" campaign in late 1957. This campaign effectively silenced critics of the regime, but it also foretold subsequent events.

A second mistake was the Great Leap Forward campaign in industry and agriculture in early 1958. This campaign was a complex event. On the one hand, it testified to the cohesive structure of the Chinese state and its hegemony over society established in earlier campaigns. Together with overambitious industrial production goals to catch up with the United States and Britain in a few years, the Leap authorized collectivization on a gargantuan scale with huge "people's communes" consisting of thousands of households (Bernstein 1984; D. Yang 1996; Domenach 1995; Lieberthal 1993). Millions of peasants were mobilized to build large irrigation facilities simply by manual labor and to produce steel in their backyard furnaces. On the other hand, despite causing a famine that claimed at least twenty million peasants' lives during 1959 and 1960,[29] the Leap did not generate significant unrest. At the same time, the campaign caused considerable discord within the leadership and tension with the Soviet Union (Lieberthal 1993, 104–8; Zhang 1999, 204–5). The Leap both weakened the internal cohesion of the CCP and foreshadowed the subsequent Sino-Soviet conflict. In 1960, following many critical exchanges between the two countries, the Soviet Union withdrew all its advisers and discontinued aid to China.

The most serious mistake was made when Mao ordered a party rectification through a "Socialist Education Campaign" in the mid-1960s (H. Y. Lee 1978; Harding 1993). Mao's motivations in launching this so-called Great Proletarian Cultural Revolution ranged from personal to ideological: he was angered by criticisms of the Great Leap failures, concerned about the return of "spontaneous capitalism" through unauthorized decollectivization, apprehensive about "Soviet revisionism" associated with Khrushchev, and manipulated by ambitious subordinates, including his wife Jiang Qing and Minister of Defense Lin Biao. Following a leadership struggle in mid-1966 that led to the removal of many top leaders whom Mao disliked, student and worker groups were mobilized to challenge the authority of the party in their units. These students and workers were primarily those who had until then been marginalized because of their class backgrounds (children of bourgeois classes) or their employment status (temporary and contract workers). Children of cadres and privileged state workers quickly galvanized to oppose them. Soon party and state authority in cities throughout China collapsed under the pressure of radical student and worker groups. After nearly two years of chaos, Mao intervened and ordered the military to suppress the radicals.

---

[29] The causes of this famine were complex. As peasants were mobilized to work away from their fields, and as their lands and animals were turned over to commune governments, less effort and care were devoted to agricultural production. Communal mess halls that allowed peasants to eat as much as they wanted reduced local reserves. Another main cause was the sharp increase in state grain procurement based on production results exaggerated by local officials (D. Yang 1996).

The costs for the developmental state were grave: between 60 and 80 percent of the nation's technocrats and officials were purged at all levels of government and, if they survived, would regain their positions only a decade later. Hundreds of thousands of intellectuals and professionals languished in labor camps.[30] By the end of the Cultural Revolution, the Maoist state had suffered serious damages, even though it did not collapse.

CONCLUSION

This chapter has studied state formation politics in China during the first half of the twentieth century when two major elite groups emerged and vied for power. The Republican state was born out of a mixture of confrontation and accommodation. Elite compromise was the predominant dynamic of alignment among the elites. Widespread mass suppression was carried out together with the incorporation of local warlords. State leaders had ambitious visions and succeeded in establishing core elements of a developmental structure, including relatively effective coercive institutions, a modern bureaucracy, and an alliance with German capital. Yet the Republican state suffered from important structural weaknesses. Opposition to Chiang Kai-shek's leadership from within the GMD and from urban intellectual groups was vigorous. Warlords were still in control of their own provinces and often conspired to challenge central authority. The Japanese invasion exposed the structural weaknesses of the Republican state and eventually brought about its defeat at the hands of its communist nemesis.

By contrast, the Maoist state followed the path of confrontation marked by elite polarization and controlled mass mobilization. This mode produced a state structure with even greater cohesion than the Korean states and the Indonesian state under Suharto discussed in Chapters 2 and 3. Over two decades, as the communists fought to survive in the face of relentless GMD pressure, the CCP and the Red Army underwent ruralization, militarization, and centralization. The outcome of these processes included a cohesive and experienced leadership under Mao, a centralized Leninist party, and a battle-tested guerrilla army of uniformly poor peasants. The communist victory in the civil war, coupled with the

---

[30] The costs in human lives and the social and political consequences of the Cultural Revolution were enormous: according to official figures, about half a million urban residents died as a result of persecution.

CCP's ideological strength, won critical Soviet support. These assets were sufficient to form a developmental state structure when the CCP established its rule over mainland China in 1949. China's involvement in the Korean War and tensions with Taiwan contributed to the rapid consolidation of the state just as it carried out massive transformation of society and the economy in a series of violent but effective campaigns. Despite the radical nature of the changes, the high degree of violence unleashed against certain groups, and the sufferings of starving peasants, the state managed to carry through its socioeconomic agenda. Toward the 1960s, a legacy of state formation politics – the cult of Mao – caused significant destruction of state structure, although the institutional pillars of the state, especially the Red Army, were not overthrown.

State formation in Vietnam, discussed in the next chapter, followed very different patterns. Accommodation but not confrontation was the dominant path. There were also consequences for this path as we would expect. Unlike the Maoist state, which pursued one radical campaign after another, the Vietnamese state lost its momentum after the first campaigns – the "land reform" and "organizational rectification." Like the Indonesian state in the 1950s but unlike the Maoist state, the Vietnamese state did not have the kind of structure to support its developmental goals.

5

Vietnam

Accommodation and Arrested Revolution

VIETNAM AND CHINA IN CONTRAST

Unlike South Korea and Indonesia, which lie far apart geographically, China and Vietnam[1] share a border, and their development paths were not always separate for both ideological and geopolitical reasons. From the 1920s through the early 1960s, the Soviet Union was a source of ideological inspiration as well as practical assistance and doctrinal guidance for both Chinese and Vietnamese communists, who studied Lenin and Stalin in translation, toured Soviet modern factories and collective farms built under Stalin, and received training from Soviet advisers in revolution and administration.

The Vietnamese also received extensive policy guidance in the 1950s from their Chinese comrades, who were more experienced in revolution and state making. Chinese experiences were useful to Vietnam because the historical contexts facing both revolutions were fundamentally similar: both sought to build socialism in predominantly rural, backward countries under the constant threat of "imperialist" attacks. "Land reform" was a particular area where Vietnam learned much from China.[2] The

---

[1] Due to limited information available for subsequent periods, this chapter focuses only on the period of 1945–60. Geographically, I limit the analysis to northern and north central Vietnam – in particular the area under communist control.

[2] "Land reforms" in China (1947–51) and North Vietnam (1953–6) were essentially rural class struggles (Moise 1983). Their ultimate goals were to overthrow the rural social order and consolidate communist rule. Redistributing land to tillers was only one of several steps in the struggle and was neither the ultimate goal nor the highest priority from the perspective of communist leaders in both countries, who were not interested in maintaining *private* ownership – equal or not. Land redistribution was a mere tactic to

Soviet Union never implemented any land redistribution; Chinese communists developed their own expertise on the issue, and their Vietnamese comrades benefited from consulting China's policies and working with Chinese advisers in Vietnam.

Despite similar conditions and so much shared knowledge among their leaders, several indicators show a striking contrast in the character of socialist development between the two countries. China's average annual economic growth rate between 1953 and 1978 was 6 percent (Lin et al. 1996, 71). An equivalent indicator for North Vietnam is not available, but on the whole Vietnam failed to expand the productive capacity of its economy, whereas China succeeded (Fforde 1999, 49). Vietnam's industrial growth, if any, was financed almost entirely by aid from the Soviet bloc, not by the mobilization of domestic resources as in China (Fforde and Paine 1987, ch. 3). This fact is demonstrated in the accumulation rates in the two economies: the Chinese rate of accumulation as a share of total output was more than 30 percent in the mid-1970s, whereas the respective rate for North Vietnam was about 12 percent, largely financed through foreign aid (Fforde 1999, 51). The rate of state procurement of grain averaged 29 percent in the Soviet Union from 1930 to 1932, 28 percent in China from 1953 to 1957, and only 17 percent in North Vietnam from 1961 to 1965 (Vickerman 1986, 7; see also Table 6).

mobilize peasants' support at a stage in the struggle for power. As soon as communist leaders felt secure, they would want to, and did, take away lands from all peasants in the name of socialist development. Unlike land reforms in other contexts (e.g., South Korea and Taiwan), which granted peasants permanent ownership of their land, "land reforms" in China and North Vietnam offered few lasting benefits to peasants, if any. These "land reforms" simply replaced landlords' exploitation with state exploitation through collectivization. Excessive state exploitation and poor management of cooperatives led to the starvation of more than 20 million peasants in China during the early 1960s and contributed to chronic hunger and the famines of 1979 and 1988 in Vietnam (D. Yang 1996 on China; interviews in Hanoi during 2002–5 and personal observation in Ho Chi Minh City during 1978–90). After fifteen years of reform, 18 percent of Vietnamese were still "undernourished" or "malnourished" by 2003 compared to the regional average of 10 percent (*Tuoi Tre* [Youth], July 10, 2003, citing United Nations Human Development Report). By killing and dispossessing landlords and rich peasants, these "land reforms" also destroyed an important source of rural entrepreneurship with long-term consequences for rural development. As shown in a study of the rural transition in China and Vietnam since decollectivization, nearly half of successful farmer households had a family tradition of moneymaking before the revolution, whereas only about 10 percent of successful households had poor peasant backgrounds (Luong and Unger 1998, 84–5). For accounts that treat Vietnam's "land reform" as a policy that benefited peasants, see C. White (1981) and Dang P. (2002). An official account that makes the same argument is Hoang U. et al. (1968).

TABLE 6. *Agricultural Stagnation in North Vietnam,*
1961–1973

Three-Year Average Based on Annual Production	1961–5	1966–9	1970–3
Production (million tons)	5.21	4.82	5.19
Procurement (million tons)	0.90	0.68	0.88
Rice import (million tons)	0.12	0.60	0.81
Procurement (as % of production)	17.3	14.2	16.9

Source: Calculated from File no. 595, Ministry of Grains and Foodstuffs, Trung Tam Luu Tru Quoc Gia III, appendix, 1, 22, and 25.

Under the Vietnamese Workers' Party (VWP),[3] collectivization was modest compared to the goals, scope, and scale of China's Great Leap Forward (Kerkvliet 2005). The latter not only built commune-level cooperatives but also mobilized massive peasant labor for irrigation and for backyard steel projects. In contrast, Vietnam's collectivization raised neither production nor procurement of surpluses. The country also reported no large-scale mobilization of peasant labor for agricultural development projects as in China's Great Leap Forward (GLF). Vietnamese state and cooperative sectors were not able to dominate domestic commerce as much as their Chinese counterparts (Abrami 2002, 9).

Vietnamese cities saw fewer political campaigns, and those that were launched were timid by Chinese standards. No national counterrevolutionary and "five-anti" campaigns were ever launched in North Vietnam. A campaign to "transform capitalism" was conducted from 1958 to 1960, as a result of which capitalists lost most of their assets to the state (Nguyen T. N. T. 1999). Many perhaps committed suicide or ended up in labor camps, but fewer public mass denunciations or trials took place than in China. During 1955 and 1956, many Vietnamese intellectuals and party members voiced bitter criticism against government policies, from rural class struggle to household registration rules to state encroachments on artistic freedoms (Ninh 2002). This was the so-called Nhan Van-Giai Pham affair, the Vietnamese version of the Chinese Hundred Flower event.[4] In response, the state imposed tighter control over artistic activities and meted out hard-labor sentences to many

---

[3] This was the name of the Indochinese Communist Party (ICP) from 1951 to 1976. After 1976, the name was changed to Vietnamese Communist Party (VCP).

[4] In contrast with the Hundred Flowers event in China, where intellectuals responded to Mao's calls for criticism, Vietnamese critics acted on their own initiatives.

intellectuals. This selective punishment was no match for the scale of terror employed in Mao's Anti-Rightist campaign.

Clearly Vietnamese socialism followed a moderate path relative to China. This phenomenon invites two hypotheses: either Vietnamese leaders as a group were more modest in their ambitions, or they were somehow hindered in their efforts to take a radical path. Those who make the first hypothesis often point to the influence of the "moderate" Ho Chi Minh (e.g., Elliott 1976). Yet the Vietnamese "land reform" campaign from 1953 to 1956, when Ho was party chairman, testified that Vietnamese communists could be as radical and murderous as their comrades elsewhere. In May 1953, on the eve of the campaign, the VWP Politburo chaired by Ho authorized the execution of landlords by a ratio of one person for every one thousand people, or 0.1 percent of the population.[5] This Vietnamese ratio approximated the ratio of actual executions in China's "land reform" campaign.[6]

According to the second hypothesis, it has been argued that the Vietnamese state after its birth was burdened with the double tasks of fighting the French and unifying the country.[7] These tasks not only diverted resources away from building socialism but also made class struggle less appropriate as a strategy (C. White 1981). On a closer look, however, this argument does not hold across all periods or in comparative perspective. No doubt the war for independence did not allow the leadership to focus exclusively on socialist construction in North Vietnam. At the height of this war in 1953, however, class struggle and social revolution were viewed by most party leaders as supporting, not contradicting, the goal of independence (Vu T. 2010b). At the same time, national unification by force was not considered the desired strategy by the leadership

---

[5] "Chi thi cua Bo Chinh Tri" (Politburo's Decree), May 4, 1953 (Dang Cong San Viet Nam, hereafter DCSVN, 2001, 14: 201). Based on other sources, Edwin Moise (2001, 7–9) accepts an estimate close to 15,000 executions. This was about 0.1 percent of the total population of 13.5 million in North Vietnam in 1955.

[6] Benedict Stavis (cited in Shue 1980, 80) estimates the official number of executions in China during 1949–52 to be between 400,000 and 800,000. (These executions may also have come from other campaigns besides land reform in the same period, and if unofficial deaths are added, the total number could reach more than a million.) If 500,000 deaths (officially and unofficially) can be assumed to be specifically related to land reform, then the proportion was also about 0.1 percent in the total population of 572 million Chinese in 1952.

[7] Here I refer to the Franco-Vietnamese War (1946–54) only, as North Vietnam's war with South Vietnam and the United States began after 1960, which lies beyond the time frame of this chapter. As I argue later, the civil war in the 1960s did divert the North Vietnamese state from its goal of socialist construction.

from the Geneva conference up to the late 1950s. How unification became a priority over the competing task of building socialism in North Vietnam hinged on an internal power struggle among elites and needs to be explained as well. Finally, in the 1950s China was just as burdened by war as Vietnam: in Korea it fought to a stalemate the most powerful army on earth, the American-led Allied forces, when the People's Republic was less than a year old.[8] What is more, the Maoist state was fighting this war while successfully carrying out a radical agenda on the mainland. As Table 6 indicates, North Vietnam's rate of grain procurement from 1961 to 1965, before the civil war and U.S. bombing escalated, was already low and equal to about half the Chinese rate in the mid-1950s.

If war does not explain the relative ineffectiveness of the Vietnamese state in the late 1950s and early 1960s, what else hindered the course of socialist development in Vietnam? This chapter focuses on the period of 1945 to 1960 and argues that the Vietnamese state's failure to carry through rural class struggle in the 1950s and the subsequent moderation in the Vietnamese socialist course resulted primarily from its lack of a developmental structure. This shortage in developmental assets in turn was the result of its pattern of state formation. We have seen in Chapter 4 how elite polarization and controlled mobilization in China produced a cohesive Maoist developmental state when it was founded in 1949. In contrast, the Vietnamese state was born out of accommodation. Similar to its Indonesian counterpart, this state attempted developmental policies prematurely without a developmental structure. This led to leadership change, the temporary suspension of socialist construction programs, and the moderate character of the subsequent course of development.

This chapter begins with a discussion of Vietnam's colonial legacies to facilitate comparison with other cases in the study. Compared to Indonesia, colonial rule did not contribute to but in fact hampered the rise of a developmental state structure in Vietnam. Then I focus on state formation processes in Vietnam, highlighting the early compromises among

---

[8] The two wars were not equivalent in every aspect. On the one hand, the Korean War (1950–3) was shorter than the Franco-Vietnamese War (1946–54), and China was fighting the Korean War on a foreign territory. On the other, the Korean War was on a much larger scale. Besides hundreds of thousands of UN troops and Korean soldiers on both sides, there were about 700,000 Chinese and 300,000 Americans (J. Chen 1994, 151; Summers 1990, 289). In the Franco-Vietnamese War, there were about 200,000 French and foreign troops fighting 291,000 Viet Minh soldiers (Goscha forthcoming; Prados 2007, 221). The Korean War was a conventional war from the start, whereas the Franco-Vietnamese War was a guerrilla war until 1950, when China helped organize and supply several Vietnamese regular divisions with sophisticated weapons.

Vietnamese elites when they established the Viet Minh state in August 1945. As in Indonesia, this state was founded by incorporating numerous spontaneous uprisings all over Vietnam following Japan's surrender. Accommodation produced divided state leadership, fractured organizations, and a decentralized structure lacking both a cohesive social base and a crucial foreign alliance. Finally, I consider the effect of these legacies of state formation politics on the structure of the Vietnamese state and its socialist construction agenda.

COLONIAL LEGACIES

The French took over Vietnam gradually in the latter half of the nineteenth century. First taking Cochinchina (southern Vietnam) as a colony in the 1860s, they set up protectorates of Tonkin (North Vietnam) and Annam (Central Vietnam) in the 1880s. The colonizing process was initially driven by French militarists and missionaries, with the French government reluctantly becoming involved. Because colonization followed a halting pattern, unified rule over the entire Indochina (the three Vietnamese regions plus Laos and Cambodia) and financial independence of the colony were not established until the last decade of the century (Ennis 1936, 80–8). Even after this period, the three regions of Vietnam kept distinct administrative regimes (Robequain 1944, 9–11). Cochinchina was a full colony directly administered by French civil servants, whereas in Annam the Vietnamese emperor retained nominal sovereignty and native officials worked side by side with the French. Tonkin was nominally a protectorate like Annam but was in fact ruled more directly by the French. While the French governor general and French residents superior in all regions had real authority, the mandarin elite and local governments were preserved in Annam and Tonkin. Toward the 1920s, the French gradually constructed a more effective modern bureaucracy while implementing many socioeconomic development projects.

Among the three countries in this study that experienced colonialism, Indochina's experience of French rule is often considered the worst relative to Dutch rule in Indonesia and Japanese rule in Korea (Sharp 1946; Kohli 2004). French rule in Indochina was relatively less intensive, more exploitative, and left behind fewer positive legacies. I examine two relevant areas in comparative terms: socioeconomic development and state building. The most impressive socioeconomic achievement under the French was infrastructural development. In Cochinchina, more than 1,200 kilometers of canals were dug through forests and marshes, which resulted in quadrupling the cultivated area for rice between 1880 and 1937 (Robequain 1944, 111, 220). The expansion of cultivated area made possible a ten-times increase in rice production, a nearly three-times increase in population in Cochinchina, and a five-times increase in rice exports from Saigon during the same period.[9] Besides canals, a trans-Indochina railroad system was built in the first decade of the twentieth century. By 1945, this system had a total mileage of 1,550 kilometers, or half the length of the Korean system built by the Japanese.[10] Indochina had about 17,500 kilometers of "metalled" roads and 27,500 kilometers of "banked" roads in 1936, whereas the comparable number for Korea was 50,000 kilometers of motor roads (Robequain 1944, 92, 99).

No comparable growth statistics are available, but various indicators suggest that Indochina lagged far behind the Dutch Indies, not to mention Korea, in foreign trade and investment. Despite large increases in rice exports and significant French investments in rubber plantations and coal mines, Indochina's per capita foreign trade volume was the lowest among Southeast Asian colonies – only 62, 42, and 36 percent of comparable volume in the Dutch Indies, the Philippines, and British Burma, respectively (Sharp 1946, 52).[11] Total European and American investments in the Dutch Indies exceeded $2 billion, whereas investment was less than $400 million in Indochina. Per capita investments still showed that the Dutch Indies enjoyed twice the level of investment of Indochina (Sharp 1946). In part, this resulted from French policy to restrict foreign investments from other countries to the exclusive benefit of French companies. French interests were to be protected at the cost of colonial development. Fears of a proletariat in the colony and concerns about unemployment in France discouraged the French government from supporting industrialization in Indochina until 1940 (Hardy 1998, 813, 818). The colonial government made no efforts to promote an indigenous entrepreneurial class, while repressive labor policies were implemented to serve the need of French capital (Murray 1980, 232–3).

With regard to state building, the French presence in Indochina paled compared to the Dutch in Indonesia and the Japanese in Korea. In 1937 about 42,000 Europeans lived in Indochina, making up less than

[9] Murray (1980, 449) mentions that rice production in Cochinchina increased from roughly 300,000 tons in 1870 to 3 million tons in 1930.

[10] The Indochinese system included another 464 kilometers of tracks located in Yunnan, China.

[11] However, note that per capita foreign trade volume in Indochina was about the same as Thailand, twice the figure in India, and higher than in China (Robequain 1944, 307n).

0.2 percent of the total population, compared to 240,000 Dutch in the Dutch Indies (0.4 percent) and 570,000 Japanese in Korea (2.6 percent) (Robequain 1944, 21; Maddison 1989, 660). French officials numbered about 3,900 (0.02 percent of total population), compared to nearly 12,000 Dutch officials (0.76 percent) (Robequain 1944, 29; Maddison 1989, 659). One exception stands out: the French overtook the Dutch in terms of coercive forces. Before 1940, the Indochinese colonial army comprised about 27,000 troops (including 11,000 French and 16,000 natives), or 1 soldier for every 852 natives (McAlister 1969, 50).[12] The comparable number for the Dutch was 38,000 (9,000 Dutch), or 1 for every 1,600 natives (Maddison 1989, 659; Elson 2001, 8). Even here the French ratio was still about half of the Japanese ratio in Korea, as cited in Chapter 3.

Overall, the French left little behind in terms of *capitalist* developmental institutions. By 1940, the Indochinese economy was kept totally dependent on France with little industrialization permitted or encouraged. The colonial bureaucracy was built on top of traditional institutions and had a shallow reach compared to other cases in this study. Yet this comparison of colonial legacies between Indochina and the other two cases in an important sense is inappropriate because some colonial legacies carried different implications for Indochina than they did for both South Korea and Indonesia. In the latter two cases, because the postcolonial elites pursued *capitalist* development, the more advanced state–capital relations and colonial bureaucratization were under colonial rule, the better the prospects were for the postcolonial construction of a developmental state. But because Vietnamese state elites espoused a *socialist* developmental vision, the development of those same colonial institutions left ambivalent and perhaps negative legacies for them because such institutions often had a conservative character, whereas elite goals required radical changes. A more developed *capitalist* colonial economy, for example, meant more powerful class enemies to deal with down the road for postcolonial *communist* leaders. So did a larger colonial bureaucracy. In fact, the inheritance of colonial elites and institutions created many problems for Vietnamese communists.

In comparative perspective, the underdevelopment of capitalism under French rule ironically gave Vietnam some advantage over Maoist China in *socialist* development. Because pre-1949 China experienced greater

---

[12] By March 1945, the colonial army had about 76,000 troops, of which 55,000 were natives (McAlister 1969, 114, 301).

capitalist development in Manchuria, in the foreign settlements and in the coastal areas, the Maoist state must have faced greater social resistance. This made Vietnam's modest performance even more puzzling.

ACCOMMODATION AND THE BIRTH OF THE VIET MINH STATE, 1945–1946

When Mao proclaimed the People's Republic of China (PRC) in October 1949, millions of communist troops were sweeping the crumbling GMD government from mainland China. When Ho Chi Minh proclaimed the founding of the Democratic Republic of Vietnam (DRV) in September 1945, his Indochinese Communist Party (ICP) had less than five thousand members scattered around Vietnam with little centralized communication and a militia of probably a few thousand poorly equipped men and women. While Mao proudly appeared in public as the leader of the Chinese *Communist* Party and forcefully declared his support for the socialist camp against imperialists, Ho was careful not to reveal that he had once been a dedicated Comintern agent. In his Declaration of Independence, Ho borrowed the language of freedom and equality from none other than the United States, the leader of the imperialist camp (Marr 1995, 533). We have seen how the proclamation of the PRC was the culmination of a decades-long confrontation; I argue in this section that the Vietnamese event was the result of a consequential accommodation long overlooked by Vietnam historians.[13]

As in Indonesia, decolonization and state formation in Vietnam began with Japan's invasion, but the role of the Japanese here was less

---

[13] The standard accounts of this event are Tonnesson (1991) and Marr (1995). Both are significant contributions but can benefit from the new sources that have since become available. As Marr (1995, 152, n. 1) admits, "We are entirely dependent on Communist Party sources for the events described here and much that follows. As indicated in the preface, I have ignored unconfirmed assertions apparently designed to convince readers of the infallibility or omnipresence of the Party." On noncommunists, Marr (1995, 92) describes Vu Dinh Hoe as "a regular contributor to *Thanh Nghi*," while he was in fact the journal's cofounder and executive manager (*chu nhiem*). Another key member of this group was Do Duc Duc, whose name is misspelled as "Do Duc Dung" in Marr (1995, 200, n. 184). My account relies primarily on the following sources, which were either unavailable or barely used in works published just a decade ago: Viet Minh newsletter *Viet Nam Doc Lap* (1941–5); communist journal *Su That* (1945–50); noncommunist journal *Thanh Nghi* (1941–5); anticommunist newspaper *Viet Nam* and journal *Chinh Nghia* (1945–6); the 1995 and 2000 memoirs of the key noncommunist leader Vu Dinh Hoe; and *Van Kien Dang Toan Tap* (Collected Party Documents), 1924–60. See the bibliography for a full list of other newspapers consulted.

straightforward. In the Dutch Indies, Japanese forces landed, quickly defeated the Dutch colonial army, and brought back prominent indigenous nationalists to work as advisers for the Japanese military government with a promise of future independence. In French Indochina, Japanese forces under a different commander "took over" the colony in 1940 not through conquest but through negotiation. The French agreed to make Indochinese ports, roads, labor, and materials available for Japanese wartime needs; in return, the French colonial government was allowed to maintain its rule over Indochina.[14] With the French still in place, the Japanese had little need for Vietnamese nationalists. The colonial regime continued its effective repression of the nationalist movement.

Only in March 1945, after the fall of the Vichy government in France and in anticipation of an imminent Allied landing in Indochina, did the Japanese decide to overthrow French rule. After having interned French colonial administrators and French soldiers, the Japanese allowed the Vietnamese emperor to declare an independent Empire of Vietnam (EVN) and set up a Vietnamese administration in April 1945. Rather than selecting experienced anticolonial nationalists as they did on Java, the Japanese picked a group of successful but politically inexperienced professionals and intellectuals to form a new government in Vietnam.[15] The prime minister of this government, Tran Trong Kim, had been trained in France and was known primarily as a school inspector and historian (Nguyen Q. T. and Nguyen B. T. 1999, 894–5).

Although its leaders had limited political experience and this government lasted only four months, its historical role was by no means inconsequential (Vu N. C. 1986). Rallying to its side were many influential urban groups such as the nationalist Greater Viet Party and the Thanh Nghi (Commentaries) group.[16] Phan Anh and Vu Van Hien, two French-trained lawyers in Thanh Nghi served as ministers of youth and justice. The group set up the New Vietnam Party (Tan Viet Nam Hoi) to

[14] Control over Indochina protected Japanese forces in southern China and gave Japan a springboard to invade other countries in Southeast Asia (Tarling 1998, 51–72). On the other hand, leaving the French to administer Indochina allowed the Japanese to economize their forces that could be deployed in other territories (Truong B. L. 1973).

[15] See Tonnesson (1991, 282–6); Marr (1995, 116–17); and Shiraishi (1992) for hypotheses about Japanese motives in Indochina.

[16] This group was composed of many lawyers, doctors, and professionals who published the journal *Thanh Nghi* in Hanoi from 1941 to 1945. Some authors translate *Thanh Nghi* literally as "clear discussion," but the phrase as an idiom means "commentaries" or "criticisms" (Nguyen K. T. et al. 1996, 780; see also Vu D. H. 1995, 46).

mobilize mass support for the new government.[17] In its brief tenure, the government greatly expanded the opportunities for mass political action by removing press censorship, releasing thousands of political prisoners, and launching a vigorous youth movement in the cities.[18] Without these moves, the nationwide spontaneous uprisings that seized power when the Japanese surrendered in August 1945 would not have happened.

The Japanese coup of March 1945 catapulted the EVN government to power, but this event was, at the same time, a gift from the Japanese to the underground communist movement (Tonnesson 1991, 247). The French police until then had been effective in suppressing communists. In 1940 colonial troops crushed a rebellion led by the ICP in southern Vietnam and executed nearly all its leaders without much difficulty. In 1941 Ho Chi Minh returned to the border area of Vietnam and China and sought to revive the movement. Ho had been a founding member of the French Communist Party in 1920. A Comintern agent in southern China and Thailand in the 1920s, Ho had trained many young Vietnamese revolutionaries and helped found the ICP in 1930. He was back in the Soviet Union for most of the 1930s, when he fell out of Stalin's favor (Duiker 2000; Quinn-Judge 2002). On his return to Vietnam in 1941, Ho and surviving leaders of the ICP's underground northern branch set up the League for Vietnam's Independence (Viet Nam Doc Lap Dong Minh, or Viet Minh), a front organization controlled by communists but open to all. Following the Chinese strategy, ICP leaders sought to build up a guerrilla force and succeeded to some degree in mobilizing local support for their cause (Tonnesson 1991, 114–25, 125–32, 144–7). Under the sponsorship of Zhang Fakui, a GMD general, Ho reluctantly worked with Vietnamese nationalist groups in southern China to form a similar front, but this amounted to nothing significant (Tonnesson 1991, 122).[19] Yet before March 1945, Viet Minh had very little formal organization and maintained a precarious resistance in the face of fierce French repression (Tonnesson 1991, 131). This situation changed after the Japanese overthrew the French in March 1945. By that time, Japanese military

---

[17] According to Mr. Vu Dinh Hoe, a founder and the general secretary of New Vietnam, "hoi" as used in Vietnamese at the time also meant "dang" (political party). The explicit political mission of the group (see Chapter 6) in fact made it more similar to a political party. Interview with Mr. Hoe, Hanoi, December 2003.

[18] Phan Anh built on previous efforts by the colonial government to mobilize colonial youths for the defense of the colony in the early 1940s (Raffin 2005).

[19] Ho traveled to southern China in 1943 and was arrested by GMD forces. He was held in prison for a year before being released and asked to collaborate with other nationalist groups.

commanders were concerned mainly about preparing for an invasion by Allied forces, not about suppressing communists. The countryside was thus left open to agitation and Viet Minh quickly filled the gap.[20] While Viet Minh publicly denounced the EVN government as a Japanese puppet,[21] behind the scenes communists sought to convert its officials to their cause (Le T. N. 2000). This effort paved the way for the later compromise between the two groups.

The EVN government was only four months old when the Japanese surrendered. In the wake of massive unrest following this event and a Viet Minh challenge in the northern part of the country, this government resigned and agreed to transfer power to its rival without a fight. This compromise was significant because the EVN government could have attempted to suppress the communists: in Hanoi, where Viet Minh was strongest, pro–Viet Minh groups had fewer than one thousand support-ers with about a hundred rifles, whereas the EVN had at its disposal fifteen hundred civil guardsmen all armed with rifles (Marr 1995, 393). In return for their compromise, many EVN officials were subsequently offered positions in the Viet Minh government as ministers and deputy ministers.[22] The colonial bureaucracy, including colonial laws, proce-dures, and employees, was incorporated almost intact in the new state (Marr 2004). Thousands of colonial troops would defect and join the Viet Minh military in late 1945 (Lockhart 1989, 150, 175–6; McAlister 1969, 300–3). The birth of the Viet Minh state occurred through these important but often overlooked compromises. When Ho was sworn in as president of the Democratic Republic of Vietnam (DRV) in early Septem-ber 1945, nearly half of his cabinet positions were given to noncom-munists. Communists took control of foreign affairs, defense, interior, and information portfolios in the coalition government while yielding real authority to noncommunists in ministries of economy, agriculture, education, and justice.

This initial compromise between the two groups was sufficiently strong to survive a challenge from the right. The DRV was about five weeks old when GMD troops marched into Hanoi to disarm Japanese forces

---

[20] In an article in *Viet Nam Doc Lap* (Independent Vietnam, hereafter *VNDL*), April 30, 1945, it was acknowledged how the movement had benefited from the fall of the French.
[21] See *VNDL*, April 21, 1945.
[22] These included Phan Anh (minister of youth), Phan Ke Toai (viceroy of North Vietnam), Nguyen Van Huong (Phan Ke Toai's chief of staff), Ta Quang Buu (Phan Anh's assis-tant), Vu Trong Khanh (mayor of Hai phong), Nguyen Manh Ha (economic chief of Hai phong), Hoang Minh Giam (chief of the Japan-Vietnam Liaison Team in North Vietnam), and others.

under the terms of the Potsdam agreement (Worthington 1995, 2). Accompanying these troops from southern China were two prominent nationalist groups in exile – the Vietnamese Nationalist Party (Viet Nam Quoc Dan Dang, or VNP) and the Vietnamese Revolutionary League (Viet Nam Cach Mang Dong Minh Hoi, or VRL).[23] The VNP was led by Nguyen Tuong Tam, a prominent French-trained intellectual and novelist (Jamieson 1993, 113–14, 176–81). In the 1930s Nguyen Tuong Tam was the leader of the Self-Strength Literary Movement in Hanoi, but left for southern China during World War II to join the VNP. The VRL was led by Nguyen Hai Than, who had been active in nationalist organizations in southern China since 1905, and who had once studied and taught at the Whampoa Military Academy (Nguyen Q. T. and Nguyen B. T. 1997, 953–4). These groups seized power in many provinces with their own militias and demanded that the Viet Minh government step down. Viet Minh forces still controlled Hanoi but daily skirmishes with their rivals seriously threatened their fragile authority.

The Chinese generals were mainly interested in keeping order and disarming the Japanese. Unlike the Americans in South Korea or the British in Saigon, the Chinese in North Vietnam recognized Ho's government. As noted earlier, during 1943 and 1944 these GMD generals had encouraged collaboration among various Vietnamese nationalist groups in exile, including Viet Minh. Now they simply continued this effort by pressuring Ho to share power with the exiled nationalist groups. Too weak to stand up to the Chinese, the communists offered these nationalist parties the vice presidency, several minister portfolios, and seventy seats in a newly elected National Assembly. Ho also was forced to appoint two "nonpartisans" as interior and defense ministers. Because ICP leaders wanted to deny accusations from their rivals that the Viet Minh government was controlled by communists, they made a gesture of compromise by announcing the dissolution of the ICP in November 1945. (In fact, the party was never dissolved; it only operated in secret from then on.) At one point, Chinese pressure was so intense that Ho considered bringing the former emperor back to lead the government and resigning his position to become an "adviser" (Vu D. H. 2000, 58).[24] What the ICP offered the

---

[23] See Chapter 8 for more discussion of these groups.

[24] My account of *Thanh Nghi* and the New Vietnam Party relies heavily on Vu D. H (1995; 2000) – the memoirs of Mr. Vu Dinh Hoe, a key participant in these events as the Viet Minh's first minister of education, then its minister of justice. Born in 1912, Mr. Vu Dinh Hoe is the only noncommunist minister who is still alive. His two volumes incorporated many memoirs written by his now deceased associates such as Phan Anh and Vu Trong Khanh. Besides the memoirs, I conducted many interviews with Mr. Vu

exiled groups was not a real compromise because the communists never really handed much power to their opponents or the nonpartisan ministers.[25] As soon as the Chinese were replaced by the French and withdrew in mid-1946,[26] Ho's government purged most of the exiled nationalists; those who escaped fled to southern China.[27]

The exiled groups failed to break the pattern of elite compromise that had shaped the Viet Minh state till then. With the exiled nationalist groups aggressively mobilizing among the urban elites, the ICP came to rely more on prominent noncommunist intellectuals and businessmen in the coalition government to reach out to urban constituencies. Former EVN officials played a critical but as yet unacknowledged role in generating support for Viet Minh. These officials were influential in colonial elite circles; their family or business ties to former mandarins, colonial bureaucrats, and local elites helped lure these to the side of Viet Minh (Vu D. H. 2000, 68, 96–100). In addition, the Viet Minh government carried out numerous arrests of nationalists on the pretext that these men broke the laws. The participation of noncommunists in the government, especially in the Ministry of Justice, helped deflect the charges that the arrests were a communist purge against nationalists. The Chinese could have used these charges as an excuse to overthrow Viet Minh rule.

Following the Indonesian pattern, the Vietnamese state was born out of mass incorporation. While early research assumed Viet Minh's centralized leadership of the revolution, recent works reveal a more complex situation. Before August 1945, Viet Minh leaders mistakenly expected a U.S.-China invasion to expel the Japanese. They thus concentrated on building a militia to fight alongside the Allies (Tonnesson 1991, 336), but the invasion never occurred. When the Japanese suddenly surrendered, creating a power vacuum in the cities, it was local groups that seized power spontaneously and bloodlessly.[28] Many local groups were organized

---

Dinh Hoe between 2002 and 2006 in Hanoi and Ho Chi Minh City and consulted *Thanh Nghi* and *Doc Lap* (Independence). The latter journal was edited by the DP leadership.
[25] On the communist efforts to take control of the Interior Ministry from the nonpartisan appointee, see Le G. (2000).
[26] Chiang Kai-shek's government yielded to American pressure to let the French army replace Chinese troops. The French in return offered Chiang certain trade privileges in North Vietnam (Worthington 1995).
[27] Those who stayed on did not fare well. For example, Chu Ba Phuong, the nationalist minister of economy, was sent to a concentration camp for trying to flee the Viet Minh area; see Van Phong Quoc Hoi (2002) for the fates of many of these nationalists.
[28] Vu Ngu Chieu (1986, 313) correctly argues that the EVN government made available to the communists thousands of youths already mobilized. He regards this movement as contributing to the strength of the communists. Here I view the youths as both a boon

by underground or recently released communist cadres, but many were also mobilized by local elites or bourgeois groups.[29] In Hanoi, for example, the Democratic Party (DP), not the local ICP branch, had the most guns (Marr 1995, 393; Vu D. H. 2000, 63).[30] Non–Viet Minh groups there also raced to seize power but, for one reason or another, lost out to pro–Viet Minh groups such as the DP. Most local communists acted on their own without central ICP instructions. In many provincial centers in southern Vietnam, Vanguard Youth groups organized earlier by Phan Anh, the minister of youth in the EVN government, seized power (Marr 1995, 375, 377, 464–6). Central Viet Minh leaders and their militias arrived days or weeks later and took control of a few main cities; in most other places, these mass groups or militias claimed to be – and were simply accepted as – local Viet Minh governments.

In his detailed account of local mass uprisings throughout Vietnam in late 1945, David Marr (1995, 402) describes the confusion: "The administration established by the Viet Minh in Hanoi became as much a prisoner of the thousands of revolutionary committees emerging from around the country as the directing authority." The central government incorporated most local groups that seized local power in late 1945 regardless of their revolutionary quality or political loyalty. Policies issued by local revolutionary governments responded more to local interests and conditions than to central orders (Marr 2004). The problem of "revolutionary mandarins" was widespread after the birth of the Viet Minh state. Village-level People's Committees in particular gained notoriety for their arrogance, nepotism, collusion, arbitrary arrests, and abuses of public property.[31] As

(then) and a burden (later) for the communists with respect to their dual goals of seizing power and building socialism.

[29] The case of Kien An province (now part of Hai Phong) is typical. In late August, two bands of Viet Minh adherents of different districts opened fire on each other in their attempts to seize power, leading to three deaths. When a new provincial revolutionary people's committee was formed, its chairman belonged to the Democratic Party (see note 30), its vice chairman an ICP member, while the others included a former colonial clerk, a former education mandarin, a former district mandarin, a member of the Vietnamese Nationalist Party, and a representative of Viet Minh's women's organization (Marr 1995, 416). The situation in South Vietnam was more complex, but the general picture did not differ from that in other parts of Vietnam.

[30] A loose party of French-trained intellectuals and student leaders that the ICP helped set up in June 1944 to mobilize support among urban elites. The ICP maintained its influence on the DP through (closet) communists planted in the DP leadership. See Chapter 6 for more on the DP.

[31] See Ho Chi Minh's letter, "Thu gui Uy ban nhan dan cac ky, tinh, huyen va lang" (Letter to regional, provincial, district and village People's Committees), n.d. (DCSVN 2000,

in Indonesia, internal fighting among local militias was common. In most cases, local Viet Minh militias did not fight the Japanese. Instead, it was "old Viet Minh" groups fighting "new Viet Minh,"[32] Viet Minh militias exchanging fire with DP militias,[33] and People's Committees challenging the authority of Viet Minh committees.[34]

In sum, the communists rose to power with little bloodshed and established a new state in a short time thanks to their accommodation of former EVN officials, local mass groups, and the colonial bureaucracy. They did not accommodate everybody: exiled nationalists and Trotskyites who were their archrivals were brutally eliminated. This behavior was not unique in Vietnam: in Indonesia, Sutan Sjahrir compromised and cooperated with Sukarno and Amir Sjarifuddin but not with Tan Malaka. At the same time, accommodation at the elite level as observed in Vietnam was substantial and different from the token presence of noncommunists in the PRC's government after 1949 on mainland China. These "patriotic personalities" played no direct role in the CCP's victory in the civil war and were brought into government afterward primarily for propaganda purposes. By contrast, EVN officials and other urban intellectuals who collaborated with communists were crucial to the latter's ascendancy and retention of power from late 1945 to mid-1946. At the mass level, the establishment of the Maoist state in China was the direct outcome of a military conquest in which the Red Army defeated GMD troops on the ground and took over, leaving few opportunities for any local mass groups to form and seize local power. In Vietnam, the predominant pattern was spontaneous mass revolts, followed by incorporation.

Elite compromise and mass incorporation shaped the structure of the emerging Vietnamese state in five major ways. First, the state had a divided leadership with communists sharing substantial power with many non-communists. In comparative perspective, the leadership of the new Vietnamese state was more inclusive and moderate than the Maoist state, although less so than its Indonesian neighbor. Ideological beliefs varied

8:16–18); also the series of critical articles in a newspaper of the VNP, "Xua va nay: Nhin qua cac Uy ban hanh chinh dia phuong" (Before and now: A glimpse at local administrative committees), *Viet Nam*, May 25–June 5, 1946.

[32] Ho Chi Minh's letter, "Thu gui Uy ban nhan dan cac ky, tinh, huyen va lang."

[33] Vu Dinh Hoe quotes from a 1948 report by Pham Tuan Khanh, DP general secretary (Vu D. H. 2000, 141). Conflicts broke out in Hai Duong Province and in southern Vietnam. See also Marr (1995, 409–10).

[34] See "Chi thi cua Ban chap hanh Trung uong" (Central Committee's Decree), November 25, 1945 (DCSVN 2000, 8:30).

among Vietnamese noncommunists and communists, but in general the former were less radical than the latter, presenting a potential site of conflict.

Second, compromise with the EVN government required the Viet Minh state to inherit the colonial bureaucracy. This bureaucracy suffered damages at local levels because of the mass revolts, but from the district level up it was largely intact. The appropriation of colonial institutions permitted the Viet Minh movement to quickly transform itself into a state. It allowed the self-proclaimed government, in the shortest time possible, to establish its branches over the entire country and to mobilize financial and human resources nationally. Yet colonial apparatuses, including laws, courts, colonial militias, central bureaucracies, and local governments, were built primarily to serve French interests and operated on principles unacceptable to communists, such as inequality, racism, and capitalism. Given its conservative character, the colonial bureaucracy posed another potential obstacle to the radical vision of social revolution espoused by the communist leadership.

Third, the public dissolution of the ICP in November 1945 had two critical consequences. As a clandestine organization, the party would have less control over the Viet Minh state at a critical moment when this state was expanding rapidly under a coalition government led in part by many noncommunists (Tonnesson 1991, 360).[35] This lack of control exacerbated the other weaknesses in state structure. Furthermore, the dissolution added to Stalin's mistrust of Vietnamese communists for lacking revolutionary commitments. Despite numerous appeals from Ho, the Soviet Union steadfastly ignored the DRV.[36] Although the dissolution of the ICP was a gesture and not a true act of compromise, this move denied the Viet Minh state a crucial foreign alliance for radical policies.[37]

Fourth, mass incorporation resulted in local governments having significant autonomy. As Chapter 6 discusses in more detail, these governments had little respect for central authority. In some cases, they refused

[35] Pham Van Dong, the DRV prime minister, would blame this dissolution on weak central control in his speech "Phai kien toan chinh quyen cong hoa nhan dan" (We must strengthen the people's republican government) at the Third National Cadre Conference, January 21–February 3, 1950 (DCSVN 2001, 11:181).

[36] The DRV also approached the United States, but as I argue elsewhere, this move does not mean that Vietnamese communists were willing to give up their radical vision (Vu T. 2009).

[37] Only in 1950, after Chinese communists had won the civil war and Mao lobbied Stalin hard on its behalf, did the DRV gain Soviet recognition (Goscha 2006).

to accept officials appointed from above.[38] In others, they harassed central tax collectors and challenged those central policies that contradicted local interests (Marr 2004). In comparative perspective, whereas the CCP had nearly a decade to accumulate centralized organizations before establishing a state in 1949, Vietnamese communists had to build a centralized state from scratch after having proclaimed it.

Finally, accommodation implied serious consequences for the ICP as a Leninist party. On the one hand, ICP leaders needed to expand the party rapidly to supply cadres for leading state positions. On the other, they also wanted to raise, or at least preserve, the revolutionary quality of the party by recruiting selectively among certain social classes. Yet accommodation made a selective recruitment policy difficult to maintain because such selectivity could discourage other groups from collaborating, and thereby defeat the very purpose of accommodation. In addition, the party center had weak control over local cells and local situations in general. Even if the party wanted to implement selective recruitment, it would be difficult to ensure compliance from below. The party's radical character would be greatly diminished as it expanded.

LEGACIES OF ACCOMMODATION AND THE ROAD TO THE GREAT PURGE, 1946–1950

Accommodation gave the Vietnamese state a particular structure. Its leadership did not share the same radical vision. Its structural integrity was compromised by the central government's and the party's weak control over local branches. It had no foreign allies that would assist in the implementation of a radical agenda. To be sure, Vietnam in 1947 or 1948 was different from Indonesia at the same time. The ICP dominated the ruling coalition, and internal challenges to its domination did not exist. Yet the structure of the Vietnamese state was much less cohesive than its Chinese counterpart in 1949. Problems in the state structure gradually became acute in three interrelated areas: land policy, leadership conflict, and the consolidation of state and party organizations.

When they established the Viet Minh state in late 1945, communists eschewed class struggle although they issued laws that required landlords to reduce rents by 25 percent, to reschedule debts, and to abolish certain rents for their tenants (Bo Canh Nong 1950, 7–12). These land laws suggested that, while the ICP was forced to accommodate landlords in the

---

[38] See Vu D. H. (2000, 236n) for an example.

Viet Minh national front, it did not sacrifice its radical vision but only bided its time.[39] Yet even this limited progressive agenda was not implemented. In a comprehensive review of party policies in the countryside in 1950, ICP secretary general Truong Chinh impatiently noted that the rent reduction program after five years was still unfinished business even in the areas under full Viet Minh control. The confiscation of land from the French to be transferred to peasants was either neglected or carried out too slowly.[40] In extreme cases, tenants reportedly sent hundreds of letters to higher-level officials to complain against unfair or arrogant cadres. Communal lands were not distributed as mandated by law. During the campaign to buy rice for the government, Truong Chinh expressed concerns that the rich were often able to avoid having to sell, whereas the poor had to borrow rice at high interest to fulfill their obligations to the government. Where the rent reduction laws were implemented, they caused considerable conflict but were not remarkably effective in helping tenants.[41] As the Viet Minh government became more dependent on peasants for labor, taxes, and other contributions, top communist leaders became increasingly impatient with the speed and manner with which these laws were being implemented.[42]

While land policy made little progress, a growing conflict emerged between communists and noncommunists at many levels of government (Vu D. H. 2000).[43] The latter resented the heavy-handed way in which the former, who were generally less educated, demanded and exercised authority over their areas of expertise, ranging from legal to economic to

---

[39] "Cach mang thang Tam: Trien vong cua Cach mang Viet nam" (The August Revolution: The prospects of Vietnam's Revolution), *Su That* (Truth), September 7, 1946.

[40] "Chinh sach cua Dang o nong thon Viet nam" (Party policy in rural Vietnam), Truong Chinh's report at the meeting of the Central Economic Committee, July 5–7, 1950 (DCSVN 2001, 11:608–12).

[41] For an example of conflict, see Vu D. H. (2000, 120–1). Another account in the party's newspaper observed that the campaign was carried out fully in the South, went sluggishly in the central region, and was ignored or neglected in the North up to 1948. Chi Thanh, *Su That*, October 30, 1950.

[42] See Truong Chinh, "Chinh sach cua Dang o nong thon (Viet Nam)," 612–13; also "Chinh sach ruong dat cua ta hien nay va cuoc van dong giam to giam tuc" (Our current land policy and the rent and interest reduction campaign). This is a report to the Third Plenum of the Central Committee circa April 1952 (DCSVN 2001, 13:126–7).

[43] See also Duong Duc Hien, "Dang Dan Chu Viet Nam trong hang ngu Mat tran" (The DP within the National Front), *Doc Lap* (Independence), February 20, 1951, and Hoang Van Duc, "Hien trang doi song vien chuc, tri thuc" (The current living conditions of intellectuals and government officials), *Doc Lap*, October 15, 1951.

literary policies. With respect to rural policy, noncommunists in the Viet Minh government supported land redistribution but were sympathetic to rich peasants.[44] Because they had sustained control of five state ministries, including Justice, Education, Trade, Agriculture, and Irrigation, their different views were translated into moderate policies. Among these, the Justice portfolio was most important because it was part of the state coercive apparatus. It was also where the bitterest conflict took place. When the Viet Minh state was established, noncommunist ministers of justice[45] appointed many French-trained professional lawyers as judges in provincial governments and in lower-level judicial positions (Vu D. H. 2000, 53–6). While the rent reduction policy was carried out, often these judges, on the basis of their own judgment and in the name of the law and judicial independence, sided with landlords against both tenants and local governments. Where they could, the judges ordered the release of people arrested illegally by local police. The judges also were not shy about arresting corrupt local officials who were members of the clandestine ICP (Vu D. H. 2000, 159–65, 196–7). As analyzed in more detail in Chapter 8, this conflict over judicial authority caused significant tension between communist and noncommunist state leaders.

Tension was exacerbated by the Viet Minh state's inheritance of the colonial bureaucracy. Unlike in China, where the CCP got rid of most GMD bureaucrats in the first year, the Vietnamese state kept colonial officials on its payroll for years. The various conflicts between executive and judicial organs in the government were known to ICP leaders as early as mid-1946.[46] By 1950, Truong Chinh was accusing the bureaucrats in the Ministry of Agriculture and its local departments of obstructing party policies. In Chinh's words, these officials were holdovers from the colonial bureaucracy who did not come from peasant backgrounds, had little understanding of rural conditions, and did not care about peasants' interests.[47]

---

[44] For example, Do Duc Duc, a member of the Thanh Nghi group and a DP leader, called for rich peasants to be protected during the land reform. *Doc Lap*, March 15, 1953.

[45] These were French-trained lawyers Vu Trong Khanh and Vu Dinh Hoe.

[46] "Nghi quyet cua Hoi nghi Can bo Trung uong" (Resolution by the Central Cadre Conference), July 31–August 1, 1946 (DCSVN 2000, 8:103).

[47] Truong Chinh, "Chinh sach cua Dang o nong thon (Viet Nam)," 612–13. In his speech at the same conference, Prime Minister Pham Van Dong also regretted that the ICP had retained colonial bureaucrats, although he did not elaborate on the problem. See "Phai kien toan chinh quyen cong hoa nhan dan."

More broadly, party documents indicated concerns that colonial bureaucrats were unenthusiastic and even deliberately sabotaged government policies. There were complaints about many "counterrevolutionary elements" among schoolteachers inherited from the colonial regime.
Predictably, the marriage between a revolutionary party and a colonial
bureaucracy did not go smoothly. As Truong Chinh wrote in 1946, the
majority of political cadres were "loyal, enthusiastic, politically astute and
resourceful, but uneducated."[48] In contrast, state bureaucrats, who were
professionals, managers, and intellectuals trained under the French, were
"educated but lacked interests in [revolutionary] politics." Conflict was
brewing: Viet Minh cadres looked down on and distrusted bureaucrats
and professionals; the latter in turn argued that, because Vietnam had
achieved independence, it was time for political cadres to be replaced by
educated professionals who had the necessary skills to manage the state.

Still, another area where problems emerged concerned the organization of the ICP. As noted, a dilemma for ICP leaders was how to maintain
accommodation while being selective in its membership policy. The ICP
expanded rapidly from 1945 to 1950. From less than 5,000 members in
late 1945, its membership had exceeded 760,000, an increase of more
than 100-fold, by 1950.[49] It turned out that accommodation trumped
selectivity: in a count by party leaders in 1952, more than 65 percent
of party members came from petty bourgeois backgrounds.[50] We have
seen that CCP members were mostly poor peasants. Not only did this
membership give the Maoist state deep roots in the peasantry, but the
social character of this membership also made it congruent with radical socioeconomic programs. With a party mostly composed of middle
peasants and higher social classes, the radical dreams of ICP leaders
were bound to meet internal opposition. The rent reduction policy was
unevenly implemented not only because of obstruction by noncommunist
bureaucrats and French-trained judges. The failure of the policy had its
origins within the ranks of the party itself.

---

[48] "Cach mang thang Tam: Nhiem vu can kip cua dan toc Viet nam" (The August Revolution: The urgent tasks of the Vietnamese nation), *Su That*, October 4, 1946.

[49] See "Nhan dan dan chu chuyen chinh o Viet nam" (The democratic dictatorship of the
people in Vietnam), a report to the Third Plenum of the Central Committee, probably
in April 1952 (DCSVN 2001, 13:95–6).

[50] See "Van de chinh Dang" (On party rectification), Le Van Luong's report to the Third
Plenum of the Central Committee, probably in April 1952 (DCSVN 2001, 13:102).
The document did not spell out what classes comprised the "petty bourgeois," which
appeared to include middle peasants, urban middle class, and higher social strata.

In sum, accommodation created many dilemmas for communist leaders espousing a radical vision of social transformation, including land policy implementation, the "contamination" of the party by bourgeois elements, and simmering conflicts with noncommunists in the coalition government and with inherited colonial bureaucrats. Beginning in 1950, Chinese assistance would offer ICP leaders the political support and the resources to rescue their vision. Rather than strengthening the structure of their state *before* launching a radical social revolution, they sought to do both at the same time; this turned out to be fatal for their socialist building agenda.

THE FAILURE OF A PREMATURE SOCIALIST REVOLUTION, 1950–1960

Vietnamese communists had long harbored dreams of a radical social revolution (Vu T. 2008) but were held back by the legacies of accommodation. The triumph of Chinese communists on mainland China in 1949 opened up a new opportunity for them to build a strong state structure and to implement their vision. They welcomed the arrival of the Cold War in Asia and volunteered to fight it on the socialist side (Vu T. 2009). Chinese aid and advisers encouraged and enabled Vietnamese communists to embark on realizing their socialist vision.

In response to the new and favorable conditions, the ICP reemerged in public in early 1951 as the Vietnamese Workers' Party (VWP). The party embarked on a radical policy course after 1948, implementing a cultural conference, a cadres' work-style reform movement modeled after the Chinese Cheng Feng campaign, a Three-Anti campaign, a campaign to establish workers' management councils in state enterprises, a "land reform," and a "party rectification" campaign (Moise 1983; Ninh 2002, 93–117; Vu T. 2005).[51] The latter two were of highest priority. Among their many goals, these campaigns sought to purge the party and bureaucracy of "contaminated elements" while mobilizing peasants' support for the war against France.[52] The overall goals were to create a more cohesive

---

[51] Subjects of the work-style reform campaign were intellectuals, soldiers, and students. The Three-Anti campaign was directed against corrupt Viet Minh cadres.

[52] As an official document stated in 1953, "To strengthen the people's dictatorship, consolidate our rear, suppress the reactionaries, stimulate production, and guarantee supplies for our resistance [against the French], [the Party will] now launch the land reform to overthrow the feudal landlord class and to destroy the social basis of imperialism in our country" (DCSVN 2001, 14:395).

party and to consolidate state power in the countryside. In the process, all power was to be centralized in the central committee of the VWP. Non-communist government leaders were effectively removed from positions of authority while disobedient local judges were dismissed.

The way the two campaigns of party purge and "land reform" were jointly launched suggests that communist leaders understood that a radical social revolution could not be implemented without a developmental state structure. Yet they chose to combine the task of building a state structure with that of leading a social revolution by embedding the party purge in the "land reform" campaign. In particular, the party set up a Land Reform Authority (LRA) with local branches down to the district level. This special agency and its branches were placed under central party leadership and were independent of existing party and state bureaucracies below the central level. It was in fact a super-bureaucracy with vast extra-institutional powers, accountable to only a few top leaders. The main task entrusted to this agency was to mobilize poor peasants to stand up not only against landlords and local elites but also against local Communist Party branches and local governments up to the provincial level. Interestingly, in its history the CCP had implemented "land reform" campaigns combined with organizational purges but had never had to establish a special institution such as the LRA separate from the party structure.

Unlike in China, the Vietnamese campaigns met an ignominious fate. The state actually achieved most objectives of the campaigns by the time they were abruptly halted in mid-1956. By then, 70 percent of the rural population had received redistributed land and thousands of landlords had been executed.[53] While official policies did not attack middle peasants, many had been wrongly classified as rich peasants or landlords and punished, in the party's own admission, "by brutal and barbaric torture."[54] Two-thirds of local party and government branches had undergone "rectification" with more than 50 percent of the cadres in these branches purged. These cadres were replaced with those poor peasants who demonstrated the highest zeal during the campaigns. The old rural power structure was thus overthrown, and state reach now penetrated more deeply into rural society than ever.

For what they had already achieved, the two campaigns would have made the countryside ready for the next radical phase of the revolution;

[53] Data cited in this paragraph are limited to the area in northern Vietnam under the control of the DRV government.
[54] See Chapter 6 for more details.

yet a conjuncture of many events led the party to suspend them by late 1956. First, personal appeals by high-ranking provincial cadres who were persecuted forced a reassessment of the two campaigns. Second, encouraged by events in the Soviet bloc,[55] prominent intellectuals outside the party and many party members began to voice bitter criticism of the campaigns in public forums (Boudarel 1990; Ninh 2002, 121–63). International events certainly affected the party's decision to halt both campaigns. Still, in comparative perspective, the same international events did not generate insurmountable trouble for the Chinese leadership. With its cohesive structure, the Maoist state absorbed the crisis in the Soviet bloc and struck back with the violent Anti-Rightist campaign. Its Vietnamese counterpart having no such cohesive structure simply could not withstand external pressures and domestic dissent.

Although no specific information is available, if we judge by the efforts to appease victims of the campaigns, conflict within the party must have been intense. The party made public apologies for its mistake of persecuting too many innocent people, including party members. It authorized a subsequent campaign to "rectify the errors," essentially to reinstate some cadres who had been wrongly persecuted and to reclassify many "landlords" who should have been treated as middle peasants. In addition, Truong Chinh was forced to resign his position as general secretary.

Unlike in China, where "land reform" was carried out without significant problems and paved the way for an even more radical collectivization drive, the suspension of rural class struggle and the "error rectification" campaign in North Vietnam arrested the momentum of socialist construction there in three ways. First, it generated intense conflicts within local party and government units that would take years to heal. Those who were wrongly classified as landlords or rich peasants during the event now demanded their property back, while the poor peasants who now owned such property resisted (Moise 1983, 260–5). Those who were reinstated after being wrongly accused of counterrevolutionary crimes, not to mention relatives of executed victims, would not have forgiven their accusers easily. Their accusers, who had been promoted to leadership positions thanks primarily to those fabricated accusations, would have felt highly insecure after the reinstatement of their victims.[56] Two years

---

[55] These events included Khrushchev's denunciation of Stalin and the revolts in Poland and Hungary.

[56] See, for example, "Dan chu va chuyen chinh" (Democracy and dictatorship), "Doi voi can bo moi" (To the new cadres), and "Kien toan chinh quyen xa" (Strengthening commune governments), *Nhan Dan*, November 9, 25, and December 25, 1956.

after the "error rectification" campaign had begun, party documents still lamented the "lack of solidarity" in the countryside.[57]

Second, the VWP's admission of mistakes led to the resignation not only of General Secretary Chinh but also of Hoang Quoc Viet, another Politburo member who was in charge of mass relations, and Le Van Luong, who handled party organization and discipline. Though Chinh was retained in the Politburo and remained influential, the Maoist mass line and radical agrarian reform had lost their chief proponents. In their places emerged Le Duan, Le Duc Tho, and Pham Hung. All three had worked for extensive periods in the South. No one replaced Hoang Quoc Viet, the mass mobilization chief. Le Duan had called for an armed struggle in the South as early as 1956 but his call was not heeded by the VWP. It was not a coincidence that the rise of Duan, Tho, and Hung marked a turning point in North Vietnam's policy toward the South. With this new team, the task of unification was no longer relegated to the back burner but was now given equal or higher priority than the task of building socialism in the North. As Nguyen Lien-Hang (2006, 10–12), who offers the most recent and systematic treatment of this topic, argues:

[In 1958,] two contending "factions" began to emerge in the [Vietnamese Communist Party] . . . the "North-firsters" wanted to continue concentrating the DRV's resources on state building: socialist development of the economy that would compete with and ultimately defeat the South. The "South-firsters" wanted to shepherd the DRV's resources into supporting the resistance in the South: reunification through war. . . . [At the Fifteenth Plenum in January 1959, it was decided that] the socialist revolution in the North was not proceeding according to plan, but the power of the South-firsters in the [party] and the Politburo was not yet absolute. [The South-firsters] had won the first round of debates, but their victory was only tentative: [the Plenum] approved the use of armed conflict primarily in situations of self-defense. . . . Although building socialism in the North remained the top goal at the [subsequent Third Party Congress in 1960], the emergent highest echelons [in the party] would subsequently privilege armed conflict in the South.

Finally, "mistakes" during "land reform" impeded collectivization at the very moment when this campaign was at a high tide in China. In 1957 euphoria was sweeping over North Vietnam with the Soviet success in launching Sputnik bolstered by Mao's calls for socialist countries to overtake the imperialists in industrial production. As Mao was exhorting the Chinese to produce "more, faster, with higher quality and more economically" (*you da, you kuai, you hao, you sheng*) in 1958 on

---

57 See "Thong tri Ban Bi Thu 158-TT/TW" (The Secretariat's Circular no. 158-TT/TW), September 3, 1959 (DCSVN 2002, 20:324).

the eve of the Leap,[58] the same slogan (*nhieu, nhanh, tot, re*) appeared repeatedly in *Nhan Dan*'s editorials, in mass conferences, and in many keynote speeches.[59] In agriculture, Vietnamese peasants and agronomists, on learning from Mao's teachings, embarked on a campaign to plant more thickly, plow more deeply, and use more fertilizers.[60] In industry, the VWP also launched a management reform campaign to mobilize workers (Vu T. 2005).

The only area where Vietnam appeared out of step with China was in collectivization. As has been noted, most mutual aid teams in North Vietnam were disbanded after the abrupt halt of rural class struggle in mid-1956. Subsequently, the "error rectification" campaign took away resources and cadres that could have been used to promote collectivization (Kerkvliet 1998). After much debate, Vietnamese leaders cautiously decided to launch the collectivization campaign in late 1958. No sooner did Vietnamese collectivization start than events in China took a sudden turn and discouraged Vietnamese leaders from taking a radical road to collectivization. Before 1959, Vietnamese newspapers were full of praise for Chinese leaps in industry and agriculture. These accounts were accompanied by enthusiastic calls from Hanoi leaders for emulation and by news of collectives eagerly applying Mao's advice.[61] Secret party documents also indicated great enthusiasm about the Chinese GLF and conveyed specific instructions for emulation.[62] By early 1959, however, such mention of China suddenly disappeared from the press.[63] Farming techniques

---

[58] Quoted in Schoenhals (1987, 9).

[59] The Second National Congress of Heroes and Heroines among Soldiers, Workers and Peasants in July 1958 selected *nhieu, nhanh, tot, re* to be its "central slogan." See "Cac xi nghiep nha nuoc phai kinh doanh cho co lai" (State enterprises must make profits), *Nhan Dan*, July 14, 1958.

[60] See, for example, "Huan thi cua Ho chu tich" (Chairman Ho's instructions), "Ruong lua thi diem cua Dai Hoc Nong Lam" (Experimented rice fields of the College of Forestry and Agriculture) and "Cay day cao do rat co loi" (Very thick planting yields great results), *Nhan Dan*, July 5, October 27, and November 11, 1958, respectively. See also Tran Luc (Ho Chi Minh) (1958a; 1958b; 1959).

[61] Calls from top leaders for emulation included, Tran Luc (Ho Chi Minh), "Danh tan phai huu" (Smashing the rightists) and Le Thanh Nghi, "May bai hoc lon trong cao trao xay dung chu nghia xa hoi cua Trung Quoc" (A few great lessons from the high tide of socialist building in China), *Nhan Dan*, September 16 and October 18, 1958, respectively.

[62] Report at the Central Committee's Fourteenth Plenum, November 1958 (DCSVN 2002, 19:434, 472, 474, and 481). Not only farming techniques but also small-scale steel furnaces were objects to emulate.

[63] A comparison of two articles authored by Tran Luc (Ho Chi Minh) is instructive. In the one titled "1959," published in *Nhan Dan* on January 21, 1959, Chinese achievements in overtaking imperialist countries were highlighted with equal emphasis to those of

were still discussed but not in the context of the GLF. Vietnamese peasants might have escaped Chinese-style massive labor mobilization for irrigation and industrial projects simply because the movement in Vietnam had just begun in early 1959. At this time, Maoist blind faith in human will ran into serious problems, and evidence of a looming famine began to mount.

Even though most North Vietnamese peasants were to join cooperatives by 1960, the movement there generated neither an intense engagement between the state and the peasantry nor the opportunity for the state to increase its exploitation of peasant labor as the communization movement in China had. If collectivization had not been delayed by the "error rectification" campaign, North Vietnam might have followed Chinese leaps (and falls) more closely. The comparison of the sequences of events in China and North Vietnam indicates an indirect relationship between the outcome of rural class struggle campaigns, on the one hand, and the more moderate course of socialist development in North Vietnam up to the early 1960s, on the other.

Thus, Chinese land reform excesses were occasionally acknowledged and led to moderation but not to leadership change in the CCP; when conditions improved, the rural revolution moved decisively on to the next, more radical, stage. The Vietnamese "mistakes" in the "land reform" campaign and party purge had far more serious consequences. Leadership changes at the top and turmoil in the villages not only delayed the next stage of collectivization but also affected the entire course of Vietnamese socialism. By 1960, the struggle in the South had been given equal or higher priority than socialist construction in the North.

In comparative perspective, the difference between the courses of social revolution in China and in Vietnam thus lay in the gap between their developmental state structures. Similar to the Korean state under Park, the Chinese state launched transformative policies when its structure had been consolidated. The Vietnamese case fell into the same category with

the Soviet Union. In another article titled "1–5-1959," published in *Nhan Dan* on May 1, 1959, Chinese achievements took less space than those of the Soviet Union and North Korea. In the absence of primary sources, one may speculate that the VWP's evaluation of the GLF must have changed radically in early 1959. There were a series of conferences of the CCP where agricultural problems were reported at the same time (the first Zhengzhou and Wuchang conferences in November and the Sixth Plenum in December 1958). Vietnamese leaders may have somehow learned about the truth behind the Chinese "miracles" at this time. They may have interpreted Mao Zedong's decision to step down as chairman of the People's Republic at the Sixth Plenum as signaling something wrong with the Leap (this Chinese event was reported in "Tu tuong Mao Trach Dong" [Mao's thoughts], *Nhan Dan*, December 26, 1958).

Indonesia of the 1950s. Without a consolidated developmental structure in place, state attempts at directing developmental changes turned out to be premature. The difference with developments in Indonesia was that in Vietnam the communist leaders were far more cohesive as a group and did not lose power. In fact, the Vietnamese state became more consolidated after the purge. Rural class struggle overthrew the old power structure and helped extend state control over rural society. Nevertheless, the developmental agenda of the party was sidetracked and was not restored as a top priority again until 1975.

CONCLUSION

This chapter has analyzed the Vietnamese pattern of state formation and its consequences. We have seen from the previous chapter that elite polarization and effective mass mobilization in China created a Chinese state with a cohesive structure. This state went on to implement perhaps the most radical social revolution ever attempted. The state formation processes in Vietnam, in contrast, were marked by elite compromise and mass incorporation. Communists rose to power through an urban coup in which noncommunist elites, colonial bureaucracy, and local mass groups were accommodated. The outcome was a state with a divided leadership, a colonial bureaucracy that did not share radical values with the revolutionary leadership, and a weak central control over local governments. Even the Communist Party – the organizational vehicle at the core of the state – lost its Leninist character and became essentially a petty bourgeois party through the process.

When the international situation became more favorable with the victory of Chinese communists in China, Vietnamese leaders decided to steer their struggle toward a radical direction. Seeking to strengthen the state structure while launching a social revolution in the countryside, Vietnamese communists achieved some goals but were forced to suspend class struggle by the late 1950s. The legacies of state formation thus played a critical role in the divergent paths of China and Vietnam. If compared to Indonesia, the Vietnamese case followed a similar pattern despite the fact that communists led the Vietnamese state, whereas pro-Western groups were in power in Indonesia in the 1950s. In both states, the elites sought to play developmental roles prematurely without a cohesive developmental structure, only to be resisted or defeated.

In Part I, examination of the macropatterns of state structures in six cases has clearly indicated the importance of state formation legacies and the role played by both confrontation and accommodation. In Part II, we look more closely into the cases of Vietnam and Indonesia up to 1960, where states were born out of accommodation. In particular, the next four chapters analyze the politics of accommodation at the microlevel. The goal is to find out how accommodation was institutionalized in the organizations and discourses of the Vietnamese and Indonesian nationalist movements as these movements were transformed into postcolonial states. The in-depth study of the Vietnamese and Indonesian cases reveals significant variations in the dynamics of accommodation, not only because the two countries had different histories but also because the political arena in each case held a different set of political actors. Communists led in Vietnam but conservative nationalists were in power in Indonesia. However, the general causal patterns of state formation identified thus far still hold.

PART TWO

VARIANTS OF ACCOMMODATION
VIETNAM AND INDONESIA COMPARED

6

Organizing Accommodation in Vietnam

Coalition Government, United Front, and Leninist Party

Among the macropatterns of state formation and development in six national cases considered in Part I, the accommodation path taken by Vietnam and Indonesia in the 1950s involved elite compromise and mass incorporation. We have seen that the outcomes in these cases were states lacking cohesive structures. Under these circumstances, the Vietnamese and Indonesian state elites implemented developmental policies only to see them backfire (as in Vietnam) or suffer defeat (as in Indonesia).

Part II probes further into the dynamics inside the nationalist movements that founded these states. The goal is to understand how accommodation became institutionalized in political organizations and in elites' discursive formulations. Political organizations and discourses that embodied accommodation can be shown to be incoherent in particular ways that reflected the particular politics of each country. To some extent, the chapters in Part II revisit points raised earlier in Part I, but a narrower focus on the accommodation path here will allow more nuanced accounts of the historical contexts and the thoughts of political actors during state formation. Most importantly, by looking at the subnational level, the analysis of organization and discourse adds causal-process observations to the macroaccounts offered in Part I.

The organizations of the Vietnamese movement, including the coalition government, the Viet Minh united front, and the political parties, are the subject of this chapter. In particular, I ask how the government and political parties evolved under conditions of compromise; and whether political leaders understood and were able to deal with organizational problems caused by accommodation.

Accommodation is found to be organized in two main ways. First, accommodation was institutionalized in the coalition government comprising communists and noncommunists. Second, accommodation led to the communists' failure to maintain distinct organizational boundaries between them and other groups. Communists accommodated other groups for tactical and strategic gains but not for ideological reasons. Accommodation forced them to play down or delay the construction of their distinct corporate identity. No clear boundaries are found between the party and its front organizations such as the Democratic Party (DP) and Viet Minh. At the same time, mass incorporation denied central leadership control over local branches, leading to leaders' inability to protect the organizational cohesion of the party in terms of its class character. In the first few years, the ICP permitted limited flexibility in membership recruitment, especially with regard to urban intellectuals and professionals whose support it needed. At local levels, recruitment was based on personal relationships more than on social class criteria. The party enjoyed rapid expansion but its membership as a whole lacked revolutionary qualities, and party structure was not centralized. The party in effect became a united front, not a Leninist party as originally designed. This problem, as we have learned from Chapter 5, provided the rationale for the party purge of the 1950s. Ultimately, this purge led to the derailment of Vietnam's socialist agenda.

A brief historical overview of the Vietnamese nationalist movement since the 1920s suggests that elite compromise had occurred before 1945 but left little organizational legacies. After this point, however, we can focus on how this movement was organized and transformed into the Vietnamese state and consider the institutionalized legacies in state structure up to the mid-1950s. Newly available data about the party purge carried out in the 1950s offer a glimpse of how its leaders perceived and handled the problem.

EARLY NATIONALIST ORGANIZATIONS, 1910s–1940s

Unlike Indonesia, Vietnam had been a unified country under centralized imperial rule before the French arrived. French colonization since the mid-nineteenth century led to numerous movements aimed at restoring imperial rule. In the first two decades of the twentieth century, the two best known groups with modernist tendencies were the Eastern Travel (Dong Du) and Dong Kinh Free School (Dong Kinh Nghia Thuc). The former raised money and smuggled many young men to Japan for military training, while the latter launched a cultural reformist movement through its teaching curriculum (Marr 1971, 120–84). Both organizations were short-lived.

After Phan Boi Chau and other leaders of the Eastern Travel movement were expelled from Japan, they moved to southern China and organized many political activities there. This region was home to many small exiled Vietnamese groups active in plotting against French rule. In 1925, Nguyen Ai Quoc (an alias used by Ho Chi Minh) founded a new organization, the Vietnamese Revolutionary Youth League (Thanh Nien Cach Mang Dong Chi Hoi). Nguyen was in southern China with the delegation sent by the Comintern to advise both the GMD and the CCP during 1923 to 1927 (Huynh 1982, 99–123). With Soviet funds, the Youth League built on existing exiled groups, recruiting young men from Vietnam for training and smuggling them back to spread the network. Some of Nguyen Ai Quoc's students went on to Moscow for further training. After Chiang Kai-shek's attack on Shanghai communists in 1927, the league stopped its operations, although league members in northern and central Vietnam, probably numbering a few dozen, continued their secret activities. With Nguyen Ai Quoc's help, various league factions in Vietnam were able to unite and form the Indochinese Communist Party (ICP) in Hong Kong in 1930.[1] However, after a wave of peasant unrest in central and southern Vietnam during 1930 and 1931, which at one point was led by local ICP members, the party was brutally repressed and would not recover until the late 1930s.

A second center of nationalist activities emerged in northern Vietnam, where the Vietnamese Nationalist Party (Viet Nam Quoc Dan Dang, or VNP) was founded in 1927. This party grew out of a book club, the Nam Dong Publishing Society, which translated several works by Sun Yat-sen before being shut down by the colonial government (Hoang V. D. 1970, 25–6; Woodside 1976, 59–67).[2] Unlike other groups at the time, VNP leaders came from middle peasant or merchant families. The party appeared to be influenced by Sun Yat-sen's ideas in naming itself after the Chinese GMD, but its programs did not mention Sun's Three Principles. The VNP also was crushed after leading an uprising in 1930.

Other centers of nationalist movements developed in France and in Cochinchina (southern Vietnam). In France, Vietnamese exiles and students formed the Annam Independence Party (AIP) that became a training

---

[1] The party was originally named Vietnamese Communist Party but changed its name to Indochinese Communist Party afterward.
[2] Vu K. (2002) contains some information on Nam Dong and reprints a booklet published in 1926 by Nam Dong on Sun Yat-sen and his ideas. Nhuong Tong (1949) provides a biography of Nguyen Thai Hoc, the VNP's founder and first leader.

ground for many prominent Trotskyites during its brief existence from
1927 to 1929 (Tai 1992, 233–40). Cochinchina was under French direct
rule and had a more open political environment than other parts of
Indochina. In the early 1920s, Cochinchina had many active collaborator groups. Organized at about the same time with the Youth League
in southern China was Nguyen An Ninh's secret society in Saigon. This
group recruited hundreds of members among existing religious sects,
secret societies, peasants, and workers (Tai 1992, 191–5). Nguyen An
Ninh was subsequently arrested and died in prison while his group gradually disintegrated. By the early 1930s, two main groups in Saigon vied for
support among the urban population (Marr 1981, 387–400; Tai 1992,
232–43). One group was the Trotskyites in the AIP who had returned
from France. For several years, this group (known as *La Lutte* for the
name of its journal) allied with the ICP, the second group, to spread leftist
propaganda, to organize demonstrations, and to run campaigns for the
elections of the Saigon Municipal Council and the Cochinchina Colonial
Council.

The movement inside Vietnam became more radical with the rise to
power of the Popular Front in France in 1936. This new French government implemented limited reforms in Indochina and released thousands of
political prisoners. Trotskyites were far more radical than ICP members
in calling for an international rather than national proletarian revolution and in rejecting alliance with the native bourgeoisie. In contrast, the
ICP focused on agitating among peasants and on organizing clandestine
activities (Marr 1981, 388–93). After the Popular Front government fell
in France, the movement was no longer tolerated by the colonial administration. Believing that the opportunity for revolution had arrived with
French surrender to Nazi Germany in Europe, the ICP launched a rebellion in 1940. This uprising failed, and almost all of its top leaders were
executed.

Before 1945, elites belonging to many of these groups had sometimes
collaborated on their anticolonial activities. Examples include the collaboration between the Vietnamese Revolutionary Youth League and exiled
nationalist groups in southern China, between the VNP and communist groups in Tonkin in the late 1920s, and between ICP leaders and
Trotskyites in Saigon in the 1930s. These efforts left few organizational
legacies. In all three examples, the relationships between collaborating
groups were short-lived and often tense. We have seen that in late 1945
conflict broke out between exiled nationalist groups and Viet Minh. ICP
leaders also ordered the assassination of many Trotskyites in late 1945.

FROM COALITION GOVERNMENT TO PARTY PURGE, 1941–1956

In the past decade, scholarly understanding of the Vietnamese nationalist movement during the crucial 1940s has shifted fundamentally. Earlier accounts equated the communists with the movement and presented the ICP as centralized and monolithic.[3] Recent studies have begun to capture the spontaneity of a movement that involved many more groups than just the ICP.[4] These studies show that communist leaders in fact had precarious control over the movement and over their own party (Marr 1995, 238–40).

The organizational character of the nationalist movement that formed the Viet Minh state in 1945 was complex.[5] Party labels such as ICP and DP, while convenient, conjure up inaccurate images of well-structured organizations. In fact, a central feature of Vietnam's nationalist movement during the late 1940s was its organizational anarchy. In the rush to expand, the ICP failed to maintain boundaries between itself and its united front organizations. Over time, it became a united front with its membership incorporating all social classes. The other political groups that shared leadership with the ICP in the movement – first the New Vietnam Party and then the Democratic Party – were also swept along by events. Eventually the movement would be transformed into a wobbly leviathan that frustrated the communists' radical ambitions. To remove obstacles to their transformative agenda, party leaders carried out a massive purge of their organizations and destroyed half of the party and state apparatuses from the provincial level down. Party and state organizations were no doubt more consolidated and centralized after the purge; the price paid, however, was the temporization of socialist programs, as Chapter 5 has argued.

Road to the Coalition Government, 1941–1945

That the ICP misapplied the united front strategy may be surprising. Vietnamese communists were no strangers to united front theory and praxis. They were serious students of Leninism and possessed years of

---

[3] For example, see Huynh (1982).

[4] E.g., Tonnesson (1991); Marr (1995; 2004); Goscha and de Treglode (2004). Vu N. C. (1984) pays more attention than most studies to the EVN government but a nonelite or movement-centered account of the event still awaits further research.

[5] Geographically the discussion will be limited to north and north central Vietnam. The ICP was best organized in these regions and if anarchy existed there, it was worse elsewhere.

experience in mass mobilizing. In Leninist doctrine, the united front is a tactic or strategy that helps a revolutionary communist party to overcome its small numbers in the face of a repressive state. The front is composed of social and functional organizations that mobilize mass support for party programs.[6] In the theoretical model of a front, the party forms the nucleus with a series of concentric layers of mass organizations all directed by the party. The distance between the center and a particular concentric circle is implicitly based on Leninist assumptions about class behavior. Organizations based on least revolutionary social classes (e.g., landlords) must be placed on a circle far away from the center. Their relationship with the party ought to be temporary and guarded in nature. Those organizations whose members were more revolutionary (e.g., the urban poor) should be closer to the center. The center, of course, is occupied by the most revolutionary class – the proletariat.

Since the ICP's birth in 1930, its leaders had created many united fronts depending on specific political needs at particular times (Huynh K. K. 1982). The Viet Minh front founded in 1941 was broader by design than all its predecessors. All "patriotic" Vietnamese, regardless of age, gender, ethnicity, social class, or profession, were invited to join. As late as 1940, the party still viewed land redistribution as a necessary component of the anticolonial struggle; Vietnamese landlords were the enemy together with France and Japan. With the new united front policy, land redistribution was to be postponed indefinitely. Landlords and the "national bourgeoisie" were welcomed into the front and permitted to have their own "national salvation associations" or to join existing peasants' groups.[7] The masses were to be mobilized to the greatest possible extent but were divided into separate groups according to gender, age, and profession to facilitate effective mobilization.

Viet Minh was to be organized horizontally as a coordinating board of all mass organizations at a particular level. It did not have its own staff but was run by representatives from the ICP and from those mass organizations at the same level.[8] By instructions from the center, ICP members in a Viet Minh organ would form a party group (*Dang doan*) and this group would lead the organ from within. The relationship between Viet Minh

[6] Huynh (1982, 137–41) presents the theoretical model but does not discuss how it was applied in practice.

[7] *VNDL*, December 1, 1941, and April 11, 1943. Also, "Trung Uong Hoi Nghi Lan Thu Tam" (The Eighth Central Committee Plenum), May 1941 (DCSVN 2000, 7:124–6).

[8] DCSVN (2000, 8:455–570) contains a collection of documents issued by Viet Minh before August 1945.

and the government was conceptualized similarly.[9] A local Viet Minh unit, once security could be assured, should establish a local National Liberation Committee (later called People's Committee). Each national salvation association in the Viet Minh would send a representative to the Liberation Committee. Viet Minh leaders determined the percentage of their representatives in these committees, and the remaining seats would be open to elected local elites or elders (*ky hao, phu lao*). Viet Minh cadres who participated in a Liberation Committee would form their own cell (*Viet Minh doan*) to lead the committee from within. In sum, party cells would lead Viet Minh organizations, whose cells in turn would direct local governments. The model was elaborate and well designed in advance.

ICP leaders wanted to expand the party and the Viet Minh front as quickly as possible; alliances with selected political parties were welcome. However, party leaders made clear to the rank and file that the internal structure of the party should not be confused with the internal structure of Viet Minh and national salvation associations.[10] Whereas the latter two were to be as open and flexible as possible, the former should be restricted and centralized. Maintaining separate organizational structures was a critical principle for the party in its alliance with other parties.[11] No explicit explanation of this principle was provided but the rationale seems obvious: coalition was never viewed as permanent, and separate organizations were necessary if the party needed to adapt its strategies and change its coalition partners under changing circumstances.[12]

Similarly, mass organizations such as national salvation associations had to be organizationally independent and separate from the party.[13] Party documents explained that separation was necessary to preserve

---

[9] "Viec to chuc cac Uy ban Dan toc Giai phong" (On the establishment of National Liberation Committees), April 16, 1945 (DCSVN 2000, 8:535–40).

[10] "Chi thi ve cong tac" (Decree on [organizational] tasks), ICP Central Committee, December 1, 1941 (DCSVN 2000, 7:206–30). This document laid out detailed instructions for the organization of Viet Minh from village to national levels.

[11] "Nghi quyet cua Ban Thuong Vu Trung Uong" (Resolution of the Standing Committee of the Central Committee), February 25–28, 1943 (DCSVN 2000, 7:292–7); "Nghi quyet cuoc hoi nghi toan xu Bac Ky" (Resolution of All-Tonkin Meeting), September 25–7, 1941 (ibid., 186); and "Nghi quyet cua toan quoc hoi nghi Dang Cong San Dong Duong" (Resolution of the national congress of the ICP), August 14–15, 1945 (ibid., 433).

[12] In fact, the party wanted its members not only to keep separate organizations but also to proselytize communism and offer "constructive criticisms" to its coalition partners.

[13] "Nghi quyet cua Ban Thuong Vu Trung Uong," 295.

the "revolutionary initiatives and autonomy" of the masses. This autonomy perhaps would allow the movement to develop with minimal party supervision. Separation was desirable because party organizations were to remain clandestine, whereas mass organizations by nature had to operate with much less secrecy.

Because of French repression, the main problem for the ICP in the early 1940s was less how to organize than how to expand. The Japanese coup in March 1945 ushered in a new situation, one favorable to the movement. As local governments in many remote areas collapsed but were not immediately replaced by the Japanese, Viet Minh local organizations seized power and established People's Committees. In the aftermath of this takeover, central leaders became alarmed by two organizational issues. First, there was no separation between Viet Minh and the newly established People's Committees. Local Viet Minh cells simply became local governments – a tendency disfavored by the party.[14] The second issue was the rise of "revolutionary mandarins" or Viet Minh cadres who became the new local despots.[15] These issues foreshadowed organizational problems that would plague the movement as it sought to take over the colonial state five months later.

Regarding the situation in March 1945, we have seen in Chapter 5 that Viet Minh groups were not alone in capitalizing on the Japanese coup. One of the most influential groups in North and Central Vietnam was the New Vietnam Party (Tan Viet Nam Hoi) founded in May 1945. At the time of its founding, this party announced a Central Committee of thirty-three prominent intellectuals and professionals (Vu D. H. 1995, 182–9). These men were part of a broad network of like-minded friends who founded or contributed to the popular journal *Thanh Nghi*. It is instructive to hear from its leaders how the New Vietnam Party was formed, as this was the common experience of many groups not only in Vietnam but also in Indonesia:

Only after March 9 could we openly organize. All of us knew that we needed to band together by forming a political party to consolidate our shaky independence. How to form? A circle of friends who had full trust of each other's true character and capacity and who had worked together before on other projects assembled to discuss an agenda and to organize a party based on [such trust]. Organizing

---

14 "Uy Ban Nhan Dan va Viet Minh" (People's Committees and Viet Minh), *VNDL*, April 30, 1945.
15 "Mot cai te phai bo!" (This practice must be condemned!), *VNDL*, June 10, 1945; "Chong cai te quan cach manh [*sic*]!" (Down with revolutionary mandarins!), *VNDL*, June 20, 1945.

took time: A party could not become big right away.... To serve the nation the only realistic way was [not to wait for all groups to join together and form a big party, but] for each group to form its own organization and start working [immediately].[16]

I return to this kind of party based on personal trust and status circles when discussing the Indonesian movement in Chapter 7; the point here is simply that New Vietnam represented a very different model from the ICP as an organization. It was not ideology but trust through prior contacts that underlay the organization; the party was correctly viewed by its leaders as "a patriotic alliance not of political parties but of personalities." Besides a common goal of winning independence for Vietnam, personal ties and the journal appeared to be the main organizational linkages.

While New Vietnam did not have as tight an organization as the communists, it was an ambitious group. Its main goal was "to preserve Vietnam's independence in the Great Asia Sphere of Co-Prosperity" by uniting "the most determined individuals" who came from all walks of life and all political camps. These individuals turned out to be prominent professionals with little political experience.[17] In terms of activity, New Vietnam had an office staffed by two Central Committee members; this office was open three hours every evening. Party finance relied on personal funds and a few wealthy donors who offered their houses and cars to the organization. Sympathetic to Viet Minh but determined to chart their own course, New Vietnam leaders used their journal and traveled to many cities to mobilize support for the EVN government. Unfortunately for the party, provocative articles in *Thanh Nghi* that called on the EVN government to adopt an autonomous foreign policy soon alarmed Japanese authorities.[18] Although they escaped arrests, key New Vietnam leaders decided to close the journal and dissolve the group in early August to join

---

[16] Vu Dinh Hoe, "Viec thong nhat cac chinh dang" (The unification of political parties), *Thanh Nghi*, May 19, 1945.

[17] There were exceptions. Two members of the Central Committee, Nhuong Tong and Ngo Thuc Dich, were founders and veteran leaders of the Vietnam Nationalist Party (VNP) (Hoang V. D. 1970). Khai Hung was another VNP member. Ton Quang Phiet and Dao Duy Anh had once been leaders of the defunct leftist Tan Viet Revolutionary Party. All these veterans did not seem to play central roles in New Vietnam, however. The network would splinter after 1945: many, such as Ton Quang Phiet and Vu Dinh Hoe, would become high-ranking officials in the Viet Minh government, whereas others became Viet Minh's opponents. Khai Hung and Nhuong Tong were said to be assassinated by Viet Minh in the late 1940s (Hoang V. D. 1970, 435, 466).

[18] Vu Dinh Hoe, "Van de ngoai giao" (The question of foreign policy), *Thanh Nghi*, June 16, 1945.

Viet Minh (Vu D. H. 1995, 197–228). After the quiet dissolution of New Vietnam, several leaders who joined Viet Minh also joined the Democratic Party (DP). The ICP helped to set up the DP in 1944 as part of its strategy to mobilize urban intellectuals, professionals, and students. Original DP members came from the Students' Association in Hanoi under the chairmanship of Duong Duc Hien (Vu D. H. 1995, 120–2, 137).

We have seen in Chapter 5 that the birth of the Viet Minh state in August 1945 was the result of compromise between the EVN government and the Viet Minh movement. A few days after Viet Minh had successfully seized power in Hanoi, Ho Chi Minh formed a cabinet with noncommunists. Among fifteen members, six were noncommunists.[19] Noncommunists helped to mobilize support for Viet Minh from urban sectors, local elites, and former mandarins. They brought into the Viet Minh government numerous urban professionals and intellectuals with similar backgrounds. Although noncommunists had no independent organization, they had long been prominent intellectuals in their own right and collaborated in the Thanh Nghi group, the New Vietnam Party, or the EVN government. Highly educated, experienced in business management, and trained in technical fields, noncommunists such as Hoang Van Duc, Vu Trong Khanh, Vu Dinh Hoe, Tran Dang Khoa, Nguyen Van Huyen, and Nghiem Xuan Yem formulated successful programs to reduce illiteracy and to fight the famine and the floods raging in northern Vietnam at the time. Their success further enhanced their influence.

Accommodation thus gave birth to a coalition government with a skewed distribution of power in favor of communists. On a closer look, this government was not composed of layers of concentric circles surrounding the party, as the theoretical model of a united front would describe. Accepting political compromises while lacking their own qualified personnel, ICP leaders had to grant noncommunist leaders full sectional authority as provincial heads and ministers of certain ministries. Rather than simply occupying positions on one of the concentric circles, these noncommunist leaders formed the centers of certain loci of autonomous activities. Although these loci were not in the realms of foreign policy or defense, they involved social, cultural, economic, and judicial policy at national and local levels. While communist domination could not be challenged, the ICP had limited control over those

---

[19] Noncommunists included Vu Dinh Hoe (Education), Duong Duc Hien (Youth), Vu Trong Khanh (Justice), Nguyen Manh Ha (Economy), Nguyen Van To (Social Affairs), and Nguyen Van Xuan (nonportfolio).

state branches concerned with social and economic management. As ICP leader and Prime Minister Pham Van Dong lamented in early 1950, "Currently our party controls only key government agencies but not most state apparatuses and technical departments. Even for an especially important agency such as the police, we don't have full control from the top to the bottom. Our grip on the judicial system is weak. Educational institutions are beyond our direct supervision."[20] Accommodation thus denied the ICP the ability to formulate and implement a radical program of socioeconomic change.

The ICP and New Vietnam Party represented very different kinds of political organization. The former was clandestine, professional, and well versed in organizational concepts. The latter was public, amateurish, and based mostly on personal trust. The ICP turned out not to follow the united front model as intended but was a mere member – albeit a dominant one – in the coalition government. Accommodation was institutionalized in the composition of this government and in the functional division between its two main components. This division did not allow the ICP to formulate and implement its socioeconomic policies as it wished.

Within the coalition government, the DP, the Viet Minh front, and the ICP were the three main organizations that came to embody accommodation. How did the ICP manage its party and front organizations from 1945 to 1950? As noted earlier, organizational separation was a central principle repeatedly emphasized by ICP leaders. In reality, however, organizational boundaries among the DP, the ICP, Viet Minh, and government entities often collapsed. The DP did not have a political identity separate from the movement until years later. Viet Minh was indistinguishable from the ICP at all levels. Instead of leading a united front as the vanguard, the ICP itself became a united front of all classes, with profound consequences.

The DP and Viet Minh

The Democratic Party (DP), the minor party in the Viet Minh government, never became an effective or autonomous organization. From the beginning, the ICP planted a secret cell within the Central Committee of the DP and more or less controlled its agenda. The DP was a useful tool of communist mobilization among urban intellectuals and professionals. After the Viet Minh government had been established, DP leaders convened the

---

[20] "Phai kien toan chinh quyen cong hoa nhan dan," 185.

first meeting of its provisional Central Committee.[21] In this meeting, the leaders declared that their party would adhere to "New Democracy-ism" (*Chu nghia Tan dan chu*), which was in fact Sun Yat-sen's Three People's Principles (although Sun was not mentioned). The party rejected the "French rotten parliamentary system and other regimes ruled by bureaucrats, financial cliques or the military." It proposed instead a republic that guaranteed freedom and equality of opportunity and that promoted social reforms and industrialization. The general secretary was a (secret) ICP member and his deputy was a former editor of *Thanh Nghi* and member of New Vietnam Party's Central Committee.[22]

The following year saw the DP undergo fast growth. Its first National Congress in October 1946 reported that the party had forty-two provincial branches and ten other branches (Vu D. H. 2000, 99, 137). By the end of 1946, the DP had about seventy-five hundred members. This success cannot be taken seriously because only two months later when war broke out between the Viet Minh government and the French, DP leaders dissolved their party at one stroke. The reasons given were that its general secretary had joined the army, and its constituency – urban businessmen and professionals – had all fled to the countryside. DP leaders thought that its members could serve the nationalist cause just as well by participating in local Viet Minh and government agencies (Vu D. H. 2000, 127, 136–45). At the insistence of Ho Chi Minh, who wanted the DP to resume as a separate organization, DP leaders convened a meeting of the DP Central Committee in mid-1947. Although DP membership reportedly grew after its resumption (Vu D. H. 2000, 138), the brief dissolution of the DP suggested that its leaders thought of themselves more as leaders of the national government than of the DP. In other words, party identity and organization had little meaning to them.

Like the DP, Viet Minh was not intended by its creators to be an autonomous organization. Before August 1945, however, it was prominent. Its General Command, or Tong Bo, issued numerous calls for mass uprisings and published two journals. Local Viet Minh groups played some role in the seizure of power in August 1945. Soon afterward, Viet Minh as an organization was sidelined. Apparently ICP cadres now in power were preoccupied with new state and party responsibilities; they

---

[21] "Chu nghia va chuong trinh cua Viet Nam Dan Chu Dang" (Ideology and agenda of the Democratic Party of Vietnam), *Doc Lap*, September 4, 1945.

[22] These men were Hoang Minh Chinh and Do Duc Duc, respectively. Other members of the committee included Nghiem Xuan Yem, Dang Thai Mai, Nguyen Duong Hong, Le Trong Nghia, Vu Minh Quang, Nguyen Thanh Le, and Hoang Van Duc.

could give Viet Minh and other mass organizations only passing thoughts. Tong Bo neither held regular meetings nor issued regular instructions to local Viet Minh as before.[23] There was actually no party cell (*Dang doan*) in Tong Bo, which suggested that it never functioned as an organization formally independent and separate from the ICP.[24] Despite several attempts by the ICP Central Committee to correct the situation, Viet Minh remained disorganized, demoralized, and neglected by party committees at upper levels.[25] Viet Minh chairman and ICP Politburo member Hoang Quoc Viet admitted in 1950 that since 1945 most party committees had viewed the united front as a mere formality (*hinh thuc, hieu hy*) and never assigned capable cadres to this line of work.[26]

Whereas Viet Minh was neglected at the central and provincial levels, at lower levels where party cells were weak or did not exist "Viet Minh" and "party" were indistinct concepts and organizations to their members. Here the evidence is sketchy owing to the unavailability of reports at low levels. Documents provide evidence of two zones in the Red River Delta and northwestern provinces, where the party was better organized; the evidence from these zones seems to reveal the general trend. In Zone 2, documents admitted that reports on Viet Minh activities and budgets for them were never separated from those of the party, as they should have been.[27] In Zone 3, district cadres reportedly knew only Viet Minh and "were not aware" of being ICP members. It was pointed out that the clandestineness of the ICP was responsible for this confusion. Because the ICP legally did not exist, party instructions from provincial to district levels were delivered not in formal meetings but by "shoulder-slapping

[23] This criticism was made in "Chi thi cua Ban Chap hanh Trung uong" (Central Committee's Decree), November 25, 1945 (DCSVN 2000, 8:30). Viet Minh's General Command at the time was headed by Hoang Quoc Viet, an ICP leader, and Hoang Van Duc, a DP leader.

[24] "Nghi quyet cua Hoi nghi can bo Trung uong" (Resolution of the Central Cadre Conference), April 3–6, 1947 (DCSVN 2000, 8:190).

[25] See "Thong cao cua Thuong vu T.U" (Announcement by the Standing Committee of the ICP Central Committee), December 31, 1947 (DCSVN 2000, 8:359–60); "Tich cuc cam cu va chuan bi tong phan cong" (Zealously holding off the enemy and preparing for the general attack phase), report by Truong Chinh at the Central Cadre Conference, January 14–18, 1949 (DCSVN 2001, 10:54), and "Ve cong tac Mat tran va dan van" (On front and mass work), report by Hoang Quoc Viet at the same conference (ibid., 111).

[26] "Ve cong tac Mat tran va dan van," 157–8.

[27] "Nghi quyet cua Hoi nghi Khu uy 2" (Resolution of Zone 2's Party Committee), July 8–11, 1947 (DCSVN 2000, 8:233, 240). Zone 2 included the provinces of Son Tay, Ha Dong, Ha Nam, Nam Dinh, Ninh Binh, Hoa Binh, Son La, and Lai Chau (Nguyen T. U. 1999, 145).

and whispering methods."[28] In many cases, local party committees were forced to disguise party organizations and activities under the cover of Viet Minh, and any difference between the two became lost (Truong Chinh 1948, 71).

The ICP

As front organizations, the DP and Viet Minh are expected not to have well-built structures. Noncommunists in the DP perhaps knew that the DP did not have real autonomy and did not want to invest in its organization. Besides, communists perhaps did not want these front organizations to develop strong structures to challenge their control one day. Then, what about the ICP?

Recall that the ICP suffered a great setback in 1940 with its failed rebellion in southern Vietnam; almost all Central Committee members were executed by the French. The Eighth Central Committee Plenum in 1941 that created Viet Minh was convened under this difficult circumstance. Its resolution lamented that the party had few active cadres left after waves of brutal French repression. Another concern was that the party did not possess the proletarian character that its leaders wished it to have. Among the membership, 25 percent were classified as "proletariat" and 70 percent came from "peasant" and "petty bourgeois" backgrounds.[29] Women (treated as a class by themselves) accounted for the remaining 5 percent. More peasants and colonial soldiers than urban workers participated in the 1940 rebellion, and the ICP blamed this "imbalance" for the failure of the rebellion.[30] The resolution of the meeting called for aggressive party penetration into mines, plantations, and urban centers to recruit more workers.

Party membership policy in subsequent years maintained two similar emphases. One was to expand into factories and the other was to strengthen the national network of party cells.[31] After Allied troops

---

[28] "Bao cao cua Khu Uy III nam 1947" (Report of Zone 3's Party Committee), n.d., probably mid-1948 (DCSVN 2000, 8:474). In original, "vo vai va ri tai thao luan." Zone 3 included the provinces of Hai Phong, Kien An, Thai Binh, Hung Yen, and Hai Duong (Nguyen T. U. 1999, 145).

[29] "Trung uong Hoi nghi lan thu 8" (Eighth Central Committee Plenum), May 1941 (DCSVN 2000, 7:132). It is not clear how party leaders came up with these percentages.

[30] Ibid., 134–5.

[31] "Nghi quyet cua Ban Thuong vu Trung uong" (Resolution of the Standing Committee of the Central Committee), February 25–28, 1943 (DCSVN 2000, 7:308–9).

landed on Normandy in June 1944, however, party leaders became impatient with the lack of progress in party work. Penetrating tightly controlled urban centers was more difficult than party leaders had expected. In an article in the party journal *Co Giai Phong* (Liberation Flag), Secretary General Truong Chinh scolded the rank and file for their passivity in the face of French terror.[32] Truong Chinh ordered that each member recruit one new member and make three "sympathizers" read the party newspaper every month. No requirements for class backgrounds were mentioned; instead, party members were told to search among their families and relatives first for new recruits. Years later this method of recruitment based on family connections would be criticized but, for the time being, it seemed that anything would do.

After having established itself in Hanoi in August 1945, ICP's recruitment was no longer difficult, and its leaders became more cautious with membership policy.[33] The party wanted to take advantage of new opportunities for growth, but it also wanted to avoid recruiting "complicated elements" into its ranks. Central leaders were irked that many local party branches (such as in Quang Ngai and many northern provinces) were still too obsessed with secrecy and did not want to admit new members. On the other hand, other party branches (such as in Ha Tinh and many southern provinces) were too lax: they simply let everybody join.

The concern about rash expansion never disappeared but ICP membership policy until 1946 allowed some flexibility. In July 1946 a conference of central leaders pointed out that local party branches (especially in central Vietnam) were still too restrictive (*co doc, hep hoi, ta khuynh*) in their membership policy and thus failed to attract urban intellectuals and professionals.[34] The resolution of this conference instructed every member to recruit a new member in the following month. The conditions for membership were to be made easier (*cham chuoc*) for those of working class, professional, and intellectual backgrounds. Clearly flexibility reflected the communists' general policy to accommodate other groups.

As noted in Chapter 5, ICP leaders announced the dissolution of the ICP in November 1945 as a gesture of compromise. After that time, internal communication channels among different party levels were kept

---

[32] "Phai tich cuc hoat dong" (Party members must act zealously), *Co Giai Phong*, June 16, 1944 (reprinted in Tran H. L. 1974, 125–7).

[33] "Chi thi cua Ban Chap hanh Trung uong" (Central Committee's Decree), November 25, 1945 (DCSVN 2000, 8:28–9).

[34] "Nghi quyet cua Hoi nghi Can bo Trung uong" (Resolution of the Central Cadre Conference), July 31–August 1, 1946 (DCSVN 2000, 8:108–11).

secret. So were identities of ICP members, except those who already had been publicly identified. The party was to be disguised as the "Association for Marxist Studies." Party meetings were concealed either as private or as government gatherings. The ability to maintain secrecy varied among party committees, but this does not contradict the fact that certain difficulties existed for all party members in mentally and physically separating party activities and functions from other realms of their work.

After war broke out in late 1946, which led to the disintegration of many army and administrative units (Lockhart 1989, 184–8), ICP leaders paid more attention to party consolidation.[35] As a result, they had in their hands the first ever detailed report of party membership and organizational development trends in north and north-central Vietnam by mid-1948.[36] Growth had been fast, at 350 percent for the entire year. Total membership in the two regions was 39,160, of whom 20,881 were provisional members. This total number included 5,715 members in the army. Calculations showed that there was 1 party member for every 30 members of national salvation associations and for every 200 ordinary Vietnamese. The ratio appeared unsatisfactory to party leaders, as the report stated that the party should become much larger to be truly "a party of the masses." The report complained that recruitment practices at local levels were still too restrictive.

Regarding members' social background, "workers" accounted for 8 percent, "middle and poor peasants" 68 percent, "intellectuals and petty bourgeois" 17 percent, and "capitalists and landlords" 0.15 percent.[37] No separate numbers were given for middle and poor peasants, but elsewhere the report stated that more party members were middle peasants than poor peasants and tenants combined, which suggested that middle peasants made up at least 35 percent of total party membership. At least more than half of all members (35 percent plus 17 percent) thus belonged

---

[35] A move to consolidate the party was the establishment of Party Organization Departments down to the provincial level. These departments would make plans for membership growth, handle personnel dossiers, and keep track of organizational issues. "Chi thi ve viec lap Ban To chuc Khu va Tinh" (Decree on the establishment of organizational departments at regional and provincial levels), September 1, 1947 (DCSVN 2000, 8:273–5).

[36] "Bao cao cua Trung Uong ve tinh hinh to chuc Hoi (Dang) o Bac Bo va Bac Trung Bo den cuoi nam 1947" (Central Committee Report on party organization trends in north and north-central regions up to the end of 1947), n.d., probably mid-1948 (DCSVN 2000, 8:361–97). According to this report, information from other regions was not available due to difficulties in communication.

[37] Ibid., 367–72.

to the less revolutionary classes. Constituting 25 percent of membership in the ICP in 1941, workers now accounted for only 8 percent. Most cadres (not regular party members) had an elementary and middle school education, suggesting that socially most belonged to local elites. Although the report noted that poor peasant and working-class members were more disciplined and resilient than those of petty bourgeois backgrounds, overall the party wanted more of all classes. For example, the small percentage of capitalists and landlords in the party was seen as a problem requiring a solution.[38] The report admitted that members of these classes were not as enthusiastic about the revolution as were others, but it faulted local party cadres for not paying enough attention to convert these groups. The complaints and admissions indicated that the central leadership tried to monitor the overall development of the party but had little actual control over local practices.

The loose central grip on grass-roots branches was similarly shown in other party-building activities. The same report noted that most local party cells from the district level down were weak in the sense that they were unable to draft their local agendas without guidance from above. An indicator of their full integration into the party structure was whether they had their own committees, as all party cells were supposed to have. The best rates of party cells with committees were found in Zone 3 in the upper Red River Delta, ranging between 40 and 60 percent.[39] In Zones 11 and 12, which were the suburbs of Hanoi and provinces northeast of the Red River Delta, the rates were close to zero.[40] These low rates cannot be attributed entirely to French repression because the ratios of party members among the general population were at or above average for these zones.[41] This situation apparently suggests that many party members had been recruited into the party for reasons unrelated to their political skills and that local party bases were far from fully integrated. Zone 10 offered further evidence of rash recruitment campaigns.[42] Since late 1947, local cadres in this zone had reportedly launched such campaigns

---

[38] Ibid., 369.

[39] In an example of a best organized province (Hung Yen), the number of party cells with leadership was 58 percent (DCSVN 2000, 8:375).

[40] Zone 11 was Hanoi and Zone 12 included Lang Son, Bac Giang, Bac Ninh, Hai Ninh, Hong Gai, and Quang Yen provinces (Nguyen T. U. 1999, 145).

[41] In Zone 11, there was 1 ICP member for every 200 people. The ratio in Zone 12 was 1 for every 160 (DCSVN 2000, 8:362). The average rate for all zones was 1 for every 200 people.

[42] Zone 10 included Lao Cai, Ha Giang, Yen Bai, Phu Tho, Tuyen Quang, and Vinh Yen provinces (Nguyen T. U. 1999, 145).

in which numerous new members were admitted on the basis of personal relationships.[43] These members were not educated about the meaning of party membership, nor were their backgrounds carefully checked.[44] This case demonstrated that central leaders had limited control over what happened at the grass-roots level in their own party.

By 1948 the civil war in China was at a turning point where communist troops had gained an upper hand in Manchuria and were about to take control of North China. Perhaps to prepare for the opportunity of linking up with Chinese communist forces, ICP Central Committee launched an ambitious membership campaign that set a 30 percent target for party growth at the district level in the following five months.[45] By now, recruitment was to be more selective: the targets were members in the army and local guerrilla forces, workers in state factories, and people in French-controlled zones and in ethnic minority regions. Not only were new members restricted to certain classes, but expansion would be accompanied by consolidation. The goal was to have 20 percent of all party cells consolidated in five months.

Thanks in part to this membership campaign, by early 1949 Indochina approached the worldwide standard in the proportion of Communist Party members in the general population. As Ho Chi Minh proudly announced in his closing speech of the Sixth Central Cadre Conference, there were 20 million communists among two billion people all over the world, or 1 per 100; the ratio in Indochina then was 1 out of 112 people.[46] Party membership increased by 300 percent in the first nine months of 1948, and 450 percent by the end of 1948.[47] From a mere 20,000 members in late 1946, the party had 50,000 a year later, and about 180,000 members by the end of 1948.[48]

---

43 The original phrase was "ket nap o at theo cam tinh rieng," which literally means to recruit en masse based on personal ties.

44 "Chi thi ve viec cung co va phat trien Hoi" (Decree on party consolidation and development), April 30, 1948 (DCSVN 2001, 9:453–62).

45 "Chi thi cua Ban Thuong vu Trung uong" (Decree by the Standing Committee of the Central Committee), signed by Le Duc Tho, June 1, 1948 (DCSVN 2001, 9:149).

46 "Bai noi chuyen trong buoi be mac Hoi nghi" (Closing speech), Central Cadre Conference, January 14–18, 1949 (DCSVN 2001, 10:166–7).

47 "Bao cao ve tinh hinh Dang nam 1948" (Report on party [organization] in 1948), Central Cadre Conference, January 14–18, 1949 (DCSVN 2001, 10:120–50). The number of 450 percent for 1948 is taken from "Hoan thanh nhiem vu chuan bi, tich cuc chuyen sang tong phan cong" (Completing preparations for the general attack phase), Truong Chinh's report at the Third National Conference, January 21–February 3, 1950 (DCSVN 2001, 11:92).

48 The growth was uneven, however: there were 70,000 members in Zone 3 alone. All of South Vietnam had about 30,000 members by the end of 1948.

While the expansion made party leaders happy, data on class back-grounds of members began to raise some concerns. About two-thirds of members came from "poor and middle peasant" backgrounds, 12 percent were "petty bourgeois and intellectuals," and 6.5 percent were "workers."[49] These data showed no significant difference from the na-tional data for the previous year. Hence, Secretary General Truong Chinh's speech at the same conference pointed to the problems of "con-taminated [class] backgrounds" of party membership.[50] Chinh warned vaguely against "mistaken ideas and tendencies" that were emerging in the party. However, the agenda on party building in 1949 still allowed for growth balanced with consolidation through the intensified political education of new recruits. The approach was to recruit first and educate later. Central ICP leaders had become more alert about the danger of contamination for their party but still hoped that political education for new members would set things straight. By September 1949 ICP member-ship would increase by another 250 percent to 430,000.[51] One-third of troops were now party members. "Workers" accounted for 8.7 percent, which was basically the same as in 1947.

In early 1950, the ICP succeeded in securing Soviet and Chinese diplo-matic recognition and assistance, thus obviating its need to maintain the earlier accommodation to other groups. Central leaders were now deter-mined to confront organizational problems and take effective control over grass-roots recruitment. At the Third National Party Conference, Truong Chinh's criticisms of party organization were harsh and direct. Recruitment campaigns that emphasized quantity but not quality and the method of recruiting among friends and families had opened up the party to "complicated elements." Rich peasants, village notables, and their children had been admitted into the party and now were sabotaging party policies on rent reduction and rice collection.[52] French spies had allegedly infiltrated some party organs. Political education fell far behind growth in membership. The party's capacity to implement its policies had been affected by the thoughts and behavior of "petty bourgeois" and "exploitative classes" allegedly prevalent among party members.

---

[49] These were data from Zone 3, the zone with nearly half of total party members and with the best organizations. Data from other zones were not reported. One would presume that middle peasants continued to outnumber poor peasants this year as in the previous year.

[50] Truong Chinh, "Tich cuc cam cu va chuan bi tong phan cong" (Zealously holding off the enemy and preparing for the general attack phase), January 14, 1949 (DCSVN 2001, 10:25–67).

[51] "Hoan thanh nhiem vu chuan bi," 92.

[52] Ibid., 93–5.

Except in the early 1940s, when French repression nearly destroyed the ICP, the party was always careful in its membership policy. From late 1945 when the ICP rose to power to mid-1948, party leaders encouraged the admission into the party of urban intellectuals and professionals. In practice, there were few barriers to people who wanted to join the ICP, regardless of their class backgrounds. The evidence presented here is sketchy but suggests that this relative openness was the result of two factors. In the first few years, maintaining strict class-based recruitment was counter to the general policy of the party to accommodate other groups. At local levels, the central party at most could monitor broad trends but had little real control over its branches. Regardless of central direction, local branches kept their own recruitment practices. The party's operation as a disguised organization exacerbated these problems. From mid-1948 to early 1950, when there was less need for accommodation, party membership policy became more restrictive and class-based. This shift coincided with the rising fortune of the communists in the Chinese civil war and eventually the success of the ICP in securing international socialist support in 1950. Yet this shift had little impact on the class character of the party. By this time, accommodation had become entrenched in party organization.

Confronting the Organizational Legacies of Accommodation

How did the ICP deal with the organizational legacies of accommodation? The ICP's organizational strategy to "rectify" the government and the party included two main elements. One was to remove noncommunists from positions of authority and to take full control of social, economic, cultural, and judicial policy apparatuses. By the early 1950s, this move was much easier than in 1945 because the ICP now had enough experienced cadres to administer the state at all levels and in all policy areas. Soon noncommunists no longer had much effective authority in the government. The coalition government at this point existed only in name. The second element of the ICP's strategy was to launch a "rectification" campaign to increase central control over local branches and to purge the "contaminated" members.

Organizational "rectification" included several measures. The first measure was to prevent further contamination with restrictive membership rules. The failure of earlier adjustments left the party with only one option, namely to close the door completely. In September 1950 a freeze on new members was put into effect that would not be lifted until seven years later.[53] When the ICP reemerged as the Vietnamese Workers' Party (VWP) in 1951, this freeze was codified in new membership rules, which made it extremely difficult to admit new members and which extended the probationary stage for all new recruits.[54] This was clearly a desperate measure: rather than the freeze, the party could have sought to replace its "contaminated" members over time by internal mechanisms such as selective promotion. Yet this measure also required central control over local promotion processes and would not guarantee that class-based recruitment and promotion would be enforced by local branches.

As a second measure to ensure organizational consolidation, political education was accelerated with radical methods taught by Chinese advisers. In May 1950 the central leadership launched a yearlong political education campaign with different curricula for party members from the highest ranking to the lowest.[55] Because this political education campaign allegedly revealed the deep penetration of bourgeois thoughts and behavior, party leaders authorized more radical measures. In subsequent campaigns during 1952 and 1953, cadres not only were asked to study party policies and Marxist-Leninist theories; they also were told to attend Maoist self-criticism sessions where they were expected and often coerced into purging their minds of "bourgeois thoughts."[56]

[53] Only exceptional cases would be considered for membership. "Chi thi cua Ban Thuong vu Trung uong" (Decree by the Standing Committee of the Central Committee), September 14, 1950 (DCSVN 2001, 11:481–3). The decision to lift the freeze was "Chi thi cua Ban Bi Thu so 05-CT/TW" (The Secretariat's Decree no. 05-CT/TW), February 12, 1957 (DCSVN 2002, 18:37).

[54] For the favored classes, an applicant for membership must be recommended by two existing members who had been in the party for at least six months (in the previous Party Constitution written c. 1941, it was three months); probationary time was six months (previously: two or four). For the less favored classes, the recommenders must have been in the party for at least a year (previously: six months) and probationary time was also one year (previously: six months). "Dieu le Dang Lao dong Viet nam" (VWP's Party Constitution) (DCSVN 2001, 12:448); "Dieu le tom tat cua Dang" (Abbreviated Party Constitution), n.d., probably 1941 (DCSVN 2000, 7:137–47). By the end of 1950, the total number of members had reached 730,000 from 480,000 in September 1949. "Dien van be mac Dai hoi Dai bieu Toan quoc lan thu II Dang Lao dong Viet nam" (The closing speech at the Second Party Congress of the VWP), February 19, 1951 (DCSVN 2001, 12:481).

[55] "Nghi quyet cua Ban Thuong vu Trung uong" (Resolution of the Standing Committee of the Central Committee), May 1, 1950 (DCSVN 2001, 11:313–20).

[56] "Van de chinh Dang" (On party rectification), Le Van Luong's report at the Third Central Committee Plenum, April 22–28, 1952, gave the broad direction of the new policy (DCSVN 2001, 13:101–6). For violent aspects of the campaign, see Ninh (2002, 101–7); and Q. Ngoc and T. Hong, "Phe binh lanh dao sinh vien" (Criticisms of student leaders), *Dat Moi* (New Land), 1956, 11–12.

As a third measure, organizational reform was implemented together with rent reduction and "land reform" campaigns.[57] "Party rectification" was first planned for implementation at the lowest level – the thousand party cells in rural areas – and then at district and provincial levels. Government apparatuses at these levels also would be retooled following the party purge at the same levels. As noted in Chapter 5, the party established the Land Reform Authority (LRA), a separate vertical organization from central to district levels with vast authority to discipline party members and dissolve "contaminated" local party cells.[58] From a pilot campaign in Thai Nguyen Province, the central party had concluded that its existing government and party apparatuses from the provincial level down could not be trusted.[59] Hence this new organization was created to ensure that new radical policies would not be "sabotaged" by "contaminated elements" as had been the fate of earlier policies.

The LRA would send teams of cadres into villages to encourage poor peasants and tenants to "struggle" with landlords and, in most cases, with ("contaminated") local party and government committees.[60] Landlords and rich peasants were to be expelled from the party even if they belonged to the local party leadership. The most zealous poor peasants in this campaign subsequently would be admitted into the party and promoted to local leadership positions. Party leaders might have been paranoid, as has been suggested (Moise 1983), but its leaders apparently felt they had no other way. Purging the "contaminated" elements and centralizing control of the party were essential if the state was to direct radical socioeconomic change effectively.

According to party documents, three-quarters (2,876) of all party cells (3,777 total) in sixteen provinces had been "rectified" in the rent

---

[57] "Bao cao cua Tong Bi thu Truong Chinh" (General Secretary Truong Chinh's report), Fourth Central Committee Plenum (Second Session), n.d., probably late January 1953 (DCSVN 2001, 14:68, 81). Also, "Cong tac to chuc doi voi cuoc van dong cai cach ruong dat" (Organizational tasks in the land reform campaign), report at the Fifth Central Committee Plenum, November 1953 (DCSVN 2001, 14:488–503). For simplicity, the discussion in this section combines rent reduction and "land reform" campaigns. Although these two campaigns were carried out separately in several stages (often rent reduction first to be followed by "land reform"), the methods and organization were similar. Both campaigns became more radical toward the end.

[58] "Cuong linh cua Dang Lao dong Viet nam ve van de ruong dat" (General party policy on land), November 1953 (DCSVN 2001, 14:502).

[59] "Chi thi cua Bo Chinh tri" (Politburo's Decree), March 20, 1954 (DCSVN 2001, 15:60–2).

[60] "Chi thi cua Ban Bi thu" (The Secretariat's Decree), December 28, 1953 (DCSVN 2001, 14:562–74).

reduction and "land reform" campaigns by the time these campaigns were suspended; 84,000 members in these cells were punished (*xu tri*) among the total of 150,000, or 56 percent.[61] "Punishment" usually meant being expelled from the party after torture and could include execution by firing squads. As Truong Chinh would admit in 1956, "most cadres and party members who were arrested were subject to brutal and barbaric torture."[62] The goal of the party was to purge only members with exploitative class backgrounds, but in practice those of working classes were purged as well. In the Ta Ngan Zone (provinces to the west of the Red River), 7,000 of the total 8,829 persecuted party members belonged to working classes. This situation appeared to result from the party decision (cited in Chapter 5) to authorize for execution the ratio of one class enemy per every 1,000 people. It also could be the result of top leaders' overall mistrust of the existing party apparatus, regardless of who, from which class backgrounds, staffed them.

Comparable destruction was found at the district and provincial levels. In the sixty-six districts and seven provinces where the party rectification campaign was carried out,[63] 720 out of 3,425 cadres and employees were purged; 80 percent of these 3,425 were party members. The number purged was 21 percent, which appeared not a particularly large proportion. However, if only cadres from provincial department levels up were counted, 105 were punished out of 284, or 37 percent. Among 36 incumbent members of provincial party committees, 19 (or 53 percent) were persecuted. At the district level, 191 out of 396 district party committee members were punished, or 48 percent. In an extreme case (Ha Tinh Province), all 19 members of the provincial party committee, police department, and district militia commanders were branded "counterrevolutionaries" and purged during the campaign. All were found later to be innocent by central authorities.

Overall, where the campaign was run, more than half of all party members and leaders at local levels were purged. The rates were the same for low-level village party cells and high-ranking provincial committees. Sometimes the best party cells were the most repressed, and the most

---

[61] The data in this paragraph came from Truong Chinh's report at the Tenth Central Committee Plenum, August 25–October 5, 1956. This Plenum issued the Error Rectification Campaign. "De cuong bao cao cua Bo Chinh tri" (Draft report of the Politburo) (DCSVN 2002, 17:432–8).

[62] Ibid., 435. In original, "nhuc hinh rat tan khoc, da man."

[63] The campaign at the provincial level was directed by the party's Central Organizational Department headed by Le Van Luong.

exemplary members received the worst punishments.[64] In Truong Chinh's own words, "The [last] phases in the rent reduction and land reform campaigns in reality were a severe purge of rural party organizations on a large scale with brutal measures."[65] He called the campaign at district and provincial levels "a massive internal purge."[66] Apparently personal appeals from high-ranking cadres at provincial level who were wrongly persecuted created conflict among top leaders, who decided to halt first the purge at the provincial and district levels and then at lower levels.[67]

As pointed out in Chapter 5, the party was forced to suspend the purge and the "land reform" campaign, apologize for the "mistakes," and order an "Error Rectification" campaign. Despite the brutalities, the ICP was able to build a more cohesive party and government structure out of the process. This structure would help the communist state to effectively mobilize popular resources for the civil war in the 1960s. For better or for worse, the event also led to severe political repercussions within the party leadership and a leadership change. Vietnam ended up missing the chance to lock steps and leap forward with the Maoist social revolution in China.

CONCLUSION

We have seen from Chapter 4 that organization was the decisive factor that brought the CCP to power. The communist victory over Chiang Kai-shek's regime in the civil war attested to its cohesive organization. ICP leaders did not lag behind their Chinese comrades in terms of

---

[64] Ibid., 433.

[65] In Vietnamese, "mot cuoc tran ap du doi bang nhung thu doan tan khoc va tren mot quy mo lon" (ibid.).

[66] In Vietnamese, "dai tran ap noi bo" (ibid.).

[67] The first document that warned of serious mistakes in the campaign dealt solely with those at the provincial and district levels. "Chi thi cua Ban Bi thu so 18/CT-TW" (The Secretariat's Decree no. 18/CT-TW), April 8, 1956 (DCSVN 2002, 14:111–13). Another order by the Secretariat four days later still called for radical measures in the campaign at the village level. "Chi thi cua Ban Bi thu so 20/CT-TW" (The Secretariat's Decree no. 20/CT-TW), April 12, 1956 (ibid.,132–9). The first decision that acknowledged mistakes at the village level was "Chi thi cua Bo Chinh tri so 33/CT-TW" (Politburo's Decree no. 33/CT-TW), July 5, 1956 (ibid., 268–74). It is not difficult to understand why top leadership paid attention first to high-ranking provincial cadres: at their ranks many of these cadres enjoyed access to and probably were known personally by top party leaders. Le H. B. (2000, 170) discusses the cases of two top provincial cadres in Phu Tho who had been persecuted but were then saved by old comrades in the party's Central Organization Department.

organizational skills. Ho Chi Minh had decades of experience in the revolutionary business spanning France, Russia, southern China, northern Thailand, and northern Vietnam. ICP leaders also learned hard lessons in two failed rebellions in 1930 to 1931 and in 1940. Truong Chinh and Le Duan spent years in colonial prisons because of these failures. No one knew better than these leaders the danger of rash actions that could provoke the colonial regime into crushing their movement. Their experience gave them the caution to resist the constant temptation among their ranks to take such actions. As Ho Chi Minh wrote to communist cadres in 1942, when they urged him to launch a revolt as soon as possible, "Comrades, you want to launch an uprising immediately. Very good! But [to do that,] we would need to have three things: The first is organization; the second is organization; the third is organization. Once we achieved these three things, we could launch a revolt and we would succeed."[68]

How wrong he was. Organization did not really help the ICP to seize power in August 1945 when the Japanese surrendered to the Allies. Accommodation to noncommunists and local mass groups brought the ICP to power as the dominant partner in the Viet Minh state. Accommodation brought support from elites in the colonial regime, collaboration from colonial bureaucrats, and nominal sovereignty over all local governments of Vietnam. The Viet Minh state could be erected and function as a state in a matter of days or weeks, with relatively little bloodshed. Noncommunist leaders and local mass groups contributed decisively to this event, although their contributions have been overlooked in most historical accounts. These groups also did not rise to power thanks to formidable organizations.

Yet accommodation had important implications for political organizations and institutions of the Viet Minh state. Accommodation was institutionalized in the coalition government comprised of communists and noncommunists. Furthermore, all political organizations were found to display blurred boundaries and corporate identities, from the DP to Viet Minh to the ICP. Given its leaders' knowledge of Leninist concepts and their organizational skills, the ICP was the most surprising case. The evidence indicates that this party accommodated urban constituencies and rich and middle peasants by relaxing its membership policies to some extent. More importantly, it lacked effective control over local recruitment. In the process of expansion, the party lost its Leninist character and became in effect a united front of all (mostly elitist) classes. By the

[68] *VNDL*, May 11, 1942.

time the party wanted to wage a social revolution, it confronted serious organizational problems. The deliberate destruction of its organization by half solved some problems but, at the same time, caused severe internal conflict and the postponement of its radical agenda.

The Indonesian state also was formed along the accommodation path. There, no political party dominated the scene as in the case of the ICP in Vietnam. Accommodation gave birth to an unstable multiparty parliamentary system of government. In this system, all political parties were poorly organized with blurred boundaries and vague corporate identities. Accommodation was institutionalized in both similar and different ways, providing an interesting contrast to Vietnam.

7

Organizing Accommodation in Indonesia

Parliament and Status-Based Parties

The broadcast of the Japanese emperor's announcement reached Indonesia at noon on August 15, 1945. The news of Japan's surrender came as a shock to those native nationalists who had collaborated with Japan (Anderson 1972, 66–9). The transfer of power from Japan to Indonesia was about to be arranged, and these Indonesian leaders expected to have a few months afterward to consolidate their government before Japan's eventual defeat. In the previous months, Sukarno, Mohammad Hatta, and others had agreed to a draft national constitution by which a presidential system would be established, based roughly on the Japanese-created administration on Java. This system would have a strong executive who would lead a state party and be advised by agencies set up by the Japanese. In other words, if things had gone as planned, especially if Sukarno had not been later sidelined,[1] there was some chance that Indonesia may have a centralized and cohesive state structure in the mold of militarist Japan.

Japan's surrender meant that no legal transfer of power would happen. It also meant that the Allies and the Dutch would arrive in Indonesia sooner than expected. Yet, after Sukarno and Hatta's proclamation of independence on August 17, it did not yet appear that Indonesia would be destined to have a state with a fragile structure. Despite numerous local uprisings, Indonesian leaders went ahead as planned and set up a government with power centered in the presidency. Only two months later

---

[1] As pointed out in Chapter 3, the constitution drafted under the Japanese would be resurrected when Sukarno regained power in 1957 and later also endorsed by Suharto. This constitution helped both leaders to centralize power in their hands.

this government was transformed into a parliamentary system, thanks to compromises among Indonesian elites.

As with the previous chapter, this chapter examines the institutionalization of accommodation in Indonesia's political organizations. We know that accommodation left serious structural problems for both Vietnam and Indonesia, and that elites would have difficulties implementing their socioeconomic agendas. We have also learned that accommodation in Vietnam was institutionalized in a coalition government and in the blurring of boundaries among political parties. The evidence in this chapter suggests that accommodation in the Indonesian case created similar yet different kinds of institutional arrangements compared to Vietnam. The difference was Indonesia's unstable parliamentary system, composed of numerous status-based political parties. The similarity between the two cases involved the blurred boundaries and weak corporate identities of political organizations.

This chapter begins with a historical overview of Indonesia's nationalist movement, which emerged at about the same time as the movement in Vietnam. As in Vietnam, political collaboration among Indonesian elites in this early period left few legacies. Following a detailed discussion of the birth of Indonesia's parliamentary institution and the evolution of political organizations since 1945, I offer an explanation for the different experiences between Vietnam and Indonesia despite sharing the same path of accommodation.

EARLY NATIONALIST ORGANIZATIONS, 1910s–1930s

In the Dutch Indies, modern political organizations appeared a decade before they did in French Indochina. The two earliest organizations were the Pure Endeavor (Budi Utomo, or BU), founded in 1908, and the Islamic League (Sarekat Islam, or SI), founded in 1912. Although these organizations have been viewed as precursors of the nationalist movement (Ingleson 1975, 1), their goal was not an independent Indonesia (van Niel 1960, 56; McVey 1965, 63; Noer 1973, 112).[2] Budi Utomo was founded by medical students of aristocratic descent and was primarily oriented toward the provision of cultural and educational services to Javanese (van Niel 1960, 56–9). Sarekat Islam was initially aimed at organizing

---

[2] Noer shows that Sarekat Islam leaders might have had conflicting views about the goals of the movement. In any case, in its first years Sarekat Islam was loyal to the colonial government.

Muslim traders to better compete with ethnic Chinese; its leaders viewed their organization as part of a Pan-Islamist movement. The only nationalist organization that demanded an independent state for the Indies was the small Indies Party (Indische Partij, or IP) founded in 1911; ironically, most of its leaders and supporters were not natives but Eurasians (van Niel 1960, 63–5). The party had barely started when the colonial government exiled its leaders two years later.[3]

During the same period, Marxism and trade unionism were imported to Indonesia by members of the Dutch Socialist Party (McVey 1965). The most prominent member of this group was Hendricus Sneevliet who founded the Indies' Social Democratic Association (Indische Sociaal-Democratische Vereniging, or ISDV) in 1914.[4] Original members of ISDV were Dutch expatriates, but six years after its founding, ISDV was transformed into the first communist party in Asia, the Communist Party of the Indies (Perserikatan Komunist di India or PKI), under local leadership.[5] Like Sarekat Islam, PKI was not nationalist but internationalist. ISDV and later PKI called for workers in the Indies to join the international struggle against capitalism and imperialism (McVey 1965, 30, 46–52, 65).

At one point Sarekat Islam achieved a membership of about half a million (Dahm 1969, 14). Sarekat Islam had a large following but suffered from a weak organization because the colonial government allowed only Sarekat Islam's local branches but not a central organization to be established (Shiraishi 1990, 69). The decentralized Sarekat Islam thus was vulnerable to penetration by other parties. In particular, ISDV (later PKI) was able to convert many younger Sarekat Islam leaders. By the early 1920s communist leaders formed an important faction within the SI leadership. However, communists' aggressive efforts to steer SI to the left led to their expulsion from SI in 1923. Four years later, PKI (with about three thousand members) was crushed after it launched a failed rebellion during 1926 and 1927. Sarekat Islam itself was broken into many small Islamic political parties and associations in the 1930s.

---

[3] IP later would revive briefly in 1918–20 under the name Insulinde, but it failed to compete with Sarekat Islam and PKI for influence (van Niel 1960, 159–63).

[4] After his expulsion from the Indies, Sneevliet would become a Comintern agent under the name Maring and would help to form the CCP and arrange for Soviet-GMD collaboration in China in the 1920s.

[5] The Dutch name was Partij der Kommunisten in Indie. Later the Indonesian name would be changed to Partai Komunis Indonesia, but the abbreviation (PKI) remained the same.

Except for the short-lived IP, secular nationalist parties emerged only after the crushing of PKI and the decline of Sarekat Islam. They were elitist and tended to be led by intellectuals rather than union organizers or Islamic leaders. Their viability depended on a few prominent and talented leaders rather than on organizational strength; the movement up to 1940 thus produced many future leaders for Indonesia but left little organizational foundation. In the mid-1920s, the two main nationalist groups were the Indonesian League (Perhimpunan Indonesia, or PI) and the Indonesian Nationalist Party (Perserikatan Nasional Indonesia, or PNI). PI was founded in Holland by Indonesian students (Ingleson 1975). This organization never had more than fifty members but it served as a valuable training ground for many future leaders, including Hatta and Sjahrir. PI would cease being a major player after Hatta and Sjahrir left the leadership in the late 1920s.[6] PI's rival from afar for much of the 1920s was PNI, founded in the Dutch Indies in 1927 by Sukarno (Dahm 1969). Thanks primarily to Sukarno's great oratorical skills, PNI would grow to about five thousand registered members before the colonial government banned it and imprisoned him in 1929 (Dahm 1969, 110).

After his arrest, Sukarno's collaborators in PNI dissolved this party and formed the Indonesian Party (Partai Indonesia, or Partindo) to circumvent the ban. Upon his release from prison, Sukarno joined Partindo. At the same time, Sjahrir and Hatta established, as an alternative, the Indonesian National Education (Pendidikan Nasional Indonesia, or "New PNI") in 1931. Despite brief efforts to build grass-roots organizations, both Partindo and New PNI did not grow into substantial movements before their respective leaders (Sukarno, Hatta, and Sjahrir) were exiled and their parties dissolved in the early 1930s (Ingleson 1979, 53–89, 141–228).

By the late 1930s, the remnants of various nationalist groups reemerged under the Great Indonesia Party (Partai Indonesia Raya, or Parindra), the more radical Indonesian People's Movement (Gerakan Rakyat Indonesia, or Gerindo), and small Islamic parties. Parindra was founded in 1935 as the successor of Budi Utomo, whereas Gerindo originated in part from Partindo (Ingleson 1979, 229). Parindra and Gerindo collaborated with the colonial government instead of opposing it as their predecessors did. Some former Sarekat Islam members founded the Indonesian Islamic League Party (Partai Sarekat Islam Indonesia, or PSII), and a faction in this party later founded the Indonesian Islamic Party (Partai Islam Indonesia, or PII) (Benda 1958, 90).

---

[6] Both actually were expelled from PI by a new group of leaders who were secret members of the Dutch Communist Party (Ingleson 1975, 68–70).

Prominent Islamic groups that were neither anticolonial nor nationalist included Muhammadiyah and Nahdlatul Ulama (Council of Islamic Teachers, or NU). Muhammadiyah, founded in 1912 as a social and educational organization, was inspired by the Islamic reformist movement in the Middle East and India and by puritanical Wahhabism in Saudi Arabia (Benda 1958, 45–8). These movements called for the renovation of Islam, a rejection of medieval scholasticism, and a return to the teachings of Mohammed. In Indonesia, reformists attacked Islamic institutions and cultural practices predominant in rural areas, which at one level were orthodox and formal and at another level "contaminated" by pre-Islamic Hindu, Buddhist, and animistic cultures. Nahdlatul Ulama was created in 1926 by rural orthodox Islamic teachers as a counter to Muhammadiyah (Noer 1960, 224–6). In 1937 the two movements established the Great Islamic Council of Indonesia (Majelis Islam A'la Indonesia, or MIAI), but this was no more than a loosely organized forum to coordinate activities (Benda 1958, 90). During the Japanese occupation, all the major leaders of these groups and still others would be brought together to work as advisers to the Japanese military government.

As in colonial Vietnam, elite collaboration occurred in Indonesia before 1940, as observed between Sarekat Islam and PKI in the 1920s and among Gerindo, Parindra, and PSII in the 1930s. Yet the organizational legacies of this period were insignificant. Besides expanding the personal networks of nationalists and offering training in mass agitation to individual leaders, collaboration left little in terms of concrete organizations. Elites may have been concerned about organization but they failed to develop cohesive ones. Agitation rather than organization was the primary focus, as in the cases of Sarekat Islam, PKI, and PNI. Or, elites were more interested in mass education than organization, as in the case of New PNI.[7]

FROM PROLIFERATION TO DISINTEGRATION, 1942–1955

Similar to its Vietnamese counterpart, the Indonesian state was born out of elite compromise and mass incorporation. Yet accommodation was

---

[7] In the early 1930s there were debates between New PNI and Partindo on organizational issues, in which New PNI leaders criticized their Partindo counterparts for violating democratic principles. See, for example, the collection of Sjahrir's articles published in *Daulat Rakyat* (People's Sovereign, New PNI's journal) in 1931–4, republished in Sjahrir (1947). Also, see Hatta (1976), "PI dan saya" (PI and me) and "Sekali lagi keterangan saya" (Let me explain one more time). For an English summary of the debates, see Ingleson (1979, 154–61). These debates revealed different views about the appropriate relationship between leaders and followers in an organization rather than indicating an interest in actual organizing activities.

arranged differently in the two cases. At the elite level, the ICP formed a coalition government to share power with noncommunists in the Thanh Nghi network. These two groups collaborated and excluded – in many cases through assassinations – other nationalist and Trotskyite leaders.

In Indonesia, nationalists led by Sukarno formed a new government in August 1945 on the basis of the structure created by the Japanese. Although the Japanese had left behind a model and components of a centralized, cohesive state, Sukarno soon had to compromise with other groups and transfer power to Sjahrir and his associates. The results of this accommodation were a multiparty parliamentary system and numerous status-based parties. No group, including the three larger parties, had any significant mass support. Built loosely out of status circles and dependent on individual leaders, these parties lacked internal cohesion and were extremely unstable. Their leaders were able to get seats in parliament and the cabinet based on personal prestige or relationships, and not on the strength of their organizations. As a result, they paid little attention to organizational matters. Even to a greater extent than in Vietnam, the boundaries among parties were blurred and their corporate identities weak.

From Totalitarianism to Parliamentarianism

During their occupation of Java, the Japanese created advisory councils and agencies led by nationalist and Muslim leaders. These organizations were centrally organized, and directed in most cases by Japanese officials. Japan's promise of independence and its limited support for Indonesian nationalism were to facilitate the mobilization of Indonesian manpower and resources for the Pacific War. After Japan's defeat, for a brief period, these organizations formed the core of the Indonesian nationalist movement. If they had been preserved, the Indonesian state may have had a centralized and more cohesive structure. Yet accommodation among elites led to the dissolution of these Japanese-built organizations and their replacement by a multiparty parliament in which numerous political groups, however small and insignificant, participated.

Among the earliest organizations created by the Japanese in early 1943 was Putera. Sukarno and Hatta shared leadership of Putera with two Muslim leaders (Benda 1958, 117). By late 1943, as the Japanese prepared for the Allies' invasion, they established a Central Advisory Council and seventeen regional councils. Indonesian politicians and professionals staffed these councils (Benda 1958, 137). The chairman and vice chairman of the

Central Advisory Council were Sukarno and Hatta. Among the council's forty-three members, six were prominent Islamic leaders. Muslim leaders also frequently chaired regional councils. Through these councils, secular nationalist and Muslim leaders received some training in state management, even though organizational matters were strictly in Japanese hands.

Putera was replaced in early 1944 by the Javanese Service Association or Jawa Hokokai, which had branches all the way down to villages and urban neighborhoods. Like Putera, Jawa Hokokai was established to mobilize manpower and resources (Benda 1958, 153–6). Sukarno and a Muslim leader served as advisers to the Japanese chief of Jawa Hokokai. At local levels, this association was staffed by local bureaucrats, thus allowing nationalist leaders limited supervision of local governments for the first time. While not autonomous, the combined advisory councils and Jawa Hokokai branches formed a shadow governmental hierarchy from central to local levels run by Indonesians.

Immediately after proclamation of independence, it appeared that the new state would be set up according to Japanese design. While the constitution drafted under the Japanese struck a delicate balance among various political ideologies, it called for the formation of a presidential system with vast powers vested in the presidency. Under Sukarno and Hatta, the new government attempted to preserve the bureaucratic structure and personnel left behind by the Japanese. Almost all of its cabinet members came from the former Japanese-sponsored advisory bodies (Anderson 1972, 110–13). With full executive and provisional legislative powers, Sukarno appointed a Central National Committee (KNIP) to advise him.[8] A government party led by the president was to be founded to mobilize the masses and coordinate the struggle (Budiardjo 1955, 37; Legge 1988, 100). Different groups would participate in this party, but it was to be centralized and directed from the top, similar to Jawa Hokokai.

Yet these Japanese-built centralized organizations were dissolved when Sukarno and Hatta accommodated Sjahrir and other groups in the KNIP. With this body being transformed into a parliament, power that previously had been concentrated in the president and the cabinet was now scattered among many factions.[9] The plan for a centralized government

---

[8]   The constitution established the People's Consultative Assembly (MPR) and People's Council of Representatives (DPR) as the supreme legislative bodies but also stated that before their establishment the president would assume legislative authority with the advice of a National Committee (Budiardjo 1955, 37; Anderson 1972, 171–2).

[9]   Sukarno as president retained the crucial power to appoint KNIP members. He would use this power to double the number of KNIP members in 1947 so that there was a majority

party was nipped in the bud. Sjahrir's subsequent call for political parties to be established led to the hasty formation of numerous parties (including his own) to gain seats in the KNIP and local councils. By one count, the republic had twenty-nine political parties participating in its parliament by the end of 1945 (Hartoni 1960, 24). This situation prompted a popular newspaper in Jakarta to call for a halt to forming new parties for fear of political chaos.[10]

Were the creators of the multiparty system – that is, Sjahrir and his associates – aware of the danger of fragmentation and instability inherent in this system? In a lengthy public announcement by the Ministry of Information published after the call for party formation, both two-party and multiparty systems were analyzed, noting their advantages and disadvantages.[11] It was pointed out that the multiparty system might cause the "disease of sectarianism" (*penyakit sectarianisme*) or the tendency to form small parties based on petty differences that could lead to chaos. Yet, because the two-party system was rejected as excluding all but two groups, the ministry argued that the best system was one that had more than two but in which the number of parties would be limited so that only the major ideologies (*aliran paham politik*) were represented. The announcement admitted that the appropriate number of political parties would be difficult to determine but went on to say that the matter could be decided later by a representative body. Apparently the disease of sectarianism was insufficient to weigh against Sjahrir's devotion to democracy and his faction's need for broad elite support to oust Sukarno's cabinet (Anderson 1972, 177). Accommodation under these conditions was institutionalized in the multiparty parliamentary form.

In comparative perspective, while both Vietnam and Indonesia walked down the path of accommodation, the struggle to transform the nationalist movement into a new state resulted in a different institutional form in Indonesia. In Vietnam, the ICP dominated politics as the best organized party. In Indonesia, no such party existed. The centralized mobilizing organizations established by the Japanese on Java formed the early

of votes approving the Linggajati Agreement with the Dutch. See Presidential Decree no. 6, *Antara*, January 2, 1947. For subsequent debates in KNIP on this decree, see *Antara*, January 4–20, 1947. See also Budiardjo (1955, 53–4).

[10] "Partai terlalu banjak!" (There are too many parties!), *Ra'jat*, January 22, 1946.

[11] Kementerian Penerangan (Ministry of Information), "Arti Partai Politik Didalam Demokrasi" (The meaning of political parties in a democracy), *Berdjuang*, January 9, 10, 14, 1946.

structure of a Republican state, but thanks to elite compromise, this budding state was replaced by one with an unstable multiparty parliamentary system at the top. Proponents of this system were well aware of its dangers but they went on to create it anyway. The system in turn encouraged the proliferation of political parties. These parties had weak boundaries and blurred corporate identities. They were built around loose status circles, not strict organizational principles. Their leaders earned parliamentary and cabinet seats thanks to personal status or relationship rather than organizational skills. Because Sjahrir's parliament did not require them to compete in elections, they had little incentive to build cohesive organizations. The rise and decline of three main parties, including PSI, PNI, and Masjumi, offer examples of how these parties were organized and operated.

The Proliferation of Parties Based on Status Circles

Most Indonesian political parties of the 1950s were founded or resurrected in late 1945 and early 1946. Most, if not all, were founded in response to Sjahrir's call in November 1945 after he successfully changed the KNIP into a sort of parliament. To understand why these parties were particularly suitable to the conditions of accommodation and why they created instability, we need to take a close look at their structures and origins.

Because colonial regimes were repressive, only two forms of organization for political activism were possible for noncollaborating elites. One form was the underground secret parties of which the ICP was an example. To survive, this kind of party needed tight discipline and highly dedicated leaders and members. Often they were professional revolutionaries subscribing to some anticolonial ideologies. These necessarily small parties operated at the margins of society and were frequently subject to police raids. The other form of political organization was progressive networks of elites formed around professional or status circles in mainstream colonial societies. These networks functioned as forums for both socialization and political discussion (but not political action in the strict sense). Participants could share some vague progressive ideas but were not required to believe in any elaborate ideologies. The networks may have had informal rules regulating behavior, but their glue was less organizational norms than personal relationship, the presence of prominent personalities, and the sense of shared social status. The Thanh Nghi network in Vietnam is an example of this network. Thanh

Nghi had many parallels in Indonesia, as historian John Legge (1988, 43) describes:

One might identify, in Occupation Jakarta [under Japanese rule], a number of centers – rival student organizations, asramas (dorms), discussion groups, groups arising from common places of employment under the Japanese – and Sjahrir's followers were to be found in many of these. But the membership of such groups overlapped to such an extent, and the paths of their leading figures crossed so frequently and in such a variety of different connections, that it might seem more correct to see them not in their attachment to this asrama or that movement, but rather as a single group loosely organized about a series of focal points, and interacting continuously with each other.

As Legge suggests, Sjahrir's group was part of the broader network of overlapping circles with nationalist tendencies. It was a major group in the network because it had a well-known leader and many followers. Its leader, Sjahrir, had acquired a significant reputation in the nationalist movement in Indonesia in the early 1930s and had been exiled for many years because of his political activities. But a group in a network, especially a local one, often did not need leaders with such stellar anticolonial credentials in order to form. A group leader could be a medical doctor or a successful businessman with a professional reputation, a personal interest in social issues, and leisure time for activism. Deliar Noer (1960, 62) describes one such person:

Abu Hanifah had never been affiliated with a Muslim party or organization in prewar days. For some time he organized an Islam study club at Medan (North Sumatra) which, however, had neither a large following nor influence among the local Muslim community. . . . But he maintained contacts with the Muslim movements in prewar days through his writings in Muslim magazines. . . . Besides, he is a [medical] doctor, which means an intellectual, and there are still not many intellectuals . . . particularly in the Indonesian Muslim community. Thus a political opening for him existed there [to become a future leader].[12]

When political opportunity was suddenly expanded, as in late 1945 in Vietnam or Indonesia, these progressive circles were often the only kind of organizations available for mobilization in a particular place – the only game in town, so to speak. But they also had certain characteristics that made them particularly suitable to the politics of accommodation at the time. First, these groups were formed on the basis of personal relationships and did not espouse any particular coherent ideologies. To exist openly under repressive colonial regimes, the networks self-selected and filtered out the most radical elements. Without clearly defined

---

[12] Hanifah's name would show up on the Masjumi leadership roster in November 1945.

ideologies, these groups were more willing to accommodate others. Second, because personal trust was abundant in the networks, it was easy and fast for political entrepreneurs to transform overlapping groups into political parties. For groups whose leaders enjoyed national prominence in colonial societies, they could multiply quickly by attracting local groups who wanted to associate with such leaders. The ease of formation and multiplication explained why they proliferated.

Yet their strengths were also their weaknesses. Because they were built on personal trust, relationships *within* personal factions were closer than those *among* them, which were needed to hold the party together. This also meant that organizational boundaries and corporate identities were not important to party members. One faction might want to be identified with a faction in another party rather than with other factions in its own party. These parties were unstable because they relied on overlapping personal relationships, and they recruited on the basis of social status within a circle rather than on organizational skills. A member was often guaranteed a place in a circle thanks to his status, regardless of whether he had any following. Because of his other professional commitments, he may even be allowed to join a party on a part-time, trial basis. Because of his well-recognized social status, he could switch parties rather easily or resign from an organization and then join it later at no loss to his status.[13] If party membership generated government positions, members might become more committed to their parties, but then they might be committed more to their government responsibilities than to party organization.

We have seen in Chapter 6 that the New Vietnam Party had little structure beyond its Central Committee. Its leaders were part-time revolutionaries. They did not share a common ideology but were involved because they all wrote for the same progressive journal and perhaps came from similar social backgrounds as urban professionals and intellectuals. Their list of committee members was public record; some on this list were veteran members of other political parties, but there was no evidence that these people played any important role in the party itself. Their names

[13] The case of Raden Achmad Subardjo was extreme: he was a leader of Perhimpunan Indonesia in Holland before Hatta but spent some time in the Soviet Union and then in Japan as a correspondent. He then worked for the colonial Economic Department in the late 1930s and for the Japanese as an adviser during the occupation. He was made minister of foreign affairs in the first cabinet under Sukarno and was involved in organizing a "state party." After this cabinet was dissolved for a cabinet headed by Sjahrir, Subardjo helped Tan Malaka organize the Union of Struggle to overthrow Sjahrir. This activity led many observers to label him a communist (McVey 1954, 26). However, in 1951, he suddenly showed up as a Masjumi member and minister of foreign affairs in Sukiman's cabinet (Noer 1960, 241). His pro-U.S. diplomacy later caused this cabinet to fall.

simply were on the roster. When conditions were no longer favorable, the leaders simply closed down their party and joined another. Many if not most Indonesian leaders were similarly unconcerned about consolidating their parties.

After independence, the three main parties in Indonesian politics up to the late 1950s – the Socialist Party (PS and later PSI), the Nationalist Party (PNI), and Masjumi – formed coalition cabinets that tried but failed to implement pro-Western and growth-oriented economic policies. The history of these parties has been well researched,[14] but the following discussion of the three parties should illuminate the microdynamics of Indonesia's unstable and fractured political organizations.

Socialist Party

The Socialist Party (Partai Sosialis, or PS) resulted from the merging of two different parties that were formed in November 1945 (Anderson 1972, 202–12). One was Partai Rakyat Sosialis (People's Socialist Party, or Paras), which was the reincarnation of the prewar Pendidikan Nasional Indonesia (Indonesian National Education) led by Sjahrir and Hatta in the early 1930s. Paras leaders also included new blood from the student group recruited by Sjahrir during the Japanese occupation. The initiative to form Paras originated from former members of Pendidikan after Sjahrir had become prime minister. Sjahrir sent a delegation to the meeting that founded Paras, but he himself did not attend (Mrazek 1994, 285–6).

The second group in PS was Partai Sosialis Indonesia (Indonesian Socialist Party, or Parsi) under Amir Sjarifuddin's leadership. Parsi was the reincarnation of the prewar Gerindo, a party of radical leftists led by Sjarifuddin. It was now supplemented with younger elements recruited by Sjarifuddin during the Japanese occupation, and several leftist returnees from Holland, the best known of whom was Abdulmajid Djojoadiningrat, an executive member of the Dutch Communist Party.[15]

---

[14] History of prewar Indonesian nationalist, communist, and Islamic parties can be found in McVey (1965); Noer (1973); and Ingleson (1975; 1979). G. Kahin (1950; 1952, 304–31); Budiardjo (1955); and Anderson (1972, 202–31) offer general accounts about postwar political parties. Myers (1959) and Legge (1988) focus on PS and PSI. Benda (1958) deals with Islamic groups during the Japanese occupation, while Noer (1960, 1987) studies Masjumi and other Islamic parties in the post-1945 period. Rocamora (1975) provides the single-best source on PNI, and an insightful paper by McVey (1954) discusses PKI during 1945–50. Less important sources are Naim (1960) on NU, and Hartoni (1960) on PKI.

[15] Abdulmajid succeeded Hatta as chairman of Perhimpunan Indonesia, the Indonesian League in Holland in the late 1920s, and turned it into a communist organization.

Both factions in PS called themselves "socialists" and were influenced by Marxism, but each believed in a different version of socialism. Sjahrir's outlook was closely aligned with European social democratic thinking and his approach to organization emphasized mass education over agitation and mobilization. In contrast, Sjarifuddin held views not unlike those of Leninists: he advocated more radical social changes and sought power in mass mobilization. One of the main reasons these two groups came together was because several key members in Sjahrir's circle had once been part of Sjarifuddin's during the Japanese occupation before Sjarifuddin was arrested by the Japanese authority in 1943 (Legge 1988, 110–18). The initiative to merge Paras and Parsi appeared not to involve Sjahrir; he was not listed as a leader when PS was founded but became PS chairman only later. Sjahrir's low-key involvement in both Paras and PS was indicative of his total disregard for organizational work.

Paras and Parsi founded PS together, but in fact the two factions were never fused (Anderson 1972, 205). Collaboration between them seemed limited to mutual support in the three cabinets under Sjahrir from October 1945 to July 1947. In these cabinets, Sjahrir was prime minister and minister of foreign affairs, and Sjarifuddin was minister of defense. Yet, whereas Sjahrir was not concerned about party matters, Sjarifuddin used his position to build up the strength of his own faction (Sjahrir 1956, 45). Recall that Sjarifuddin launched a youth congress in late 1945 and founded Pesindo, the youth militia.

The minimal interaction between the two factions did not help to harmonize the different views of their members. Furthermore, the gradual move by Sjarifuddin's group to take full control of Pesindo and other mass organizations raised suspicion within Sjahrir's camp about Sjarifuddin's intention to seize control of PS (Sjahrir 1956, 35). Disagreement between the two factions over the concessions Sjahrir made in the Linggajati Agreement signed with the Dutch in mid-1947 was the last straw (G. Kahin 1952, 207–8; Legge 1988, 112–19). In this dispute, Abdulmajid, Sjarifuddin, and other Parsi leaders joined with other parties in parliament to criticize Sjahrir for the concessions, which they viewed as excessive. After Sjahrir resigned as prime minister, Amir Sjarifuddin was appointed to form a new cabinet. The Sjarifuddin cabinet with several Parsi members as ministers fell after only eight months in power. This time the role was reversed: Sjahrir's Paras faction joined the opposition in parliament to attack the Renville Agreement, which Sjarifuddin negotiated with the Dutch (G. Kahin 1952, 230–1). As a result of this fallout, Paras withdrew from PS and set up a new party, the Socialist Party of Indonesia (PSI) in February 1948. Later that year, Sjarifuddin and Abdulmajid brought the remaining PS to join Musso's PKI, rebelled against the republican government, and were both executed.

Given Sjahrir's negligence of party building, PSI remained a small elite party as the Paras faction had been. Too dependent on Sjahrir, PSI became increasingly irrelevant now that he was no longer prime minister.[16] In February 1950, when PSI convened its first executive committee meeting ever, the party had only a few thousand members (Sjahrir 1956, 47). Despite two party congresses between 1952 and 1955, where suggestions were made to open up and expand the party, PSI never developed any mass following. In the first election for the parliament held in 1955, PSI had about fifty thousand members and won only 2 percent of total votes, which translated into 5 out of 257 seats in the parliament (Mrazek 1994, 409–11; Feith 1962, 434–5). Two PSI leaders joined cabinets in the early 1950s, most notably the influential economist Sumitro Djojohadikusumo, who was minister of trade and industry in the Natsir cabinet and minister of finance in the Wilopo cabinet. Yet these leaders' link to PSI was loose, and PSI offered little support for these cabinets in their economic policies (Mrazek 1994, 406).

Indonesian Nationalist Party

The Indonesian Nationalist Party (Partai Nasional Indonesia, or PNI) was founded in early 1946 and based in part on the prewar PNI. Unlike PS, which was small and elitist, PNI was much larger and more diverse, with three main factions and several less stable groupings. A significant faction in PNI included older leaders who worked with Sukarno when the original PNI was founded in 1927. The leader of this faction, Sartono, was deputy chairman of the prewar PNI. Another major faction consisted of young lawyers who had joined the nationalist movement in the mid-1930s. The most prominent member of this faction was Wilopo, who would become a prime minister in the early 1950s (Rocamora 1975, 48–9). Cohesion for this faction came from the fact that its leading members graduated from the same law school within a year or so of each other.

In terms of social backgrounds and personal beliefs, the Sarmidi-Sidik faction stood out from the others. Members of the other factions were highly educated professionals, came mostly from the upper *priyayi* class, and were drawn to socially conservative nationalism but not to radical

---

[16] In late 1949, when the Round Table Conference Agreements were signed that recognized Indonesia's formal independence, PSI abstained from voting for it on the grounds that the agreements made too many concessions to the Dutch (Mrazek 1994, 400).

Marxism.[17] In contrast, the faction led by Sarmidi Mangunsarkoro and later Sidik Djojosukarto were less educated and mostly came from families of petty traders, village officials, and other low-rung members in the colonial bureaucracy (Rocamora 1975, 48). These leaders had the least Westernized outlook and were the strongest supporters in PNI of an armed struggle against the Dutch. This faction was built mostly from the youth groups mobilized in the Barisan Pelopor during the Japanese occupation. While national PNI leaders were mostly conservative regarding social changes, the youths in many provinces and districts who came from lower *priyayi* and other marginalized strata were far more radical in their outlook. They also were more willing to collaborate with local communist groups to attack local governments dominated by the upper *priyayi* class.[18]

Why these factions joined PNI is unclear. In fact, they made few efforts to reconcile their differences so that the party could become more cohesive and united. One major source of factional conflicts in PNI concerned the strategy for the struggle for independence. The Sarmidi faction was staunchly anti-Dutch and frequently sided with those from other parties that opposed the Sjahrir government's diplomatic negotiations. The other PNI factions vacillated on this issue and were ready to accept cabinet positions under Sjahrir when such positions were offered to them. In early 1946 PNI, led by the Sarmidi faction, joined Tan Malaka to call for a total war with the Dutch and other Western powers. However, Sjahrir was able to persuade a minor PNI leader to help him defeat Malaka.[19] Six months later, when Sjahrir needed to persuade the parliament to accept the Linggajati Agreement that he had negotiated with the Dutch, he reshuffled the cabinet and offered four ministries to PNI leaders (G. Kahin 1952, 193–5). These four leaders accepted the offers, even though the PNI leadership council (then dominated by radical leaders) opposed the agreement.[20]

In part thanks to the prestige gained from their cabinet positions, the leaders of the moderate factions were able to seize control of the party

[17] *Priyayi* is a Javanese term to indicate the upper class on Java, which supplied bureaucrats for the colonial administration (Anderson 1972, 17).

[18] The role of these youth groups in the uprisings in Solo, East Sumatra, and Aceh against the royal families and traditional elites is analyzed in Soejatno (1974); Morris (1985); and van Langenberg (1985).

[19] The PNI leader was Herling Laoh (Anderson 1972, 319–20).

[20] The four leaders were A. K. Gani (minister of prosperity), Susanto Tirtoprodjo (minister of justice), Lukman Hakim (deputy minister of finance), and Herling Laoh (minister of public works).

leadership council for a brief period from March to November 1947. After Sjahrir fell from power, moderate PNI leaders were retained in Sjarifuddin's cabinet and held the First Deputy Prime Ministership and four ministerial portfolios of Economy, Education, Justice, and Labor (Rocamora 1975, 24–7). When the Dutch launched an attack on the republic in violation of the Linggajati Agreement, the moderate factions in PNI that supported negotiation lost out. A new leadership council that was elected in November 1947 withdrew PNI support for Sjarifuddin's cabinet and caused it to fall, despite the fact that four PNI leaders held important posts in this cabinet.

In the next two years, PNI did not stick to a consistent pattern of opposing or supporting the government, whether its members served in the cabinet or not.[21] It supported the government when the latter was under attack by PKI in late 1948 but, especially after the rise of Sidik as party chairman in May 1950, sided with the opposition in parliament. Under Sidik's leadership, PNI generally pursued a radical nationalist foreign and economic policy platform. PNI's Fourth Congress in 1949 called for the formation of an "anticapitalist bloc" with the leftist parties (Rocamora 1975, 27–32, 37). The oppositionist policy of PNI alienated its most moderate Parindra faction, which broke away and formed a new party, PNI-Merdeka (Free PNI) in mid-1950.[22]

In Indonesia's first independent parliament, PNI was the second-largest party after Masjumi. In the Natsir cabinet (August 1950–March 1951), PNI was not represented. It opposed the government on the Papua issue and on Indonesia's entry into the United Nations. Its leaders helped to engineer the downfall of this cabinet (Rocamora 1975, 40–1). In the subsequent Sukiman cabinet, PNI secured six posts in return for more moderate stands on foreign policy and other issues.[23] For the first time in its history, the PNI party council nominated and supported PNI ministers, all of whom came from the Sartono faction, which led the

---

[21] Five PNI members served in the special Hatta cabinet (January 1948 to December 1949) including Susanto Tirtoprodjo (Justice), Maramis (Finance), Ali Sastroamidjojo (Education and Culture), and Herling Laoh (Public Works) (G. Kahin 1952, 232). Four PNI members served in the Hatta cabinet (of the Republic of the United States of Indonesia, December 1949–August 1950), including Wilopo (Labor), Laoh (Communications and Public Works), Arnold Mononutu (Information), and (after May 1950) Sarmidi Mangunsarkoro (Education) (Feith 1962, 46–7; Rocamora 1975, 32).

[22] Former leaders of Parindra in PNI were Jody Gondokusumo and Syamsuddin St. Makmur (Rocamora 1975, 23, 28, 37).

[23] These posts included deputy prime minister and ministers of interior, information, trade and industry, and public works and utilities (Feith 1962, 180). Sidik of PNI and Sukiman of Masjumi were the *formateurs* of this cabinet.

leadership council. However, the decision of the national party council to support this cabinet was not well received among its local branches, which were more radical (Rocamora 1975, 52–4). In several controversial policies of the Sukiman cabinet, including the government raid against the communists in August 1951, compliance with the United Nations' embargo on China, and the signing of the San Francisco Treaty with Japan and the United States, the PNI leadership council was forced to be on the defensive (Feith 1962, 187–98). In the case of the treaty, the party council called for PNI ministers to reject it, but this call was ignored (Rocamora 1975, 58).

The first cabinet headed by a PNI prime minister was inaugurated in April 1952. Wilopo became prime minister, and men of his faction took Foreign Affairs and Economy portfolios (Feith 1962, 229). However, Wilopo was immediately ostracized by the PNI leadership council for yielding too much to the demands of Masjumi, which shared power in the cabinet. Although Wilopo was PNI deputy chairman at the time, his faction was not able to defend his cabinet within the party on a wide range of issues, from Papua to the Round Table Conference Agreements (Rocamora 1975, 61–2). PNI joined the opposition to protest the army leadership for its demobilization program; Wilopo resisted but in the end had to dismiss many top officers in the army's general staff. The decision by the PNI minister of the economy to return oil installations to their prewar foreign owners was severely criticized at party meetings and never implemented. The Wilopo cabinet also was attacked in PNI meetings for being too close to PSI and Masjumi leaders while neglecting PNI interests. Then, North Sumatran squatters, supported by local PNI and PKI branches, clashed with police. Under pressure from the North Sumatran PNI branch, the PNI leadership council withdrew its support for the Wilopo cabinet, which fell in June 1953.

PNI did not disintegrate as did PS. Neither did it become more cohesive. Because of a weakened Masjumi, PNI emerged from the national election in 1955 as the largest party, winning 22.3 percent of all votes (Feith 1962, 434). PNI led two more cabinets, with Ali Sastroamidjojo as prime minister. While Wilopo pursued pro-Western capitalist development, Ali cabinets were more responsive to the radical nationalist factions of Sidik and Sartono at the expense of economic growth.

Masjumi

Masjumi (Partai Majelis Syuro Muslimin Indonesia, or Indonesian Muslim Council Party) was larger and its organization more complex than both PS and PNI. Recall that the Japanese authorities created Masjumi as an umbrella organization of all Muslim groups, the two most prominent being Muhammadiyah and Nahdlatul Ulama (NU). In November 1945, Masjumi was reborn under leaders of the prewar Islamic party PSII and those of the Japanese-sponsored Masjumi (Anderson 1972, 219–24). The new party inherited from the old Masjumi not only the name but also its federal structure. It had two kinds of members: Islamic organizations and individuals. Member organizations such as Muhammadiyah and NU were represented in the Central Committee and the Leadership Council, but they were allowed to keep their own organizations and maintained independent operations. No efforts were made to integrate the various organizations in the party; on the contrary, the organizational structure of Masjumi institutionalized this cleavage. NU leaders predominated in the Consultative Council (Majelis Syuro), which advised the leadership and which was empowered to issue religious edicts binding on the party. On the other hand, the leaders of Muhammadiyah and other Islamic political groups had control of the Youth Department and were better represented in the Leadership Council (Noer 1960, 59–60).

Similar to PS and PNI, Masjumi leadership was split into several personal factions. The dominant faction when the party was formed in 1945 was led by Sukiman Wirjosandjojo, the leader of the prewar Islamic Party of Indonesia (PII). Another faction was led by the former leaders of the prewar Islamic League Party of Indonesia (PSII), which was the successor of Sarekat Islam. Because of personal conflicts, Sukiman and others broke away from PSII and formed PII (Noer 1973, 138, 157–61). In the course of the struggle with the Dutch, these older factions lost their influence to a younger group of leaders led by Mohammad Natsir (Noer 1960, 150–7). All three factions were identified with reformist Islam, although the Natsir faction had the worst relationship with NU (Feith 1962, 137).

The groups and factions in Masjumi shared several important interests. First, in the competition with secular nationalist and communist parties for influence, Muslim groups had a common interest in promoting a greater, if not dominant, role for Islam in the state. Second, the constituency of most Islamic groups was local elites and property owners, although Muhammadiyah appealed mainly to urban traders, especially in West Java and the outer islands, whereas NU's support came primarily from landlords and better-off peasants in rural East and Central Java. Yet these shared interests were insufficient to hold Masjumi together.

Similar to PNI, Masjumi as a party had no power to bind its members to party platforms decided by the Leadership Council. In early 1946, Masjumi opposed making concessions to the Dutch and supported Tan

Malaka. However, Sjahrir was able to defeat Malaka by luring four Masjumi leaders to his side with positions in a new cabinet.[24] At the same time, two other Masjumi leaders continued to oppose the government and later were arrested with Tan Malaka on the charge of plotting a coup. Sjahrir's third cabinet, formed in late 1946, had seven Masjumi ministers.[25] While the Masjumi Leadership Council called for a cabinet based on a coalition among parties, the party did not object to its members joining a cabinet "as individuals" (Noer 1960, 89–90, 96).

Similar to other parties, the factions in Masjumi often pursued contradicting policies. When Masjumi ministers (from the Natsir faction) negotiated the Linggajati Agreement with the Dutch, the Sukiman-dominated Leadership Council denounced the agreement without giving its ministers a chance to explain (Noer 1960, 98). Opposition to this agreement in parliament eventually caused the cabinet to fall. When Amir Sjarifuddin of PS formed a new cabinet in mid-1947, he was able to lure six Masjumi members of the PSII faction into his cabinet over the objection of the Masjumi leadership. The PSII faction later would break away and reestablish the prewar PSII (Noer 1960, 106).

The Natsir faction played prominent roles in the diplomatic negotiations that brought Indonesia formal independence in late 1949. By then, support for this faction in Masjumi surpassed support for the Sukiman faction. Yet the Natsir faction was not sufficiently strong to remove Sukiman and others in his faction from the Leadership Council. The struggle between these two cliques would cause the collapse of two Masjumi cabinets when this party was at the zenith of its power in postcolonial Indonesia.

The first Masjumi cabinet was headed by Natsir and included three members of his faction and an NU leader (Feith 1962, 150). In forming this cabinet, Natsir sought alliance with smaller parties and excluded PNI. This cabinet was immediately criticized by Sukiman for not being representative. When a vote of confidence in the cabinet was cast in the parliament, Masjumi's acting chairman Wibisono of the Sukiman faction walked out to indicate his disagreement (Noer 1960, 224). A similar

---

[24] These were ministers Mohammad Natsir (Information) and Hadji Rasjidi (Religion), and vice ministers Arudji Kartawinata (Defense) and Sjafruddin Prawiranegara (Finance) (Noer 1960, 89).

[25] The ministers were Mohammad Roem (Interior), Sjafruddin Prawiranegara (Finance), Mohammad Natsir (Information), Faturrachman (Religion), and Wachid Hasjim (State). The two vice ministers were Jusuf Wibisono (Economic Affairs) and Harsono Tjokroaminoto (Defense) (G. Kahin 1952, 194–5).

confrontation between the two factions erupted, causing the Natsir cabinet to fall only six months later. This confrontation took place when Natsir implemented the regulations for the elections of interim regional councils that had been approved by the previous cabinet. These councils would be elected not directly by the people but by an electoral college composed of representatives from locally established organizations (Feith 1962, 165–6). As the organization with the best social and religious grassroots network, Masjumi unsurprisingly came to dominate the regional legislatures where the elections had been carried out. Alarmed by this development, PNI won a vote in the parliament to halt the elections. Natsir chose a confrontational strategy and called for a no-confidence vote. Rather than supporting fellow Masjumi leader Natsir, Wibisono publicly called on him to resign. This contributed to the fall of this cabinet in March 1951 (Noer 1960, 230–5).

The role was reversed when Sukiman became the new prime minister and Wibisono became minister of finance in the succeeding cabinet (Feith 1962, 180). Natsir's faction now joined the opposition to attack Sukiman's foreign policy. More anticommunist than Natsir, Sukiman wanted to pursue a closer relationship with the United States, as opposed to adopting a neutral foreign policy by which Indonesia would join neither Cold War bloc. When Indonesia was invited to sign the San Francisco Peace Treaty that committed Japan to pay reparations to Southeast Asian countries, the Sukiman faction managed to win a narrow vote in the Leadership Council of Masjumi over objections from the Natsir camp (Noer 1960, 245–53). The Sukiman cabinet was under fire again when its foreign minister secretly signed an agreement by which Indonesia would receive American aid under the terms of the U.S. Mutual Security Act of 1951. This act was aimed at making aid recipients more responsive to the American Cold War needs and the agreement signed by Sukiman's foreign minister met adamant protests from the parliament after it became known. While debates were going on, Masjumi Leadership Council under Natsir ruled that the party would not be responsible for the agreement, although it would not automatically withdraw its ministers from the cabinet (Noer 1960, 257). Under pressure from opponents of the agreement, including Natsir, the Sukiman cabinet resigned in February 1952, only ten months after it had taken office.

The viability of Masjumi as a party suffered not only from factional conflicts but also from its federal structure. Acceptance of entire well-established organizations such as NU into the party made Masjumi resemble a united front rather than a political party. A membership that included both organizations and individuals made power-sharing rules difficult to achieve. Finally, a major cleavage existed between the orthodox NU and the modernist Muhammadiyah. Party leaders were aware of the problems but had no solutions. A special committee of Masjumi in 1947 considered the question of whether the party should accept only individuals and not organizations as its members. This committee decided to maintain the concept of "the Masjumi family" and to accept the role of Masjumi as the coordinator and facilitator of cooperation among the members of this family (Noer 1960, 49). For the sake of cooperation, the institutional separation of NU and Muhammadiyah within Masjumi was set up. NU leaders dominated the Consultative Council, whereas reformists dominated the Leadership Council. Yet this separation did not solve the problem. NU leaders proposed that the Consultative Council be made into a party legislature, which would be authorized to issue binding instructions to the Leadership Council. However, this council viewed the Consultative Council only as an advisory body except on religious matters.[26] *Ulama* (Islamic teachers) who led NU were dismissed as politically naive by Islamic politicians of both the Sukiman and Natsir factions (Noer 1960, 50).

Conflicts between NU and the rest of Masjumi simmered for many years but broke out in the open while a new cabinet to succeed Sukiman was being formed. In past cabinets in which Masjumi participated, an NU leader always had control of the Ministry of Religion. This time Muhammadiyah leaders demanded their turn in controling the Ministry of Religion, but NU did not want to concede. The Leadership Council was unable to bridge both demands and eventually acquiesced to the decision made by the *formateur* – Wilopo, a PNI leader. Wilopo picked a Muhammadiyah leader to be the minister of religion. A few weeks after the announcement of the cabinet, NU decided to secede from Masjumi to set up a separate party (Noer 1960, 259–71). In the first national election of 1955 for a new parliament, NU won nearly seven million votes or 18.4 percent, whereas Masjumi won almost eight million votes or 20.9 percent (Feith 1962, 434–5). Had the two parties not split, their combined strength would have been close to 40 percent, not a majority but large enough compared to other parties to have a dominant position in parliament.

---

[26] Not surprisingly, NU leaders complained that the Consultative Council was merely "a jeweled ring worn only for going to the feast and locked in the drawer when they are finished" (Naim 1960, 14).

Thus, because their leaders had contradicting political beliefs and came from diverse backgrounds, Indonesian parties were generally divided into personal factions. There were real ideological and religious differences between the major parties, but these differences were not sufficient to give each of them a cohesive political identity. PS was divided into two factions with little interaction and little joint action. PNI was more integrated and its factional divisions were less clear-cut. Masjumi was one of a kind, whose weaknesses came not only from factional cleavages but also from its unwieldy federal structure. These parties, and numerous others, were born or resurrected in late 1945 to take advantage of expanding political opportunities. They mainly emerged out of status circles and were built on personal factions rather than on deeply shared ideological platforms. They were particularly suited to the politics of accommodation but in many cases functioned more as convenient labels than as real organizations. Politicians gained their parliamentary and cabinet seats thanks less to their parties than to personal relationships reaching across party boundaries. The frequent crossing over of party lines indicated blurred boundaries and the weak corporate identity of political parties. In a parliament that included virtually all political factions, however minor and marginal, these parties simply created one more layer of confusion and exacerbated the underlying instability.

CONCLUSION

Indonesia was not predestined to have a fractured state structure. The Japanese had constructed elements of a centralized frame, but these collapsed in the wake of Japan's sudden surrender. Because of particular compromises among key leaders, the unstable multiparty parliamentary system came into being. Because of elite compromise, political parties formed on the basis of status circles proliferated in response to the opportunity. These parties had weak boundaries and blurred corporate identities. Their leaders had little incentive to build cohesive organizations because they could get parliamentary and cabinet seats through personal relationships rather than on the basis of their organizational skills. Even the smallest parties were allowed to claim seats in the appointed parliament, resulting in instability at the apex of the political system.

Thanks to the Japanese, Indonesian nationalists were more prepared than the Vietnamese in forming a state. Ironically, the state they got in the end had a more fragile structure. The ultimate outcome also was less favorable to those Indonesian factions that sought to implement developmental policies. We saw in Chapter 3 that they lost power by the mid-1950s, and many among them went down in history as rebels against the very state they helped to found.

Why the differences between Vietnam and Indonesia? While both countries took the accommodation path, the two cases differed in terms of the kinds of groups and the balance of power among them. In Vietnam, the ICP was better organized than all others, even if its eventual domination was not inevitable. The ICP was able to claim some support from the Allies, whereas Sukarno and Hatta could not. Chinese recognition of the Viet Minh state was also more forthcoming than what the Indonesian republic received from the British. Second, the ideology of the dominant faction was important. Sjahrir's and Hatta's belief in democratic socialism led them to support a parliamentary system of government. It would have been extremely unlikely for the ICP to act in the same way; all they were willing to accept was a rubber-stamp National Assembly.

Different circumstances were thus imposed upon the Vietnamese and Indonesian movements. Remarkably, the general pattern still holds for both cases: accommodation generated poorly integrated political organizations and institutions. With the in-depth stories as told in Chapter 6 and this chapter, I have shown how the macropattern of accommodation operated at a microlevel. Furthermore, through the efforts of revolutionaries to cope with organizational dilemmas, human actors and their particular social contexts can be observed more clearly. The next two chapters focus on a different aspect of accommodation politics in the nationalist movements in Vietnam and Indonesia. In particular, I examine how accommodation politics was institutionalized in certain formulations of the political discourses that created ideological incongruence in the structure of both states.

8

Talking Accommodation in Vietnam

Nation, the People, and Class Struggle

As a Comintern agent with decades of experience, Ho Chi Minh accumulated considerable organizing skills. Yet he did not simply organize people in the physical sense but also wrote and spoke to rally their support for the communist cause. Over his long career, he wrote for or edited numerous newspapers and journals under various names and in at least three languages (Nguyen T. 2005). Whether he was effective or not in mobilizing the masses, there is no doubt that he spent as much of his time writing as he did organizing. This point is clear from a brief excerpt in which Nguyen Ai Quoc (i.e., Ho Chi Minh) graphically described "colonial sadism": "[After the raping, killing and burning by two colonial troops,] the three corpses lay on the flat ground...the eight year old girl naked, the young woman disemboweled, her stiffened left forearm raising a clenched fist to the indifferent sky, and the old man, horrible, naked, like the others, disfigured by the roasting with his fat which had run, melted and congealed with the skin of his belly, which was bloated, grilled and golden, like the skin of a roast pig."[1] Clearly Nguyen Ai Quoc displayed through this piece a great flair for constructing a discourse imbued with violent images. The quality of the work makes clear that he devoted significant energy to the job.

We have seen from Chapters 6 and 7 that accommodation was institutionalized in political organizations and government structures. The goal of this chapter and the next is to show how accommodation was institutionalized in discursive formulations and created ideological incongruence or inconsistency for the emerging states in Vietnam and Indonesia.

---

[1] "Annamese women and French domination" (1922), in Ho C. M. (1960, 1:26).

Here I treat political discourses as another tool of political struggle, just like arms, manpower, or organizations. Even though all the tools are to achieve political power, the functions of discourses in a struggle obviously differ from other tools. Political actors use a particular discourse for various purposes – for example, to explain their actions, to legitimize their claims to authority, to affect the behavior of others, and to build a community of supporters. As noted in Chapter 1, the literature on developmental states has neglected ideological factors in general and political discourses in particular. Given the wide-ranging utility of discourses and the efforts that political actors such as Ho Chi Minh put into constructing them, this neglect cannot be justified.

The tricky issues are these: how does one analyze political discourses, and what value does this kind of analysis add to causal arguments? While everyday discourse is unbounded and unfocused, "the language of politics is a restricted code, one in which options with respect to formal qualities such as vocabulary, style, syntax, and trope are far more restricted than in ordinary language" (Schoenhals 1992, 1). Given this characteristic of political discourses, a discursive analysis can zoom in on a few key formulations in a particular discourse; these formulations can be assumed to represent larger political forces at work.[2] More broadly, the composition of discursive formulations, their histories, and the vigorous contests among them[3] reveal certain aspects of the broader political struggle. These aspects are either unobservable in other activities or corroborate observations made elsewhere. Hence, an in-depth discursive analysis, even though by itself may not be proof of a causal relationship, can add another layer of "causal process observations" to a hypothesis (Brady and Collier 2004).

Some of the formulations analyzed in this study can be found in many contexts. For example, "the nation" is a common theme in the political discourse of most countries today. "The people" is another. Formulations do not have to be simple concepts but can also take the form of thematic arguments or assumptions. "Anticapitalism," "class struggle," and "family values" are such formulations. Many of these categories or formulations have the same core meaning in many languages, but in each political context at a particular time they convey unique images and specific meanings. They also have different histories as they interact with

---

[2] Discourse in this case can be thought of as a "dependent variable."
[3] This is when discourse acts as an "independent variable" that shapes subsequent discourses (Tarrow 1998, 106–22).

political events and with other formulations in a particular discursive context.

In Vietnam, "the nation" dominated the political discourse early on; Marxist discourses arrived in the late 1920s but did not have much popular appeal. Populist themes slowly developed in the early 1940s among intellectuals, while the clandestine discourse produced by the ICP shelved class themes to focus on national unity. Accommodation was expressed and embedded in the emphasis on either "the nation" or "the people" in the discourses of many groups. The ICP, the party that should have promoted class struggle, was ironically silent about this theme. From late 1945 to mid-1946, a media war erupted between exiled nationalists and the communists. This war of words exposed significant ideological incongruence in the communist discourse. The incongruence resulted from the ICP's need to maintain national solidarity on the one hand, and its eagerness to defend its belief in class struggle on the other. The need for accommodation explains why, in their defense of class struggle, communists had to justify it by its contribution to national interests. Yet this incongruence made it difficult for the ICP to formulate and communicate a clear and consistent discourse. Inconsistency would persist even during the period when the party sought to emulate Maoist institutions and discourses in which class struggle was central. Discursive formulations in this period are found to display a mixture of populist and class struggle themes and were more moderate than similar formulations found in China. This mixture exposed the persistent ideological incongruence in the state structure, even though no evidence is available to suggest how this incongruence was used within the party to obstruct a radical socialist transformation based on class struggle.

EARLY NATIONALIST DISCOURSES, 1900–1940

Vietnam was unified under the Nguyen dynasty before being colonized by France. Until the late nineteenth century, resistance to French rule was led mainly by Nguyen kings and the mandarins. Modern anticolonial movements that emerged at the beginning of the twentieth century continued to stress the goal of an independent Vietnam.[4] "Homeland" (*nuoc, quoc gia,*

---

[4] Among English sources, Marr (1971; 1981) offers the best discussions of intellectual changes from the late nineteenth century to the 1940s, including the thoughts of Phan Boi Chau, Phan Chu Trinh, and Nguyen Ai Quoc. Tai (1992) focuses specifically on Nguyen An Ninh and southern intellectuals.

non song) was the dominant figure in the discourse of many anticolonial groups and originally was closely bound up with loyal sentiments to the Nguyen monarch. Perhaps because of a preoccupation with the practical task of liberating the nation from foreign rule, earlier leaders made little effort to explore modern revolutionary theories and concepts. Phan Boi Chau, leader of the Eastern Travel movement, was interested mostly in foreign military assistance, even though he befriended many socialists in Japan and twice met Sun Yat-sen (Marr 1971, 126, 217). Phan praised Lenin's revolutionary strategy but did not write about Marx and socialism until the late 1920s, when he was under house arrest in Vietnam.[5] His booklet about socialism was perhaps among the first scholarly analyses about the topic available in Vietnam.[6] The first publications of Sun Yat-sen's thoughts appeared in Vietnam at about the same time, thanks to the men who would later found the VNP (Hoang V. D. 1970, 25–6; Vu K. 2002). Judged from the scant information available, many VNP leaders seemed to be influenced more by Social Darwinism than by Sun's principles.[7]

For a younger generation of Vietnamese who lived in France in the early 1920s, however, radical revolutionary ideas had more appeal. Some became adherents to European anarchist thought. Others were attracted to socialism. Nguyen An Ninh, who was suspicious of violent revolutionary methods and opposed to socialism, belonged to the former group (Tai 1992, 72–84). Nguyen Ai Quoc, on the other hand, joined French socialist circles in Paris and helped to found the French Communist Party in 1920. Disappointed by the indifference of the French Left toward colonial Indochina, Nguyen Ai Quoc was initially attracted more to Lenin's thesis on the colonial question than to the Marxist theory of class struggle (Quinn-Judge 2000, 31). Although he started with anticolonial nationalism, internationalism increasingly emerged as the key theme in his writings in the early 1920s, even before starting his work for the Comintern. His articles published in the French leftist press in this period were overwhelmingly focused on the inhumanity of colonialism, especially

[5] See Phan Boi Chau, "Luoc truyen Liet Ninh – vi nhan cua nuoc Nga Do" (The story of Lenin, the great man of Red Russia), published in a military journal in China in 1921, in Chuong T. (2000, 5:317–23); and "Xa hoi chu nghia" (Socialism), published as a booklet in Vietnam sometime between 1927 and 1938, in Chuong T. (2000, 7:131–72).

[6] McHale (2004, 120) also notes that the first Marxist text appeared in Vietnam in the late 1920s and apparently did not attract great attention.

[7] This is based on a letter sent by Nguyen Thai Hoc, chairman of the VNP, to the French Parliament after his arrest (Nhuong T. 1949, 138).

the French colonial system. Yet the Vietnamese revolution was not viewed simply as a national struggle. Nguyen wrote: "Colonialism is a leech with two suckers one of which sucks the metropolitan proletariat and the other that of the colonies."[8] He discussed not only "An Nam" and Indochina in his writings but also other French and English colonies where exploitation and the mistreatment of indigenous peoples were widespread.[9] He also attacked racism in the United States and English capitalism in China.[10] One of his pieces discussed the labor movement in Turkey, where a national revolution had taken place but which, he noted, had been "profitable only to one class: the moneyed class."[11] He went on to call for "the Turkish proletariat... to embark on class struggle."

While the discourse found in Nguyen Ai Quoc's writings did not fully embrace international class struggle, the communist discourse throughout the 1930s inside Vietnam did (Marr 1981, 347–52; McHale 2004, 102–30). A new class discourse that called for a "proletarian revolution" to "struggle against French imperialism" and to serve "the toiling masses" emerged during the peasant rebellions in Nghe Tinh during 1930 and 1931. A notable aspect of this discourse was its novelty and foreignness in the Vietnamese context and its failure to strike a chord with peasants in the way its producers intended (McHale 2004, 118–27). Placed in perspective, the event indicated that the discourse conveyed in Nguyen Ai Quoc's lessons to Youth League members in southern China had begun to take on a life of its own inside Vietnam.

The late 1930s witnessed many new actors on the scene and the continuing evolution of the Marxist discourse in Vietnam. The sufferings and struggles of peasants (*dan cay*) and workers (*tho thuyen*) were the central topic in ICP's publications from the time, such as *Dan Chung* (The Masses), a biweekly journal published during 1938 and 1939 (Bao Tang Cach Mang Viet Nam 2000b).[12] In most issues of *Dan Chung*, there was a regular column called "Echoes from the Countryside" that discussed rural poverty and the exploitation of peasants and plantation workers.

---

[8] Nguyen Ai Quoc, "The U.S.S.R. and the colonial peoples" (1924), translated in Ho C. M. (1960, 1:80).

[9] See, for example, "Uprising at Dahomey" (1923), "Condemned Colonialism" (1924) "Imperialists and China" (1924), and "Rule Britannia" (1925) in Ho C. M. (1960, vol 1). "An Nam" was one of the older names of Vietnam.

[10] See "English 'colonization'" (1923), "Lynching, a Little Known Aspect of American Civilization" (1924), and "The Ku-Klux-Klan" (1924) in Ho C. M. (1960, vol. 1).

[11] See "The Workers' Movement in Turkey" (1924) in Ho C. M. (1960, 1:59).

[12] "Dan chung" can also be translated as "the people," but the usage of the time seemed to mean "the masses."

Specific cases of landlords oppressing peasants were raised but there were no calls for land redistribution, only calls for the colonial government to distribute communal lands to poor peasants.[13] Another regular column was "Workers' Front," where issues concerning the rights and interests of workers were discussed. On international issues, *Dan Chung* attacked Japanese aggression, supported the Soviet-led world peace movement, and defended the Molotov-Ribbentrop Pact. Domestically the journal called for the formation of a Popular Front to unite the people in opposing fascism and war and in demanding press freedom, "in the interests of the people and the country."[14]

The class discourse in *Dan Chung*, while appearing radical, was in fact mild compared to the program of rival Trotskyites.[15] The latter criticized Stalin, rejected any alliance with the national bourgeoisie, and called for curbing the power of big capitalists. They supported the formation of a Front of Workers and Peasants rather than a popular front that united all people. Trotskyites such as Ta Thu Thau and Huynh Van Phuong had long called for redistributing land to peasants, while they were still in France (Tai 1992, 236–7). In contrast, ICP leaders Truong Chinh and Vo Nguyen Giap refrained from calling for such redistribution. While pointing out in their 1938 study of "the peasant question" that "the central issue was how to let peasants have [their own] land to till," in the section on policy recommendations, the authors asked only that the French government "listen to peasants and implement policies that would improve their living conditions."[16] Overall, Trotskyites placed ICP leaders on the defensive and perhaps forced them to be publicly more radical than they would have preferred.[17]

An independent nation, whether under a Vietnamese monarch or a republican government, was the dominant theme in the anticolonial movement early on. Revolutionary theories such as Marxism were introduced into Vietnam in the late 1920s by way of southern China. A leader of a major radical faction of the movement in this period, Nguyen Ai

[13] See, for example, *Dan Chung*, August 20 and September 10, 1938.

[14] See "Mat tran cong nong duy nhat cua Trot-kit" (The Trotskyist front for workers and peasants), *Dan Chung*, September 28, 1938.

[15] See "Phe binh bai tra loi nhut bao cua ong Hai Phong" (A critique of the responses by Mr. Hai Phong) and "Mat tran cong nong duy nhat cua Trot-kit," *Dan Chung*, August 28 and September 28, 1938, respectively.

[16] Truong Chinh and Vo Nguyen Giap ([1937] 1959, 16–20).

[17] For example, see A Dong, "May loi cung cac ban dan chu" (A few words for our friends in the Democratic Front), *Dan Chung*, August 24, 1938. Trotskyites were far fewer in number compared to ICP members.

Quoc, began to embrace internationalism. Up to the end of the 1930s, however, ICP theorists combined class themes with those that stressed popular or national solidarity. Although social classes and "the masses" were more prominent than either "the people" or "the nation," the ICP's discourse displayed some degree of accommodation. The party was silent about class struggle, and its rhetoric was focused as much on national independence from colonialism as on the need for an international proletarian revolution.

The ICP's failed uprising in 1940 decimated its leadership of the 1930s. The pre-1940 legacy was limited in part because of this event. Most formulations found in the discourse during this period are not to be found again as different factions rose to lead the ICP. Under new leadership, class themes disappeared entirely and "the nation" returned as the dominant figure in the communist discourse from 1941 onward. This sharp turn in the discourse indicated an unprecedented level of ideological accommodation.[18] At the same time, noncommunist discourse gave more prominence to "the people" but not to "the nation" in part because of colonial censorship. Both noncommunist and communist discourses were accommodative, albeit in different ways: the former displayed a compromising attitude (a willingness to accommodate debate), whereas the latter displayed a compromising policy platform (the promotion of national unity among all social classes).

THE STRUGGLE BETWEEN NATION AND CLASS, 1941–1956

The discourse of the Vietnamese nationalist movement evolved through many stages. Before the movement seized power in August 1945, several streams of discourse existed, out of touch with one another. The clandestine discourse produced by Viet Minh promoted "the nation" and "revolution" while suppressing all other themes, including classes. Another important stream found in the journal *Thanh Nghi* did not aggressively promote "the nation." *Thanh Nghi*'s main focus was on social reforms but not revolution; "the ordinary people," "peasants," and social equity issues figured prominently in its discourse.

In late 1945, the ICP engaged in sharp polemics with exiled nationalist groups returning from China. Under their attacks, communist leaders

---

[18] This did not mean the communists' rejection of Marxism and Stalinism. The move away from class themes corresponded with the ICP's revolutionary strategy to form a national united front; in internal documents ICP leaders continued using class categories in their analysis (Vu T. 2009).

were forced to openly defend class struggles as legitimate. However, class interests had to be defended not in their own right but as contributing to national interests. The public exchange exposed the difficulty facing communists in the formulation of a clear and consistent discourse that promoted the nation on the one hand while defending class struggle on the other.

By the late 1940s, "the people" replaced "the nation" as the dominant figure in the discourse. This discursive transformation occurred through two events. First, as communists clashed with noncommunists in the Viet Minh government, both groups sought to claim that only they represented "the people." The second event that transformed the discourse was the overwhelming influence of the Maoist discourse in the early 1950s that emphasized class struggle but also paid "the people" some lip service. The ideological inconsistency in the official discourse was intensified with this transformation. While the ICP needed to promote class struggle together with its "land reform" and party purge, widespread reservations emerged about the legitimacy of class struggle, even among the top leaders.

As it turned out, themes of class struggle by the early 1950s dominated the discourse but the Vietnamese orthodox formulations as written in the party's constitution were less class-based compared to those found in China. I argue that the debate leading to these moderate formulations suggested that ICP leaders were aware of the ideological inconsistency or incongruence in their discourse. Party leaders were able to circumvent this inconsistency only by relying on extra-institutional means to bring the class struggle discourse directly to peasants during the "land reform."

1941–1945

In the period from 1941 to 1945, I focus on two distinct streams of discourse in the nationalist movement. One stream was created by the ICP-led Viet Minh in their hideout. This discourse is found mainly in Viet Minh's secret publications, including *Viet Nam Doc Lap* (Independent Vietnam, or *VNDL*), *Cuu Quoc* (Save the Country), and *Co Giai Phong* (Liberation Flag).[19] These publications mobilized public support and sympathy for Viet Minh; the discourse was oriented toward

---

[19] *VNDL*'s first issue was published in August 1941. Until August 1942 Nguyen Ai Quoc was its main contributor, editor, and illustrator. Pham Van Dong took over this job until mid-1945. The newspaper was published three times a month with two pages in each issue and a circulation of four hundred (Bao Tang Cach Mang 2000a, 6).

stirring emotion and provoking action. Readers were always called on to act immediately, whether to donate money or join the organization. The discourse targeted all social strata but especially less educated people.

The second discourse was found in *Thanh Nghi*, a Hanoi-based journal for the public-minded elites of the colonial society.[20] *Thanh Nghi* was aimed at sharing thoughts and educating the (already educated) elites about social issues. Through the journal, a loose network of contributors was formed in an indirect relationship with a broader circle of readers. Constrained by censorship, *Thanh Nghi* did not discuss political issues directly. Before the Japanese coup against the French in March 1945, the calm and scholarly discourse in *Thanh Nghi* provoked thoughts but not emotions, and it avoided direct agitation for actions. While Viet Minh leaders certainly read *Thanh Nghi*, *Thanh Nghi* writers did not have access to most Viet Minh publications. Although they do not interact closely, the two kinds of discourses displayed interesting contrasts in how the key themes of "the nation" and "the people" were constructed by the two major groups that later would join to lead the nationalist movement.

Chapter 5 noted that after 1941 the ICP eschewed class struggle for the sake of national unity. "Class" had been the central concept in the communist discourse during the 1930s but disappeared without a trace in Viet Minh's publications. Instead, Viet Minh propagandists invested much effort in building up the "nation" (*dan toc*) as the central accommodative figure. This nation had two foundations. First was a long tradition mystically dated back thousands of years. Members of the nation shared the same roots: *VNDL* repeatedly called Vietnamese "children of the Dragon and the Fairy" and "children of the Hong and Lac tribes," referring to Vietnam's myths of national creation. Vietnamese also shared a common history of successful fights against foreign invaders. Patriotic traditions and well-known but long dead national heroes frequently appeared in the discourse.[21]

---

[20] For an insightful analysis of *Thanh Nghi* content, see Pierre Brocheux, "A Group of Vietnamese Intellectuals and the Problems of Their Nation: The Review of *Thanh Nghi* (1941–1945)" (translated in Vu D. H. 1995, 448–78). *Thanh Nghi* (Commentaries) debuted in late 1939 but came to be under the management of Vu Dinh Hoe and his group in 1941. It was first published monthly, then bimonthly, and eventually weekly. It was not published during March–May 1945 and was closed for good in early August of the same year. Its circulation was five hundred in 1940, two thousand in 1942, and three thousand in 1944 (ibid., 452).

[21] For example, see *VNDL*, February 1 and May 1, 1942, March 1 and May 1, 1943. See also "Tuyen Ngon" (Manifesto), October 25, 1941 (DCSVN 2000, 7:458–63).

More importantly, the Vietnamese nation was based on shared sufferings under French and Japanese "imperialists." With Nguyen Ai Quoc as the editor and chief contributor, graphically described colonial sadism was unsurprisingly a frequent topic in *VNDL*. Japanese troops did not just burn, plunder, arrest, rape, torture, and kill. They drew blood from indigenous children to treat their wounded soldiers, and those poor children died when they had no blood left. The Japanese buried people alive, cut out their tongues, made them kill each other, and eat their own flesh.[22] The Vietnamese nation was compared to a "piece of delicious meat" for the foreign "wild beasts," "wolves," and "hunting dogs." Vietnamese people were compared to dogs, horses, and water buffaloes – animals that in popular perceptions lived hard lives or had to perform hard labor. These violent and beastly images were clearly aimed at stirring up emotions and highlighting the sharp line dividing the Vietnamese nation from its foreign enemies.

The hard fate of the Vietnamese nation justified the sacrifices needed for its liberation: all Vietnamese, including women and children, were called on to contribute to the revolution as much as possible. Wives and old parents were specifically asked to lend their husbands and sons. Balanced against these immediate sacrifices were promises of concrete future rewards. The promises went beyond the abolishment of heavy taxes, forced labor, and restrictions on freedom. The picture of independent Vietnam depicted in *VNDL* displayed the populist side of the Viet Minh discourse: because Vietnam was already rich (in natural resources), it would be much richer once independence was achieved.[23] Peasants would then have all the land they needed, and no workers would be unemployed. There would be schools, theaters, electricity, automobiles, hospitals, kindergartens, and nursing homes in both cities and the countryside. At break times, workers would read newspapers, play guitar, or listen to performances on the radio. Women would have equal rights with men; they would study, become mandarins [*sic*], and share household and national responsibilities with men. In this vision, the state was to be both interventionist and populist. It would nationalize and run factories, launch irrigation schemes, enforce labor laws, help those families with many children, feed the handicapped, and manage hospitals and kindergartens.[24]

---

[22] *VNDL*, October 1, 1941, February 21 and April 1, 1942.
[23] *VNDL*, September 11, 1943.
[24] "Tuyen Ngon."

Viet Minh's populist discourse did not separate "the people" (*dan, dan ta, dong bao, dan chung*) from "the nation" (*dan toc*).[25] The people were viewed as a collective of groups separable by ascription or status (age, gender, nationality, profession, and social status). This differentiation was not as important as the fact that they all suffered as one nation under foreign rule. Conflicts among different strata within "the people" never appeared in Viet Minh's discourse. Neither did such themes as "social justice" or "equity." In Viet Minh's program, capitalists would be free to get rich, while workers would have to work only eight hours a day. Landlords could keep their land, and tenants would get their rents reduced. While Viet Minh promised freedoms and material benefits to everybody, it specifically warned its cadres that the goal of the revolution was not to take from the rich to distribute to the poor.[26]

Claiming to be the champion of popular interests, Viet Minh demanded in return that the people show it respect and loyalty. As *VNDL* taught its readers,

If the organization [i.e., Viet Minh] did not exist, how would our people know how to fight the French and the Japanese? The organization is the teacher of our people.... Our parents gave us our lives, and we don't forget that. The organization saves us from death [from French and Japanese brutalities], and we can't forget that either. To pay back our debt, we have to love and respect the organization. We have to obey it, be loyal to it, sacrifice for it, and work enthusiastically for it.[27]

In this formulation, the relationship between the masses and their leadership (as embodied in "the organization") was hierarchical; people owed the leadership, and they ought to repay their debt by being obedient and loyal. This was the unpopulist aspect of the Viet Minh discourse, as it elevated "the organization" above the people even while it claimed to serve their interests. "The people" thus had a secondary status in the discourse compared to "the nation."

In contrast with Viet Minh's discourse, "the nation" did not appear frequently in *Thanh Nghi*.[28] The concept of the nation, when it was

---

[25] *Dan* is a Vietnamized word borrowed from Chinese *min* (the people). *Dan* can stand by itself (e.g., *yeu dan*, or "love the people"), be combined with other Vietnamese words (e.g., *dan ta*, or "our people"), or appear in original Chinese compounds (e.g., *dan chung* [Chinese *minshu*], *nhan dan* [Chinese *renmin*], or *dan toc* [Chinese *minzu*]). *Dong bao* (literally, "fellows of the same ovary") refers to Vietnam's creation myth.

[26] *VNDL*, July 30, 1945.

[27] *VNDL*, July 1, 1943.

[28] A rare exception was Vu Van Hien, "Tin Nguong" (Religion), *Thanh Nghi*, March 16, 1943, 2–3.

discussed, also was defined by a common origin and fate.[29] However, one does not find the myths of national creation in *Thanh Nghi*. Instead, the discourse was framed in Social Darwinist terms: "the survival instincts" of the Vietnamese race (*sinh ton luc cua noi giong*) were viewed as the key to the future of the Vietnamese nation.[30] There was no direct criticism of the French colonial system before the Japanese coup in March 1945, and there was no attack on the Japanese throughout the life of the journal. The inhumanity of French colonial rule was a prominent topic between May and August 1945, but even then (when French censorship no longer existed) the language was passionate but not graphic.[31] The strongest words ever used were "tears," "smashed bones," and "barbaric French." *Thanh Nghi* also called for personal sacrifices for national interests but did not suggest a specific course of action.[32] Clearly the discourse was not used for agitation purposes, as was the case with Viet Minh.

Thanh Nghi's treatment of "the people" allowed for more internal diversity than the Viet Minh view. Although "the people" also appeared as a collectivity, the collective will was founded first on individual efforts and only later on the alliance of social strata.[33] Collective will thus was based on an elite core: the individuals able to make such efforts were not lower social classes but educated intellectuals. *Thanh Nghi* accepted the legitimacy of different political views among elites and denounced those who attempted to impose on the movement a single ideology or vision of the national future.[34] Their attitude was accommodative.

Thanh Nghi discourse was simultaneously elitist and populist. Lower strata (*dam binh dan, ke thu dan*) were consistently portrayed as illiterate and simple-minded but at the same time diligent and brave.[35] They lived

[29] Vu Dinh Hoe, "Giai thoat trong dau kho" (Escape from sufferings), *Thanh Nghi*, January 1944, 3–4.

[30] Vu Dinh Hoe, "Song" (To live), *Thanh Nghi*, February 1943.

[31] Trong Duc (Do Duc Duc), "Mot cuon hac thu de ket an che do thuoc dia cua nuoc Phap tai Dong Duong" (A black book to indict French colonial rule in Indochina), *Thanh Nghi*, May 5, 1945, 11–12. See also Nghiem Xuan Yem, "Nan dan doi" (Famine) in the same issue, and Vu Dinh Hoe, "Mot chinh sach bao nguoc cua thuc dan Phap" (A cruel policy of the French colonial government), *Thanh Nghi*, May 26, 1945.

[32] Vu Dinh Hoe, "Song," and Vu Van Hien, "Tin Nguong."

[33] Vu Dinh Hoe, "Giai thoat trong dau kho."

[34] See Phan Anh, "Di kien, dong tam" (Different views, shared interests), *Thanh Nghi*, March 25, 1944, 3–4.

[35] Do Duc Duc, "Du luan chan chinh" (A rightful popular opinion), and Vu Dinh Hoe, "Nghe nong trong cuoc kinh doanh moi" (Farming in the new economy), *Thanh Nghi*, June 1 and July 22, 1943, respectively.

hard lives and sorely needed elite leadership: "Peasants suffer from hunger
and cold; they want [the elites] to return to the villages to lead them out
of miseries and to educate them. If left alone, they never changed because
they are constrained by corrupt customs."[36] Change had to begin with
education: suffrage would hurt rather than help "uneducated people"
(*bon dan vo hoc*) because they would use such a right unwisely (*kho
dai*).[37] However, there was no blunt demand as in the Viet Minh discourse
for mass loyalty and submission to elite leadership. On the contrary,
Thanh Nghi discourse placed greater responsibility on leadership than
on the masses. Urban upper classes and the intellectual elites were often
chided for looking down on peasants and for destroying the traditional
value system while not being able to create a new system for lower classes
to adhere to.[38] This view of the masses in *Thanh Nghi* was more populist
than in Viet Minh and, as will be seen in Chapter 9, quite similar to the
way Indonesian nationalist elites treated their *rakyat*.

Thanh Nghi discourse was populist in another different way from that
of Viet Minh. The latter was populist by offering rosy visions of a *future*
Vietnam. *Thanh Nghi* was populist in its efforts to draw attention to the
harsh living conditions of peasants *at present*. While Viet Minh avoided
any discussion of social inequity in its discourse,[39] poor peasants and their
unjust sufferings were an important topic in *Thanh Nghi*. The journal
was especially critical of social institutions in the countryside that were
corrupt, oppressive, and unfair to ordinary peasants.[40] As the colonial
government was intervening into the rice market to fight rising prices
in urban centers, *Thanh Nghi* called on the government to implement
forced collection from large landlords "for the sake of social equity."[41]
The quota approach, which assigned collection responsibilities through
local administrative bodies, was viewed as vulnerable to abuses by local
elites and would cause peasants to suffer. Economic analyses in *Thanh*

---

[36] Nghiem Xuan Yem, "Thanh nien tri thuc voi nghe nong o xu nha" (Young intellectuals and farming in our country), *Thanh Nghi*, April 16, 1943, 6–10.

[37] Vu Dinh Hoe, "Van de giai cap binh dan" (On the lower classes), *Thanh Nghi*, May 1, 1943.

[38] Nghiem Xuan Yem, "Thanh nien tri thuc voi nghe nong o xu nha," and his "Ai pha hoai, ai xay dung" (Who destroys, who builds?), *Thanh Nghi*, November 16, 1943.

[39] A rare exception was Phi Son, "Nong dan voi cach mang" (Peasants and revolution), *Cuu Quoc*, Spring 1945, 4.

[40] Nghiem Xuan Yem, "Thanh nien tri thuc voi nghe nong o xu nha."

[41] Tan Phong (Vu Van Hien), "Van de gao va dan que" (The rice problem and peasants), *Thanh Nghi*, June 16, 1943, 2–4.

Nghi also supported a larger state role in economic development once the country won independence, but the discussion of state roles in *Thanh Nghi* was not as specific as that in Viet Minh.

As the opportunity for liberation approached, the Vietnamese national-ist movement in the early 1940s was evolving. Discourse was a critical tool for movement leaders to mobilize the masses (for Viet Minh) and to build an intellectual community devoted to nationalist goals (for *Thanh Nghi*). These two separate efforts within the movement operated under differ-ent leaderships and conditions. Viet Minh's discourse was constructed by seasoned political activists constantly on the run. "The nation" domi-nated this discourse, which indicated accommodation on the communists' policy platform. The discourse promoted violence and was aimed at pro-paganda and agitation. Class conflicts were not mentioned, nor were social issues. In contrast, the discourse on *Thanh Nghi* was to exchange ideas and build shared understanding and values; it was made by and for the progressive elites in the colonial society. The discourse allowed for debate and conflicting voices, unlike the narrowly focused and carefully scripted Viet Minh discourse. While no figure dominated *Thanh Nghi* discourse, peasants and "the little people" were frequent heroes.

1945–1946

Thanh Nghi was closed for good in early August 1945. At the same time, Viet Minh leaders left *VNDL* behind to march to Hanoi on the news of Japan's surrender. Under Viet Minh's contested rule from late 1945 to late 1946, a confrontation took place between communist and anticommu-nist discourses. As noted in Chapter 5, several exiled Vietnamese political groups returned to Vietnam from southern China in late 1945 and com-peted with the Viet Minh government for power. At one level the struggle between the two camps in Hanoi was fought with assassination and kid-napping teams, demonstrations and counterdemonstrations, and many gun battles on the streets. At another level, tense polemical exchanges took place in their newspapers. Unlike the discourses of *Thanh Nghi* and Viet Minh that were aimed primarily at exchanging thoughts (the for-mer) and mobilizing supporters (the latter), here discourses became elites' weapons of words to attack the credibility and legitimacy of their oppo-nents in public forums. Harsh accusations by opposition parties came out daily; the Viet Minh government responded not only with equally harsh words but also with censorship and plainclothes police who harassed and arrested distributors of opposition newspapers.[42] In the polemic exchange between communists and exiled nationalists, "the nation" was overshadowed by ideological categories. We have seen in Chapter 6 that the struggle for power between the ICP and the exiled nationalists strengthened the position of noncommunists in the Viet Minh government, thus weakening communist domination. On the discourse front, the exchange appeared to have a similar impact. The polemics disrupted Viet Minh's accommodative discourse until then. The way communists responded exposed some serious incongruence in the ideological infrastructure of the Viet Minh state.

The confrontation between communists and exiled nationalists displayed a radical face of the nationalist movement unseen in the previous period. Both sides claimed to speak for "the nation," but the communists were more effective than their opponents in constructing a unified discourse linked to the main themes in the national struggle for independence.[43] This can be observed in the labeling game. While the exiled groups labeled the Viet Minh government "fascist" and "communist," the communists accused their enemies of being *Viet gian* (Vietnamese traitors) for opposing the government.[44] *Viet gian* had long been a category used in communist discourse to lump all Vietnamese who disagreed with communist policy or leadership. With *Viet gian*, communists sought to associate their opponents with foreign interests, especially the Japanese. They sought to deny their opponents the right to represent the nation and to make them bear the popular hatred against foreign oppressors. In contrast, the labels "fascist" and "communist" used by anticommunist groups had no mental association with the national struggle.

---

[42] See criticisms of press censorship under Viet Minh in "Dan chu voi bao chi" (Democracy and the press), *Y Dan* (The People's Will), December 29, 1945. This newspaper was published by Catholic intellectuals in Hanoi. Also, "Kiem duyet va tu do ngon luan" (Censorship and freedom of expression), *Viet Nam*, June 27, 1946. *Viet Nam* was published by the VNP.

[43] To be sure, the power of the label *Viet gian* also came from the barrel of the gun. Viet Minh's police apparatus was used to arrest political opponents on charges of being *Viet gian*. These arrests caused an uproar in the opposition press, which called on Ho's government to have the accused tried fairly in court, not just arrested and sent to Viet Minh's newly established concentration camps. See "The nao la Viet gian?" (Who is a Viet gian?), *Viet Nam*, December 8, 1945.

[44] See "Phong trao chong phat xit Viet Minh tai cac tinh" (The movement against the fascist Viet Minh in the provinces), *Viet Nam*, December 18, 1945, and "Buc thu ngo cung anh em Viet Nam Quoc Dan Dang" (An open letter to VNP brothers), *Su That*, December 5, 1945.

Anticommunists' use of the "fascist" and "communist" labels was not without reason. It appears that their primary goals were to discredit Viet Minh in the eyes of foreign powers, especially the GMD and American governments, and to rob Viet Minh of the support from upper-class Vietnamese. Anticommunist groups used such labels also because, unlike Thanh Nghi leaders, they were ideological and held a strong enmity toward communism. The strategy of the exiled nationalists was to portray the communist-led Viet Minh government as promoting class interests at the expense of national, family, and individual values. Their polemicists dismissed Marxism as irrelevant to Vietnam where social differentiation was stunted by French colonization. Under the colonial system, it was argued, all classes were exploited and suppressed.[45]

In the anticommunist discourse, "the people" were composed of classes whose interests might conflict. Nevertheless, class struggle was not inevitable thanks to the role played by a populist state that guaranteed social equity and development. Rather than Marxism, Sun Yat-sen's third principle on the people's livelihood was touted as a doctrine better suited to Vietnamese conditions.[46] According to this principle, capitalism and exploitation should be restricted, while land should be gradually nationalized and distributed to all peasants.[47] The state was at the center of this vision, and it stood above all classes. By its control of all productive sectors, the state would be financially equipped to build roads, schools, houses, and hospitals to serve "the people." The state would take surplus rice from landlords to distribute to landless peasants, impose price control to keep goods affordable, and reform the system of communal land distribution to guarantee rural equity.[48] Briefly, there was no need for class struggle and no legitimacy to communist causes.

---

[45] To Khanh, "Giai cap tranh dau hay dan toc tranh dau" (Class struggle or national struggle?), Uu Thien, "Nguoi tho Viet nam va cuoc tranh dau quyen loi" (Vietnamese workers and the struggle for their rights and interests), and "De ky niem Cach mang thang 8" (To commemorate the August Revolution), *Chinh Nghia* (The Just Cause), June 3, July 8, and August 26, 1946, respectively. *Chinh Nghia* was the theoretical journal of the VNP.

[46] Q. H., "Chu Nghia Dan Sinh" (The principle of people's livelihood), *Chinh Nghia*, November 4, 1946.

[47] X., "Chu Nghia Dan Sinh" ([Sun Yat-sen's] principle of people's livelihood), *Chinh Nghia*, November 11, 1946.

[48] "Van de lao cong" (The labor issue), "Mot chuong trinh kien thiet dia phuong" (A program to develop the local economy), and "Van de cong dien" (The communal land issue), *Chinh Nghia*, December 2, 1945, July 8 and July 30–31, 1946.

Under vicious attacks by their ideological opponents, communists could no longer hide their belief in class struggle as they had done until then. While there certainly were different opinions among communist leaders on how and when to respond, the actual responses followed a general strategy of defending class struggle *on the basis that it supported the national struggle against colonialism*. In the editorial of its debut issue in late 1945, the biweekly journal of the ICP, *Su That* (Truth), claimed that one of its missions was "to show all fellow Indochinese a basic truth: there is only one way to achieve freedom, peace and happiness *for mankind, for every nation and for the working class*. This way is through the thorough execution of Marxism."[49] The formula of class and national interests being one and the same was a common theme throughout the communist discourse in this period. Dismissing Sun Yat-sen as mistaken, *Su That* argued that national struggle was a form of international class struggle.[50] In this view, colonialism was the means for Western capitalists to consolidate their domestic rule; anticolonial wars for national independence would weaken imperialism and strengthen the world proletarian movement. Opposing class struggle was the same as defending imperialism.

Communists mounted a vigorous defense of class struggle, but their responses exposed many inconsistencies in their discourse. First, they were silent about domestic class struggle. This silence did not make the issue go away because their opponents relentlessly hammered on it. Second, they were forced to *publicly* justify class struggle based on national interests. Thus far they had pretended that class conflicts did not exist, so that they would not have to say whether class or national interests were more salient to them. Being forced to make a public choice would make it harder if one day they wanted to raise class interests above national ones. In fact, even though they had to publicly place "the nation" above class struggle, occasionally they lost patience and hinted that limits existed. Such an occasion came when Truong Chinh warned that the ICP promoted "class solidarity" (*doan ket giai cap*) for the sake of national unity, but that it would not support "compromises on class interests" (*giai cap thoa hiep*);[51] and when he promised his readers that one day land would be redistributed to peasants and that a social revolution would be launched

---

[49] *Su That*, December 5, 1945 (emphasis added).

[50] B. C. T. (likely Bui Cong Trung), "Thuyet giai cap tranh dau va van de dan toc" (Class struggle theory and the national issue), *Su That*, July 5–12, 1946.

[51] *Su That*, June 30, 1946. "Class compromises" meant making concessions that would hurt fundamental class interests.

to end the exploitation of men by men.[52] At the same time, he called on tenants to struggle against landlords "within the framework of the National United Front" to make sure the Viet Minh policy of rent reduction was honored.[53] Yet rent reduction was said to aim at "improving peasants' living conditions" rather than ending exploitation or feudalism. The argument of "yes, class struggle was relevant; yes, national unity was still more relevant" clearly exposed the ICP's difficulty in formulating and communicating a clear and consistent discourse.

Discourses became weapons in the sharp exchanges between communists and anticommunists during 1945 and 1946. Communists tried to show that they were with the nation and their enemies were not. They attempted to defend class struggle while preserving their nationalist credentials. The salience of "class" was not denied but had to be defended by its association with "the nation." In contrast, anticommunists played up ideologies to make communists look bad with foreign powers and with certain domestic constituencies. That anticommunists were able to force communists to come out of their nationalist disguise to defend class struggle was an indication of anticommunists' effectiveness. The communist defense exposed serious ideological inconsistencies in their discourse.

1947–1956

The exiled nationalists created much trouble for the ICP, but they were defeated by mid-1946. Yet a new conflict soon emerged within Viet Minh between communists and noncommunists in the Viet Minh government. Unlike the previous polemic between communists and anticommunists, which was direct, vicious, and ideological, the subsequent debate between communists and noncommunists was generally indirect, civil, and policy oriented.[54] This change did not mean that the stakes of this debate were low. Noncommunists had control of the government apparatus in social, economic, cultural, and judicial policy realms; urban intellectuals also played prominent roles in all branches of the government and had many supporters in the colonial bureaucracy and even in the ranks of the ICP.

---

[52] Truong Chinh, "Cach mang thang tam" (The August Revolution), *Su That*, September 7, 1946.
[53] Truong Chinh, "Giam dia to" (Rent reduction), *Su That*, November 15, 1946.
[54] The debate took place in *Su That* (Truth), the ICP's journal, and *Doc Lap* (Independence), a weekly journal of the Democratic Party (DP).

Chapter 5 showed that by 1948 conflict was brewing between communists and noncommunists over land policy and local law enforcement. The debate, which lasted for nearly two years, was the rare public expression of this conflict at the top level of the Viet Minh state. Publicly this debate involved only a few people but was in fact closely watched by the top echelons of leadership, local officials, and those in law enforcement. The front man for the communists was Quang Dam, a protégé of Truong Chinh, an editor of *Su That* and the translator of many of Mao's works into Vietnamese (Quang Dam 2002).[55] Quang Dam wrote with veiled authority as a public spokesman for the party. On their part, noncommunists delegated Vu Trong Khanh, a French-trained lawyer and the attorney general of Zone 10, to be their chief representative. Vu Trong Khanh had been the mayor of Hai Phong under the EVN government and the first minister of justice in the Viet Minh government in late 1945. On the same side with him were Vu Dinh Hoe, the current minister of justice, and Hoang Van Duc, a French-trained agricultural engineer and a top DP leader. The debate exposed and exacerbated the ideological incongruence of the Viet Minh state and the depth of the ideological cleavage between communists and noncommunists. After the event, the ICP gradually removed all noncommunists from positions of authority.

The debate started with the communist criticisms directed against the principle of judicial independence. With this principle, local judges justified their actions to curb the abuses of power by local government and party cadres. The judges, as Chapter 5 has shown, refused to follow the instructions of local administrative or party committees and released people illegally arrested for political reasons. In his first two articles that started the debates, Quang Dam launched two lines of attack, one against the capitalist judicial system and the other against French-trained intellectuals.[56] First, he argued that law and justice, as part of the state, were to serve class interests. Nothing was above class struggle in societies with classes. Judicial independence (*tu phap doc lap*) and the separation of powers (*phan quyen*) might have helped the European bourgeoisie initially to restrain arbitrary royal authority but had since served as a

---

55 Quang Dam is the pen name of Ta Quang De, who had been a clerk in the colonial administration and had no connection with *Thanh Nghi*. His brother, Ta Quang Buu, was far better known, had served in the EVN government and was a Viet Minh deputy minister.

56 "Tu phap voi nha nuoc" (The judicial branch and the state), *Su That*, April 15, 1948; "Tinh chat chuyen mon trong tu phap" (The specialized knowledge of judicial work), *Su That*, May 19, 1948.

myth to cover up the oppressive nature of the capitalist system there. In colonial societies, the colonial government also touted this myth, but its courts never granted justice to the colonized people and meted out thousands of cruel verdicts for nationalist revolutionaries. Judicial independence and separation of powers were no sacred and neutral principles as their proponents asserted.

Quang Dam's second line of attack was directed at noncommunist leaders who had been trained in colonial schools. He denounced "many intellectual elements" who stayed aloof from "the masses" and "the people." These "elements" were trained by the French and poisoned by old bourgeois theories that had been designed to serve the interests of colonial rulers and exploiting classes. They were full of self-love and believed in excessive individual freedom. They were motivated by envy, ambition, and desire for social status and political power. Their specialized knowledge of law was simply experience in implementing complicated legal procedures and did not guarantee the realization of justice, but they expected that such specialized knowledge was sufficient to afford them unrestricted freedom from any political control. Knowingly or not, they helped the counterrevolutionaries by their insistence on judicial independence and by their criticisms of local administrative committees. Clearly, Quang Dam was speaking for the uneducated party cadres who were frustrated with the seemingly arrogant French-trained intellectuals. But his arguments also betrayed the ideological incongruence of the Viet Minh state. He raised class struggle as a theoretical issue and attacked the colonial legal system, but he could not aggressively promote class struggle. It was the interests of "the people" and "the masses" that he claimed to defend, not class interests.

In response to Quang Dam, his opponents denied the relevance and legitimacy of class struggle even as a theory. In particular, Vu Trong Khanh argued that law was not only a tool of the ruling class but also a tool to protect the weak against the strong and the powerful.[57] Law transcended class struggle. Civil law, for example, was to mediate conflicts among ordinary people and had nothing to do with politics. Law was built on and reflected not only the will of the ruling class but also social customs practiced by the masses of "the people." Similarly, judicial independence was to protect "the people" who were above any classes and to prevent

---

[57] "Y kien ban doc ve van de tu phap" (Readers' opinion about the judicial system), *Su That*, August 19–September 2, 1948; and "Van de tu phap" (The judicial system issue), *Su That*, June 20, July 10, and August 1, 1949.

officials from abusing power in any regime, democratic or not. Vu Dinh
Hoe pointed out that Vietnam had never had an independent judiciary
from the ancient ages to the colonial period.[58] It was "thanks to the
August Revolution" that "the people" now could enjoy this progressive
legal system. In other words, Vu Dinh Hoe implied that he was with "the
revolution," not against it. Judicial independence was neither feudalistic
nor a colonial fig leaf; it was revolutionary.

Vu Dinh Hoe claimed that the judicial system he oversaw since the
beginning of the revolution was entirely with "the people." In principle, all judges were elected by people's *representative* institutions such
as the National Assembly and local People's Councils. At local levels, he
noted that his ministry had already implemented a jury system by which
"the people" could participate directly in trying specific cases. Vu Dinh
Hoe indirectly reminded the communists that according to the constitution drafted in 1946 and still in force, popularly elected bodies, not
the Communist Party or the government, held supreme power. Judges
were accountable only to these bodies. In other words, the message to the
communists was, you are not the same as "the people," and you ought
to be held accountable to "the people," too. In Vu Dinh Hoe's arguments, "the people," not social classes, were brought out clearly as the
only basis of legitimacy. He forced communist leaders to confront their
own rhetoric and the still-legitimate institutions created by their earlier
accommodation with noncommunists.

Vu Trong Khanh and Vu Dinh Hoe put Quang Dam on the defensive:
the latter had to justify that he was on the side of "the people."[59] Quang
Dam argued that the government and "the people" were one because
the former was made up of the best representatives of the people. To
honor "the people" meant to follow the government, especially local
governments. Local committees were closest to "the people"; they knew
the "desire of the people" even better than the central government. It was
not these committees but "the people" who arrested *Viet gian* because
they hated them. The arrests did not conform to due process because of
special circumstances, but how could legal procedures be more important
than "the desire of the people"? Local committees did not abuse their
power; they were only acting in the interests of the people by helping

58 "Tu phap trong che do dan chu moi" (The judicial system in the new democracies), *Doc
Lap*, July 1948.
59 "Vai diem can ban ve van de tu phap" (Some basic points about the judicial issue), *Su
That*, November 15, 30, and December 19, 1948; and "Ve cuoc thao luan Van de tu
phap" (On the debate about judicial issues), *Su That*, January 6, 1950.

with the arrests. Judicial officials should support rather than oppose those committees.

Although he launched the debate with class struggle theory, Quang Dam was now forced to cling to a fuzzy concept of "the people," which took him further away from class struggle. "The people" (*nhan dan*) was imagined by Quang Dam as a collective (*tap doan*), indivisible and resolutely committed to the struggle. The people had a "collective will" that represented the supreme form of justice; "the interests of the people" should serve as the supreme principle of law. The people had a "collective desire," which was that judicial cadres be loyal to them. Unable to match his opponents' theoretical arguments, Quang Dam turned to threats: "Under the Supreme Court, which was the People's Court, under the Supreme Law, which was the People's Collective Will, those who advertently or inadvertently used legal formalities to oppose the spirit of the law would be punished by the people."

Seeking to further blur class lines (and thus imply that class categories were neither relevant nor legitimate), Hoang Van Duc joined the debate with an intellectuals-centered history of the Vietnamese "revolution."[60] He noted that, because social stratification was not severe in colonized Vietnam, the majority of Vietnamese intellectuals originated from the working classes. There were those who came from indigenous petty bourgeois and capitalist classes, but under the colonial system these were exploited just like the working classes. This was the social basis for the formation of a special group, what Hoang Van Duc called "people's intellectuals" (*tri thuc nhan dan*), who were leading "the revolution." The early enlightened "people's intellectuals" (read: the communists) led the revolution at the beginning but since then a new crop of "people's intellectuals" had emerged. These were trained under the French but they had said good-bye to the old theories and accepted the people's interests as their guiding principle. They now belonged to "the people" and were in fact leading "the revolution." They did not serve any class; they served only "the people."

Hoang Van Duc's view was subversive because it denied the myth, which communists had been constructing, about the revolution being led by "the proletariat." It insinuated that most current communist leaders themselves did not come from working classes as they often claimed; what distinguished them from him was that they had joined "the revolution"

---

[60] "Tri thuc Viet nam trong cuoc cach mang dan chu" (Vietnamese intellectuals in [our] democratic revolution), *Doc Lap*, November 1949.

at an earlier point. Even from a Marxist theoretical standpoint, they had no right to monopolize its leadership. Hoang argued that intellectuals like him were with "the people," the collective that was above class. Class categories were once again denied both relevance and legitimacy.

Hoang Van Duc elicited a strong response from Quang Dam, who called the former's view "a dangerous misunderstanding."[61] By then (early 1950), the DRV had joined the socialist camp and Vietnamese communists were no longer reticent about class struggle. Quang Dam now could point out that "the nation" and "the people" were in fact composed of many classes. Specifically, there were classes that led the revolution, classes that were allied with them during the course of the revolution, and classes that were counterrevolutionary. Yet the communists appeared not sufficiently confident to fully drop "the people" from their discourse. Quang Dam denied that a "class-based perspective" conflicted with a "people-based perspective." In the revolution, "the people" would be lost without the leadership of the proletariat. Classes mattered. Current communist leaders had long left their original petty bourgeois backgrounds and had now become "true proletariats" through their activities and training in the Communist Party. They were leading the revolution, and intellectuals like Hoang Van Duc were only their (temporary) allies. Intellectuals might one day become proletariats but that remained to be proved by their individual performance in the revolution.

The debate showed an increased confidence among communists to advance themes of class struggle in their discourse. Ironically, the inconsistency in the discourse did not disappear through the debate. Communists were still forced to justify class struggle by appealing to "the people." Discourse had limited influence as a causal factor: although communists lost the debate, noncommunists were soon removed from power. Yet this analysis of discourse has offered additional evidence of the ideological incongruence in the state structure and the illegitimacy of class struggle, which posed obstacles to the ICP's socialist ambitions.

The Timid Rise of a Class Discourse

We have seen that class discourse was suppressed up to 1948, especially in public communication channels, to accommodate other groups in the

---

[61] Quang Dam, "Nguoi tri thuc trong xa hoi va trong cach mang" (Intellectuals in society and in the revolution), *Su That*, March 15, 1950.

nationalist coalition. To the extent possible, the communists avoided any discussion of class struggle. When they had to defend it, the emphasis was on international class struggle against imperialism and not domestic class struggle against landlords or capitalists. In this sense, class struggle had to be justified by the national struggle for independence from imperialist rule. By late 1948, however, class terms returned to the political discourse at the same time when translations of the Soviet and Chinese "theory of new democracy" and the Maoist Land Law based on class struggle appeared in the party journal.[62] Yet the rise of this new discourse was not smooth, as shown in the debate on key texts such as the Party Constitution.

When ICP leaders met in the Second Party Congress in 1951, they looked to China for guidance. They decided that Vietnam's communist regime was to be a "people's democratic dictatorship led by the proletariat," similar to Mao's republic (Truong Chinh 1948, 9–11).[63] Yet supporters of a new discourse centered on class struggle failed to persuade their comrades to go along with respect to two important formulations. First was the class base of the party. After considerable debate, ICP leaders settled for the formulation that defined the Communist Party as "the organized vanguard of the working class and working people" of Vietnam.[64] Note that in the CCP's Party Constitution, the party belonged only to the working class. There was no fuzzy phrase "working people" attached to "the working class."[65] Admitting contradicting views within the Central Committee, Secretary General Truong Chinh tried to put a positive spin on the ideological inconsistency in this formulation. What mattered, he pointed out, was not whether the party belonged to the working class, or to the working class and the working people. What mattered was that

[62] Mao Trach Dong, "Tinh hinh hien thoi va nhiem vu cua chung ta" (On the current situation and our tasks), and "Dai cuong phap luat ruong dat Trung quoc" (A general description of Chinese land law), *Su That*, May 1, 1948; and Truong Bat (a Chinese author), "Chu nghia Dan chu moi va nha nuoc dan chu moi" (Theory of new democracy and new democratic states), *Su That*, July 30, 1948.

[63] See also "Phat bieu cua dong chi Truong Chinh sau khi ket thuc thao luan Luan cuong chinh tri" (Comrade Truong Chinh's remarks following the discussion about [the party's] Political Manifesto) (DCSVN 2001, 12:415). This discussion followed the presentation of Truong Chinh's draft manifesto at the Second Party Congress in January 1951. On the Chinese formulation, see Mao Zedong, "On the People's Democratic Dictatorship," July 1, 1949 (Brandt et al. 1973, 449–61).

[64] "Phat bieu cua dong chi Truong Chinh," 412–13.

[65] "Constitution of the Chinese Communist Party," June 11, 1945 (Brandt et al. 1973, 422).

the Party Constitution was as strict as that of any Marxist-Leninist revolutionary party.[66] Yet in fact, as Truong Chinh admitted, although many leaders wanted to adopt the Chinese formulation, the majority opted to add "working people" to the phrase.

Another deviation from a strictly class struggle discourse was the formulations that defined "the people" and the class alliance at the heart of the revolution. "The people" who were "the motor of the revolution" were now defined to include four classes (workers, peasants, petty bourgeois, and national capitalists) and "prominent personalities (including landlords) who were patriotic and progressive."[67] Leading the revolution was an alliance of workers, peasants, and "working intellectuals." These formulations did not go as far as Chinese ones, in which there were only four classes and no prominent personalities. These personalities, as the party newspaper explained to a confused reader, referred to several former mandarins and big landlords who were still serving as ministers in the government.[68]

The new formulations suggested the continuing ideological inconsistency and confusion in the structure of the Vietnamese state. Even though the party had adopted class struggle in practice, elements of its previous discourse constructed under accommodation lingered for years. Despite the pressure to adopt the Chinese model, a full-blown class struggle discourse was resisted by many party leaders, indicating its lack of legitimacy. As a result, on the eve of the social revolution, "class" had to be attached to and borrow legitimacy from "the people."

Although evidence of ideological inconsistency is clear, its impact is less so. The Party Constitution was more moderate in Vietnam than in China, but the purge from 1953 to 1956 still took place, unleashing proportionately as much violence as in China. Hence the power of formal institutions such as Party Constitution or official laws should not be exaggerated. In the party purge, the formal discourse was circumvented by two measures. First, the Land Reform Authority, the independent super-agency, organized and circulated teams of cadres who entered villages, identified "backbone elements," and stayed with them for extended periods to convert them and mobilize them in later class struggle campaigns. Through this Maoist "three-togethers" method, the new radical

---

[66] "Phat bieu cua dong chi Truong Chinh," 412–13.

[67] "Chinh cuong Dang Lao Dong Viet Nam" (Program of the Vietnamese Workers' Party) (DCSVN 2001, 12:434).

[68] "Tra loi thac mac ban doc" (Reply to readers' questions), *Nhan Dan*, July 12, 1951.

discourse of class struggle was brought directly to individual peasants, bypassing all formal channels of the state.

The second measure was a massive media campaign that also bypassed formal institutions. This campaign promoted class struggle by coaxing peasants into telling in public forums personal stories about real or imagined sufferings caused by landlords. These graphic accounts of landlords beating, killing, raping, and maiming their tenants in numerous forms and by various sharp or blunt objects were read again and again through the ubiquitous public address system and published in government newspapers and in pamphlet form.[69] One source of stories came from China.[70] Ho Chi Minh was an active contributor as the author of several articles in *Nhan Dan*.[71] His flair for describing heartrending scenes of colonial sadism was put to good use with scenes of landlords torturing peasants, for example, by ramming sharp sticks down peasants' throats and burning peasants with candles. In one story, members of the landlord's family (a mother and her two sons) were accused by Ho of having killed 260 peasants by such medieval methods. These publications and their reproductions in various forms were clearly aimed at raising class awareness and legitimizing class struggle. Although "land reform" laws prohibited the use of torture and violence, the media campaign directed from the center encouraged such behavior as it desensitized the population to cruel behavior and justified revenge by violence.

Thus, the Vietnamese nationalist discourse during 1941 to 1956 displayed a strong influence of accommodation despite periods of intense contention. This was evidenced in the domination of "the nation" and "the people" in the discourse. By elites' conscious efforts, themes of class conflict were disguised under nationalist or populist themes. When they

---

[69] See, for example, "Dia chu hai gia dinh toi" (Landlords harmed my family), told by Nguyen thi Chien, written by Vu Cao, Van Nghe Trung Uong (1953); "Vach kho" (Telling [our] sufferings), Van Nghe Trung Uong (1955); and "Vach mat hai ten dia chu gian ac phan dong Nguyen Thi Nam va Tran Thuc Cap" (Uncovering two cruel and reactionary landlords, Nguyen Thi Nam and Tran Thuc Cap), *Doc Lap*, September 2, 1953.

[70] See, for example, "Vuong Quy va Ly Huong Huong: Truyen tho Trung quoc" (Vuong Quy and Ly Huong Huong: Verses from China), trans. Hoang Trung Thong and Ly Quy, Van Nghe Trung Uong (1953); and "Co gai toc trang: Tap bai hat phim" (The white-haired girl: Songs from the [Chinese] movie [with same title]), trans. Dao Vu, Van Nghe Trun Uong (1955).

[71] See, for example, C.B. (Ho Chi Minh), "Dia chu ac ghe" (How cruel landlords are!); "Thanh nien nong dan" (Young peasants); and "Dan ba de co may tay" (How many women could be compared to her?), *Nhan Dan*, July 21, 1953, January 11 and February 21, 1954, respectively. No similar writings by other Politburo members can be found.

eventually emerged, formulations of class struggle were more moderate than those in China and they indicated a continuing ideological incongruence in the state structure. Using extraordinary methods, top ICP leaders were able to circumvent this ideological incongruence and unleash a violent class struggle. Available documents do not reveal the internal debate leading to the decision to halt the party purge, and we do not know how ideological arguments were employed in party debates by opponents to class struggle. Still, discursive analysis is helpful in showing the tension and weakness in the ideological structure of the state, even though the question remains as to how and whether ideological incongruence in this case contributed to the final outcome.

CONCLUSION

The analysis of discourses in the Vietnamese nationalist movement in this chapter suggests that these discourses played important roles in the power struggle among indigenous elites. Discourses explained political programs, built community, and were used as weapons to fight one's enemies and defend oneself in the battle for hearts and minds. Discourses were dependent on the human agents who promoted them, but once produced, they could take on lives of their own, constraining subsequent discourses and sometimes constraining state policy. For analysts, discourses showed how actors thought and justified their actions. Most important for our purpose, discourses provided clear evidence of the ideological basis of the state and its consistency or lack thereof.

As this chapter demonstrates, the Vietnamese state lacked cohesion not only in its administrative infrastructure but also in its ideological infrastructure. This lack of cohesion was revealed in the rivalry between "the nation" and "the people," on the one hand, and "class struggle," on the other. The former pair conveyed a sense of unity and solidarity, whereas the latter terms implied division and conflict. To seize power, the ICP pursued accommodation and was silent about class struggle. Yet the communists never gave up class struggle and came out to defend it against exiled nationalists. This tension between the two themes made it difficult for the ICP to formulate a clear and consistent discourse. On the eve of the social revolution when radical party leaders sought to promote class struggle, top party cadres still held strong reservations about a discourse centered solely on "class struggle."

The following chapter examines the political discourse in the Indonesian nationalist movement. The Indonesian state also suffered from ideological incongruences or inconsistencies due to accommodation. Yet the inconsistencies were between different formulations. State leaders sought to promote respect for central authorities, but this contradicted their discourse on democracy and "people's sovereignty." We have seen that Vietnamese communists had to justify class struggle by national or popular interests but not by class interests. Similarly, Indonesian leaders had to promote capitalism not on its own terms but by associating it with positive Islamic values and even with socialism.

9

Talking Accommodation in Indonesia

Nation, the People, God, and Karl Marx

When the nationalist movements of Vietnam and Indonesia are compared in terms of leadership and discourses, an intriguing irony emerges. Concerning leadership, the Vietnamese movement was dominated by a communist party, whereas nationalists and Muslims led in Indonesia. When we turn to movement discourses, a reverse situation is found. The previous chapter has shown that formulations commonly associated with leftist discourses, such as social justice and class struggle, were suppressed in Vietnam until the late 1940s. Ho Chi Minh did not breathe a word about social justice, socialism, or class struggle in his oft-cited Declaration of Independence. Even in 1950, top Vietnamese communists still had reservations about these themes, indicating their lack of legitimacy. In this chapter, we find that radical leftist discourses dominated the Indonesian movement in the same period. Even Islamic parties such as Masjumi, the largest political party, professed a belief in "socialism" and called its ideology "religious socialism." Smaller but radical communist parties such as Tan Malaka's Murba Party never failed to proudly proclaim their allegiance to Marx. Despite having a nationalist and Muslim leadership, everything other than "socialism" lacked legitimacy in Indonesia.

What explains this irony? Why did this mismatch occur between movement leadership and discourses, and what is the significance of this mismatch? We have seen in the preceding chapter that "the nation" dominated the Vietnamese anticolonial movement from day one. In contrast, Marxist and populist discourses were popular early in Indonesia, long before native elites started calling themselves "Indonesians." Once nationalism arrived in the mid-1920s, it had to borrow the language of Marxist internationalism and anticapitalism to be accepted as legitimate. Even Islamic political movements were deeply affected by Marxist and populist discourses. Thus, the cause of the reverse situation between Vietnam and Indonesia must be found in the early histories of these movements. At the same time, this mismatch between leadership and discourses suggests that political actors were not free to create whatever discourses they wanted but were constrained to some degree by existing discourses. Discourses influenced the ways actors framed their interests and constructed legitimizing narratives of their movements. Most important for our purpose here, the mismatch implies an ideological incongruence in the structure of the Indonesian state – in the same way we have found for the Vietnamese state.

The evolution of the Indonesian discourse during state formation can be summarized as follows. Thanks to elite compromise and mass incorporation during state formation, discursive formulations built on a mixture of socialist, anticapitalist, religious, and populist themes were created to serve as the ideological foundation of the new Indonesian state. Yet the ideological structure of this state soon revealed serious incongruence. Although state leaders spoke often of "the people," "democracy," and sometimes even "workers" and "peasants," they condemned mass spontaneous actions. While they denounced imperialism and capitalism for impoverishing Indonesia, they pursued diplomacy and acknowledged the legitimate rights of foreign capital in Indonesia. This incongruence made it difficult for the state to produce a coherent and consistent legitimizing discourse. In the late 1940s, state leaders for the first time expressed their support for capitalism, while at the same time they pursued progrowth economic policies. Nevertheless, capitalism had to be justified as legitimate by linking it to positive Islamic and socialist values. The official discourse was fraught with ideological inconsistencies to be exploited by those who opposed state-directed capitalist development.

EARLY NATIONALIST DISCOURSES, 1900–1942

Marxism was introduced to the Dutch Indies at least a decade earlier than in French Indochina. Dutch socialists and labor organizers brought Marxist ideas to the Indies in the mid-1910s with the creation of ISDV/PKI. This was at about the time the Islamic revival movement began, as seen in the founding of Sarekat Islam and Muhammadiyah. Significantly, Marxism had arrived in the Indies several years before the Russian Revolution

(1917), the founding of the Comintern (1919), and the publication of Lenin's famous thesis on the colonial question (1920). Even more important, this was a decade before a nationalist group first used the term "Indonesia" in the name of its party. Until then (1925), the term used by all political organizations to indicate today's Indonesia was still the Dutch Indies (Hindia Belanda).[1] In other words, "Indonesian" political activists in the second decade of the twentieth century had known Marx before they started calling themselves "Indonesians." The import of Marxist ideas at a very early phase of Indonesian political development, together with the late arrival of nationalism, were crucial differences from Vietnam. By 1918, the Marxist discourse, including themes of class struggle, anticapitalism, and world revolution, was popular not only among radical circles or political organizations but also in the moderate press outside Java (McVey 1965, 178).

With the founding of Budi Utomo and Sarekat Islam, such concepts as "the people" (*rakyat*) also emerged.[2] These concepts had some roots in traditional cultures of the Indies but now conveyed a significant socialist tone imported from Europe (McVey 1967, 137–8). *Rakyat* did not yet dominate the discourse as it would in later decades. Instead, the Marxist concept of "the masses" (*massa*) seemed more popular among leftist circles: from mass will (*kemauan massa*) to mass action (*massa actie*) to "from the masses and for the masses" (*dari massa dan untuk massa*) (Malaka [1925] 1947, iii, 50).

When the nationalist Indies Party (IP) and the socialist ISDV competed for the control of Sarekat Islam during 1919 and 1920, a brief clash erupted between nationalist and Marxist themes. Recall that the Indies Party was created by Eurasians, who were the only advocates at the time of an Indies independent from Dutch rule. Douwes Dekker, its leader, called for the replacement of colonial rule by a nationalist regime based on social justice but not on socialism. He argued that class struggle must be secondary to national struggle. In contrast, the ISDV rejected national independence and supported a world proletarian revolution. Whereas Indies Party leaders called for Sarekat Islam to change its name to Sarekat

---

[1] This group was PI, or Perhimpunan Indonesia (Ingleson 1975, 7). PKI was founded in 1920 – five years earlier than PI – but its name then was Perserikatan Komunist di India (McVey 1965, 46).

[2] McVey (1967, 137) also mentioned another concept that emerged at about the same time. This was the "family principle," which referred to the idealized organization of a group, the state, or society as a family, that is, as an organism that functioned harmoniously and that satisfied the interests of both individual members and the entire group.

India (League of the Indies), PKI wanted Sarekat Islam to adopt the name Sarekat Internasional (McVey 1965, 63–5).

While the Indies Party attracted some support from Sarekat Islam, it eventually lost the debate to the communists. PKI's victory further reinforced its opposition to nationalism. To communists, nationalism was a nineteenth-century European phenomenon and not a real issue in the Dutch Indies at the time (McVey 1965, 178). The concept of revolution among PKI leaders in the 1920s was a singular struggle that did not distinguish between the national and proletarian phases and that aimed directly at establishing a classless socialist state. This can be contrasted to Nguyen Ai Quoc and a generation of Vietnamese communists after him, whose concept of revolution would be just as Lenin pointed out in 1920: a two-stage struggle, with a national revolution followed by a socialist one. Even though both groups were communists, for the Vietnamese the concept of "the nation" had greater relevance in their strategic thinking than it had for Indonesians.

ISDV and Sarekat Islam were united in the early 1920s. By the late 1910s, "Red Sarekat Islam" members had already formed a significant faction in both the top leadership and local branches of SI (McVey 1965, 84–6, 171–7). The success of ISDV in infiltrating Sarekat Islam boosted the Marxist discourse in the latter. Under pressure from ISDV, Sarekat Islam leader H. O. S. Cokroaminoto came out forcefully in 1917 to declare his opposition to capitalism (Shiraishi 1990, 104).[3] Note that Sarekat Islam was originally founded as an organization of Muslim traders; in its first constitution in 1912, the promotion of commerce, Muslim brotherhood, progress, and religion was declared to be the goal of the organization (Noer 1973, 111). Despite Marx's disparaging attitude toward religion, his ideas won the support of many devout Muslims who found creative ways to harmonize the two apparently conflicting discourses. One of these ways was to divide Islam into three class-based streams: Islamic communism, Islamic capitalism, and Islamic imperialism as Islam understood by the poor, the rich, and the nobility, respectively. To "Red Haji" Misbach, a Muslim communist leader in Solo, fighting against capitalism and imperialism was identical to fighting against Satan and proving his faith to Allah (Shiraishi 1990, 255, 265).[4] The communist appeals were so popular that, as McVey (1965, 179–80) points out, their conservative opponents in Sarekat Islam would prefer criticizing PKI

---

[3] Cokroaminoto was also Sukarno's mentor and (for a few years) father-in-law.
[4] *Haji* is the title reserved for those who have made the pilgrimage to Mecca.

on any issue except on communism itself. Even after they were able to expel the communists from SI in 1923, these leaders of SI would stress that they supported socialism but only opposed the tactics of PKI (Noer 1973, 124).

If the 1930s marked the decline of nationalism and the rise of internationalism in Vietnam, the opposite trend was found in anticolonial politics in the Dutch Indies. The rise of nationalism in Indonesia was due to the work of a new batch of young activists such as Sukarno and Hatta. But the cause these activists promoted did not go unchallenged. "The nation" as their favorite theme was vigorously contested from day one. We have seen that communists attacked nationalism as an outdated bourgeois ideology. Dutch suppression of PKI following its failed rebellion in 1926 and 1927 loosened the communist stranglehold on nationalist ideas. But resistance to nationalism came also from conservative Sarekat Islam leaders who believed in Pan-Islamism. In their view, "the nation" (*bangsa*) and "homeland" (*tanah air*) were simply the masks of chauvinism that led countries to fight each other.[5]

How did the young nationalists justify the legitimacy of "the nation"? In a major tract on the history of Indonesia's nationalist movement, Hatta labored to explain why the creation called "Indonesia" was a real one.[6] The reason given was not the existence of a significant national tradition, as is common in nationalist movements, but an international trend of nationalist awakening in Turkey, Japan, and India that "Indonesia" should follow. Nationalism was thus justified not on its own merits but by way of an appeal to internationalism. Hatta in effect said that, "as internationalists, we should be nationalists." Out of either true conviction or mere convenience, nationalism also took cover under socialism. Marxist concepts peppered the discourse of young nationalists with varying degrees of significance. Most nationalists of this period, whether secular or Muslim, claimed that they were socialists. Sukarno did not simply preach nationalism, which he believed by itself was inadequate. Instead he called for *sosio-nasionalisme*.[7] Sjahrir's vision was an

---

5 Cited in Sukarno, "Kearah persatuan! Menjambut tulisan H. A. Salim" (Let's unite! A response to H. A. Salim), first published in 1928 and reprinted in Sukarno (1964, 109–14).
6 Hatta, "Tujuan dan politik pergerakan nasional Indonesia" (The goals and politics of Indonesia's nationalist movement), published circa 1930 and reprinted in Hatta (1976, 1:37–87).
7 See, for example, Sukarno, "Sekali lagi tentang sosio-nasionalisme dan sosio-demokrasi" (One more time about socio-nationalism and socio-democracy), first published in *Fikiran Ra'yat* (Thoughts of the people) in 1932 and reprinted in Sukarno (1964, 187–91).

independent Indonesia where ownership of the means of production was socialized.[8]

Nevertheless, the budding nationalist stars of the early 1930s made three important modifications of the Marxist discourse. First, visceral anticapitalist sentiments superseded utopian communist expressions in the discourse, while serious class struggle was downplayed. Rather than promising a utopian classless society or calling for a violent class struggle, nationalists preferred spending their energies on attacking capitalism, particularly its exploitative and oppressive character.[9] In an influential thesis that sought to unify nationalist, Marxist, and Islamic groups, Sukarno pointed out that these groups should unite because they all shared the same enemy, Western capitalism.[10] Like Marxists, nationalists naturally opposed Western capitalism, which colonized Indonesia. For Muslims, Westerners were infidels, and Islamic teachings of wealth sharing and injunctions against usury meant capitalism must be opposed. Anticapitalism, not class struggle, was promoted as the common denominator of all three ideologies.

The second modification of the earlier Marxist discourse by nationalists was the increased importance attached to democracy (*demokrasi* or *kerakyatan*).[11] No nationalists called for Western-style democracy. Instead, their ideal was *sosio-demokrasi*, or a democracy that combined political rights with socioeconomic equality. A third contribution of the rising nationalist discourse concerned the promotion of "the people" (as a discursive figure) and non-Marxian ways of disaggregating society. Two new concepts heralded this change, including *kedaulatan rakyat* (people's sovereignty) and *Marhaen* (the common people). Hatta promoted *kedaulatan rakyat* as the fundamental principle of the nationalist movement. As he explained, people's sovereignty was not the same as the

---

[8] Sjahrir, "Perjuangan kita dalam pengertian perjuangan sosialistis umum" (Our struggle within the context of the general socialist struggle), first published in *Daulat Rakyat* (People's Sovereign) during 1931–4 and reprinted in Sjahrir (1947, 63–6).

[9] See Hatta, "Pengaruh kolonial kapitaal di Indonesia" (The impact of colonial capital in Indonesia), first published in *Daulat Rakyat*, November 11, 1931, and reprinted in Hatta (1976, 1:356–70); and Sukarno, "Kapitalisme bangsa sendiri?" (What about our own Indonesian capitalism?), first published in *Fikiran Ra'yat* (1932) and reprinted in Sukarno (1964, 181–5).

[10] The original first appeared in *Suluh Indonesia Muda* (1926) and was reprinted in Sukarno (1964, 1–23).

[11] See, for example, Sukarno, "Sekali lagi tentang sosio-nasionalisme dan sosio-demokrasi" and Hatta, "Kearah Indonesia merdeka" (Towards a free Indonesia), manifesto of the New-PNI, published circa 1930 and reprinted in Hatta (1976, 1:90–117).

Western concept of democracy, which was based on individualism and liberal capitalism, which in turn led to exploitation.[12] The basis of people's sovereignty was "collectivism," by which "the people" controlled not only the government but also national wealth. In contrast, *Marhaen* was a fictitious character created by Sukarno. Marhaen was said to be a peasant whom Sukarno once met who owned his land and his tools but who was nonetheless very poor. Sukarno argued that *marhaens*, including small peasants, petty traders, and government employees, made up 90 percent of the Indonesian population. They, rather than the "proletariats" (defined as those who owned nothing but their labor), should be the source of legitimacy for the nationalist movement.[13]

By 1940, on the eve of the Japanese invasion, nationalism was still a contested concept but had largely prevailed over both communism and Pan-Islamism. The debate now shifted to a secular versus Islamic state. Exuding a new confidence, Sukarno did not apologize for "the nation" this time but was on the offensive toward what he termed "old-fashioned Islam." While in exile in Sumatra, Sukarno wrote several passionate articles, calling for Islam to accept nationalism and for Indonesia to adopt the model of Kemalist Turkey where state and religion were separated.[14] In his view, the interpretations of Islam varied not only according to individuals but also according to nations (hence, "the nation" was more salient than Islam) (Sukarno 1964, 377). In the old Turkey, Islamic laws, while well intentioned, had been practiced in superstitious ways that led to corruption, laziness, and economic backwardness (Sukarno 1964, 415–19). For example, because of religious reasons, peasants did not work on Tuesdays and Fridays. Ramadan and daily prayers took priority over work. The state wanted to ban coffee for causing liver and spleen sicknesses, but it could not do so because Islam prohibited only alcoholic drinks. Because of Islamic restrictions on usury, a modern banking system could not develop. How could one be proud of an Islamic state, Sukarno (1964, 409) asked, if the national economy collapsed, if politics

---

[12] Hatta, "Kearah Indonesia merdeka."

[13] See Sukarno, "Maklumat dari Bung Karno kepada kaum Marhaen Indonesia" (Greetings from Brother Sukarno to Indonesian Marhaens), first published in *Fikiran Ra'yat* (1932) and reprinted in Sukarno (1964, 167–70). For his explanation of the origins of Marhaen, see his speech in 1957 titled "Marhaen dan Proletar" translated in Sukarno (1960).

[14] For example, see Sukarno, "Me-'muda'-kan pergertian Islam" (Rejuvenating our understanding of Islam) and "Apa sebab Turki memisah negara dari agama?" (Why does Turkey separate state from religion?), first published in *Panji Islam* (1940) and reprinted in Sukarno (1964, 1:369–402, 403–43).

was anarchic, and if society fell into chaos? National interests, he argued, must be placed above religious considerations.

Sukarno was rebutted in several, no less passionate, articles by a young Mohammad Natsir, a Masjumi leader and first prime minister in post-struggle Indonesia.[15] Natsir argued that corruption and backwardness in the Ottoman Empire were not due to Islam but to the failure of its rulers to implement Islamic laws correctly.[16] Islam was relevant to the state because it taught people about their rights and responsibilities in society. Specifically, the Koran had rules about the rights and responsibilities of rulers and the ruled, how decisions regarding public affairs should be made, the appropriate relationship between husbands and wives, and why the rich were obliged to help the poor.[17] For Natsir, the most important criterion for someone to be the head of an Islamic state should not be his race, nationality, or ancestry but his religiosity. "The nation" did not appear at all in Natsir's writings; instead, it was the Islamic community (*ummat Islam*).

In Sukarno's opinion, separation between state and religion in a democratic system would not preclude the possibility that Islamic laws would be respected; he suggested that if Muslims wanted these laws they should work hard to secure a majority of votes to pass them. Natsir countered that, for Muslims, the state was not a goal in itself but was only a tool to promote Islam.[18] Natsir did not trust the parliamentary system to be able to implement Islamic laws; its members would never have the devotion required for the task.[19] In any case, an Islamic state could not be 100 percent democratic: Islamic laws as written in the holy Koran were not debatable. At the same time, Turkey under Mustafa Kemal was not a democracy as Sukarno claimed; it was a "fascist regime." Although many Islamic politicians had by 1940 accepted a secular state, the debate between Natsir and Sukarno suggested that "the nation" was by no means accepted as legitimate by all Muslim leaders.[20]

---

[15] Noer (1973, 275–95) discusses the fine points of the Sukarno-Natsir debate. There were others besides Natsir who joined the debate but for the sake of simplicity I only discuss Natsir here. See Dahm (1969, 174–96) for a fuller discussion.

[16] Natsir, "Arti agama dalam negara" (The meaning of religion in state [affairs])," published circa 1940 and reprinted in Natsir (1968, 7–18).

[17] Natsir, "Mungkinkah Quran mengatur negara?" (Can the Koran be state laws?), published circa 1940 and reprinted in Natsir (1968, 21–5).

[18] Natsir, "Arti agama dalam negara."

[19] Natsir, "Islam demokrasi?" (Islamic democracy?), published in 1941 and reprinted in Natsir (1968, 26–31).

[20] This was the view of the leaders of Partai Islam Indonesia, or PII, a splinter group from SI (Noer 1973, 160).

The foregoing discussion of early Indonesian political discourse reveals an important contrast to the Vietnamese case. Marxism arrived late in Vietnam, and up to the late 1920s the class discourse in Vietnam had little appeal as it had to confront a far more entrenched concept of "the nation" in either traditional or modern forms. In Indonesia, Marxism enjoyed early popularity; "the masses" and international class struggle competed with the Islamic "community" for influence. "The nation" and "Indonesia" arrived late and at first lacked legitimacy. These formulations had to hide behind internationalism and mix with anticapitalist and Islamic values to justify their legitimacy. The sharp exchanges between Sukarno and Natsir in 1940 revealed the depth of resistance to secular nationalism among Islamic leaders. In hindsight, these pre-1940 formulations by Sukarno were significant because they offered the foundation for future accommodation. Anti-Western capitalism could unify various groups, from left to right and from secular to religious. The theme also resonated with the popular leftist discourse that preceded it. Sukarno's formulations of anticapitalism indicate that a particular discourse does not operate in a vacuum but interacts with and is constrained by what has preceded it. But discourse is also dependent on the political context and on human agents. What made Sukarno's formulations significant was the politics of accommodation after 1942 and the prominent role he played in the movement. In this sense, discourse is not autonomous but reflects political events.

THE STRUGGLE BETWEEN CAPITALISM AND ANTICAPITALISM, 1942–1955

The discourse of the Indonesian nationalist movement underwent significant changes within the next decade. Under Japanese occupation, "the nation" became the most prominent formulation. Accommodation continued to be embedded in such formulations as "the people" and anticapitalism. There were also new formulations that associated "the nation" with "God," which reflected the accommodation between nationalists and Islamic leaders. All these formulations were institutionalized in the draft constitution accepted by most elites on the eve of Japan's surrender.

The examination of the political discourse after the founding of the Indonesian state uncovers considerable ideological incongruence in the state structure. State leaders continued to exploit anticapitalist themes and claim to stand on the side of workers and peasants. An amalgam of socialist, democratic, and populist ideas dominated the official discourse. At the same time, these leaders offered to protect the interests of foreign capital in Indonesia in exchange for diplomatic recognition. Part of their discourse was aimed at countering raging mass demands for war with "Western imperialists." These inconsistencies in the state discourse were exposed and attacked by challengers to those leaders. The opposition discourse ran the whole gamut from class struggle to anticapitalist to populist themes. By the early 1950s, some state leaders began to voice their support for capitalism for the first time, but they had to do so by linking it to Islamic and socialist values. This incoherent ideological infrastructure of the Indonesian state posed a significant obstacle to progrowth policies.

1942–1945

The nationalist discourse during the three and a half years of Japanese occupation underwent several important changes. As a result of accommodation among elites, "the nation" (*bangsa*) and "Homeland" (*tanah air*) were more prominent than ever in the discourse. "Indonesia" came to acquire a richer mythical past. By 1945, many Muslim leaders had accepted these nationalist notions and placed them alongside Allah and other Islamic concepts. "The people" continued to be popular, as were anticapitalist and antiimperialist themes.

Historians of the Japanese occupation have noted how the Japanese were especially wary of Indonesian nationalism even while they claimed to support Indonesian independence. Although the occupation authority used nationalist leaders to mobilize native support, independence was not permitted as a goal in official statements by organizations such as Putera. Even the name "Indonesia" was not allowed to be used in official contexts: the objective of Putera was to "construct a new Java as an integral part of the Greater Asia Co-Prosperity Sphere" (Sato 1994, 51–3). Sukarno and others specifically requested that "Indonesia" be used in the name of Putera and that the red-and-white flag and the song "Indonesia Raya" (Great Indonesia) be used as official symbols of the organization, but their requests were denied.

Surprisingly, statements of Indonesian leaders revealed that "the nation" (*bangsa*), "Indonesia," and "Homeland" (*tanah air*) yielded no ground to other concepts such as "the people" (*rakyat*) or "society" (*masyarakat*). This was certainly true with firebrand nationalists like Sukarno. In his speech to inaugurate Putera, for example, he called on "Indonesia" fifteen times, "the nation" twenty-three times, "our country" (*negeri kita*) four times, and "our Homeland" twice.[21] In contrast, "the people" was mentioned sixteen times and "our society" seven times. A similar pattern was found in the speech given at this occasion by Ki Hadjar Dewantoro, a former leader of the Indies Party and an early committed nationalist like Sukarno.[22] In his speech, "the nation" and "the people" each appeared six times, while "Indonesia" and "society" three times each. If indeed nationalists were not permitted to speak of independence, there appeared to be no constraints on the use of certain words in their speeches. In fact, Sukarno spoke more of "the nation" than he had in the 1930s.

Nationalist concepts now appeared frequently in the *Islamic* discourse. Speaking at the same Putera event, K. H. Mas Mansur, the former chairman of Muhammadiyah and one of the top four leaders of Putera, mentioned "God" (*Tuhan, Allah*) five times, just as often as "Indonesia" and "the nation" combined.[23] The trend increased in later years of the occupation, as the Japanese conceded more and more to the nationalists. In a speech given after the Japanese premier stated that independence would be granted to Indonesia in the future, A. K. Muzakkir, a prominent Muhammadiyah leader, spoke of "Indonesia" twenty times, "the nation" seventeen times and "homeland" eight times.[24] The number was fifteen times for God and the Prophet Mohammed combined (*Allah, Nabi Mohammad*) and twelve for "the Islamic community" (*ummat Islam*).

We have seen in the Sukarno-Natsir debate that, as late as 1940, "the nation" was still ignored, if not opposed, by many Islamic leaders. The strikingly high frequency with which nationalist concepts appeared in the discourse of Islamic leaders after 1942 was clearly the result of the Japanese efforts to bring these two groups together and the accommodation between them. Many nationalists now called the Japanese war with the Allies a "holy war" (*perang suci*) similar to the struggle of the Prophet centuries ago.[25] Some combinations such as *rakyat Islam murba*

---

[21] See Sukarno, "Putera membangunkan kembali! (*Putera* is reestablished!), *Asia Raya*, March 9, 1943. *Asia Raya* (Greater Asia) was one of the few dailies permitted to publish under the Japanese occupation. Its articles were certainly censored by Japanese officials.

[22] See Dewantoro, "Tentang kemajuan kebudayaan" (On cultural progress), *Asia Raya*, March 9, 1943.

[23] See Mansur, "Allah mentakdirkan tentara Nippon datang ke Indonesia" (It was predestined by God that Japanese forces came to Indonesia), ibid.

[24] Muzakkir, "Mihal-'Aidin Wal-Faidzin Kokullu 'Amin wa antum bichair," *Asia Raya*, September 18, 1944.

[25] See, for example, Dewantoro, "Tiap2 orang harus merasa berbakti kepada Tanah Air" (Everybody must be loyal to the Homeland) and "Rasullulah S. A. W.," *Asia Raya*, August 16, 1944, and February 23, 1945, respectively.

(common Muslim people), *tanah air Islam* (Islamic homeland), and *ummat Islam Indonesia* (Indonesian Muslim community) found in Muzakkir's speech were novel. We know that *Indonesia* and *tanah air* had been nationalist concepts, whereas *rakyat murba*, which conveyed a populist spirit, had been the favorite term of nationalists and communists. The new formulations embodied the accommodation among various groups.

"The nation" did not merely appear more frequently; it also acquired a lengthier and more polished résumé. Indonesia had no tradition of independent and unified statehood as Vietnam did, but this did not prevent the reconstruction of its past. In the 1920s Muslim leaders attacked "the nation," while secular nationalists defended it by associating it with an international trend. Now both groups had found and become proud of the native sources of their nationalism. Whereas Islamic leaders cited anti-Dutch movements in earlier centuries, purportedly led by Muslim sultans and scholars such as Diponegoro and Imam Bonjol, secular nationalists picked their national heroes (*pahlawan*) among those nationalists exiled by the Dutch in the 1930s.[26] "Indonesians" were said to have enjoyed the freedom of thought, action, and the pursuit of happiness long before Thomas Jefferson wrote the American Declaration of Independence.[27] Because freedom was a right given by Allah, historically there had been no native tradition of slavery on Java and Sumatra. There were slaves, but they came from other places such as Africa and Champa "outside Indonesia." From Western paintings several centuries old, it was concluded that "Indonesian people" originally lived clean and healthy lives. Their bodies looked big and strong; they lived long and did not die prematurely then as they did now. Through these various efforts to reconstruct the past, a national tradition was discovered and a sense of pride and optimism was apparent. Even though the tradition was lost under colonialism, it was thought to be recoverable.

The rise of "the nation" was accompanied by the sharp condemnation of the West. As I have mentioned, Indonesian nationalists in the 1930s inherited a well-developed Marxist discourse but gradually softened it into broad but vague themes of anticapitalism and antiimperialism. These remained robust themes under the Japanese occupation, even

[26] See, for example, Muzakkir, "Mihal-'Aidin Wal-Faidzin Kokullu 'Amin wa antum bichair" and "Organisasi kita" (Our organization), speech at a rally in Jakarta on March 9, 1943, reprinted in Hatta (1981, 25–32).
[27] "Menegakkan penghidupan baru" (Promoting a new life), editorial in *Asia Raya*, February 22 and 24, 1945.

though Japan was very much both capitalist and imperialist.[28] In fact, antiimperialism was often not separated from sweeping and visceral anti-Western sentiments, especially in regard to England, the United States, and Holland. All these three not coincidentally were Japan's enemies. Nevertheless, Sukarno deployed so much of his oratorical skills to incite popular hatred against "the West" that it was unlikely that he was just trying to please the Japanese.[29] Often denounced in the discourse were not only Western "corrupt" values such as "egoism," "materialism," and "intellectualism" but also the white race itself.[30]

The new themes developed under conditions of accommodation among Indonesian elites were institutionalized in the future constitution drafted near the end of the Japanese occupation. Recall from Chapter 3 that the Japanese set up the Study Commission for the Preparation of Independence in March 1945. From late May until mid-July, this commission of sixty-two members debated a draft constitution written mainly by Supomo, a legal scholar. As chair of this commission, Sukarno proposed five main principles (*Pancasila*) for the future Indonesian state.[31] These five included "nationalism" (a unified nation), "internationalism" (respect for the family of nations and for humanity), "democracy" (based on representation and consultation for consensus), "social justice" (prosperity and welfare for all), and "belief in God" (God of any religions). The first two combined would be nationalism without chauvinism; the third and fourth principles combined would be representative democracy[32]

---

[28] See, for example, S. Ratu Langi, "Tiga Arus: Imperialisme modal Barat terkandas di Utara" (Three currents: Imperialism based on Western capital foundered in northern [Asia]), *Asia Raya*, February 3–4, 1943; and Hatta, "Harapan dan kewajiban rakyat di masa datang" (The hopes and responsibilities of the people in the future), radio speech on March 5, 1943, reprinted in Hatta (1981, 18–25). Actually only Western capitalism and imperialism were allowed to be denounced; Japan's invasion of other Asian countries was called "liberation."

[29] One of the most famous phrases coined by Sukarno was "Amerika kita setrika, Inggris kita linggis!" (We will iron out America and bash England), *Asia Raya*, April 30, 1943. See also Sukarno, "Putera membangunkan kembali!"

[30] See, for example, Dewantoro, "Pendidikan dan kesusilaan untuk lembaga puteri" (Education and morality for youth organizations), *Asia Raya*, February 2, 1943, and "Memperluas, memperdalam dan mempertinggi pengajaran rakyat" (Broadening, deepening, and raising the education of the people), *Asia Raya*, April 6, 1945; and Hatta, "Harapan dan kewajiban rakyat di masa datang" and "Organisasi kita."

[31] See Yamin (1959, 1:61–81). An English translation of the speech can be found in Sukarno (1961, 3–21).

[32] Rather than Western-style democracy, Sukarno actually used three concepts: *mufakat* (discussion to reach consensus), *musyawarat* (consultation), and *perwakilan* (representation). See Yamin (1959, 1:74).

without capitalist exploitation. The last principle about "God" was an effort to accommodate both Muslims and non-Muslims.

The role of Islam in the new state was the most contested issue in the discussion. Three particular questions arose: whether the importance of Islam should be recognized in some specific way; whether there should be an Islamic Court besides state courts; and whether the president should be a Muslim.[33] Underlying the debate on these issues was the old contention between "the nation" and "the Islamic community." The compromising solutions reached between secular and Muslim nationalists were, first, that "belief in one God" became the first of all principles, to be followed by the phrase "with the obligation for adherents of Islam to practice Islamic laws," and, second, that only a Muslim can be president. Significantly, Muslim leaders no longer demanded Islam to be the state religion as Natsir did in 1940. The debate had narrowed down to specific issues. Accommodation crystallized in a formulation that all could accept: belief in one God, with God left undefined. Other demands by Muslim leaders were accepted then but later would be dropped at the last minute.[34]

Islamic and secular nationalist discourses mingled in novel ways in the discourse under the Japanese occupation. While independence was a taboo subject, "the nation" emerged as the dominant figure in the discourse. Anticapitalist and antiimperialist themes continued to be popular. Furthermore, many new compromising formulations such as *Pancasila* were institutionalized to become the basis of an official discourse of the future Indonesian state.

1945–1948

After the Indonesian state was founded, accommodation among the elites led to the inclusion of many groups previously excluded by the Japanese.

---

[33] The full transcripts of the constitutional debates are in Yamin (1959, vol. 1). Analyses of the debates relating to the role of Islam can be found in van Dijk (1981, 45–68) and Noer (1987, 34–43).

[34] The sixty-two-member Study Commission in which Javanese were overrepresented was dissolved by late July to make way for the Committee for the Preparation of Independence, a twenty-seven-member body that had representatives from all regions of Indonesia. This committee met a day after the proclamation of independence (August 17, 1945), and with pressure from the Japanese and from the chaotic situation at the time, Hatta was able to persuade the only four Muslim leaders in this committee to drop all references to Islam or Muslims in the draft constitution that was finally adopted (Noer 1987). Years later this would become a contentious issue as Islamic leaders demanded that the terms originally negotiated and approved by the Study Commission be reinstated.

Many new actors were radical fringe groups, adding higher levels of decibels to anticapitalist and populist themes. State leaders were under some pressure to sing the same tunes. They had done so before but were reluctant now because these themes did not sit well with their need to appeal for diplomatic recognition from Western countries. This situation soon created a serious incongruence in the official discourse and suggested the wobbly ideological foundation on which the young Indonesian state rested.

Before Sutan Sjahrir became prime minister, he published a pamphlet titled *Our Struggle* in October 1945 (Sjahrir 1988). This was an eloquent statement of his views, which soon became part of the official discourse.[35] The primary message of the pamphlet was a call for order. At the time, many spontaneously organized local youth groups were taking revenge on Chinese, Dutch, Eurasians, and other foreigners as well as fighting British and Japanese forces in the name of "revolution."[36] Sjahrir (1988, 9, 21) viewed the anarchy in general and the violence against foreign civilians in particular as a direct result of the indoctrination of youth with a Japanese "fascistic" culture based on "hierarchical and feudalistic solidarity" between leaders and followers.

One can easily detect certain inconsistencies in Sjahrir's pamphlet concerning socialist ideals and pragmatic considerations. A self-proclaimed socialist, Sjahrir (1988, 27–30) appeared to be defending the interests of workers and peasants in his pamphlet. Workers were urged to demand full democratic rights and better living conditions. Peasants, he wrote, must be liberated from "feudalism." At the same time, Sjahrir was concerned about order and realpolitik. He did not call on workers or peasants to lead the revolution or to overthrow any oppressing classes. Neither did he advocate land redistribution. Rather, he argued that the government should organize rural transmigration and industrialization to help peasants. He also warned workers not to let themselves be manipulated by other groups (Sjahrir 1988, 28). While he claimed that Indonesia's "democratic revolution" could contribute to the demise of world capitalism and imperialism, he cautioned that this potential was

---

[35] Existing literature on the Indonesian revolution commonly mentions Sjahrir's pamphlet as primarily a condemnation of Sukarno. Because Sjahrir became prime minister right after its publication, here I treat it as a part of the state discourse.

[36] See Anderson (1972, 147, 151, 169) on the situation in Semarang, Surabaya, and Tanggerang. Frederick (1989, 241) discusses a case of mass murder of Dutch and Eurasians in Surabaya by local youth groups.

limited by the fact that Indonesia lay within the sphere of "Anglo-Saxon capitalist-imperialist power" (Sjahrir 1988, 17). Yet how workers' and peasants' legitimate demands could be harmonized with the forces of capitalism and imperialism was not discussed. It is true that the tensions in Sjahrir's arguments could have merely reflected his honest efforts to adjust his socialist thinking to economic and political realities. Yet, radical leaders such as Malaka would capitalize on the incompatible components in Sjahrir's positions and portray them as mismatches between his words and deeds. And Malaka was not Sjahrir's only critic. Honest or not, Sjahrir certainly was not given the benefit of the doubt by the youths who were attacking British forces in Surabaya and by the peasants who were overthrowing local governments in numerous towns and villages.

Sjahrir's inconsistency became a problem for the state after he took the prime minister's job in November. While his Socialist Party (PS) claimed in its program to oppose capitalism and imperialism (Sutter 1959, 324), the government issued a political manifesto calling for world powers to recognize Indonesia's independence and pledging that Indonesia would assume all debts by the Dutch colonial government, return properties owned by foreigners, and remain open to foreign investment, especially from the United States, Australia, and the Philippines (Kementerian Penerangan 1945, 10–11). Despite the anticapitalist rhetoric of its leaders, Indonesia was willing to protect the interests of Western capital in return for diplomatic recognition.

We can observe the same incongruence in the discourses of leftist groups such as PKI that participated in the coalition government under Sjahrir and Sjarifuddin.[37] PKI's "Program of National Defense and Development" opposed "fascism and colonialism" but did not mention capitalism and imperialism.[38] PKI supported Article 33 of the Indonesian Constitution that called for government ownership and supervision of important industries, but the party was silent about the issue of foreign assets in Indonesia. As late as June 1948, top PKI leader Alimin still maintained that PKI would not oppose American capitalism; rather, it would welcome American loans, not so large that the United States could control

---

[37] PKI used some anticapitalist rhetoric when the party was first resurrected under Mohammad Jusuf in late 1945. See PKI program in "P.K.I. (Partai Komunis Indonesia) bangun kembali" (PKI resurrected), *Ra'jat*, November 8, 1945. Jusuf was a mystical character who had no connection to PKI in the 1920s.

[38] "Program pembelaan dan pembangunan nasional" (A program for national defense and construction), *Antara*, March 6, 1947, 8–9.

Indonesia but large enough to help Indonesia to develop its economy.[39] Alimin did not think that Indonesia was ripe for socialism. Echoing some government leaders of the time,[40] Alimin also urged unity and support for the government in its struggle against the Dutch.

After Sjahrir created a parliament and issued a call for political parties to be formed, the inconsistency in the ideological structure of the state became more severe when various groups with radical ideologies joined the parliament. On the agenda of the numerous emerging "parties," "fronts," and "congresses," anticapitalism and antiimperialism were dominant themes. The program of the Indonesian Workers' Front (Barisan Buruh Indonesia, or BBI), for example, included the formation of an anticolonial front of workers and peasants to fight for "an independent country free from capitalism," the abolition of land tax, and other welfare measures such as the establishment of a Workers' Fund to which workers, the government, and employers would contribute.[41] The Indonesian Workers' Party (Partai Buruh Indonesia, or PBI) founded by BBI claimed that the party "struggles on the basis of its understanding of the conflict between employers and workers, and endeavors by revolutionary methods to eliminate capitalism and to make progress towards socialism" (Anderson 1972, 214).

As anticapitalism surged with the emergence of groups such as BBI, Tan Malaka sought to seize power by exploiting the ideological inconsistencies in the official discourse. Malaka and his supporters presented a "minimum program,"[42] which demanded that (1) the government negotiate with the Dutch only on the basis of 100 percent independence; (2) a government and military be established that would be responsive to

---

[39] "Komunis dan Indonesia" (Communism and Indonesia), interview, *Berita Indonesia*, June 9, 1948.

[40] See, for example, Sukarno's "Nasionalisme dasar perjuangan anti-penjajahan" (Nationalism based on the anticolonial struggle) and "Bersatu untuk merdeka, merdeka untuk sejahtera" (Unity for freedom, freedom for prosperity), *Berita Indonesia*, May 12 and 22, 1948, respectively.

[41] "Pembentukan front anti-penjajahan dan fonds buruh" (Forming the anticolonial front and workers' fund), *Ra'jat*, November 8, 1945. This program was made at a meeting of the BBI in Bandung to be submitted at the Conference of Workers and Peasants in Surakarta later that would found the PBI.

[42] See "Membangoenkan Volksfront" (Building a People's Front), "Permusjawaratan kedua pembentukan Volksfront" (The second consultation to form a People's Front), and "Berunding atas pengakuan Kemerdekaan 100 pct" (Negotiation based on 100 percent independence), *Ra'jat*, January 12, 14, and 18, 1946. Tan Malaka's speech at the Solo conference appeared in "Diplomasi rakyat ialah diplomasi bambu runtjing" (People's diplomacy is bamboo spears' diplomacy), *Ra'jat*, January 19, 1946.

"the wish of the people"; (3) authorization be given for Indonesian forces to disarm the Japanese and take control of European internees; and (4) all enemy-owned enterprises and properties be confisticated.[43] The first demand appeared important but was no more than an empty slogan that later would be quickly accepted by the government.[44] The second demand was truly subversive, given Sjahrir's repeated talk of democracy. Malaka's group pointed out in this demand that the Sjahrir government was never elected (it was appointed by Sukarno and Hatta, who in turn were appointed by the Japanese), and that state leaders ignored the wishes of the people when ordering youth groups to stop fighting British and Japanese forces in Semarang and Surabaya in October 1945. The last demand assaulted the government where it appeared most inconsistent, namely, its solemn pledge to return properties owned by foreign capitalists and its vague talks about protecting workers and peasants.

Malaka failed to topple Sjahrir but the wide support he received showed that the government was vulnerable in its ideological structure. Even while Malaka and many of his radical collaborators spent the next two years in jail for their alleged coup against the republican government, this small faction of the left continued to attack capitalism, demand nationalization of foreign properties, and call for armed struggle.[45] By 1948, they were joined by other leftists now radicalized by the emerging Cold War. As noted in Chapter 7, the Sjarifuddin cabinet fell in early 1948 because of strong opposition to the Renville Agreement in the parliament. A new cabinet was formed under Hatta and supported by PNI and Masjumi. At the same time, Sjahrir's faction broke away from the Socialist Party (PS) and founded the Indonesian Socialist Party (PSI). As opposition parties, Sjarifuddin's remaining PS and its leftist allies such as PKI now switched to militant anticapitalist and antiimperialist rhetoric. They called for the abolition of wage and land taxes and accused the

[43] The English translation of the program and a brief explanation of its demands accepted at the Purwokerto conference that founded PP can be found in Malaka ([1948] 1991, 113–19).

[44] Malaka's original demand was to make the withdrawal of all foreign troops from Indonesian soil a precondition for negotiation but he failed to persuade his supporters to go along (Malaka [1948] 1991, 138–9). Without this specific precondition the demand was simply empty words. See Anderson (1972, 290) for a different interpretation.

[45] See Malaka's ([1948] 1991) three-volume memoir that made his case against the Sukarno-Hatta government and PKI and his booklet on the strategy of guerrilla war ([1948] 2000). Both were published after Malaka was released from prison in late 1948. For a theoretical discussion of Marxism by Ibnu Parna, an associate of Malaka, see Parna ([1947] 1950).

Hatta government of favoring the middle class while neglecting workers and peasants.[46]

Musso's return in August 1948 from the Soviet Union further radicalized PKI and its affiliated groups. In his rallies, Musso accused the Sukarno-Hatta government of being an "agent of foreign capital and imperialists."[47] Internationally, Musso demanded the government to join the Soviet camp to oppose the "imperialist bloc" led by the United States.[48] The new program for the revamped PKI stated that the party wanted to return to its tradition of the 1920s of being "the vanguard of the working people" (*rakyat pekerja*) and "a party of the poor and the oppressed."[49] The goal was to establish a republic based on "People's Democracy" (*Demokrasi Rakyat*) free from imperialism. Toward this goal, the party pledged to stop the government from making further concessions to the Dutch. It also promised to defend workers' and peasants' interests by organizing them at grass-roots levels and by smashing the old local state apparatus. The party would also struggle for the improvement of working people's daily lives, democratic rights for workers, and the abolition of "feudal and imperialist laws." There were too many peasants for the land available on Java to make "land to the tiller" an appropriate slogan, but the party would support the distribution of land taken from "feudal and imperialist" estates. Obviously, Musso's language reflected the rising Cold War discourse. At the same time, we can observe clear continuity with Malaka's program that sought to exploit the ideological inconsistencies in the state discourse.

Despite their defeats, both Malaka and Musso posed serious threats to the Indonesian state in part because they knew how to tap into a serious ideological incongruence in the state structure. On the one hand, the government needed to provide guarantees to Western capitalist interests in return for diplomatic recognition. On the other, it continued to preach socialism and pretended to protect the interests of workers and peasants. In the last two years of the struggle, the government's appropriation of some economic assets from former colonial masters brought it into direct confrontation with the working classes and further exacerbated the ideological inconsistencies in its legitimizing discourse.

[46] "Keterangan Politik Biro Partai Sosialis" (Announcement by the Political Bureau of PS), *Berita Indonesia*, March 11, 1948.

[47] For a report of one of Musso's rallies in Yogyakarta, see "Putuskan perundingan dengan Belanda" (Stop negotiating with the Dutch), *Berita Indonesia*, August 28, 1948.

[48] This was what distinguished the PKI program from Malaka's Minimum Program. On domestic issues, the two programs did not differ significantly.

[49] See Partai Komunis Indonesia ([1948] 1953).

The Timid Defense of Capitalism

The Madiun revolt of 1948 created a bad name for communism. Many elites now denounced this ideology and made an effort to separate their socialist, populist, and anticapitalist rhetoric from that of PKI. For the first time, there were also defenders of capitalism among the ranks of state ministers who wanted to promote economic growth and foreign capital investment. Yet they continued to be hamstrung by the existing discourse that was centered on anticapitalist and populist values. Their defense of capitalism was a timid one: capitalism was legitimate only when it was complemented by Islamic and socialist values.

Masjumi, whose militias fought against PKI militias in Madiun, became the most anticommunist party after the event. Sjafruddin Prawiranegara, a young Masjumi leader and first minister of finance of post-struggle Indonesia, wrote two sophisticated manifestoes about what he labeled "religious socialism"; yet the ideology could be more accurately called Islam-inspired capitalism. Prawiranegara claimed that Islam was a spiritual force and a set of principles that stood above the two materialistic ideologies of capitalism and communism. While he admitted that both communism and Islam shared concerns about social justice, to him class struggle was an inhumane strategy to achieve such a goal because in this struggle capitalists would be treated not as human beings but as animals to be slaughtered (1948, 15; 1950, 13). At the same time, Islamic law on *zakat* (donations by the rich to the poor as a religious obligation) could prevent the worst of liberal capitalism without having to rely on a proletarian dictatorship and class warfare.

We have seen that Sukarno found in anticapitalism a common denominator for Marxism, nationalism, and Islam and that this formula of accommodation created a serious inconsistency in the official discourse. Prawiranegara's new formula of religious socialism sought to reduce this inconsistency now that the state was assuming an active role in capitalist development. For "religious socialism," he argued, the nationalization of the means of production was not a goal in itself but only one of the tools to achieve social justice (1948, 17). This tool was not needed, Prawiranegara asserted, because Indonesia's wartime experience had shown that state control and distribution led only to scarcity and the thriving of black markets. Competition as found in Western liberal economic systems was a better alternative than nationalization. At earlier stages of development, competition might lead to inequality but these could be prevented by government action or through the Islamic institution of *zakat*.

Going further than Prawiranegara in returning a good name to capital-ism was Jusuf Wibisono, another Masjumi leader and minister of finance who succeeded Prawiranegara. Making arguments similar to Prawirane-gara's, Wibisono pointed out that Marxism and Leninism were pro-foundly contrary to Islam despite superficial similarities. Building on arguments made by Cokroaminoto, the leader of Sarekat Islam, when he was defending this organization against the criticisms of ISDV in the late 1910s, Wibisono (1950, 55–7) noted that unlike Western capitalism, Islamic capitalism permitted wealth accumulation only within certain limits set by the "principle of humanity." Islamic capitalism also prohib-ited market monopolies and employers' exploitation of workers. With Prawiranegara and Wibisono, capitalism for the first time in more than a decade appeared in a positive light. Yet capitalism was still not the best choice but only a better alternative than communism. It had to be complemented by Islamic and socialist values.

Despite these timid defenders of capitalism, the political discourse of the elites was still overwhelmingly anticapitalist, socialist, or populist. The discourse of PNI, a rival of Masjumi, was still dominated by pop-ulist themes although its leaders made an effort to distance their ideas from communism. To PNI chairman Sarmidi Mangunsarkoro (1952, 5), *Marhaen* (the ordinary person) comprised 91 percent of the population, including small farmers, workers, and government employees.[50] They were all poor. Mangunsarkoro (1949, 33, 34) believed that *Marhaenisme* or "socialism à la Indonesia" shared the same goal with Marxism-Leninism for a socialist society in which there was no capitalist oppression and exploitation. To achieve this goal, Mangunsarkoro proposed a ban on inheritance rights and maximum limits on private ownership of land and capital. These assets must be owned by society as a whole and supervised by the state and by workers' councils. Together they would decide pro-duction levels, wage levels, and number of work hours to allow workers time for entertainment. *Marhaenisme* viewed class struggle as unnecessary in Indonesia because Indonesia did not yet have an industrial revolution and there was no class division. PNI also rejected dictatorship; the Soviet Union, Mangunsarkoro (1952, 66) noted, had economic equality but no political democracy and was not a model for PNI.

Further to PNI's left was PKI. Madiun did not destroy PKI, and the party gradually recovered in the early 1950s under a new, young leadership whose militant rhetoric continued to combine class struggle

---

[50] The remaining 9 percent included middle peasants and traders.

and populist themes.[51] Musso was dead, but his program remained the essence of PKI's program and strategy. New and surviving PKI leaders viewed postindependence Indonesia as a semicolony run by "agents of Dutch and American imperialism."[52] PKI called for the abrogation of the Round Table Agreements, the nationalization of key enterprises, and the confiscation of large estates to be distributed to workers and peasants.[53] At the same time, the party also claimed to speak for the majority of the people (*rakyat banyak*), including workers, peasants, soldiers, youth, small traders, national entrepreneurs, and "progressive intellectuals." It demanded democratic rights for workers, tax abolition for peasants, and fair wages, work opportunities, and housing for all.

The parliamentary debates on the minimum wage bill and on the nationalization of Aminem, the Dutch electricity firm, demonstrated how isolated and easily defeated the government was in its defense of capitalism. Recall that the Round Table Agreements (RTA) acknowledged Indonesia's sovereignty but restored the control of most modern industrial assets in Indonesia to Dutch and other Western firms. As these firms returned, they faced a different workforce. From a few labor disputes in 1948, the number rose to about two hundred by 1950 and to four thousand by 1956 (see Chapter 3). The government imposed a State of Siege Law in early 1950 and issued a ban on strikes in January 1951, but these measures did not stem rising conflicts.

The protests against Aminem took place within this context. In late 1950, Aminem requested and received government approval for an increase in electricity tariffs by 58 percent.[54] Urban groups in Balikpapan, Bukittinggi, Semarang, Surabaya, and Yogyakarta responded with massive demonstrations. The statements drafted by urban protest groups and other labor organizations displayed visceral anticapitalist sentiments. For example, the Yogyakarta Committee to Protest Aminem that included

---

[51] For the politics of post-1950 PKI, see Hindley (1964); van der Kroef (1965); and Mortimer (1974).

[52] See "Bekerja untuk kemerdekaan politik" (Working for political freedom), editorial in *Bintang Merah*, December 1, 1950, 228, and "Bahaya Fascisme dan kerjasama dengan partai2" (The danger of fascism and collaboration among parties), *Bintang Merah*, June 15, 1951, 294. *Bintang Merah* (Red Star) was the theoretical journal of PKI.

[53] See, for example, "Program PKI untuk pemerintah nasional koalisi" (PKI program for a national coalition government), *Bintang Merah*, March 5, 1951, 166–7, and "Program umum Partai Komunis Indonesia" (General program of PKI), *Bintang Merah*, April 15, 1951, 220–2.

[54] For a discussion of the nationalization of public utilities and the parliamentary debates on Aminem, see Sutter (1959, 3:867–91).

representatives from local Masjumi, PNI, SOBSI,[55] and other groups blamed the RTA for the presence of "big foreign capital" (*modal besar asing*) in Indonesia.[56] "Big foreign capital" was facing an international crisis, causing it to raise the prices of everything. The committee rejected the new tariffs and demanded that the government nationalize Aminem immediately.[57] To counter the government's charge that labor strikes caused production damages and price increases, SOBSI declared that it was not because of workers that strikes occurred; it was because "big foreign capital" was stubborn in defending its profits.[58] The ban on strikes had taken away this means from the hands of the working class to oppose "big foreign capital."

In parliament, opposition leaders, including many from the ruling parties, lambasted the government for its neutral stand in labor disputes[59] and its approval of the tariff increase for Aminem. In debating a motion to establish minimum wage and other benefits for estate workers, labor leader Ahem Erningpraja argued that, given centuries of colonial exploitation, Indonesian labor organizations were no match for "big foreign capital"; the government's neutral stand would only favor capital.[60] Workers, in the metaphors of their representatives, were "animals" and "machines" under colonial regimes; they were "mice," while big capitalists were "cats."[61]

Calling capitalists "shrewd and dangerous," Kobarsjih of Malaka's radical Murba Party accused the government of behaving like the Dutch colonial government when the latter quelled a popular protest against Aminem in 1932.[62] He sponsored a bill that would cancel the tariff

---

55 SOBSI (Sentral Organisasi Buruh Seluru Indonesia or Indonesian Central Workers' Union) was the largest union in the 1950s and had close links with PKI.

56 "Putusan₂ Rapat P.P.A. Daerah Yogyajarta" (Decisions of PPA Meeting in Yogyajarta), October 19, 1950, attachment to "Rapat Pleno Terbuka ke-41 DPR RI" (mimeo transcript of the forty-first open plenum parliament meeting), evening session, December 15, 1950. This document and all the transcripts of parliamentary debates and deliberations cited in this section are available at Perpustakaan Nasional (National Library).

57 "Pengumuman" (Announcement), October 17, 1950, ibid.

58 "Pernyataan SOBSI terhadap larangan mogok" (Statement of SOBSI about the ban or strike), February 27, 1951, attachment to "Rapat 79 DPR RI Sidang 1951" (mimeo transcript of the seventy-ninth parliament meeting in 1951), June 1, 1951, 39a.

59 Minister of Labor's reply to questions from parliamentary members; see "Sidang Pertama Rapat Ke-20 DPR-RIS" (mimeo transcript of the first meeting of the twentieth session of parliament), March 23, 1950, 145.

60 "Sidang 1950 Rapat 13 DPR-RI" (mimeo transcript of the thirteenth meeting of 1950 parliament session), September 23, 1950, 11–12.

61 Ibid., 11, 21.

62 "Rapat Pleno Terbuka ke-40 DPR RI" (mimeo transcript of the fortieth open plenum parliament meeting), December 14, 1950, 15–15a.

increase and nationalize utilities firms in the shortest time possible. Joining the anticapitalist tirade was Wondoamiseno, a leader of the Muslim PSII. He called capitalists "criminals" who, under the law of "Allah the Supreme," would be "painfully tortured in hell."[63] The "revolution" and "the spirit of the proclamation on August 17, 1945" became other symbols that government critics used to demand changes.[64] Wondoamiseno asked, "What was the good of the revolution if colonial exploitation remained in place?"[65] The Estate Labor Union (Sarbupri) picked August 17, 1950, as the day for large-scale demonstrations, and this choice touched a sensitive nerve among many government supporters.[66]

In response, the government's discourse sought to redefine workers' claims as countering the interest of "the people." Prime Minister Natsir accused strikers of being "groups acting in their selfish interests and causing damages to the people" (Kementerian Penerangan 1950, 14). The minister of public works claimed that many people were threatened (by radical groups) if they did not join the protests against Aminem.[67] Government officials on various occasions asserted that the goal of "the revolution" was to improve people's living conditions and that hostilities toward foreign capital would destroy productive facilities and add more burden on "the ordinary people" (*rakyat biasa*) who had suffered for many years.[68] In parliament, government supporters such as Kasimo, the leader of the Catholic Party, and Lacuba, a Masjumi representative, similarly claimed that workers were not "the people" and "social justice" involved the society as a whole but not any particular group. The government's job was to raise the national income that would benefit "the people" broadly; the minimum wage, in contrast, only benefited workers.[69] Throughout the debate, the government was put on the defensive. We have seen that even the most articulate supporters of capitalism

---

[63] "Rapat Pleno Terbuka ke-41 DPR RI" (mimeo transcript of the forty-first open plenum parliament meeting), morning session, December 15, 1950, 28. In original, in "the other world" (*acherat*).

[64] "Rapat Pleno Terbuka ke-42 DPR RI" (mimeo transcript of the forty-second open plenum parliament meeting), December 16, 1950, 20.

[65] "Sidang 1950 Rapat 15 DPR-RI" (mimeo transcript of the fifteenth meeting of 1950 parliament session), September 25, 1950, 46.

[66] Ibid., 11. The Republic was founded on August 17, 1945.

[67] "Rapat Pleno Terbuka ke-40 DPR RI," 6.

[68] See Sjafruddin Prawiranegara, "Apakah modal Asing berbahaya bagi Bangsa dan Negara kita?" (Is foreign capital dangerous for our nation and country?), *Suara Penerangan* 2, 10 (March 16, 1951): 3–4 (this is a newsletter issued by the Office of Information of North Sumatra); also Sumitro Joyohadikusumo, "Jalan Selanjutnya" (The road ahead), part III, *Antara*, April 17, 1951.

[69] "Sidang 1950 Rapat 15 DPR-RI," 8, 12.

viewed it only as a second-best option. It was not surprising that Erningpraja's motion for a minimum wage was passed with 74 yeas and 33 nays.[70] The government accepted Kobarsjih's motion for nationalizing Aminem without even the need for a vote.[71]

CONCLUSION

After the spread of Marxism to the colony in the 1910s, socialist, populist, and anticapitalist themes dominated the discourse of the Indonesian nationalist movement, unifying to some extent diverse groups from radical Marxists to Muslims to nationalists. Voices in support of capitalism were few and especially rare after the decline of SI in the 1930s. Under the Japanese, accommodation sustained the earlier formulations of compromise while promoting "the nation" as a unifying concept.

After the state was formed, its ideological structure revealed serious inconsistencies. Although state leaders spoke often of "the people," "democracy," and sometimes even "workers" and "peasants," they condemned mass spontaneous actions. While they denounced imperialism and capitalism for impoverishing Indonesia, they pursued diplomacy and conceded the rights of foreign capital in Indonesia. In the late 1940s, some state leaders for the first time expressed their support for capitalism at the same time as they pursued progrowth economic policies. Nevertheless, capitalism had to be justified as legitimate by linking it to positive Islamic values and by contrasting it with the negative practices of communism.

The study of political discourses in Vietnam and Indonesia in this and the previous chapter offers important insight into two relationships, one methodological and the other substantive. The methodological relationship concerns discourse and other explanatory factors. Any discourse is crucially dependent on the fortunes of the groups that promote it. Colonial suppression of the internationalist faction of the ICP in Vietnam in 1940 and of PKI in Indonesia in the late 1920s had profound consequences for the later development of the political discourses in both colonies. Nevertheless, the evolution of a new discourse is shaped by the discourses that preceded it and by the bounded universe of political ideas and formulations in which it is embedded. Vietnamese nationalism never displayed fervent anticapitalist sentiments. Unlike Indonesian

---

[70] Ibid., 59.
[71] "Rapat Pleno Terbuka ke-43 DPR RI" (mimeo transcript of the forty-third open plenum parliament meeting), December 18, 1950, 10.

communism, Vietnamese communist discourse took "the nation" seriously even while communists were drawn to the internationalism of the 1930s. In contrast, the Indonesian nationalist discourse was strongly anticapitalist in part because it was developed in the shadow of a Marxist-communist movement.[72]

The substantive relationship is between the politics of accommodation and the ideological infrastructure of the state to be formed. Accommodation not only affects the administrative infrastructure of the state, as analyzed in Chapters 6 and 7, but also shapes its ideological infrastructure. The Vietnamese and Indonesian cases suggest that accommodation encourages political actors to search for, promote, and disseminate corresponding formulations. In other words, elite politics ought to be reflected in elite discourses under the constraints of preexisting discourses. The more elites accommodate one another, the more frequently their discourses carry such formulations. Yet, because these formulations accommodate but do not integrate different discourses, they result in inherent inconsistencies in the ideological infrastructure of the emerging state. Discourses alone do not determine behavior: in the Vietnamese case, the formal discourse of compromise was circumvented by media and institutional tools during the violent purge of the 1950s. Still, the Indonesian case suggests that political groups can exploit ideological inconsistencies to challenge the legitimacy of state leaders or their policies, sometimes to great effect.

---

[72] To be sure, there were widespread anticapitalist feelings throughout the colonial world, not just in Indonesia. The point here is to highlight the contrast between Indonesia and Vietnam. Vietnamese political discourses were strongly anticolonial but generally not anticapitalist.

10

Rethinking Developmental States

In this book I have been concerned with the origins of developmental states. The state is by far the most important of all political institutions, and its role in economic development has long been central in the study of modern politics. However, this book leaves aside policy explanations for rapid economic growth. Nor do I engage in the debate between neoclassical economists and many political economists concerning the appropriate economic roles for states. The literature on developmental states has produced excellent studies that address these issues (e.g., Evans 1995, esp. ch. 2). Rather, I am interested in the structures of these states. The puzzle is, what gives, or gave, successful developmental states their cohesive bureaucracies, centralized government organizations, progrowth class alliances, and firm ideological foundations? This question has rarely been asked in the political economics literature. Cohesive structures do not guarantee that state leaders at any point in time are committed to economic growth. Yet without cohesive state structures, growth-conducive policies are unlikely to generate the intended impact.

In this chapter, I revisit the assumptions underlying my conceptual framework of state formation politics. These assumptions are about elite alignment patterns, the role of foreign forces, and the ability of the framework to predict events. I also consider three implications of this study for understanding developmental states: the role of colonial legacies, the importance of ideologies, and the conditions under which state elites choose to launch developmental policies. Finally, I discuss the relationship between development and regime types with a brief examination of the case in India, which suggests the need to rethink developmental states.

EXPLAINING STATE STRUCTURES

The politics of state formation lies at the center of my explanation for the varying degrees of structural cohesion among the states under study. State formation is treated here as those critical junctures when unprecedented possibilities emerge for new national identities to take shape, for interstate boundaries to be drawn or redrawn, and for entire governments to be established. Existing literature on state formation has been preoccupied with sociological variables such as war, colonization, and commercialization (Tilly 1990; Migdal 1988; Kohli 2004). While these processes are important, I claim that they are less relevant for most states that were formed as a result of imperial or colonial disintegration. Under these circumstances, native elites and the masses could take advantage of suddenly expanding opportunities to participate in politics. These opportunities typically were enormous but brief. The nature of the state system and the kinds of opportunities available provided additional incentives for the hasty creation of formal state institutions that lacked substance or cohesion.

Yet states formed under these conditions are not predestined to have wobbly foundations. Historical cases indicate that each circumstance brought numerous possibilities, depending on how the particular elites and masses on the ground acted and interacted among themselves. For simplification, my conceptual framework distinguishes five kinds of elite alignment and also five kinds of elite–mass engagement modes. Elites may act or not act. If they act, they may unify, fragment, compromise, or polarize. The masses may not act, or they may be mobilized by elites. If the masses act spontaneously, elites may choose to incorporate or suppress them. There can be many combinations, but my six cases displayed three patterns: confrontation, accommodation, and a mixture of both. Confrontation combines elite polarization and either mass suppression or effective mobilization, whereas accommodation joins elite compromise and mass incorporation.

Confrontation gave birth to the Korean, Maoist Chinese, and Suharto's Indonesian states. In Korea, elites were polarized and carried out mass suppression. The process created North and South Korea – each ruled by a narrow group of elites coming from opposing ideologies. By the early 1950s, the South Korean state already possessed a centralized structure with a cohesive bureaucracy and police force inherited from the Japanese but reorganized during state formation. Former colonial elites, including landlords, industrialists, and bureaucrats, either dominated or supported the state. A crucial character of this narrow and exclusive social foundation was its progrowth orientation. After the early and systematic removal of communists, the South Korean state enjoyed relative stability and hegemony over society for decades afterward.

Like its neighboring Koreas, the Maoist state was born out of confrontation. Throughout the 1930s and 1940s, the Chinese Communist Party was under constant siege by GMD forces. Polarization produced a cohesive leadership with the radical Mao Zedong on top. During the decades of struggle for survival, the CCP developed a cohesive party organization and an army whose million members were mostly poor peasants. The communists also accumulated considerable mass following and mass mobilization experience. By the time it emerged victorious in the civil war, the CCP had earned Soviet support and amassed sufficient developmental assets to erect a cohesive state structure right away. This structure helped the PRC fight effectively in the Korean War and oversee perhaps the most radical transformation in Chinese history.

The rise of Suharto and the Indonesian developmental state in the late 1960s was not strictly a state-forming experience. At the same time, this event involved massive coordinated violence that approached the level observed even in extremely violent state-forming cases such as Korea and Maoist China. More importantly, this violence indicated the sharp polarization in the mid-1960s between conservative political and military elites, on the one hand, and radical communists, on the other. As in Korea and China, through polarization and suppression Suharto was able to build a cohesive developmental structure that allowed the state to take on developmental roles effectively throughout the 1980s and 1990s.

Confrontation in these three cases thus is found to be associated with cohesive state structures. By contrast, accommodation during the formation of the Indonesian and Vietnamese states in the 1940s was linked to wobbly structures. In Indonesia, the state was born without a developmental structure. Authority was fragile at the top with ruling coalitions composed of unstable political factions and reflecting the broad multiclass foundation of the state. Unlike Korea, this social base was inclusive and oriented toward redistribution, not growth. The state was highly decentralized: local militias and political groups were well organized and practically autonomous. The state bureaucracy and the military were thoroughly infiltrated by political factions. A progrowth coalition was in power initially and attempted to play developmental roles but was quickly defeated because it lacked a cohesive state structure to carry out its policies.

In Vietnam, the Indochinese Communist Party rose to power thanks not to superb organization or military might, as with the CCP, but to a decisive compromise with the government of the Empire of Vietnam. Elite compromise and mass incorporation denied the communists crucial foreign alliance as well as centralized and unified control over policy and government apparatuses. Noncommunists enjoyed significant authority in the realms of social, economic, cultural, and judicial policies. At the same time, local governments and party branches enjoyed de facto autonomy. The inheritance of the colonial bureaucracy created an ideological incongruence as evidenced in the clashes between revolutionary leaders and conservative bureaucrats. In comparative perspective with South Korea and Maoist China, accommodation hindered the creation of a cohesive state structure in Indonesia and Vietnam.

China's Republican state is the only case study in this book that exhibited a mixture of accommodation and confrontation, with accommodation being the primary mode. This state was born out of a compromise between conservative nationalists and leftists, including radical communists. It then underwent a brief confrontation when communists were purged; yet the basic pattern of compromise did not change for elites within the GMD's top leadership. At the mass level, the state was built on both mass suppression and mass incorporation. While state leaders accumulated considerable military and bureaucratic power thanks to mass suppression, the incorporation of local warlords was the greatest cause of weakness in the state structure. This state contained many effective organizations but lacked a cohesive structure overall.

The six case studies suggest that state formation politics is responsible for the varying degrees of cohesiveness in the structures of emerging states. States are simply not born equally: some are better endowed with developmental assets in the form of cohesive structures, while others are not. Endowment is not destiny: state formation is not the only moment when elites and the masses act. Their subsequent actions and interactions can reverse the situation. For example, the Indonesian state was born with a wobbly structure but confrontation in the 1960s transformed it into a developmental state. The case of the Republican state conveys a similar lesson. This state was expelled from the mainland in 1949, but this defeat removed weaknesses in the state structure, including a vigorous opposition faction within the GMD leadership and numerous disloyal provincial warlords. These legacies of accommodation were left behind on the mainland. The cohesive core of state leadership and military-bureaucratic apparatus moved to Taiwan, where it erected a formidable developmental state.

The in-depth study of the Vietnamese and Indonesian cases offers nuanced accounts of how accommodation politics became institutionalized in state structures in each case. In terms of government system, accommodation was expressed in coalition government (Vietnam) and a multiparty parliamentary system (Indonesia). In both cases, political organizations such as parties and fronts possessed blurred boundaries and weak corporate identities. Even a tightly knit Leninist party like the ICP was turned into a united front by accommodation. Indonesia witnessed the proliferation of status-based parties that were little more than unstable coalitions of personal factions. In both cases, serious ideological incongruences were found in official discourses. The ideological problem was different for each state: in Vietnam it was the tension between the nation and class struggle, whereas in Indonesia it was between socialism and capitalism. This difference between Vietnam and Indonesia had origins not just in accommodation but also in the histories of the nationalist movements in both cases. Nevertheless, in both, the incongruences were initially sustained by accommodation but later would become significant legitimizing problems for these states as they adopted developmental policies.

ASSUMPTIONS ABOUT THE POLITICS OF STATE FORMATION

The framework of state formation politics advanced in this study gives primacy to two critical dynamics of intraelite and elite–mass interaction. Like all theories, this framework makes many assumptions; the three most important ones are reviewed and clarified here.

The first assumption concerns the way patterns of elite compromise and polarization are conceptualized in this study. Elite compromise is viewed here as resulting in wobbly state structures, whereas polarization results in cohesive structures when this pattern culminates in the elimination of a major elite group or in the breakup of the state into separate territories ruled by opposing elites. This formulation of elite compromise requires further clarification. On the one hand, it appears to contradict the central tenet of democratic theories in political science. Theorists from Robert Dahl to Juan Linz have regarded accommodative elites as the prerequisite of strong and stable democracies. On the other hand, the literature on democratization suggests that the causal link between elite compromises and stable democracies is tenuous, and that the benefits of such compromises can be appreciated only in the long term. First, in studying historical cases of sustainable compromise – from the English Glorious Revolution of 1688 that undergirded the first modern democracy to the South African pact of the 1990s that ended apartheid – John Higley and Michael Burton (2006, 22) have found that shared conditions that facilitated these compromises included the prior experience of protracted but inconclusive elite conflict, a sudden crisis that exacerbated that conflict, the alignment of opposing elite factions in ways that aided negotiations, and the ability of factional leaders to control their followers. Given these difficult conditions, it is unsurprising that elite settlements that culminated in stable democracies have been so infrequent. Second, elite pacts in the short term may not seem all that honorable: they are decided by a few elites behind closed doors, often exclude the masses, contain provisions that absolve incumbents of past crimes and protect their future interests, and in some cases may even block the full transition to liberal democracy (Higley and Burton 2006, 100–2). For example, it has been argued that Mexico's 1928–9 elite pact produced only an inclusive authoritarian regime but not a consolidated democracy (Knight 1992, 139). For this reason, scholars have distinguished between liberalization and democratization (Linz and Stepan 1996, 4). Elite compromises may lead only to the former but not to the latter. Finally, it may take decades and even centuries to make elite pacts stick. Two hundred forty years elapsed between the English settlement of 1688 and the establishment of Britain's modern liberal democracy. To produce stable democracies, elite compromises need not only time but many fortuitous factors such as economic prosperity or the absence of deep ethnic cleavages (Higley and Burton 2006, 101–2). Thus, the causal relationship between elite compromises and democratic outcomes is by no means as straightforward as it seems on the surface. The only straightforward aspect appears to be the fact that elite compromises save lives: millions of Koreans, Chinese, Vietnamese, and Indonesians could have been spared their violent deaths if the elites involved had been more accommodative to one another.[1]

The second assumption of my framework involves the role of foreign forces in state-forming situations. In most cases since the eighteenth century, foreign intervention has been present at different levels. In our cases,

---

[1] Even this may not be straightforward on a closer look: Vietnamese revolutionaries considered the heavy sacrifice of human lives under their rule to be justified by "noble" goals, such as "national independence" and "socialism."

foreign intervention ranged from substantial (Republican China, 1923–7; Korea, 1947–9), to significant (Sukarno's Indonesia, 1942–6; Vietnam, 1945–6), to insignificant (Maoist China, 1945–9; Suharto's Indonesia, 1965).

Nevertheless, as I have argued in this study, there are reasons to direct our attention to native elites and the masses rather than to foreign forces. These forces explained the behavior of native elites only to some extent and in some but not all cases. Many indigenous elites chose to resist foreign pressure rather than comply. Chiang Kai-shek and Mao Zedong were notorious for not listening to their foreign advisers. Rhee Syngman called for two separate Korean governments before American officials did. After the United States accepted separate elections for two Koreas, Kim Ku opposed them and sought to overturn the American occupation government. This was also the case of Vietnamese communists who succeeded in resisting Chinese pressure in late 1945. Even if they complied with foreign pressure, native elites still had a range of options, including whom to pick as an ally and whom to fight, and where to accommodate the masses and where not to accommodate them. With respect to the masses, spontaneous mass actions had even less to do with foreign factors. Mass revolts were often directed against foreign occupying forces (in Korea, 1947–8; in Indonesia, 1945–9). In sum, while I regard foreign forces as important, the case studies suggest that native elites and the masses could and often did act autonomously during state formation.

The third assumption of my framework concerns the difficulties in determining a state-forming event a priori and in predicting the outcome of an ongoing state-forming case. Yet the difficulty lies not with the framework but with inherent complexities in the situations under study: Tremendous uncertainties are involved. As circumstances change, elites and the masses change their behavior accordingly, making things difficult to predict. This unpredictability has prompted some scholars to question the usefulness of "normal science methodology" in studying phenomena such as regime change or state formation. The question then becomes, should we just give up? What can this class of events teach us even if we may not be able to predict the future?

The answer is, we should not give up because of the theoretical and methodological advantages that make the study of state formation politics worthwhile. Theoretically, I have noted the enormous possibilities in these events for wholesale institutional change. State formation politics left critical consequences for the states under study here. Many similarities and differences among these political entities today can be traced back to state-forming periods. While we cannot predict the future, we can at least explain the present. Methodologically, state-forming events provide us with useful, clear-cut points of comparison, as in the case of states that once belonged to an empire but now are going separate ways, such as the former Soviet Republics. The collapse of the Soviet Union is a logical point for comparing these states. The cases examined in this study can be regarded as originating from one single empire (Japan), which makes the comparison an efficient one.

COLONIAL LEGACIES AND DEVELOPMENTAL OUTCOMES

By advancing an explanation based on state formation politics, I do not deny the importance of colonial legacies for some cases such as South Korea. The Japanese in fact left significant legacies in Korea. Even if the material progress under colonial rule was much destroyed by the Korean War, Japanese contributions were still substantial. In particular, the Japanese removed the ineffective traditional state; fostered the emergence of industrial workers, entrepreneurial capitalists, and modern bureaucrats; and left behind a model of statecraft and economic development. Western colonies generally underwent much less change.

Nevertheless, colonial legacies should not be exaggerated. Empirical evidence from the Korean case suggests that the preservation of colonial legacies was not a simple matter, as often assumed. Because of Japanese brutalities, colonial institutions were bitterly resented in Korea. These colonial assets further disintegrated because of the political turmoil following the collapse of Japanese rule. In this context, the preservation of colonial legacies required extraordinary efforts of both American occupiers and emerging Korean elites as they sought to cope with mass revolts and communist threats. Rhee Syngman had to coerce the National Assembly, itself already purged of most leftists by then, into pardoning many Japanese-trained police commanders and officers. The fact that Rhee himself was no Japanese collaborator but a towering nationalist with impeccable anticolonial credentials made this move puzzling. Colonial institutions were not destined to be preserved under this man, as often assumed.

In Indonesia, the continuity between the colonial state and Suharto's regime was also apparent, but the links here were even more tenuous than those in Korea. Dutch colonial legacies were more limited than Japanese legacies and created many new problems for postcolonial developmentalism. A major problem left behind by the Dutch was the creation of an entrepreneurial class of ethnic Chinese mediating between the colonial administration and native subjects. While the Chinese contributed substantially to economic development under Suharto, they became a source of resentment and a political target often exploited by opponents of the regime.

Another insight from this study concerns the different impacts of colonial legacies on postcolonial capitalist and socialist states. In particular, whether colonial legacies acquired positive values in a postcolonial context depended on the kind of legacies and the ideological correspondence between colonial and postcolonial regimes. All physical legacies of colonialism would benefit postcolonial states regardless of regime. Yet if colonial governments fostered *capitalism*, as were the cases of all colonies before World War II, the social and political legacies of colonialism were likely to create problems for postcolonial elites if these elites pursued *socialist* development, as was the case in Vietnam. Inherited political institutions such as the colonial bureaucracy were likely to resist socialism. Similarly, inherited capitalist entrepreneurs were likely to oppose central planning and the nationalization of productive assets. This happened to Vietnam as its leaders sought to implement rent reduction and land redistribution. The "rule of thumb" is this: for postcolonial *capitalist* states, the more aggressive the colonial regime was in establishing centralized authority and in promoting capitalist development, the more beneficial its legacies would be. For *socialist* states, the relationship was reversed.

IDEOLOGY AND DEVELOPMENTAL STATES

By including socialist cases in this study of developmental states, we can see colonial legacies playing a more ambivalent role. Furthermore, by matching these cases with capitalist ones, this study hopes to break down some paradigms that exist in the scholarship of these two types of systems. Sinologists now widely accept that the communist state on the mainland shared many critical traits with the Republican state. Yet students of the South Korean state are far less likely to acknowledge its essential similarities with its North Korean *twin* brother during the early years. It is also common for most Southeast Asianists to place Indonesia in the same box with South Korea.[2] Vietnam tends to be compared only with North Korea and China. There are good reasons to treat capitalist

---

[2] Four rare article-length attempts at comparing Indonesia and Vietnam include Harvey (1977); Tonnesson (1995); Antlov (1995); and Frederick (1997). None of these authors command primary sources of both Indonesia and Vietnam, however.

and socialist countries separately, but I believe that comparing them is also fruitful.

An insight drawn from this study is that building a cohesive state structure in a short period of time involved violent confrontations regardless of regime ideology. Different circumstances were involved in the deaths of tens of millions of Chinese under Mao and Liu Shaoqi in the 1950s, the brutal purge of tens of thousands of class enemies under Ho Chi Minh and Truong Chinh, the massacre of a quarter million communists under Suharto, and the tens of thousands of deaths caused by the Korean War and Rhee Syngman's repression of communists. These events took place at different times and the perpetrators of violence espoused different ideologies. Yet the politics of state building was a compelling logic that underlined all these tragic events.

This is not to say that ideology can be ignored. That ideological congruence is part of state structure is another insight for the literature on developmental states. Existing literature fails to take into account ideological factors systematically. In Korea, conservative colonial institutions contributed much to the internal cohesion of the state because this state was led by conservative nationalists. In Vietnam, the same colonial assets did not help but rather hurt when radical leaders led the state. Given the circumstances of these two cases, one can speculate that the Maoist state would have possessed a weak ideological infrastructure, had it inherited GMD institutions. In Indonesia, nationalists there were more progressive than Korean leaders but less radical than their Vietnamese and Chinese counterparts. The evidence in this case does not show as clearly the impact of inherited colonial apparatus on state structure.

Yet the correspondence between new elites and inherited colonial institutions is only one aspect of ideological congruence. The ideological consistency of official legitimizing discourses is another aspect of congruence. Although the impact of this congruence on the possibility of success for developmental policies is hard to isolate and evaluate, it is clear that ideological inconsistencies made it difficult for Vietnamese and Indonesian ruling elites to be clear and persuasive, even when they needed to promote transformative policies aggressively. Inconsistencies also offered vulnerable points for their opponents to exploit.

WHY GOVERNING ELITES CHOOSE TO BE DEVELOPMENTALIST

This study has sought to explain the origins of developmental structures, and assumes that at some point governing elites would be willing to undertake developmental roles. To restate a point made earlier, successful developmentalism depends as much on state structures as on the commitments of state leaders to promote developmental goals and policies. In Korea, Rhee contributed decisively to building a developmental structure but failed to embrace developmental roles. (Yet without Rhee's prior work, Park would have lacked the necessary structure to launch his developmental policies only a few years after assuming power.) Similarly, the Suharto regime implemented growth-conducive policies in its first years but for nearly a decade in the 1970s was distracted by oil windfalls. (Yet the cohesive structure of the state allowed the government to limit the harmful impact of "the Dutch disease" and return to progrowth policies in the 1980s and 1990s.)

Still, one may wonder about the conditions under which state elites may choose to play developmental roles. For the Republican state and the two socialist cases under study, nationalism and ideological beliefs were a driving force behind elite agendas. GMD leaders, including Sun, Wang Jingwei, and Chiang, were inspired by nationalism and by a mixture of Chinese, Japanese, American, and Russian reformist thoughts (Bergère 1998, ch. 10; Shirley 1962; Boorman 1964; T. Yang 2002; M. Yu 2002). Fascist ideas and methods also influenced Chiang (Wakeman 2000). For Chinese and Vietnamese communists, Stalinism was viewed as the model to emulate. Many among the first generation of Vietnamese communist leaders viewed the Soviet Union as Vietnam's desired destiny and were committed to Stalinism to their deaths (Vu T. 2008).

Yet even these committed revolutionaries were sensitive to political conditions. War and foreign alliances created new political realities, affecting the timing of key decisions. In Maoist China, the Korean War affected the timing and intensity of many political campaigns such as the Three-Antis, the Five-Antis, and the campaign against counterrevolutionaries. The need to mobilize resources and mass loyalty for the war brought the state into more intense engagement with social groups. The same conditions existed in Vietnam in the early 1950s when the state sought to mobilize peasant manpower and resources more intensively. The establishment of a Sino-Vietnamese alliance in 1950 also influenced Vietnam's decision to implement a radical agenda sooner rather than later. Communist China offered Vietnam crucial political and material assistance to launch its "land reform" and collectivization.

Political conditions similarly and more conspicuously shaped Korean and Indonesian governing elites' commitments to progrowth policies. Park and Suharto were professional military men but not committed revolutionaries as were Mao Zedong and Ho Chi Minh. Contingent events and conscious strategizing under changing political conditions arguably played a bigger role in their embrace of economic development. Most accounts of these two cases indicate that the process by which they became committed developmentalists was incremental and lacked clear direction: no single decision or key speech signaled their commitments to developmental policies at a particular point in the first year or two of their ascendance.[3] A detailed analysis of these events is beyond the scope of this study, but three interrelated factors driving this ambivalent process can be noted: the political contexts facing these leaders, their personal choices of strategies for consolidating their power, and the character of the political coalitions that they assembled.

First, the political contexts in which Park and Suharto rose to power suggested certain powerful political imperatives. Both leaders inherited economic decline (South Korea) or crisis (Indonesia). Both rose to power by means of military coups and faced formidable political challenges or rivals (for Park, the popular movement to overthrow Rhee, and for Suharto, the popular Sukarno and powerful PKI). As major generals, both Park and Suharto had supporters in the military but their domination of this institution was by no means guaranteed. The contexts of their ascendance thus provided them with neither secure power nor sufficient legitimacy. These contexts were important in shaping their short-term maneuvers, in particular by creating the urgent imperatives to stabilize the economy and to build broad political support.

Still, contextual factors were insufficient, rendering their personal choices of appropriate strategies equally crucial. Both Park and Suharto showed great respect for the constitutional process, either out of convenience, cautious personality, the need to maintain delicate power balances, or their concerns about the long-term legitimacy of their regimes. Rather than relying entirely on martial law, they allowed existing legitimate institutions to function while seeking to manipulate them. The junta under Park declared that it would allow civilian rule to return after order had been established. The junta then subjected itself to popular elections in 1963 in which it barely won, thanks in great part to a split among the opposition. Suharto did not proclaim himself president right away but removed his predecessor from power gradually through a combination of popular pressure and legislative means. Despite being professional

---

[3] The accounts below are based on (for South Korea) Douglas (1964); Henderson (1968); Y. C. Han (1969); T. Park (2005); and Brazinski (2005); and (for Indonesia) Pauker (1965); Lev (1966a); Legge (1968); and Elson (2001).

soldiers, both Park's and Suharto's willingness to play politics (as opposed to an inclination to apply coercion) was remarkable. Combined with contextual factors, this willingness perhaps disposed them further toward choosing economic development (as opposed to security, which could have been achieved by coercive means) as their regimes' legitimizing goal.

Finally, the strategies these leaders picked in turn helped them to gather political coalitions of a particular character. Their allies included technocrats of various backgrounds, leaders of big businesses, and Western governments and Western institutions such as the IMF and the World Bank. Both governments could draw on a pool of technocrats accumulated but marginalized under their predecessors. Money and technical advice from foreign and domestic supporters helped them to buy off other factions, win elections, implement economic stabilization measures, and build a momentum to stay in power.

Overall, our cases suggest that the conditions under which state elites chose to play developmental roles were complex. While ideas were important for some elites, political calculations were the primary logic in all cases. Elites formulated their strategies on the basis of the historical contexts in which they found themselves and over time assembled political coalitions whose interests converged on economic growth or development. Suharto had a tougher job than Park, as the Indonesian general had to build a cohesive state structure while taking on developmental policies. Park's more spectacular success should not obscure the fact that he was able to launch his policies from a cohesive structure built by Rhee.

DEVELOPMENT AND AUTHORITARIANISM

In explaining the origins of developmental states, this study primarily has been concerned with state structures. Understanding the importance of state structures in successful developmentalism is crucial to go beyond the inconclusive debate about the relationship between authoritarianism and development.[4] Because developmental states tend to be authoritarian, students of these states have been put in the morally uncomfortable and quantitatively untenable position that authoritarianism is correlated with or necessary for development. As Chalmers Johnson (1987, 143), who coined the concept of developmental states, admits, "It should... not be forgotten that authoritarianism is the most common form of political

---

[4] For reviews of this debate, see Przeworski and Limongi (1993) and Przeworski et al. (2000, 1–3, 142–5).

regime on earth but one that is only rarely accompanied by the trade-off of very high-speed, equitably distributed economic growth."

Many quantitative studies have since confirmed that the relationship is not a general law. For example, Adam Przeworski and his associates (2000) examine data for 141 countries during 1950 to 1990 and conclude that regime type, whether democratic or authoritarian, does not affect growth rates, even in poor countries. Regimes also have no overall effect on investment: poor countries invest less regardless of whether under a democracy or a dictatorship (Przeworski et al. 2000, 146–51).

Yet both sides of the debate seem to miss the point. The problem lies not with the relationship between development and authoritarianism but with the concept of authoritarianism itself. "Authoritarianism" covers a wide range of regimes from modern military dictatorships to traditional patrimonial systems. Even fascist and communist states are sometimes referred to as authoritarian. Yet there is a critical difference between regimes where a cohesive and purposive Weberian bureaucracy exists and those where bureaucrats are only personal servants of patrimonial rulers (Kohli 2004, 9). Both kinds of regimes may be equally repressive, but only the former possess developmental structures.

Furthermore, what Rhee and Suharto did with their communist and other opponents was not simply repression; it was the systematic coordination of large-scale violence, political control, and the concomitant mobilization of support from foreign and domestic capital. Their success in this task helped them to build a cohesive bureaucratic structure, institutionalize social submission, and develop a close relationship with domestic producer classes (and with foreign capital in Suharto's case). At the same time, the structures they built were sufficiently cohesive to avoid being captured by private interests.

For communist parties in China and Vietnam, repression was inseparable from state building. Mass campaigns were designed not only to destroy class enemies but also to set up local state structures staffed by loyal cadres. It was not a few hundreds or even thousands of counterrevolutionaries who were shot. It was a *percentage* of the total population *planned in advance* to be executed in the case of Vietnam's "land reform." Furthermore, most of those to be killed were only *potential* enemies *as a social class*, not individual opponents of the regime.

The systematic character of repression in these states is found not only in the way they defined their enemies but also in the way violence was organized. Similar to Suharto's Indonesia where local military commanders collaborated with local Muslim groups to mass-murder or imprison every suspected communist, the struggle against potential regime enemies in China and Vietnam was launched in *every* village and urban neighborhood. The victims of state violence did not go to district or national capitals to protest and be shot by the police; violence was *brought* to them in their homes and often carried out by neighbors or members of their own families.

The kind of repression carried out by most authoritarian regimes pales in contrast with these cases. Most authoritarian regimes can kill their opponents or suppress occasional antigovernment demonstrations, but few dare to define their enemies in systematic terms. Few are able to build cohesive bureaucratic and coercive institutions or to develop a close but independent relationship with producer classes or foreign capital. While repression is reprehensible, the debate about regime types and development distracts students of political economy from the real issue: authoritarianism refers to a particular pattern of relationship between rulers and the ruled, but more important than this pattern is the level of institutionalization of the relationship. It is an institutional structure that gives *any* state a basis for playing developmental roles effectively.

RETHINKING "DEVELOPMENTAL STATES"

The case studies in this book are taken from a small sample that is geographically bounded within Pacific Asia and historically limited to the middle decades of the twentieth century. My central theoretical inquiry – the historical origins of developmental state structures – is inspired by the literature on developmental states. In connection with the debate about democracy versus authoritarianism, this concluding section looks briefly at India, a democratic country not included in the sample but too important to neglect. India is valuable also because its experience indicates the limits of the very concept of "developmental states" in the literature.

In the contemporary developing world, late-industrializing India seems to present a big anomaly in theories of developmental states. Independent India has had a fairly broad-based state, a functioning democratic regime, and a federal system (Kohli 2004, chs. 6 and 7). India enjoyed moderate economic growth from the time of independence (1947) up to the 1970s. Since the 1980s and especially after economic liberalization in 1991, federal and democratic India has seen rapid growth rivaling centralized and authoritarian China. Does India contradict the main argument of this book about the importance of developmental state structures for growth?

The answer is no. The varying degrees of cohesion in state structure over time still explain the broad contour of India's pattern of development since independence. Indian leaders from Jawaharlan Nehru to Indira Gandhi pursued developmental, not laissez faire, policies. Yet the Indian state under these leaders failed to bring about rapid economic growth (when compared to South Korea) because of its incoherent, multiclass structure (Herring 1999; Kohli 2004). Indian performance was not a total failure because India did have some elements of a developmental state structure, for example, a competent colonial bureaucracy inherited intact from the British and a relatively cohesive Congress Party, which dominated India's politics for the first three decades (and still does to a lesser extent) (Jalal 1995, 9–38). These elements helped developmental policies to have some impact but were not sufficient to compensate for the key weakness in the state structure, namely the multiclass base of the state.

Since the 1980s, India's rapid economic growth has been possible thanks precisely to changes that strengthened that structure (Kohli 2007). While India is still democratic, the state has become markedly more probusiness in the past two decades at the expense of labor and the rural poor. Since the 1990s, India has also found crucial foreign allies that support its pursuit of capitalist development. A leader of the Non-Aligned Movement in the 1960s and a Soviet ally in the 1970s, India supported U.S. president George W. Bush's call for an Alliance against Terror in 2001 and is now a key strategic partner of the United States (Rothermund 2008, ch. 4). The overall Indian experience since Nehru thus confirms the argument of this book, namely, that effective developmental roles require not only committed leaders but also a developmental state structure based in part on a progrowth class alliance with domestic and foreign capital.

While the Indian case does not contradict the argument in this book, India's rise to becoming an economic powerhouse has exposed the narrow conceptual base of the literature on developmental states. "Development" has been defined narrowly in most studies with too much emphasis placed on material prosperity. "Developmental states" in turn are defined by their role in industrialization, as if industrialization equaled development. To be sure, material wealth is part of, and contributes to, total well-being, but it is not the same as well-being. Political freedoms and social equality also are essential components of human welfare that may or may not be brought about by material wealth.[5] The debate on democracy versus authoritarianism exaggerates the trade-offs between material prosperity

---

[5] Pioneering studies that reformulate the concepts of "development" and "developmental states" are Drèze and Sen (2002) and Robinson and White (1998).

and political freedoms, ignoring first of all that material prosperity and political freedoms are often complementary and mutually reinforcing and, second, that political freedoms are intrinsically valuable as a component of human well-being. For example, the rise of "backward castes" in India is due in part to their growing economic prosperity. Yet economic change has nothing to do with the ability of India's displaced tribal communities to demand fair compensation for their lands (Drèze and Sen 2002, 357–8). This ability has more to do with their rights to organize and protest. This ability brings these communities a sense of efficacy and dignity even though their levels of income are stagnant.

The popularity of many social movements among India's poor indicates that people at all levels of economic prosperity value the ability to do something for themselves or for others through political action (Drèze and Sen 2002, 359). At the very least, Edward Friedman (2005, 193) argues that "freedom, both in the sense of knowledge as the basis for rational choice and of physical mobility as a capacity to get away from what is awful are central to well-being." Friedman's comparison of India and China highlights this particular point:

The Chinese hinterland villager in the Mao era, limited in information by a single political line, either believed, wrongly, that all Chinese were equal in condition and living better than the exploited of Taiwan (imagined as living on banana skins), or helplessly raged at being locked into the equivalent of an apartheid caste society. In contrast, the marginalized Indian villager, joining an opposition political party, a protest movement or an exodus to the city, had capabilities forcibly denied to the virtually enserfed Chinese villagers. In ways that matter to human dignity, the Indian villager was much better off.[6]

Political freedom improves people's well-being just as material wealth does.

India suggests an alternative version of what has been known thus far as "developmental states." In the ideal type of this version, state elites are expected to create various class coalitions to work on joint developmental projects, not only for industrialization but also for social equality and for political liberalization. Elites' task is to negotiate among different developmental goals rather than to define development narrowly, to favor one group over another, or to call for violent class struggles. Economic growth may not be spectacularly rapid but is attained with improvements

[6] See Friedman et al. (1991) for more details on Chinese peasants' sufferings under and after Mao.

(or at least the preservation of past achievements) in social equality and political freedoms.

This alternative model of developmental states does not imply lesser state roles in the economy or in society. Rather, it involves a redefinition of state roles. This book opened with the image of states' rising in public and scholarly imagination at the dawn of a new millennium. As human societies grapple with old and new challenges, the issue to be debated is not whether states are relevant but whether there are alternative ways they can make a positive difference.

References

Archival Sources

Arsip Nasional (National Archive), Jakarta
Bao Tang Cach Mang (Museum of the Vietnamese Revolution), Hanoi
Perpustakaan Badan Perencanaan Pembangunan Nasional (Library of the Ministry of National Development Planning), Jakarta
Perpustakaan Lembaga Penjelidikan Ekonomi dan Masyarakat Fakultas Ekonomi UI (Library of the Institute of Economic and Social Research, Department of Economics, University of Indonesia), Jakarta
Perpustakaan Nasional (National Library), Jakarta
Thu Vien Quoc Gia (National Library), Hanoi
Trung Tam Luu Tru Quoc Gia III (National Archive III), Hanoi

Newspapers Consulted

Indonesian

Antara, 1945–50 [national news service]
Asia Raya (Jakarta), 1942–5
Berita Indonesia (Yogyakarta), 1947–8
Berjuang (Malang), 1945–6
Bintang Merah (Jakarta), 1950–3 [Communist Party's journal]
Harian Indonesia (Jakarta), 1951–3
Keng Po (Jakarta), 1946–8 [Chinese-owned]
Min Pao (Jakarta), 1946–8 [Chinese-owned]
Pantja Raya (Jakarta), 1945–6
Pemandangan (Jakarta), 1951–3
Ra'jat (Jakarta), 1945–8
Star Weekly (Jakarta), 1946 [Chinese-owned]
Siasat Warta Sepekan (Jakarta), 1948, 1950 [pro-Socialist Party]
Sikap (Jakarta), 1953 [Sjahrir's Socialist Party]

Suara Rakjat (Mojokerto), 1945
Suara Rakjat (Surabaya), 1945
Tanah Air (Semarang), 1949–50

Vietnamese

Canh Nong Tap San (Hanoi), 1946 [Ministry of Agriculture journal]
Chinh Nghia (Hanoi), 1946 [Vietnamese Nationalist Party journal]
Co Giai Phong (Ha Dong?), 1944–5 [Communist Party; predecessor of *Su That*]
Cuu Quoc (Ha Dong?/Hanoi), 1944–6 [Communist Party]
Dan Chung (Saigon), 1938–9 [Indochinese Communist Party, Southern branch]
Dan Thanh (Hanoi), 1946 [nonparty]
Dat Moi (Hanoi), 1956 [student publication]
Doc Lap (Hanoi/Viet Bac), 1945–53 [Democratic Party]
Du Luan (Hanoi), 1946 [nonparty]
Giai Pham (Hanoi), 1956 [private]
Ha Noi Hang Ngay (Hanoi), 1955–7 [private daily]
Hinh Su Cong Bao (Hanoi), 1945 [Ministry of Interior]
Hoc Tap (Hanoi), 1956–7 [Communist Party journal]
Lang Son Thong Tin (Lang Son), 1949–54 [Communist Party, Lang Son province]
Lien Hiep (Hanoi), 1945–6 [Vietnamese Revolutionary League]
Nhan Dan (Viet Bac/Hanoi), 1951–61
Nhan Van (Hanoi), 1956 [private]
Su That (Hanoi/Viet Bac), 1945–50 [Communist Party; predecessor of *Nhan Dan*]
Tap San Cong Thuong (Viet Bac), 1952–4 [Ministry of Economy journal]
Thanh Nghi (Hanoi), 1941–5
Thoi Moi (Hanoi), 1955–7 [private]
Tien (Thanh Hoa), 1945 [Viet Minh]
Tien Manh (Viet Bac), 1950 [Communist Party; Viet Bac Interzone branch]
Tin Cai Cach Ruong Dat (Thanh Hoa, Phu Tho, Bac Giang-Bac Ninh), 1954–5
Tin Noi Bo (Bac Giang), 1950–1 [Internal local Communist Party newsletter]
Tin Noi Bo (Cao Bang), 1950 [Internal local Communist Party newsletter]
To Quoc (Hanoi), 1956–7 [Socialist Party]
Tram Hoa (Hanoi), 1956–7 [private]
Truyen Thanh (Vinh), 1946 [Communist Party/Viet Minh]
Van (Hanoi), 1957 [Writers' Association journal]
Viet Nam (Hanoi), 1945–6 [Vietnamese Nationalist Party daily]
Viet Nam Doc Lap (Cao Bang), 1941–5, 1951–4 [Viet Minh/Communist Party]
Y Dan (Hanoi), 1945–6 [Catholic]

Books, Articles, and Unpublished Theses

Abrami, Regina. 2002. "Self-Making, Class Struggle and Labor Autarky: The Political Origins of Private Entrepreneurship in Vietnam and China." Ph.D. dissertation, University of California, Berkeley.

Allen, Richard. 1960. *Korea's Syngman Rhee: An Unauthorized Portrait*. Rutland, VT: Charles E. Tuttle.

Amsden, Alice. 1989. *Asia's Next Giant: South Korea and Late Industrialization*. New York: Oxford University Press.

Andaya, Barbara, and Leonard Andaya. 1982. *A History of Malaysia*. London: Macmillan Education.

Anderson, Benedict. 1972. *Java in a Time of Revolution*. Ithaca: Cornell University Press.

1983. "Old State, New Society: Indonesia's New Order in Comparative Historical Perspective." *Journal of Asian Studies* 42: 477–96.

Antlov, Hans. 1995. "Rulers in Imperial Policy: Sultan Ibrahim, Emperor Bao Dai and Sultan Hamengkubuwono IX." In Antlov and Tonnesson 1995, 227–60.

Antlov, Hans, and Stein Tonnesson, eds. 1995. *Imperial Policy and South East Asian Nationalism*. Richmond, Surrey: Curzon Press.

Apter, David, and Tony Saich. 1994. *Revolutionary Discourse in Mao's Republic*. Cambridge, MA: Harvard University Press.

Aspinall, Edward. 2005. *Opposing Suharto: Compromise, Resistance and Regime Change in Indonesia*. Stanford: Stanford University Press.

Ban, Sung Hwan, et al. 1980. *Rural Development: Studies in the Modernization of the Republic of Korea: 1945–1975*. Cambridge, MA: Harvard University Press.

Bao Tang Cach Mang Viet Nam (Museum of the Vietnamese Revolution). 2000a. *Bao Viet Nam Doc Lap, 1941–1945* (Collection of *Viet Nam Doc Lap* newspaper). Hanoi: Lao Dong.

2000b. *Bao Dan Chung, 1938–1939* (Collection of *Dan Chung* newspaper). Hanoi: Lao Dong.

Barrett, David. 1982. "The Role of Hu Hanmin in the 'First United Front': 1922–1927." *China Quarterly* 89 (March): 34–64.

Bedeski, Robert. 1981. *State-Building in Modern China: The Kuomintang in the Prewar Period*. Berkeley: Institute of East Asian Studies, University of California.

Benda, Harry. 1958. *The Crescent and the Rising Sun: Indonesian Islam under the Japanese Occupation, 1942–1945*. The Hague: W. Van Hoeve.

1966. "The Patterns of Administrative Reform in the Closing Years of Dutch Rule in Indonesia." *Journal of Asian Studies* 25, 4 (August): 589–605.

Bergère, Marie-Claire. 1986. *The Golden Age of the Chinese Bourgeoisie, 1911–1937*. Trans. Janet Lloyd. Cambridge: Cambridge University Press.

1998. *Sun Yat-sen*. Trans. Janet Lloyd. Stanford: Stanford University Press.

Bernstein, Thomas. 1967. "Leadership and Mass Mobilization in the Soviet and Chinese Collectivization Campaigns of 1929–30 and 1955–56: A Comparison." *China Quarterly* 31 (July–September): 1–47.

1984. "Stalinism, Famine and Chinese Peasants: Grain Procurements during the Great Leap Forward." *Theory and Society* 13, 3 (May): 339–77.

Bo Canh Nong (Ministry of Agriculture). ca. 1950. *Giam To Giam Tuc, The Le Linh Canh* [Rent and interest reduction and tenancy regulations]. Viet Bac (?).

Bodenhorn, Terry, ed. *Defining Modernity: Guomindang Rhetorics of a New China, 1920–1970*. Ann Arbor: Center for Chinese Studies, University of Michigan.

Boorman, Howard. 1964. "Wang Ching-Wei: China's Romantic Radical." *Political Science Quarterly* 79, 4: 504–25.

Booth, Anne. 1994. "Growth and Stagnation in an Era of Nation-Building: Indonesian Economic Performance from 1950 to 1965." In Lindblad 1994, 401–23.

1998. *The Indonesian Economy in the Nineteenth and Twentieth Centuries: A History of Missed Opportunities*. New York: St. Martin's Press.

Boudarel, George. 1990. "Intellectual Dissidence in the 1950s: The *Nhan Van Giai Pham* affair." *Vietnam Forum* 13: 154–74.

Brady, Henry, and David Collier, eds. 2004. *Rethinking Social Inquiry: Diverse Tools, Shared Standards*. New York: Rowman & Littlefield.

Brandt, Conrad, et al. 1973. *A Documentary History of Chinese Communism*. New York: Atheneum.

Brazinski, Gregg. 2005. "From Pupil to Model: South Korea and American Development Policy during the Early Park Chung Hee Era." *Diplomatic History* 29, 1 (January): 83–115.

Brown, Gilbert. 1973. *Korean Pricing Policies and Economic Development in the 1960s*. Baltimore: Johns Hopkins University Press.

Budiardjo, Miriam. 1955. "Evolution towards Parliamentary Government in Indonesia: Parties and Parliament." M.A. thesis, Georgetown University.

Case, William. 2002. *Politics in Southeast Asia: Democracy or Less*. Richmond, Surrey: Curzon Press.

Cathie, J. 1989. *Food Aid and Industrialization: The Development of the South Korean Economy*. Brookfield, VT: Avebury.

Centeno, Miguel. 2002. *Blood and Debt: War and the Nation-State in Latin America*. University Park: Pennsylvania State University Press.

Chan, Anita, et al., eds. 1999. *Transforming Asian Socialism: China and Vietnam Compared*. New York: Rowman & Littlefield.

Ch'en, Jerome. 1991. "The Communist Movement, 1927–1937." In Lloyd Eastman et al., eds., *The Nationalist Era in China, 1927–1949*, 53–114. Cambridge: Cambridge University Press.

Chen, Jian. 1994. *China's Road to the Korean War*. New York: Columbia University Press.

Chen, Yungfa. 1986. *Making Revolution: The Communist Movement in Eastern and Central China, 1937–1945*. Stanford: Stanford University Press.

Choi, Jang Jip. 1993. "Political Cleavages in South Korea." In Hagen Koo, ed., *State and Society in Contemporary Korea*, 13–50. Ithaca: Cornell University Press.

Chung, Dooeum. 2000. *Elite Fascism: Chiang Kai-shek's Blue Shirts in 1930s China*. Burlington, VT: Ashgate.

Chuong Thau, ed. 2000. *Phan Boi Chau Toan Tap* (Collected writings by Phan Boi Chau). 10 vols. Hanoi: Trung Tam Van Hoa Ngon Ngu Dong Tay.

Coble, Parks. 1979. "The Kuomintang Regime and the Shanghai Capitalists, 1927–29." *China Quarterly* 77 (March): 1–24.

1985. "Chiang Kai-shek and the Anti-Japanese Movement in China: Zou Taofen and the National Salvation Association, 1931–1937." *Journal of Asian Studies* 44, 2 (February): 293–310.

Collier, Ruth. 1998. *Paths toward Democracy: The Working Class and Elites in Western Europe and South America*. Cambridge: Cambridge University Press.

Cribb, Robert, ed. 1990. *The Indonesian Killings, 1965–1966: Studies from Java and Bali*. Monash Papers on Southeast Asia no. 21. Clayton, Victoria: Centre for Southeast Asian Studies, Monash University.

1991. *Gangsters and Revolutionaries: The Jakarta People's Militia and the Indonesian Revolution, 1945–1949*. Honolulu: University of Hawaii Press.

1994. Introduction. In Robert Cribb, ed., *The Late Colonial State in Indonesia*, 1–9. Leiden: KITLV Press.

Crouch, Harold. 1988. *The Indonesian Army in Politics*. Rev. ed. Ithaca: Cornell University Press.

Cumings, Bruce. 1981. *The Origins of the Korean War*. Vol. 1. Princeton: Princeton University Press.

1987. "The Origins and Development of the Northeast Asian Political Economy: Industrial Sectors, Product Cycles, and Political Consequences." In Deyo 1987, 44–83.

Dahm, Bernhard. 1969. *Sukarno and the Struggle for Indonesian Independence*. Trans. Mary Heidhues. Ithaca: Cornell University Press.

Dang, Phong. 2002. *Lich Su Kinh Te Viet Nam 1945–2000* (Economic history of Vietnam, 1945–2000). Hanoi: Khoa Hoc Xa Hoi.

Dang Cong San Viet Nam (Vietnamese Communist Party). 2000–6. *Van Kien Dang Toan Tap* (Collection of party documents). 45 vols. (1924–85). Hanoi: Chinh Tri Quoc Gia.

Deyo, Frederic, ed. 1987. *The Political Economy of the New Asian Industrialism*. Ithaca: Cornell University Press.

Dick, Howard. 2002. "Formation of the Nation-State, 1930–1966." In Dick et al. 2002, 153–93.

Dick, Howard, et al., eds. 2002. *The Emergence of a National Economy: An Economic History of Indonesia, 1800–2000*. Honolulu: University of Hawaii Press.

Dirlik, Arif. 1989. *The Origins of Chinese Communism*. New York: Oxford University Press.

Dogan, Mattei, and John Higley, eds. 1998a. *Elites, Crises, and the Origins of Regimes*. Lanham, MD: Rowman & Littlefield.

1998b. "Elites, Crises, and Regimes in Comparative Analysis." In Dogan and Higley 1998, 3–27.

Domenach, Jean-Luc. 1995. *The Origins of the Great Leap Forward*. Trans. by A. M. Bennett. Boulder, CO: Westview Press.

Doner, Richard, Bryan Ritchie, and Daniel Slater. 2005. "Systemic Vulnerability and the Origins of Developmental States: Northeast and Southeast Asia in Comparative Perspective." *International Organization* 59, 2 (Spring): 327–61.

Douglas, William. 1964. "South Korea's Search for Leadership." *Pacific Affairs* 37, 1 (Spring): 20–36.

Drèze, Jean, and Amartya Sen. 2002. *India: Development and Participation.* 2nd ed. New York: Oxford University Press.

Duiker, William. 2000. *Ho Chi Minh: A Life.* New York: Hyperion.

Eastman, Lloyd. 1974. *The Abortive Revolution: China under Nationalist Rule, 1927–1937.* Cambridge, MA: Harvard University Press.

   1991. "Nationalist China during the Nanking Decade, 1927–1937." In Lloyd Eastman et al., eds., *The Nationalist Era in China, 1927–1949,* 1–52. Cambridge: Cambridge University Press.

Eckert, Carter, et al. 1990. *Korea Old and New: A History.* Cambridge, MA: Harvard University Press.

Edmonds, Richard. 1997. "The State of Studies on Republican China." *China Quarterly* 150 (June): 255–9.

Elias, Norbert. [1939] 1982. *Power and Civility.* Vol. 2 of *The Civilizing Process.* 2 vols. Trans. Edmund Jephcott. New York: Pantheon Books.

Elliott, David. 1976. "Revolutionary Re-integration: A Comparison of the Foundation of Post-Liberation Political Systems in North Vietnam and China." Ph.D. dissertation, Cornell University.

Elson, R. E. 2001. *Suharto: A Political Biography.* Cambridge: Cambridge University Press.

Emmerson, Donald. 1978. "The Bureaucracy in Political Context: Weakness in Strength." In Karl Jackson and Lucian Pye, eds., *Political Power and Communications in Indonesia,* 82–136. Berkeley: University of California Press.

Ennis, Thomas. 1936. *French Policy and Developments in Indochina.* Chicago: University of Chicago Press.

Esherick, Joseph. [1971] 1998. *Reform and Revolution in China: The 1911 Revolution in Hunan and Hubei.* Ann Arbor: University of Michigan Center for Chinese Studies.

   1994. "Deconstructing the Construction of the Party-State: Guilin County in the Shaan-Gan-Ning Border Region." *China Quarterly* 140 (December): 1052–79.

   1995. "Ten Theses on the Chinese Revolution." *Modern China* 21, 1 (January): 45–76.

   1998. "Revolution in a Feudal Fortress: Yangjiagou, Mizhi County, Shaanxi, 1937–1948." *Modern China* 24, 4 (October): 339–77.

Evans, Peter. 1995. *Embedded Autonomy: States and Industrial Transformation.* Princeton: Princeton University Press.

Feith, Herbert. 1962. *The Decline of Constitutional Democracy in Indonesia.* Ithaca: Cornell University Press.

Feith, Herbert, and Lance Castles, eds. 1970. *Indonesian Political Thinking, 1945–1965.* Ithaca: Cornell University Press.

Fforde, Adam. 1999. "From Plan to Market: The Economic Transition in Vietnam and China Compared." In Chan et al., 1999, 43–72.

Fforde, Adam, and Suzanne Paine. 1987. *The Limits of National Liberation.* London: Croom Helm.

Fincher, John. 1981. *Chinese Democracy: The Self-Government Movement in Local, Provincial and National Politics, 1905–1914*. London: Croom Helm.

Fitzgerald, John. 1990. "The Misconceived Revolution: State and Society in China's Nationalist Revolution, 1923–26." *Journal of Asian Studies* 49, 2 (May): 323–43.

———. 1996. *Awakening China: Politics, Culture, and Class in the Nationalist Revolution*. Stanford: Stanford University Press.

Frederick, William. 1989. *Vision and Heat: The Making of the Indonesian Revolution*. Athens: Ohio University Press.

———. 1997. "Brothers of a Kind: Perspectives on Comparing the Indonesian and Vietnamese Revolutions." In Taufik Abdullah, ed., *The Heartbeat of Indonesian Revolution*, 271–93. Jakarta: PT Gramedia Pustaka Utama.

Friedman, Edward. 2005. "Why Democracy Matters." In Edward Friedman and Bruce Gilley, eds., *Asia's Giants: Comparing China and India*, 183–210. London: Palgrave Macmillan.

Friedman, Edward, Paul Pickowicz, and Mark Selden. 1991. *Chinese Village, Socialist State*. New Haven, CT: Yale University Press.

Fukuyama, Francis. 1992. *The End of History and the Last Man*. New York: Free Press.

Fung, Edmund. 1985. "Anti-imperialism and the Left Guomindang." *Modern China* 11, 1 (January): 39–76.

———. 2000. *In Search of Chinese Democracy: Civil Opposition in Nationalist China, 1929–1949*. Cambridge, MA: Harvard University Press.

Galbiati, Fernando. 1985. *P'eng P'ai and the Hai-Lu-Feng Soviet*. Stanford: Stanford University Press.

Gardner, John. 1969. "The *Wufan* campaign in Shanghai." In Doak Barnett, ed., *Chinese Communist Politics in Action*, 477–539. Seattle: University of Washington Press.

Garver, John. 1992. "China's Wartime Diplomacy." In James Hsiung and Steven Levine, eds., *China's Bitter Victory: The War with Japan, 1937–1945*, 3–32. Armonk, NY: M. E. Sharpe.

Geisert, Bradley. 2001. *Radicalism and Its Demise: The Chinese Nationalist Party Factionalism and Local Elites in Jiangsu Province, 1924–1931*. Ann Arbor: University of Michigan Center for Chinese Studies.

George, Alexander, and Andrew Bennett. 2005. *Case Studies and Theory Development in the Social Sciences*. Cambridge, MA: MIT Press.

Gerschenkron, Alexander. 1966. *Economic Backwardness in Historical Perspective*. Cambridge, MA: Harvard University Press.

Glassburner, Bruce, ed. 1971. *The Economy of Indonesia*. Ithaca: Cornell University Press.

Goldman, Merle. 1967. *Literary Dissent in Communist China*. Cambridge, MA: Harvard University Press.

Goldman, Merle, and Andrew Gordon, eds. 2000. *Historical Perspectives on Contemporary East Asia*. Cambridge, MA: Harvard University Press.

Goodman, David. 2000. *Social and Political Change in Revolutionary China: The Taihang Base Area in the War of Resistance to Japan, 1937–1945*. New York: Rowman & Littlefield.

Gorski, Philip. 1999. "Calvinism and State-Formation in Early Modern Europe." In Steinmetz 1999, 147–81.

———. 2003. *The Disciplinary Revolution: Calvinism and the Rise of the State in Early Modern Europe*. Chicago: University of Chicago Press.

Goscha, Christopher. 2006. "Courting Diplomatic Disaster? The Difficult Integration of Vietnam into the Internationalist Communist Movement (1945–1950)." *Journal of Vietnamese Studies* 1, 1–2 (Fall): 59–103.

———. Forthcoming. *Historical Dictionary of the Indochina War (1945–1954): An International and Interdisciplinary Approach*. Honolulu/Copenhagen: University of Hawaii Press/Nordic Institute of Asian Studies.

Goscha, Christopher, and Benoit de Treglode, eds. 2004. *Naissance d'un Etat-Parti: Le Viet Nam depuis 1945/ The Birth of a Party-State: Vietnam since 1945*. Paris: Le Indes Savantes.

Haggard, Stephan. 1990. *Pathways from the Periphery*. Ithaca: Cornell University Press.

Haggard, Stephan, and Chung-In Moon. 1993. "The State, Politics, and Economic Development in Postwar South Korea." In Hagen Koo, ed., *State and Society in Contemporary Korea*, 51–93. Ithaca: Cornell University Press.

Haggard, Stephan, et al. 1997. "Japanese Colonialism and Korean Development: A Critique." *World Development* 25, 6: 867–81.

Han, Ki-Shik, 1971. "Political Leadership and Development in Postwar Korea: Continuity and Change between the Rhee and Park Regimes." Ph.D. dissertation, University of California, Berkely.

Han, Sungjoo. 1972. "Political Dissent in South Korea, 1948–61." In Kim and Cho 1972, 43–69.

———. 1980. "Student Activism: A Comparison between the 1960 Uprising and the 1971 Protest Movement." In Chong Lim Kim, ed., *Political Participation in Korea: Democracy, Mobilization and Stability*, 143–61. Santa Barbara: CLIO Books.

Han, Y. C. 1969. "Political Parties and Political Development in South Korea." *Pacific Affairs* 42, 4 (Winter): 446–64.

Harding, Harry. 1993. "The Chinese State in Crisis, 1966–9." In Robert MacFarquhar, ed., *The Politics of China, 1949–1989*, 148–247. Cambridge: Cambridge University Press.

Hardy, Andrew. 1998. "The Economics of French Rule in Indochina: A Biography of Paul Bernard (1892–1960)." *Modern Asian Studies* 32, 4 (October): 807–48.

Harper, T. N. 1999. *The End of Empire and the Making of Malaya*. Cambridge: Cambridge University Press.

Harrison, John. 1972. *The Long March to Power: A History of the Chinese Communist Party, 1921–1972*. New York: Praeger.

Hartford, Kathleen. 1989. "Repression and Communist Success: The Case of Jin-Cha-Ji, 1938–1943." In Steven Goldstein and Kathleen Hartford, eds., *Single Sparks: China's Rural Revolution*, 92–127. Armonk, NY: M. E. Sharpe.

Hartoni K. 1960. "The Indonesian Communist Movement, 1945–1948." M.A. thesis, Columbia University.

Harvey, Barbara. 1977. *Permesta: Half a Rebellion.* Ithaca: Modern Indonesia Project, Cornell University.

Hatta, Mohammad. 1976. *Kumpulan Karangan* (Collection of papers). Vol. 1. Jakarta: Bulan Bintang.

    1981. *Kumpulan Pidato* (Collection of speeches, 1942–49). Jakarta: Yayasan Idayu.

Hawkins, E. 1963. "Labor in Transition." In McVey 1963, 248–71.

Henderson, Gregory. 1968. *Korea: The Politics of the Vortex.* Cambridge, MA: Harvard University Press.

Herring, Ronald. 1999. "Embedded Particularism: India's Failed Developmental State." In Woo-Cumings 1999, 306–34.

Higgins, Benjamin. 1957. *Indonesia's Economic Stabilization and Development.* New York: Institute of Pacific Relations.

Higley, John, and Michael Burton. 2006. *Elite Foundations of Liberal Democracy.* New York: Rowman & Littlefield.

Higley, John, and Richard Gunter, eds. 1992. *Elites and Democratic Consolidation in Latin America and Southern Europe.* Cambridge: Cambridge University Press.

Hill, Hal, ed. 1994. *Indonesia's New Order.* Honolulu: University of Hawaii Press.

    2000. *The Indonesian Economy.* 2nd ed. Cambridge: Cambridge University Press.

Hindley, Donald. 1964. *The Communist Party of Indonesia, 1951–1963.* Berkeley: University of California Press.

Ho, Samuel. 1979. "Rural-Urban Imbalance in South Korea in the 1970s." *Asian Survey* 19, 7 (July): 645–59.

    1984. "Colonialism and Development: Korea, Taiwan, and Kwantung." In Ramon Myers and Mark Peattie, eds., *The Japanese Colonial Empire, 1895–1945,* 347–98. Princeton: Princeton University Press.

Ho Chi Minh. 1960. *Selected Work.* Vol. 1 (1922–6). Hanoi: Foreign Language Publishing House.

Hoang Uoc, Le Duc Binh, and Tran Phuong. 1968. *Cach Mang Ruong Dat o Viet Nam* (Land revolution in Vietnam). Hanoi: Khoa hoc Xa Hoi.

Hoang Van Dao. 1970. *Viet Nam Quoc Dan Dang* (The Vietnamese Nationalist Party). Saigon: Tuan Bao Tan Dan.

Hong, Yong-pyo. 2000. *State Security and Regime Security: President Syngman Rhee and the Insecurity Dilemma in South Korea, 1953–1960.* New York: St. Martin's Press.

Hsueh, Chun-tu. 1961. *Huang Hsing and the Chinese Revolution.* Stanford: Stanford University Press.

Huynh Kim Khanh. 1982. *Vietnamese Communism, 1925–1945.* Ithaca: Cornell University Press.

Ingleson, John. 1975. *Perhimpunan Indonesia and the Indonesian Nationalist Movement, 1923–1928.* Monash Papers on Southeast Asia no. 4. Melbourne: Center of Southeast Asian Studies, Monash University.

    1979. *Road to Exile: The Indonesian Nationalist Movement, 1927–1934.* Singapore: Heineman Educational Books (Asia).

Jackson, Karl. 1980. *Tradition, Authority, Islam and Rebellion*. Berkeley: University of California Press.

Jalal, Ayesha. 1995. *Democracy and Authoritarianism in South Asia*. Cambridge: Cambridge University Press.

Jamieson, Neil. 1993. *Understanding Vietnam*. Berkeley: University of California Press.

Johnson, Chalmers. 1962. *Peasant Nationalism and Communist Power*. Stanford: Stanford University Press.

——— 1982. *MITI and the Japanese Miracle: The Growth of Industrial Policy, 1925–1975*. Stanford: Stanford University Press.

——— 1987. "Political Institutions and Economic Performance: The Government-Business Relationship in Japan, South Korea, and Taiwan." In Deyo 1987, 136–64.

Jordan, Donald. 1976. *The Northern Expedition: China's National Revolution of 1926–1928*. Honolulu: University of Hawaii Press.

Jun, Niu. 1999. "The Origins of the Sino-Soviet Alliance." In Odd Arne Westad, ed., *Brothers in Arms: The Rise and Fall of the Sino-Soviet Alliance, 1945–1963*, 47–89. Washington, DC, and Stanford: Woodrow Wilson Center Press and Stanford University Press.

Jun, Sang In. 1991. "State-Making in South Korea, 1945–1948: U.S. Occupation and Korean Development." Ph.D. dissertation, Brown University.

Kahin, Audrey, ed. 1985. *Regional Dynamics of the Indonesian Revolution*. Honolulu: Hawaii University Press.

Kahin, George. 1950. *Some Aspects of Indonesian Politics and Nationalism*. New York: Institute of Pacific Relations.

——— 1952. *Nationalism and Revolution in Indonesia*. Ithaca: Cornell University Press.

Kang, David. 1995. "South Korean and Taiwanese Development and the New Institutional Economics." *International Organization* 49, 3 (Summer): 555–87.

Kau, Ying-mao. 1969. "The Urban Bureaucratic Elite in Communist China: A Case-Study of Wuhan, 1949–1965." In Doak Barnett, ed., *Chinese Communist Politics in Action*, 216–67. Seattle: University of Washington Press.

Keating, Pauline. 1997. *Two Revolutions: Village Reconstruction and the Cooperative Movement in Northern Shaanxi, 1934–1945*. Stanford: Stanford University Press.

Keim, William. 1979. *The Korean Peasant at the Crossroads: A Study in Attitudes*. Bellingham, WA: Center for East Asian Studies, Western Washington University.

Kementerian Penerangan (Ministry of Information). 1945. *Maklumat Pemerintah Republik Indonesia/Political Manifesto of the Government of the Republic of Indonesia* (November 1). Yogyakarta.

——— 1950. *Membangun diantara Tumpukan Puing dan Pertumbuhan* (Rising up between ruins and growth). Statement by Prime Minister Mohammad Natsir at Parliament (October 10).

Kerkvliet, Benedict. 1998. "Wobbly Foundations: Building Cooperatives in Rural Vietnam." *South East Asia Research* 6, 3 (November): 193–251.

2005. *The Power of Everyday Politics: How Vietnamese Peasants Transformed National Policy.* Ithaca: Cornell University Press.

Kerkvliet, Benedict, et al. 1998. "Comparing the Chinese and Vietnamese Reforms: An Introduction." *China Journal* 40 (July): 1–7.

Kihl, Young Whan. 1979. "Politics and Agrarian Change in South Korea: Rural Modernization by 'Induced' Mobilization." In Raymond Hopkins et al., eds., *Food Politics and Agricultural Development*, 133–69. Boulder, CO: Westview Press.

Kim, Ilpyong. 1969. "Mass Mobilization Policies and Techniques Developed in the Period of the Chinese Soviet Republic." In Doak Barnett, ed., *Chinese Communist Politics in Action*, 78–98. Seattle: University of Washington Press.

Kim, Joung Won. 1975. *Divided Korea: The Politics of Development, 1945–1972.* Cambridge, MA: Harvard University Press.

Kim, Kyong-Dong. 1981. "Toward a Sociology of War: The Social Impact of the Korean War." *Korea & World Affairs* 5, 2 (Summer): 243–67.

Kim, Quee-Young. 1983. *The Fall of Syngman Rhee.* Berkeley: Institute of East Asian Studies, University of California.

Kim, Se Jin. 1971. *The Politics of Military Revolution in Korea.* Chapel Hill: University of North Carolina Press.

Kim, Se Jin, and Chang Hyun Cho. 1972. *Government and Politics of Korea.* Silver Spring, MD: Research Institute on Korean Affairs.

Kim, Son-ung, and Peter J. Donaldson. 1979. "Dealing with Seoul's Population Growth." *Asian Survey* 19, 7 (July): 660–73.

Kim, Stephen Jin-Woo. 2001. *Master of Manipulation: Syngman Rhee and the Seoul-Washington Alliance, 1953–1960.* Seoul: Yonsei University Press.

Kirby, William. 1984. *Germany and Republican China.* Stanford: Stanford University Press.

1990. "Continuity and Change in Modern China: Economic Planning on the Mainland and on Taiwan, 1943–1958." *Australian Journal of Chinese Affairs* 24 (July): 121–41.

2000a. "The Nationalist Regime and the Chinese Party-State, 1928–1958." In Goldman and Gordon 2000, 211–37.

2000b. "Engineering China: Birth of the Developmental State, 1928–37." In Wen-Hsin Yeh, ed., *Becoming Chinese: Passages to Modernity and Beyond, 1900–1950*, 137–60. Berkeley: University of California Press.

Knight, Alan. 1992. "Mexico's Elite Settlement: Conjuncture and Consequences." In Higley and Gunter 1992, 113–45.

1998. "Historical and Theoretical Considerations." In Dogan and Higley 1998a, 29–45.

Koh, Kwang-Il. 1963. "In Quest of National Unity and Power: Political Ideas and Practices of Syngman Rhee." Ph.D. dissertation, Rutgers University.

Kohli, Atul. 1997. "Japanese Colonialism and Korean Development: A Reply." *World Development* 25, 6: 883–8.

2004. *State-Directed Development: Political Power and Industrialization in the Global Periphery.* Cambridge: Cambridge University Press.

2007. "State, Business, and Economic Growth in India." *Studies in Comparative International Development* 42: 87–114.

Koo, Hagen. 1993. "The State, *Minjung*, and the Working Class in South Korea." In Hagen Koo, ed., *State and Society in Contemporary Korea*, 131–62. Ithaca: Cornell University Press.

2001. *Korean Workers: The Culture and Politics of Class Formation*. Ithaca: Cornell University Press.

Krasner, Stephen. 1978. *Defending the National Interest*. Princeton: Princeton University Press.

Kuhn, Philip. 2002. *Origins of the Modern Chinese State*. Stanford: Stanford University Press.

Le Gian. 2000. *Nhung Ngay Song Gio: Hoi Ky* (Those stormy days: A memoir). Hanoi: Cong An Nhan Dan.

Le Huy Bao. 2000. "Anh Le van Luong voi viec phat hien va sua chua sai lam ve chinh don to chuc" (Le van Luong with the discovery and rectification of errors in the party organization reform campaign). In *Le Van Luong Tron Doi Vi Su Nghiep Cua Dang* (All his life for the cause of the party), 166–74. Hanoi: Chinh Tri Quoc Gia.

Le Trong Nghia. 2000. "Cac cuoc tiep xuc giua Viet Minh voi Chinh phu Tran Trong Kim" (The meetings between Viet Minh and the Kim Government). In Tap Chi Xua Va Nay, *Lich Su, Su That va Bai Hoc* (History, truth and lessons), 459–71. Hanoi: Tre.

Lebra, Joyce. 1975. "The Significance of the Japanese Military Model for Southeast Asia." *Pacific Affairs* 48, 2 (Summer): 215–29.

Lee, Chong Sik. 1965. *The Politics of Korean Nationalism*. Berkeley: University of California Press.

trans. and ed. 1977. *Materials on Korean Communism, 1945–1947*. Honolulu: Center for Korean Studies, University of Hawaii.

Lee, Ha Woo. 1975. "The Korean Polity under Syngman Rhee: An Analysis of Its Culture, Structure, and Elite." Ph.D. dissertation, American University.

Lee, Hahn Been. 1968. *Korea: Time, Change, and Administration*. Honolulu: East-West Center Press, University of Hawaii.

Lee, Hong Yung. 1978. *The Politics of the Chinese Cultural Revolution: A Case Study*. Berkeley: University of California Press.

Lee, Y. C. 1999. "Labor Policy Change in a Developmental Authoritarian State: A Case of Korea, 1961–1987." Ph.D. dissertation, University of Notre Dame.

Legge, John. 1968. "General Suharto's New Order." *International Affairs* 44, 1: 40–7.

1972. *Sukarno: A Political Biography*. Harmondsworth, Middlesex: Penguin Books.

1988. *Intellectuals and Nationalism in Indonesia*. Ithaca: Modern Indonesia Project, Cornell University Press.

Lev, Daniel. 1966a. "Indonesia 1965: The Year of the Coup." *Asian Survey* 6, 2 (February): 103–10.

1966b. *The Transition to Guided Democracy: Indonesian Politics, 1957–1959*. Ithaca: Modern Indonesia Project, Cornell University.

1967. "Political Parties in Indonesia." *Journal of Southeast Asian History* 8, 1 (March): 52–67.

Levine, Steven. 1987. *The Anvil of Victory: The Communist Revolution in Manchuria, 1945–1948.* New York: Columbia University Press.

Lieberthal, Kenneth. 1980. *Revolution and Tradition in Tientsin, 1949–1952.* Stanford: Stanford University Press.

1993. "The Great Leap Forward and the Split in the Yan'an Leadership." In Robert MacFarquhar, ed., *The Politics of China, 1949–1989,* 87–147. Cambridge: Cambridge University Press.

Liew, Kit Siong. 1971. *Struggle for Democracy: Sung Chiao-jen and the 1911 Chinese Revolution.* Berkeley: University of California Press.

Lin, Justin Yifu, et al. 1996. *The China Miracle: Development Strategy and Economic Reform.* Hong Kong: Center for Economic Research.

Lindblad, Thomas, ed. 1994. *Historical Foundations of a National Economy in Indonesia, 1890s–1990s.* Amsterdam: Royal Netherlands Academy of Arts and Sciences.

2002. "The Late Colonial State and Economic Expansion, 1900–1930s." In Dick et al. 2002, 111–52.

Linz, Juan, and Alfred Stepan. 1996. *Problems of Democratic Transition and Consolidation.* Baltimore: Johns Hopkins University Press.

Lockhart, Greg. 1989. *Nations in Arms: Origins of the People's Army of Vietnam.* Wellington: Allen & Unwin.

Luong Van Hy and Jonathan Unger. 1998. "Wealth, Power, and Poverty in the Transition to Market Economies: The Process of Socio-Economic Differentiation in Rural China and Northern Vietnam." *China Journal* 40 (July): 61–93.

Lyons, Gene, and Michael Mastanduno, eds. 1995. *Beyond Westphalia: State Sovereignty and International Intervention.* Baltimore: Johns Hopkins University Press.

Mackie, J. A. C. 1967. *Problems of the Indonesian Inflation.* Ithaca: Cornell University Press.

1971. "The Indonesian Economy, 1950–1963." In Glassburner 1971, 16–69.

Maddison, Angus. 1989. "Dutch Income in and from Indonesia, 1700–1938." *Modern Asian Studies* 23, 4: 645–70.

Mahoney, James, and Dietrich Rueschemeyer, eds. 2003. *Comparative Historical Analysis in the Social Sciences.* Cambridge: Cambridge University Press.

Malaka, Tan. [1925] 1947. *Massa Actie* (Mass action). Jakarta: Pustaka Murba.

[1948] 1991. *From Jail to Jail.* Trans. and introd. Helen Jarvis. Athens: Ohio University Center for International Studies.

[1948] 2000. *Gerpolek.* Jakarta: Jambatan.

Mangunsarkoro, Sarmidi. 1949. *Masjarakat Sosialis* (A socialist society). Medan: Toko Buku Sarkawi.

1952. *Politik Marhaenis* (Marhaenist politics). Yogya: Usaha Garuda.

Marr, David. 1971. *Vietnamese Anticolonialism, 1886–1925.* Berkeley: University of California Press.

1981. *Vietnamese Tradition on Trial, 1920–1945.* Berkeley: University of California Press.

1995. *Vietnam 1945: The Quest for Power*. Berkeley: University of California Press.

2004. "Beyond High Politics: State Formation in Northern Vietnam, 1945–1946." In Goscha and Treglode 2004, 25–60.

Martin, Brian. 1996. *The Shanghai Green Gang: Politics and Organized Crime, 1919–1937*. Berkeley: University of California Press.

Matray, James. 1995. "Hodge Podge: American Occupation Policy in Korea, 1945–1948." *Korean Studies* 19: 17–38.

McAlister, John. 1969. *Vietnam: The Origins of Revolution*. New York: Alfred Knopf.

McCord, Edward. 1993. *The Power of the Gun: The Emergence of Modern Chinese Warlordism*. Berkeley: University of California Press.

McGinn, Noel, et al. 1980. *Education and Development in Korea*. Cambridge, MA: Harvard University Press.

McHale, Shawn. 2004. *Print and Power: Confucianism, Communism and Buddhism in the Making of Modern Vietnam*. Honolulu: University of Hawaii Press.

McVey, Ruth, ed. 1963. *Indonesia*. Ithaca: Cornell University Press.

1954. *The Development of the Indonesian Communist Party and Its Relations with the Soviet Union and the Chinese People's Republic*. Cambridge, MA: Center for International Studies, Massachusetts Institute of Technology.

1965. *The Rise of Indonesian Communism*. Ithaca: Cornell University Press.

1967. "Taman Siswa and the Indonesian National Awakening." *Indonesia* 4 (October): 128–49.

1971. "The Post-Revolutionary Transformation of the Indonesian Army." *Indonesia* 11 (April): 131–76.

1972. "The Post-Revolutionary Transformation of the Indonesian Army." *Indonesia* 13 (April): 147–82.

Meade, Grant. 1951. *American Military Government in Korea*. New York: King's Crown Press, Columbia University.

Merrill, John. 1980. "The Cheju-do Rebellion." *Journal of Korean Studies* 2: 139–97.

Migdal, Joel. 1988. *Strong Societies and Weak States: State-Society Relations and State Capabilities in the Third World*. Princeton: Princeton University Press.

2001. *State in Society: Studying How States and Societies Transform and Constitute One Another*. New York: Cambridge University Press.

Moise, Edwin. 1983. *Land Reform in China and North Vietnam*. Chapel Hill: University of North Carolina Press.

2001. "Land Reform in North Vietnam, 1953–1956." Paper presented at the 18th annual conference on SE Asian Studies, Center for SE Asian Studies, University of California, Berkeley, February.

Moore, Barrington. 1966. *Social Origins of Dictatorship and Democracy*. Boston: Beacon Press.

Morris, Eric. 1985. "Aceh: Social Revolution and the Islamic Vision." In A. Kahin, 1985, 83–110.

Mortimer, Rex. 1974. *Indonesian Communism under Sukarno: Ideology and Politics, 1959–1965*. Ithaca: Cornell University Press.

Mrazek, Rudolf. 1994. *Sjahrir: Politics and Exile in Indonesia*. Ithaca: Modern Indonesia Project, Cornell University Press.

Murray, Martin. 1980. *The Development of Capitalism in Colonial Indochina (1870–1940)*. Berkeley: University of California Press.

Myers, Robert. 1959. "The Development of the Indonesian Socialist Party." Ph.D. dissertation, University of Chicago.

Naim, Mochtar. 1960. "The Nadlatul Ulama Party (1952–1955): An Inquiry into the Origins of Its Electoral Success." M.A. thesis, McGill University.

Nam, Koon Woo. 1989. *South Korean Politics: The Search for Political Consensus and Stability*. Lanham, MD: University Press of America.

Natsir, Mohammad. 1968. *Persatuan Agama dengan Negara: M. Natsir versus Soekarno* (Unify religion with the state: Natsir versus Sukarno). Padang: Yayasan Pendidikan Islam.

Nguyen Kim Than, et al., eds. 1996. *Tu Dien Han Viet Hien Dai* (Modern Chinese-Vietnamese dictionary). Rev. ed. Ho Chi Minh City: The Gioi.

Nguyen Lien-Hang. 2006. "The War Politburo: North Vietnam's Diplomatic and Political Road to the Tet Offensive." *Journal of Vietnamese Studies* 1, 1–2 (Fall): 4–58.

Nguyen Quoc Thang and Nguyen Ba The. 1997. *Tu Dien Nhan Vat Lich Su Viet Nam* (Dictionary of Vietnamese historical figures). Ho Chi Minh City: Van Hoa.

Nguyen Thanh. 2005. *Su Nghiep Bao Chi cua Chu Tich Ho Chi Minh* (President Ho Chi Minh's journalist career). Hanoi: Ly Luan Chinh Tri.

Nguyen Thi Ngoc Thanh. 1999. "The Reform of Capitalists and Capitalism in North Vietnam (1958–1960)." Unpublished paper, Hanoi.

Nguyen To Uyen. 1999. *Cong Cuoc Bao Ve va Xay Dung Chinh Quyen Nhan Dan o Viet Nam trong nhung nam 1945–1946* (The construction and defense of the people's government, 1945–1946). Hanoi: Khoa Hoc Xa Hoi.

Nhuong Tong. 1949. *Nguyen Thai Hoc (1902–1930)*. Saigon: Tan Viet.

Ninh Kim. 2002. *A World Transformed: The Politics of Culture in Revolutionary Vietnam, 1945–1965*. Ann Arbor: University of Michigan Press.

Noer, Deliar. 1960. "Masjumi: Its Organization, Ideology and Political Role in Indonesia." M.A. thesis, Cornell University.

— 1973. *The Modernist Muslim Movement in Indonesia, 1900–1942*. Singapore: Oxford University Press.

— 1987. *Partai Islam di Pentas Nasional 1945–1965* (Islamic parties on the national stage 1945–1965). Jakarta: PT Pustaka Utama Grafiti.

North, Robert (with the collaboration of Ithiel de Sola Pool). 1952. *Kuomintang and Chinese Communist Elites*. Stanford: Hoover Institution Studies and Stanford University Press.

O'Brien, Kevin. 1990. *Reform without Liberalization: China's National People's Congress and the Politics of Institutional Change*. Cambridge: Cambridge University Press.

O'Donnell, Guillermo, and Phillippe Schmitter. 1986. *Transitions from Authoritarian Rule: Tentative Conclusions about Uncertain Democracies*. Baltimore: Johns Hopkins University Press.

Oh, B. H. 1975. "Students and Politics." In Wright 1975, 111–52.

Oh, John Kie-Chang. 1968. *Korea: Democracy on Trial.* Ithaca: Cornell University Press.

Orloff, Ann Shola. 1999. "Motherhood, Work, and Welfare in the United States, Britain, Canada and Australia." In Steinmentz 1999, 321–54.

Paauw, Douglas. 1963. "From Colonial to Guided Economy." In McVey 1963, 155–247.

Pak, Chi-Young. 1980. *Political Opposition in Korea, 1945–1960.* Seoul: Seoul National University Press.

Park, Chung Hee. 1979. *Saemaul: Korea's New Community Movement.* Seoul: The Secretariat for the President.

Park, Tae-gyun. 2005. "Different Roads, Common Destination: Economic Discourses in South Korea during the 1950s." *Modern Asian Studies* 39, 3: 661–82.

Parna, Ibnu. [1947] 1950. *Undang Berpikir Rakyat Berjuang* (Invitation to think about [our] struggling people). Jakarta: Wijaya.

Partai Komunis Indonesia (Communist Party of Indonesia). [1948] 1953. *Djalan Baru untuk Republik Indonesia* (The new road for Indonesia). Jakarta: Yayasan Pembaruan.

Pauker, Guy. 1958. "The Role of Political Organizations in Indonesia." *Far Eastern Survey* 27, 9 (September): 129–42.

———. 1965. "Indonesia in 1964: Toward a 'people's democracy'?" *Asian Survey* 5, 2 (February): 88–97.

Pepper, Suzanne. 1978. *Civil War in China.* Berkeley: University of California Press.

Perry, Elizabeth. 1980. *Rebels and Revolutionaries in North China, 1845–1945.* Stanford: Stanford University Press.

———. 1985. "Rural Violence in Socialist China." *China Quarterly* 103 (September): 414–40.

Prados, John. 2007. "Assessing Dien Bien Phu." In Mark Lawrence and Fred Logevall, eds., *The First Vietnam War,* 215–39. Cambridge, MA: Harvard University Press.

Prawiranegara, Sjafruddin. 1948. *Politik dan Revolusi Kita* (Politics and our struggle). Jakarta: Indonesia Raya.

———. 1950. *Islam dalam Pergolakan Dunia* (Islam in a tumbling world). Bandung: Al Ma'arif.

Przeworski, Adam, and Fernando Limongi. 1993. "Political Regimes and Economic Growth." *Journal of Economic Perspectives* 7, 3 (Summer): 51–69.

Przeworski, Adam, et al. 2000. *Democracy and Development: Political Institutions and Well-Being in the World, 1950–1990.* Cambridge: Cambridge University Press.

Quang Dam. 2002. *Quang Dam: Nha Bao, Hoc Gia* (Quang Dam: A journalist and scholar). Hanoi: Lao Dong.

Quinn-Judge, Sophie. 2002. *Ho Chi Minh: The Missing Years, 1919–1941.* Berkeley: University of California Press.

Raffin, Anne. 2005. *Youth Mobilization in Vichy Indochina and Its Legacies, 1940 to 1970.* Lanham, MD: Lexington Books.

Reeve, David. 1963. *The Republic of Korea: A Political and Economic Study.* New York: Oxford University Press.

Reid, Anthony. 1974. *The Indonesian National Revolution, 1945–1950.* Hawthorne: Longman Australia.

———. 1979. *The Blood of the People: Revolution and the End of Traditional Rule in Northern Sumatra.* Kuala Lumpur: Oxford University Press.

Richardson, Philip. 1999. *Economic Change in China, c. 1800–1950.* Cambridge: Cambridge University Press.

Robequain, Charles. 1944. *The Economic Development of French Indo-China.* Trans. Isabel Ward. New York: Oxford University Press.

Robinson, Mark, and Gordon White, eds. 1998. *The Democratic Developmental State: Politics and Institutional Design.* New York: Oxford University Press.

Robison, Richard. 1986. *Indonesia: The Rise of Capital.* Sydney: Allen & Unwin.

Rocamora, J. Eliseo. 1975. *Nationalism in Search of Ideology: The Indonesian Nationalist Party, 1946–1965.* Quezon City: University of the Philippines.

Roosa, John. 2006. *Pretext for Mass Murder: The September 30th Movement and Suharto's Coup d'état in Indonesia.* Madison: University of Wisconsin Press.

Rothermund, Dietmar. 2008. *India: The Rise of a Giant.* New Haven: Yale University Press.

Saich, Tony, ed. 1994. *The Rise to Power of the Chinese Communist Party: Documents and Analysis.* Armonk, NY: M. E. Sharpe.

Sato, Shigeru. 1994. *War, Nationalism and Peasants: Java under the Japanese Occupation, 1942–1945.* Armonk, NY: M. E. Sharpe.

Schoenhals, Michael. 1987. "Saltationist Socialism: Mao Zedong and the Great Leap Forward." Ph.D. dissertation, University of Stockholm.

———. 1992. *Doing Things with Words in Chinese Politics: Five Studies.* Berkeley: Institute of East Asian Studies, University of California.

Schoppa, R. Keith. 2000. "The Search for Social Cohesion in China, 1921–1958." In Goldman and Gordon 2000, 238–71.

Schran, Peter. 1976. *Guerrilla Economy: The Development of the Shensi-Kansu-Ninghsia Border Region, 1937–1945.* Albany: State University of New York Press.

Schurmann, Frank. 1966. *Ideology and Organization in Communist China.* Berkeley: University of California Press.

Selden, Mark. 1971. *The Yenan Way in Revolutionary China.* Cambridge, MA: Harvard University Press.

Seo, Joong-Seok. 1996. "The Establishment of an Anti-Communist State Structure Following the Founding of the Korean Government." *Korea Journal* 36, 1 (Spring): 79–114.

Shapiro, Michael, and Hayward Alker. 1996. *Challenging Boundaries: Global Flows, Territorial Identities.* Minneapolis: University of Minnesota Press.

Sharp, Lauriston. 1946. "Colonial Regimes in Southeast Asia." *Far Eastern Survey* 15, 4 (February 27): 49–53.

Shiraishi, Masaya. 1992. "The Background to the Formation of the Tran Trong Kim Cabinet in April 1945: Japanese Plans for Governing Vietnam." In

Takashi Shiraishi and Motoo Furuta, eds., *Indochina in the 1940s and 1950s*, 113–41. Ithaca: Southeast Asia Program, Cornell University Press.

Shiraishi, Takashi. 1990. *An Age in Motion: Popular Radicalism in Java, 1912–1926*. Ithaca: Cornell University Press.

Shirley, James. 1962. "Political Conflict in the Kuomintang: The Career of Wang Ching-Wei to 1932." Ph.D. dissertation, University of California, Berkeley.

Shue, Vivienne. 1980. *Peasant China in Transition*. Berkeley: University of California Press.

———. 1988. *The Reach of the State: Sketches of the Chinese Body Politic*. Stanford: Stanford University Press.

Sjahrir, Sutan. 1947. *Pikiran dan Perjuangan* (Thoughts and struggle). Jakarta: Pustaka Rakyat.

———. 1949. *Out of Exile*. Trans. Charles Wolf. New York: John Day.

———. 1956. *Indonesian Socialism*. Rangoon: Asian Socialist Publishing House.

———. 1988. *Perjuangan Kita* (Our struggle). Banda Naira: Rumah Syahrir.

Smail, John. 1964. *Bandung in the Early Revolution, 1945–1946: A Study in the Social History of the Indonesian Revolution*. Ithaca: Modern Indonesia Project, Cornell University.

So, Wai-chor. 1991. *The Kuomintang Left in the National Revolution, 1924–1931*. Hong Kong: Oxford University Press.

Soejatno. 1974. "Revolution and Social Tensions in Surakarta, 1945–1950." Trans. Benedict Anderson. *Indonesia* 17 (April): 99–112.

Spence, Jonathan. 1990. *The Search for Modern China*. New York: W. W. Norton.

Spruyt, Hendrik. 1994. *The Sovereign State and Its Competitors: An Analysis of System Change*. Princeton: Princeton University Press.

Steinberg, David. 1989. *The Republic of Korea: Economic Transformation and Social Change*. Boulder, CO: Westview Press.

Steinmetz, George, ed. 1999. *State/Culture: State Formation after the Cultural Turn*. Ithaca: Cornell University Press.

Strange, Susan. 1996. *The Retreat of the State: The Diffusion of Power in the World Economy*. Cambridge: Cambridge University Press.

Strauss, Julia. 1998. *Strong Institutions in Weak Polities: State Building in Republican China, 1927–1940*. Oxford: Oxford University Press.

———. 2002. "Paternalist Terror: The Campaign to Suppress Counterrevolutionaries and Regime Consolidation in the People's Republic of China, 1950–1953." *Comparative Studies in Society and History* 44, 1 (January): 80–105.

Suh, Dae-Suk. 1967. *The Korean Communist Movement, 1918–1948*. Princeton: Princeton University Press.

Sukarno. 1960. *Marhaen and Proletarian*. Ithaca: Modern Indonesia Project, Cornell University.

———. 1961. *Toward Freedom and the Dignity of Man: A Collection of Five Speeches*. Jakarta: Department of Foreign Affairs.

———. 1964. *Dibawah Bendera Revolusi* (Under the revolutionary flag). Vol. 1. Jakarta: Panitya Penerbit Dibawah Bendera Revolusi.

Summers, Harry. 1990. *The Korea War Almanac*. New York: Facts on File.

Sundhaussen, Ulf. 1982. *The Road to Power: Indonesian Military Politics, 1945–1967*. Kuala Lumpur: Oxford University Press.

Sutter, John. 1959. *Indonesianisasi: Politics in a Changing Economy, 1940–1955*. 4 vols. Ithaca: Modern Indonesia Project, Cornell University.

Swift, Ann. 1989. *The Road to Madiun: The Indonesian Communist Uprising of 1948*. Ithaca: Modern Indonesia Project, Cornell University.

Tai, Ho Hue-Tam. 1992. *Radicalism and the Origins of the Vietnamese Revolution*. Cambridge, MA: Harvard University Press.

Tarling, Nicholas. 1998. *Nations and States in Southeast Asia*. Cambridge: Cambridge University Press.

Tarrow, Sidney. 1998. *Power in Movement: Social Movements and Contentious Politics*. Cambridge: Cambridge University Press.

Teiwes, Frederick. 1990. *Politics at Mao's Court*. Armonk, NY: M. E. Sharpe.

1993. "The Establishment and Consolidation of the New Regime, 1949–57." In Robert MacFarquhar, ed., *The Politics of China, 1949–1989*, 5–86. Cambridge: Cambridge University Press.

1994. *The Formation of the Maoist Leadership*. Research Notes and Studies no. 10. London: Contemporary China Institute, School of Oriental and African Studies.

Thee, Kian Wee. 1994. "Economic Policies in Indonesia during the Period 1950–1965, in Particular with Respect to Foreign Investment." In Lindblad 1994, 315–29.

2002. "The Soeharto Era and After: Stability, Development and Crisis, 1966–2000." In Dick et al. 2002, 194–243.

Thompson, Roger. 1995. *China's Local Councils in the Age of Constitutional Reform, 1898–1911*. Cambridge, MA: Harvard University Council on East Asian Studies.

Tilly, Charles. 1990. *Coercion, Capital and the European States, AD 990–1990*. Cambridge, MA: Blackwell.

Tonnesson, Stein. 1991. *The Vietnamese Revolution of 1945*. London: Sage Publications.

1995. "Filling the Power Vacuum: 1945 in French Indochina, the Netherlands East Indies and British Malaya." In Antlov and Tonnesson 1995, 110–43.

Tran Huy Lieu, ed. 1974. *Ngon Co Giai Phong* (The liberation flag). Hanoi: Su That.

Tran Luc (Ho Chi Minh). 1958a. *Cong Xa Nhan Dan Kinh Nghiem Trung Quoc* (People's communes, the Chinese experience). Hanoi: Su That.

1958b. *May Kinh Nghiem Trung Quoc Ma Chung Ta Nen Hoc* (Some Chinese experiences worthy of emulating for us). Hanoi: Su That.

1959. *Kinh Nghiem ve Hop Tac Hoa Nong Nghiep cua Trung Quoc* (China's experiences on agricultural collectivization). Hanoi: Su That.

Truong Buu Lam. 1973. "Japan and the Disruption of the Vietnamese Nationalist Movement." In Walter Vella, ed., *Aspects of Vietnamese History*, 237–69. Honolulu: Asian Studies Program, University Press of Hawaii.

Truong Chinh. 1948. *Chung ta chien dau cho doc lap va dan chu* (We fight for independence and democracy). Speech at the Fifth Cadre Conference, August 8–16. Ban Chap hanh Lien Khu Dang bo Lien khu X.

Truong Chinh and Vo Nguyen Giap. [1938] 1959. *Van De Dan Cay* (The peasant question) 2nd ed. Hanoi: Su That.

van Creveld, Martin. 1999. *The Rise and Decline of the State*. Cambridge: Cambridge University Press.

van de Ven, Hans. 1991. *From Friends to Comrades: The Founding of the Chinese Communist Party, 1920–1927*. Berkeley: University of California Press.

   1995. "The Emergence of the Text-Centered Party." In Tony Saich and Hans van de Ven, eds., *New Perspectives on the Chinese Communist Revolution*, 5–32. Armonk, NY: M. E. Sharpe.

   2000. "The Military in the Republic." In Wakeman and Edmonds 2000, 98–120.

   2003. *War and Nationalism in China, 1925–1945*. New York: RoutledgeCurzon.

van Der Kroef, Jusuf. 1965. *The Communist Party of Indonesia*. Vancouver: University of British Columbia Publications Centre.

van Dijk, C. 1975. "The Hariman Siregar Trial." *Review of Malaysian and Indonesian Affairs* 9, 1 (January–June): 1–33.

   1981. *Rebellion under the Banner of Islam: The Darul Islam in Indonesia*. The Hague: Martinus Nijhoff.

van Langenberg, Michael. 1985. "East Sumatra: Accommodating an Indonesian Nation within a Sumatran Residency." In A. Kahin 1985, 113–43.

van Niel, Robert. 1960. *The Emergence of the Modern Indonesian Elite*. The Hague: W. Van Hoeve.

Van Phong Quoc Hoi (Office of the National Assembly). 2002. *Dai Bieu Quoc Hoi tu Khoa I den Khoa X* (National Assembly Deputies from the First to the Tenth Session). Hanoi: Chinh Tri Quoc Gia.

van Slyke, Lyman. 1967. *Enemies and Friends: The United Front in Chinese Communist History*. Stanford: Stanford University Press.

   1991. "The Chinese Communist Movement during the Sino-Japanese War, 1937–1945." In Lloyd Eastman et al., *The Nationalist Era in China, 1927–1949*, 177–290. Cambridge: Cambridge University Press.

Vandenbosch, Amry. 1943. "The Effect of Dutch Rule on the Civilization of the East Indies." *American Journal of Sociology* 48, 4 (January): 498–502.

   1944. *The Dutch East Indies: Its Government, Problems and Politics*. Berkeley: University of California Press.

Vickerman, Andrew. 1986. *The Fate of the Peasantry: Premature 'Transition to Socialism' in the Democratic Republic of Vietnam*. Monograph Series no. 28. New Haven, CT: Yale University SE Asia Studies.

Villalon, Leonardo, and Peter VonDoepp, eds. 2005. *The Fate of Africa's Democratic Experiments: Elites and Institutions*. Bloomington: Indiana University Press.

Vogel, Ezra. 1969. *Canton under Communism*. Cambridge, MA: Harvard University Press.

Vogel, Steven. 1996. *Freer Markets, More Rules: Regulatory Reform in Advanced Industrial Countries*. Ithaca: Cornell University Press.

Vu Dinh Hoe. 1995. *Hoi Ky Thanh Nghi* (Memoir about *Thanh Nghi*). Hanoi: Van Hoc.

2000. *Phap Quyen Nhan Nghia Ho Chi Minh* (Ho Chi Minh's concepts of humanistic law). Hanoi: Van Hoa Thong Tin.

Vu Khieu, ed. 2002. *Pham Tuan Tai: Cuoc Doi va Tac Pham* (Pham Tuan Tai: Life and Work). Hanoi: Chinh Tri Quoc Gia.

Vu Ngu Chieu. 1986. "The Other Side of the Revolution: The Empire of Vietnam (March–August 1945)." *Journal of Asian Studies* 45, 2 (February): 293–328.

Vu Tuong. 2003. "Of Rice and Revolution: The Politics of Provisioning and State-Society Relations on Java, 1945–49." *South East Asia Research* 11, 3: 237–67.

2005. "Workers and the Socialist State: North Vietnam's State-Labor Relations, 1945–1970." *Communist and Post-Communist Studies* 38 (September): 329–56.

2008. "Dreams of Paradise: The Making of a Soviet Outpost in Vietnam." *Ab Imperio* 2 (August): 255–85.

2009. "From Cheering to Volunteering: Vietnamese Communists and the Arrival of the Cold War, 1940–1951." In Christopher Goscha and Christian Ostermann, eds., *Connecting Histories: The Cold War and Decolonization in Asia (1945–1962)*, 172–204. Stanford: Stanford University Press.

2010a. "Studying the State through State Formation: A Review Article." *World Politics* 62, 1 (January).

2010b. "To Be Patriotic Is to Build Socialism: Communist Ideology in Vietnam's Civil War." In Tuong Vu and Wasana Wongsurawat, eds., *Dynamics of the Cold War in Asia: Ideology, Identity, and Culture*, 32–52. New York: Palgrave.

Wade, Robert. 1992. "East Asia's Economic Success: Conflicting Perspectives, Partial Insights, Shaky Evidence." *World Politics* 44, 2 (January): 270–320.

Wakeman, Frederic. 1995. *Policing Shanghai, 1927–1937*. Berkeley: University of California Press.

2000. "A Revisionist View of the Nanjing Decade: Confucian Fascism." In Wakeman and Edmonds 2000, 141–78.

Wakeman, Frederic, and Richard Edmonds, eds. 2000. *Reappraising Republican China*. Oxford: Oxford University Press.

Waldner, David. 1999. *State-Building and Late Development*. Ithaca: Cornell University Press.

Waldron, Arthur. 1995. *From War to Nationalism: China's Turning Point, 1924–1925*. Cambridge: Cambridge University Press.

Wang, Ke-wen. 1985. "The Kuomintang in Transition: Ideology and Factionalism in the 'National Revolution,' 1924–1932." Ph.D. dissertation, Stanford University.

Wei, William. 1985. *Counterrevolution in China: The Nationalists in Jiangxi during the Soviet Period*. Ann Arbor: University of Michigan Press.

Weiss, Lawrence. 1981. "Storm around the Cradle: The Korean War and the Early Years of the PRC, 1949–1953." Ph.D. dissertation, Columbia University.

Weiss, Linda. 1998. *The Myth of the Powerless State*. Ithaca: Cornell University Press.

Westad, Odd Arne. 2003. *Decisive Encounters: The Chinese Civil War, 1946–1950*. Stanford: Stanford University Press.

White, Christine. 1981. "Agrarian Reform and National Liberation in the Vietnamese Revolution: 1920–1957." Ph.D. dissertation, Cornell University.

White, Gordon. 1983. "Revolutionary Socialist Development in the Third World: An Overview." In Gordon White, Robin Murray, and Christine White, eds., *Revolutionary Socialist Development in the Third World*, 1–34. Lexington: University Press of Kentucky.

White, Gordon, ed. 1988. *Developmental States in East Asia*. London: Macmillan.

White, Gordon, and Robert Wade. 1988. Introduction. In G. White 1988, 1–29.

Wibisono, Jusuf. 1950. *Islam dan Sosialisme* (Islam and socialism). Jakarta: Sinar Ilmu.

Wilbur, Martin. 1983. *The Nationalist Revolution in China, 1923–1928*. Cambridge: Cambridge University Press.

Wilbur, Martin, and Julie How. 1989. *Missionaries of Revolution: Soviet Advisers and Nationalist China, 1920–1927*. Cambridge, MA: Harvard University Press.

Wong, R. Bin. 1997. *China Transformed: Historical Change and the Limit of European Experience*. Ithaca: Cornell University Press.

Woo-Cumings, Meredith, ed. 1999. *The Developmental State*. Ithaca: Cornell University Press.

Woodside, Alexander. 1976. *Community and Revolution in Modern Vietnam*. Boston: Houghton Mifflin.

Worthington, Peter. 1995. "Occupation and Revolution: The Chinese Nationalist Army in Northern Vietnam, 1945–1946." Ph.D. dissertation, University of Hawaii.

Wou, Odoric. 1994. *Mobilizing the Masses: Building Revolution in Henan*. Stanford: Stanford University Press.

    1999. "Community Defense and the Chinese Communist Revolution: Henan's Du Eight-Neighborhood Pact." *Modern China* 25, 3 (July): 264–302.

Wright, Edward, ed. 1975. *Korean Politics in Transition*. Seattle: University of Washington Press.

Wuthnow, Robert. 1987. *Meanings and Moral Order: Explorations in Cultural Analysis*. Berkeley: University of California Press.

Wylie, Raymond. 1980. *The Emergence of Maoism*. Stanford: Stanford University Press.

Yamin, Muhammad, ed. 1959. *Naskah Persiapan Undang-Undang Dasar 1945* (Documents related to the preparation of the 1945 Constitution). Vol. 1. Jakarta: Yayasan Prapanca.

Yang, Benjamin. 1990. *From Revolution to Politics: Chinese Communist on the Long March*. Boulder, CO: Westview Press.

Yang, Dali. 1996. *Calamity and Reform in China*. Stanford: Stanford University Press.

Yang, Jonghoe. 2004. "Colonial Legacy and Modern Economic Growth in Korea: A Critical Examination of Their Relationship." *Development and Society* (Seoul) 33, 1: 1–24.

Yang, S. C. 1972. "Political Ideology and Korean Politics." In Kim and Cho 1972, 25–42.

Yang, Tianshi. 2002. "Perspectives on Chiang Kai-shek's Early Thought from His Unpublished Diary." In Mechthild Leutner et al., eds., *The Chinese Revolution in the 1920s*, 77–97. New York: RoutledgeCurzon.

Young, Ernest. 1977. *The Presidency of Yuan Shih-k'ai: Liberalism and Dictatorship in Early Republican China*. Ann Arbor: University of Michigan Press.

2002. Introduction. In Bodenhorn 2002, 1–9.

Yu, George. 1966. *Party Politics in Republican China: The Kuomintang, 1912–1924*. Berkeley: University of California Press.

Yu, Miin-ling. 2002. "A Reassessment of Chiang Kai-shek and the Policy of Alliance with the Soviet Union, 1923–1927." In Mechthild Leutner et al., eds., *The Chinese Revolution in the 1920s*, 98–124. New York: RoutledgeCurzon.

Zeon, Y. C. 1973. "The Politics of Land Reform in South Korea." Ph.D. dissertation, University of Missouri, Columbia.

Zhang, Shu Guang. 1999. "Sino-Soviet Economic Cooperation." In Odd Arne Westad, ed., *Brothers in Arms: The Rise and Fall of the Sino-Soviet Alliance, 1945–1963*, 189–225. Washington, DC, and Stanford: Woodrow Wilson Center Press and Stanford University Press.

Index

accommodation pattern, as path of
state formation, 18–19. *See
also specific countries*
Acehnese secessionist movement
(Indonesia), 61
administrative infrastructure, 5
agriculture
in China, 101, 104, 124–6
in South Korea, 44–5
in Vietnam, 101, 104, 124–6
Alimin, 223–4
Alliance against Terror (2001),
249
Aminem, 229–32
Annam (central Vietnam), 100–5
Annam Independence Party (AIP),
133–4
Australia, 223

Bai Chongxi, 84
Barisan Banteng (PNI), 59–60
Barisan Buruh Indonesia. *See*
Indonesian Workers' Front
BBI (Indonesian Workers' Front),
224
Blue Shirts (China), 81–2
Bo Gu, 88–9
Bolshevik Party model, 78–9
Bonjol, Imam, 219
BU. *See* Pure Endeavor

Budi Utomo. *See* Pure Endeavor
Bukharin, Nikolai, 6
Burma (British), 106
Burton, Michael, 239
Bush, George W., 249

Cambodia, 105
capitalist economic systems
Bukharin on, 6
producer classes in, 5–7
resistance to
in China, 102
in Indonesia, 62–9, 213–14,
228–9
in Vietnam, 102
socialist states vs., 5–7
Weiss on, 6
case selection, 19–21
Central Council for the Acceleration
of Korean Independence
(CCAKI), 36
Central Executive Committee
(CEC/GMD), 79–80, 81
Central National Committee (KNIP)
(Indonesia), 56–8, 163–5
Chang Myon, 46–7
Cheju Island rebellion (South Korea),
38, 61
Chen Duxiu, 78–9
Chen Gongbo, 82–3

63590456R00189

Made in the USA
Lexington, KY
13 May 2017